BUSINESS
Superbrands

AN INSIGHT INTO SOME OF BRITAIN'S STRONGEST B2B BRANDS 2008

www.superbrands.uk.com

Chief Executive
Ben Hudson

Brand Liaison Directors
Fiona Maxwell
Claire Pollock
Liz Silvester

Brand Liaison Manager
Heidi Smith

Administrative Co-ordinator
Nia Roberts

Head of Accounts
Will Carnochan

Managing Editor
Angela Cooper

Assistant Editor
Laura Hill

Authors
Karen Dugdale
Jennifer Small

Other publications from Superbrands (UK) Ltd:
Superbrands 2006/07 ISBN: 978-0-9554784-1-3
CoolBrands 2006/07 ISBN: 1-905652-03-8

To order these books, email brands@superbrands.uk.com
or call 01825 767396.

Published by Superbrands (UK) Ltd.
44 Charlotte Street
London
W1T 2NR

© 2008 Superbrands (UK) Ltd published under licence
from Superbrands Ltd.

www.superbrands.uk.com

Printed in the UK.

ISBN: 978-0-9554784-3-7

Contents

Endorsements

We are very pleased to be including comments from several well respected industry bodies and thank them for their support of the programme.

John Noble
Director
British Brands Group

The benefits of branding are clearly showcased in the case studies that follow. Quality and performance are givens in modern markets but these organisations go further, based on an understanding of and a connection with their customers that goes well beyond the norm. As a result many have created formidable reputations that are the envy of the business world.

While these brands offer superior performance, their value extends beyond their customers. Their success creates a halo effect, benefiting employees, suppliers and the communities, both business and social, in which they operate. This is in addition to the benefits to shareholders and others who have a direct stake.

The management of brands, adding value in the long term while building strong reputations, is crucial to the competiveness of both companies and economies and indeed to the health of our society. We all have an interest in ensuring that brands have the right climate to innovate, to compete, to deliver for their customers and to create value, in all forms.

Paul Gostick
Chairman
The Chartered Institute
of Marketing

It is tempting to think of a brand as something that only matters to consumer goods, but branding is important to all organisations. In the business to business sector, customers do not make decisions on the facts and figures alone, and often irrational, intangible forces will prompt them to choose one product or service over the other.

Today's markets are fiercely competitive and brand identity may be all that differentiates one company from its competitors. Strong brands are clear about what they are and understand their unique promise of value. They appeal to the heart as well as the head, inspire confidence and loyalty and play a crucial role in influencing customer choice. They prompt a customer to return time and time again and help to maintain a price premium.

The Chartered Institute of Marketing is pleased to support Business Superbrands 2008 in promoting greater recognition and best practice in branding. In reading this book, you will gain insight into how the featured companies build loyalty and trust into their brands, set the standard and elevate themselves above the pack. I hope you find it valuable.

Jack Wallington
Programmes Manager
Internet Advertising
Bureau

The Internet Advertising Bureau (IAB) – the trade association for online advertising – sees the UK's leading brands increasingly pushing internet advertising to the forefront of their marketing campaigns on a daily basis. In 2008, a brand not online is a brand that isn't in tune with today's consumer. It is therefore extremely encouraging to see initiatives such as Business Superbrands recognising brands that have not only made the leap into the online arena, but in some instances, focus their marketing predominantly online.

With more than 380 members, the IAB is run for the leading media owners and agencies in the UK internet industry, placing us in the perfect position to identify what brands are doing online, and who is seeing the most success.

Business Superbrands is a useful and interesting publication highlighting the brands that are using today's marketing tools most effectively.

Shane Redding
Chair
IDM B2B Council

We're extremely pleased to support Business Superbrands 2008. Within its pages you will not only find great business brands, but also some invaluable insights into the winning marketing strategies behind them.

Over the last 5-10 years we've seen the business to business landscape change almost beyond recognition. New media, new markets, new channels – even a new breed of customer, have all contributed to the evolution of the UK B2B sector into the sophisticated and distinct discipline that it is today.

The IDM, and the IDM B2B Council, have been working tirelessly towards bringing the B2B discipline the recognition and rewards that it deserves. Business Superbrands 2008 proves that there is some fantastic work being done in the sector and we applaud the publishers for providing such an impressive platform that both showcases and celebrates business to business marketing at its best.

James Aitchison
Managing Editor
World Advertising
Research Center

When we think of leading brands, we typically think of them in their most ostensible form – as the public face of the consumer goods and products that crowd our TV screens, line our high streets and fill our supermarket shelves. But that's just part of the story, especially when you consider recent research that values marketing spend in the UK's business to business sector at some £10 billion per annum.

Browse the pages of this latest edition of Business Superbrands and you will see the very finest fruits of this investment, illustrated cover-to-cover by countless examples of B2B brand and branding excellence – and, more importantly, how it contributes to business success.

Increasing our understanding of this crucial dynamic between marketing spend and its commercial result is at the heart of WARC. So congratulations to Superbrands for yet another great contribution to our collective knowledge.

About Superbrands

The Superbrands organisation presents expert and consumer opinion on branding through three annual programmes, namely Business Superbrands, Superbrands and CoolBrands. Using a comprehensive selection process, both experts and consumers – in this case business professionals – identify the country's strongest B2B brands; these are the only brands eligible to join the programme. Through identifying these brands and presenting their case studies, the organisation hopes that people will gain a greater appreciation of the discipline of branding and have an increased admiration for the brands themselves.

Full details on Superbrands in the UK can be found at www.superbrands.uk.com.

The Business Superbrands Stamp

The brands that have been awarded Business Superbrands status and participate in the programme, are given permission to use the Business Superbrands Stamp.

This powerful endorsement provides evidence to existing and potential consumers, media, employees and investors of the exceptional standing that these Business Superbrands have achieved.

Member brands use the Stamp on marketing materials such as product packaging, signage, advertising, websites and annual reports, as well as other external and internal communication channels.

Business Superbrands Selection Process

Independent researchers use a wide range of sources to compile a list of the UK's leading B2B brands. From the thousands of brands initially considered, a list of approximately 1,100 brands is forwarded to the Business Superbrands Council.

The independent and voluntary Business Superbrands Council considers the list and members individually award each brand a score from 1-10. Council members are not allowed to score brands with which they have a direct association or are in direct competition to. The lowest-scoring brands (approximately 50 per cent) are eliminated at this stage.

A panel of approximately 1,500 individual business professionals are surveyed by YouGov, the UK's most accurate online research agency. These individuals are asked to vote on the surviving 700 brands.

The remaining brands are ranked based on the combined score of the Business Superbrands Council (50 per cent) and the panel of business professionals (50 per cent). The 200 lowest-scoring brands are eliminated and the leading 500 brands are awarded 'Business Superbrand' status and are invited to join the Business Superbrands programme.

Business Superbrands Council 2008

Jonathan Allan
Managing Director
OMD UK

Anthony Carlisle
Executive Director
Citigate Dewe Rogerson

Steve Cooke
Marketing Director
BMRB

Nadia Cristina
Partner
Practice Management
International LLP

Jonathan Cummings
Director
Start Creative

BJ Cunningham
Director
Georgina Goodman

Michelle Dewberry
Founder
Michelle Dewberry Ltd

Paul Edwards
Chairman
Research International UK

Simon Gruselle
Corporate Marketing Director
Datamonitor

Joel Harrison
Editor
B2B Marketing

Joanna Higgins
Group Editor
Director Publications

Darrell Kofkin
Chief Executive
Global Marketing Network

Kate Manasian
Managing Director
Saffron Consultants

John Mathers
Ex-CEO, UK
The Brand Union

Ruth Mortimer
Editor
Brand Strategy

Lee Murgatroyd
Director
Cohn & Wolfe

Marc Nohr
Managing Partner
Kitcatt Nohr Alexander Shaw

Phil Nunn
Partner
Trinity

David Parsley
Editor
City A.M.

Andrew Pinkess
Strategy Director
Rufus Leonard

Shane Redding
Managing Director
Think Direct

Tom Stevenson
Journalist
The Daily Telegraph

Matthew Stibbe
Writer-in-Chief
Articulate Marketing

Morvah Stubbings
Managing Director
BPRI

Jack Wallington
Programmes Manager
Internet Advertising Bureau

Tim Weber
Business Editor
BBC News Interactive

Simon Wylie
Founding Partner &
Managing Director
Xtreme Information

Stephen Cheliotis
Chairman
Superbrands Councils UK

**Full biographies for all
Council members can be
found on page 144**

Foreword
Angela Cooper, Managing Editor

It gives me great pleasure to introduce this, the sixth edition of Business Superbrands.

The challenges facing the brands that you will find detailed in this publication are, as ever, numerous. However, there is one issue that transcends all sectors, all brands and indeed, all of us.

Concern over environmental issues needs little introduction, but the steps being taken in the corporate social responsibility (CSR) arena are both encouraging and innovative. Details of such activities can be found in the case studies which follow; further to which we are very pleased to be introducing a separate section in this edition focusing specifically on CSR. This project has been undertaken in association with Business in the Community (BITC), to provide some

of the organisations tackling these issues head on with the opportunity to tell their stories in more detail.

I am also very pleased to report that the new Business Superbrands voting process, now in its second year, incorporating the opinions of both the Business Superbrands Council and business professionals has again been a great success.

So how are brands awarded Business Superbrand status? They are rated on the following three factors:
Quality – does the brand represent quality products and services?
Reliability – can you trust the brand to deliver consistently against its promises and maintain product and service standards across all customer touch points?
Distinction – is the brand well known in its sector, is it suitably differentiated from its competitors

and does it have a personality and values that make it unique within its marketplace?

All three factors are considered essential ingredients in a Business Superbrand. In addition all highly rated brands must stand up against the following definition:
'A Business Superbrand has established the finest reputation in its field. It offers customers significant emotional and or tangible advantages over its competitors, which (consciously or sub-consciously) customers want, recognise, and are confident about investing in. Business Superbrands are targeted at organisations (although not necessarily exclusively so).'

I hope that you find the case studies that follow informative and inspiring.

QUALITY   RELIABILITY   DISTINCTION

High performance. Delivered.

The essence of Accenture, a global management consulting, technology services and outsourcing company, can be summarised in three words: 'High Performance Delivered.' Since launching in 2001, Accenture has achieved extraordinary success. Leveraging insights from the company's ground-breaking research into what drives high performance along with the power of its unmatched experience, Accenture helps clients become high-performance businesses and governments.

MARKET

Industry analyst International Data Corporation (IDC) expects worldwide business consulting spending to increase at a compound annual growth rate (CAGR) of 4.2 per cent from 2006 to 2011. IDC also expects spending on IT and business services worldwide to reach US$911 billion in 2011, reflecting a CAGR of 7.3 per cent from 2006 to 2011.

ACHIEVEMENTS

Known for launching one of the largest and most successful rebranding campaigns in corporate history in 2001, Accenture's rise to global prominence as a brand has been truly remarkable. Some recent accolades that Accenture has received include a July/August 2005 Harvard Business Review survey, which recognised Accenture's High Performance Business strategic initiative as one of the 10 most notable initiatives in the field during the past quarter century. In 2006, International Data Corporation recognised Accenture as the worldwide leader in Systems Integration Services.

More recently, in 2007 Accenture was placed at number 50 in BusinessWeek/Interbrand's annual ranking of the 100 Best Global Brands, with a brand value of nearly US$7.3 billion – a 40 per cent increase since 2002. Accenture was also ranked at 62 in the 2007 BRANDZ™ Top 100 Most Powerful Brands by Millward Brown, with a brand value of US$10.5 billion. Fortune's list of Most Admired Companies ranked Accenture number one in Information Technology Services for the fourth straight year. Accenture also made the Fortune

We know what it takes to be a Tiger.
To see insights from our research and experience, including our study of over 500 high performers, visit accenture.com/research

• Consulting • Technology • Outsourcing

right brain 50%   left brain 50%

High performance. Delivered.

Global 500 for the sixth consecutive year. Accenture's commitment to the environment and the community in the UK earned it a gold ranking by the Business in the Community (BITC) Corporate Responsibility Index. CRM magazine named Accenture the consulting market leader for the fifth consecutive year and CIO magazine ranked Accenture on their CIO 100 list for excellence in IT.

PRODUCT

Combining the company's research-based knowledge with its unmatched experience, Accenture helps clients on their journey to

becoming high-performance businesses and governments. Accenture's High Performance Business strategy builds on its expertise in consulting, technology and outsourcing to help its clients perform at the highest levels so they can create sustainable value for their customers and shareholders. Accenture identifies new business and technology trends to develop and implement solutions for its clients through the use of its industry knowledge, service-offering expertise and technology capabilities. Accenture helps its clients around the world identify and enter new markets, increase revenues in existing

1954	1989	1989-2000	2001		2008
Innovation is part of Accenture's heritage, as the company traces its roots back to 1954 with the installation at General Electric of the first computer for business application.	Accenture is established when a group of Consulting division partners of various global Arthur Andersen firms form a new organisation, initially called Andersen Consulting.	The company focuses on consulting and technology services related to managing large-scale systems integration and enhancing business processes.	On 1st January, the company changes its name to Accenture – executing one of the most extraordinary and successful rebranding campaigns in corporate history.	In July Accenture becomes a public company when it lists on the New York Stock Exchange under the symbol ACN.	Accenture is a global management consulting, technology services and outsourcing company, with approximately 170,000 people in 49 countries and net revenues of US$19.7 billion.

markets, improve workforce and operational performance, and deliver the company's products and services more effectively and efficiently.

To drive growth and bring services and solutions that help deliver high performance to clients, Accenture balances and leverages the strengths of the three dimensions of its business – operating groups, growth platforms and geography. Accenture has vast and relevant hands-on experience across all industries and business functions, broad global resources and a proven track record. Accenture can mobilise the right people, skills and technologies at the right time and in the right place to help clients become high-performance businesses.

RECENT DEVELOPMENTS

Accenture launched its High Performance Business strategic initiative in 2003, with the vision of not just identifying high performers, but explaining the forces that shape them. Accenture achieved great success with this goal through the careful analysis of more than 6,000 companies, including more than 500 high performers, into the characteristics that create high performance. This significant research effort, combined with Accenture's unparalleled experience, has been important, not only in terms of the company's ability to help its clients on their journey to become high-performance businesses, but also in the context of the larger marketplace of ideas. A recent Harvard Business Review survey recognised Accenture's High Performance Business strategic initiative as one of the 10 most notable initiatives in the field during the past quarter century.

Accenture began this journey with the stated belief that high-performance businesses are not only born – they can be made. Accenture's research has produced evidence that companies can, through sheer force of will, propel themselves along the paths to high performance. Through the

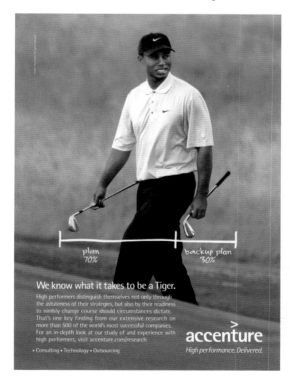

company's High Performance Business strategic initiative and its unmatched experience, Accenture is committed to deepening and expanding the development of routes to high performance for its clients.

PROMOTION

In 2003 Tiger Woods became, and remains today, the centerpiece of Accenture's advertising and marketing activities. As perhaps the world's ultimate symbol of high performance, he serves as a metaphor for Accenture's commitment to helping companies become high-performance businesses. Now in its fifth year, the campaign has become widely recognised around the globe. Armed with findings from its comprehensive High Performance Business research of over 500 high performers, as well as the company's unparalleled experience, the ongoing campaign is built around Accenture's understanding of the world's elite companies, and the company's ability to channel that knowledge on behalf of its clients. This unique position and capability is summarised in the company's campaign headline: 'We know what it takes to be a Tiger.'

Accenture's sponsorships range from major sporting events, such as the Accenture Match Play Championship, to the arts, with the Royal Shakespeare Company's 2007 International Tour of King Lear. More than just lending the company's name and financial support, Accenture strives to make a difference in each of its sponsorships by lending its technology and consulting services expertise.

Accenture's experts are often asked to speak and participate in a range of business events and industry conferences, such as the World Economic Forum.

BRAND VALUES

Accenture's brand is comprised of numerous dimensions, including the organisation's position in the marketplace, the work it does,

its internal and external communications and the behaviour of its employees. The positioning of the organisation has evolved over time to ensure that the brand remains closely aligned with its business strategy. Guided by a clear understanding of its essential capabilities and its aspirations for the future, Accenture realises that the most powerful component of its brand is the company's people. Accenture's employees give energy and support to the central brand premise, from how they interact with clients to how they 'live the brand' every day. They also bring to life the Accenture High Performance Business strategy, making it real to their clients through their experience and pragmatic, innovative solutions that deliver measurable results. Accenture's people help clients become high-performance businesses.

www.accenture.com

AccountancyAge

Since launch in 1969, Accountancy Age has remained the leading weekly newspaper for accountants. Over this period it has grown into one of the most influential, innovative and respected business titles in the UK delivering high quality, must-have financial information across a variety of platforms in print, in person and online, earning commercial success for three different publishing houses.

MARKET

Publishing has become increasingly competitive – especially as the internet continues to change the way readers, publishers and advertisers relate to one another. Nevertheless just as the influence of accountants has grown over the last 38 years, so has that of Accountancy Age.

It has faced numerous competitors in that time, but by giving readers and advertisers access to the information they need each week, in multiple formats, it has seen off all head to head competition. However the presence of national newspapers and a growing number of web start-ups ensure that Accountancy Age isn't complacent commercially or editorially.

Despite the numerous changes that the title has both led and witnessed, the goal of connecting buyers and sellers remains unchanged.

ACHIEVEMENTS

In the last six years alone, Accountancy Age's journalists have won or been short-listed for more than 50 major publishing awards, spanning print and online, writing and design.

In 2007 AccountancyAge.com was the only website outside the US – and the only non-technology title – to win one of just three B2B website awards from international publishing organisation Tabpi. There were 700 entrants in the awards and the judges said: "Accountancy Age does everything that a website must do, and nearly everything it should do."

Accountancy Age has strived to lead all media on stories in its field – from the fallout of the spate of recent corporate scandals to football's financial problems and tax controversies. Journalists on the title are sought-after commentators for other media on these and other issues.

Sir David Tweedie, who, as chairman of the International Accounting Standards Board, has been one of the most influential UK accountants of the last 20 years, has described Accountancy Age as being "a great force for good" which, "unlike many national papers actually tries to analyse the issues to determine who is right rather than merely report on disputes".

PRODUCT

For its first 30 years, Accountancy Age was an extremely successful print weekly servicing the needs of UK qualified accountants. Over the last decade it has grown into one of the most pioneering B2B titles in the UK. Accountancy Age has been posting jobs online since 1995 and content since 1996. However, AccountancyAge.com has grown significantly since those early days. It now combines an award-winning breaking news and information website with one of the most comprehensive jobsites in the sector.

1969	1994	1999	2004	2006	2007
Accountancy Age is launched as "the voice of the profession" by Michael Heseltine.	The Accountancy Age Awards are launched.	AccountancyAge.com goes live offering a comprehensive news and jobs service.	Digital editions are launched – including regional and specialist ebooks; Best Practice, a title serving the needs of high street advisers, becomes a monthly spin-off.	A comprehensive redesign of the print edition takes place. The launch of a pioneering ebook, Young Professional, takes place, as does the launch of a weekly web conference – the Insider Business Club.	Incisive Media acquires VNU's UK publishing operations, including Accountancy Age. AccountancyAge.com is named as one of the three best B2B media websites in the world and undergoes a fundamental redesign.

So much so that it now attracts more than 220,000 readers a month (equivalent to the number of qualified accountants in the UK) and more than one million page impressions. In addition, a comprehensive daily newswire offering covers everything from tax to technology, practice to business as well as general news.

Accountancy Age also stages face-to-face events, including Softworld, the UK's premier accounting and finance technology show since launch 15 years ago, and the Accountancy Age Awards. Launched in 1994, these are the most respected in the field, attended by more than 1,200 senior industry players.

RECENT DEVELOPMENTS

Young Professional is the most successful of Accountancy Age's digital editions with a circulation of 52,000. Launched in 2006 and incorporating audio and video, the product was created to serve the needs of part and newly qualified accountants and to grow the next generation of Accountancy Age readers.

Over the last 12 months its virtual conference and round table offerings have grown in number. As well as the Accountancy Age Talent E-Symposium, other virtual conferences include the first for advisers to small businesses.

Accountancy Age has also launched the Insider Business Club, a weekly web conferencing club for finance directors and senior

members of their teams; more than 3,000 have signed up.

Through KnowledgeBank, readers can access white papers and other material, a process that generates leads for advertisers.

Meanwhile Accountancy Age TV is acquiring a growing reputation for delivering exclusive interviews, essential analysis and careers advice. The head of HM Revenue & Customs, the finance director of Tesco and the chairman of BT have been among recent interviewees.

PROMOTION

With a circulation of 66,000, the weekly newspaper remains the brand's most effective promotional vehicle. However, Accountancy Age promotes itself through many of the accountancy institutes that train students, and uses on and offline adverting campaigns to promote its products.

BRAND VALUES

Accountancy Age sets out to equip its professional readers – from the most senior finance directors and partners to newly qualified accountants – with all they need for their next meeting or indeed their next job. Careers coverage – through editorial coverage and job ads – remains at the heart of much of what it does.

It is the only independent title dedicated to keeping accountants – in practice, business as well as the public and voluntary sectors – up-to-date with financial and accountancy news as it happens and in the most appropriate format. This

may be in print, online, via digital editions or through regular careers guides, management briefings and events – on and offline.

Coverage is every bit as broad as the diverse roles in which the audience works. It covers business, practice and the public and voluntary sectors as well as tax, audit, corporate finance, business recovery and consultancy.

At times Accountancy Age may be considered as the irksome, independent voice of the profession and at others, its conscience. Always, however, it aims to mirror the industry in which it operates.

www.accountancyage.com

Things you didn't know about Accountancy Age

Accountancy Age has won or been shortlisted for 49 awards in the last five years.

Accountancy Age's tax coverage dominated the 2007 autumn Budget with the PM, the chancellor of the exchequer and Conservative leader David Cameron using its coverage to support their arguments – everywhere from the floor of the Commons to the GMTV sofa.

33,000 readers have provided their details to make Accountancy Age's salary checker one of most comprehensive around.

Accountancy Age is tracking the careers of a group of trainee and newly qualified accountants. The trials and tribulations of The Apprentices are covered in the monthly ebook Young Professional.

Allied Irish Bank (GB)

Our business is business banking.

The Allied Irish Bank (GB) brand is not simply the monolithic face of the organisation, but an evolving aspiration that relies on understanding and engagement with customers. Listening, and continuously responding to customer needs, combined with relevant innovation has built the brand to what it is today. Allied Irish Bank (GB)'s business is business banking.

MARKET

Allied Irish Bank (GB) is a specialist business bank offering a full range of products and services for growing and expanding mid-corporate businesses, companies trading across geographies and professional customers.

The Bank has a broad spectrum of business customers and has developed specialist teams in its key sectors, which include healthcare, medical, education, hotels & leisure, environmental services, public sector & charities and the professional sector.

The Bank continues to establish itself as 'first choice for growing businesses and professionals' and a serious alternative to the traditional British banks. It aims to achieve these goals through a personalised service and a continued commitment to its key business principals of: providing a tailored service and adjusting this as customers' requirements develop and change; developing long term relationships with customers; local bankers who are interested, knowledgeable, experienced and fully involved with all decisions; short lines of communication and speedy decision making; having a branch management team who work closely with centralised specialists.

ACHIEVEMENTS

Allied Irish Bank (GB) has been awarded the title of Britain's Best Business Bank in an independent survey by the Forum of Private Business on each consecutive occasion since 1994. This impressive accolade recognises the Bank's ability to consistently deliver superior customer service and is testimony to the long-standing commitment from the Bank, and its people, to delivering true relationship banking.

The Bank regularly tracks customer opinion using detailed customer satisfaction surveys. The 2007 survey found that 94.8 per cent of customers interviewed were satisfied with the quality of service that they had received during the year and over 90 per cent of respondents said that they are likely or very likely to approach Allied Irish Bank (GB) for their future financial needs, with 62.6 per cent of respondents expecting to increase the level of business they have with Allied Irish.

Furthermore, the Bank remained in the top quartile of suppliers for the fifth consecutive year, with a score of 83.4 per cent in the Satisfaction Index™ – a cross-industry benchmark of an organisation's ability to meet customer requirements. More than 68 per cent of customers reported Allied Irish Bank (GB) to be better or 'the best' when compared to other business banks.

Allied Irish Bank (GB)
Our business is business banking.

Working with top-flight businesses throughout the country.

1825	1970s	1980s	1991	2001	2007
The Bank's first London office opens in Throgmorton Avenue.	AIB Group grows to create a strong branch network in Britain.	International success brings about Group investment in branches in the US.	In July, the merger of AIB Group's interests in Northern Ireland with those of TSB Northern Ireland, create First Trust Bank.	AIB Group completes the merger of Wielkopolski Bank Kredytowy S.A. and Bank Zachodni S.A. in Poland. AIB Group has a 70.5 per cent shareholding in the new Bank Zachodni WBK S.A. (BZWBK).	As at 31st December 2006, AIB Group assets total 133 billion euros, reflecting the Group's growth since 1966 when AIB's aggregate assets were 323.8 million euros. 2007's results are announced in February 2008, published on the Group website.

It is a testament to the Bank's long-standing commitment to staff development that it has consistently achieved the recognition of the Investors in People (IiP) standard across its office network since 1995, exceeding 90 per cent of the measures set down by the new IiP national benchmark. Continuing investment in staff development has been the key to its success in not only retaining employees, but also providing the high quality service that its customers receive.

PRODUCT
Allied Irish Bank (GB) is committed to tailoring products and services to meet a customer's specific needs – with capabilities at every level the Bank strives to provide continuity and ingenuity in adapting these products as business requirements change. All managers are decision-makers, developing long term relationships with their customers in providing day-to-day banking, and are closely involved with their local business community.

Traditional banking continues to be at the core of Allied Irish Bank (GB)'s Wealth Management service, which provides comprehensive advice for business customers of the Bank and has offices in Edinburgh, Manchester, Birmingham and London.

Allied Irish Bank (GB) has specialist corporate banking teams across the country who work closely with branches to provide a seamless service in key sectors, underpinned by a solid understanding of the complexities of corporate and institutional business. The

Bank's strategy is to deliver a first class service through business innovation, knowledgeable staff and short lines of communication, ensuring customers' business needs are met quickly and efficiently.

RECENT DEVELOPMENTS
In line with the Bank's mid-corporate business positioning, branches have been restyled to reflect the needs of modern day business banking for corporate customers, with meeting rooms and open office space. With 31 full service branches and seven business development offices, the Bank has invested heavily in key business areas and larger, more customer friendly premises. This has allowed for greater access to teams of specialists who are available to inform on all areas of finance including Corporate Banking, Wealth Management, Global Trade Services, Asset Finance and Independent Financial Advice.

Performance remains strong and AIB Group (UK) plc has been assigned standalone credit ratings by both Standard & Poor's and Fitch. Assigned in 2004 and up-graded in May 2005, Standard & Poor's Long Term rating is A+ with a Short Term rating of A-1. In October 2007 AIB Group (UK) plc was assigned a Long Term Fitch rating of AA-, a Short Term rating of F1+ and Support rating of '1'.

PROMOTION
With an objective of achieving growth, the Bank recognises the need to continue raising its profile. It has taken an integrated approach to this and has created a strong presence in its local markets through advertising campaigns. Engaging with the media on a daily basis, building relationships and providing expert opinions on key business topics has been the underlying focus of the communication plan.

The Bank has been advertising on one of the UK's largest 'poster' sites since 1999. At just over a third of a kilometre in length and situated at Heathrow Airport Terminal 1, the

advert is seen by more than four million passengers per year travelling to and from the Republic of Ireland.

Business sponsorship is a key part of the Bank's promotional activity and it actively seeks opportunities to work with business organisations and professional bodies. Proving that business and the arts can also work together successfully, the Bank continued its partnership with LAMDA in their annual Communication and Performance Awards.

Allied Irish Bank (GB) has a sound horseracing heritage, and is a key provider to the racing industry – 27 of the 59 racecourses in the UK bank with them. A natural progression for the Bank was to become the first Founding Partner of Ascot Racecourse, an agreement that will see the Bank partner the racecourse until 2010.

BRAND VALUES
The Bank has a strong commitment to upholding its core brand values – Dependable, Engaging and Pioneering.

As part of AIB Group, the Code of Business Ethics for all employees reaffirms the general principles that govern how the Bank conducts its affairs. It recognises that maintaining the trust and confidence of customers, staff, shareholders and other stakeholders by acting with integrity and professionalism, as well as behaving with prudence and skill, is crucial to the continued growth and success of the Bank.

Allied Irish Bank (GB) has an active Corporate Social Responsibility programme and currently supports activities in the workplace, the marketplace, the local community and in the environment.

www.aibgb.co.uk

Things you didn't know about Allied Irish Bank (GB)

AIB Group, Ireland's leading banking and financial services organisation, operates principally in Ireland, Britain, Poland and the US, employing more than 24,000 people worldwide in over 750 offices.

Allied Irish Bank (GB) was one of the first business banks to obtain the Investors in People standard, holding it since 1995.

Allied Irish Bank (GB) has been voted Britain's Best Business Bank on seven consecutive occasions since 1994.

In 2007, 17 staff celebrated 25 years of service with the Bank.

Allied Irish Bank (GB) banks 15 of the top 100 universities, 15 of the top 50 independent schools, 17 of the top 50 housing associations in the UK and 27 of the 59 racecourses in Britain.

■ BASF

The Chemical Company

BASF, the world's leading chemical company, is a major supplier to the chemical, automotive, energy and construction industries worldwide. Headquartered in Germany, BASF posted sales of 52.6 billion euros in 2006, has production sites in 41 countries, customers in 170, and employs approximately 95,000 people around the world. In the UK, BASF has plants producing construction chemicals, fibre intermediates, polyurethane raw materials, and industrial coatings.

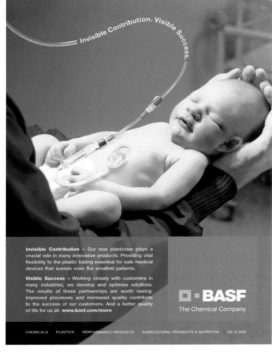

MARKET

BASF's portfolio includes chemicals, plastics, performance products, agricultural products, fine chemicals, crude oil and natural gas. Its most important customers include the agricultural, health and nutrition sectors as well as electrical/electronics, textile, packaging and paper companies. BASF is one of the few corporations with processes and products along the entire chemical value-adding chain. The extremely broad product range, and the extraordinary number of different industries supplied, makes the company relatively resilient to factors affecting individual industries.

ACHIEVEMENTS

When Friedrich Engelhorn founded the company back in 1865, he had a vision – to bring dye research and production under one roof. Each production facility would be linked to other plants so that the products and leftover material from one plant could serve as raw materials in the next. The original site in Ludwigshafen, Germany, is today the world's largest chemical complex.

BASF reduces its impact on the environment, and saves money, by using raw materials, by-products, energy and intermediates efficiently. From a few raw materials, BASF manufactures several dozen basic materials, which in turn are used to produce several hundred intermediates. After passing through a network of value-added production chains, these intermediates give rise to approximately 8,000 different products.

The company has a history of scientific innovation. It produced the first synthetic dyes, including the indigo used to colour jeans, the first polystyrene and the first magnetic recording tape. In another first for the company, a BASF employee who helped to develop the process for synthesising ammonia, which led to synthetic production of nitrogen fertilisers, won a Nobel Prize in 1931.

Today BASF is a world leader in new fields of development such as biotechnology and nanotechnology. The company is quick to act on market impulses, thanks to its strong network of employees collaborating with research and industry partners to develop solutions tailored to customer requirements. BASF shares have performed considerably better than the DAX 30 and the FURO STOXX50 indexes over the past 10 years.

PRODUCT

BASF uses its integrated approach to produce a full range of chemicals. The products are organised in five segments: Chemicals, Plastics, Performance Products, Agricultural Products & Nutrition, and Oil & Gas.

BASF is one of the leading global producers of styrenics, engineering plastics and polyurethanes. Its broad range of Performance Products includes high-value performance chemicals, coatings and

1865	1901	1929	1965	1995	2006
Badische Anilin & Soda-Fabrik is founded in Germany to produce coal tar dyes. Soaring population growth leads to strong demand for dyes, and BASF becomes a world-leading supplier.	BASF pioneers lightfast and washfast indanthrene dyes, which soon take over the supremacy of indigo in dyeing and printing.	BASF pioneers the first polystyrene, ushering in the 'plastics age'.	The acquisition of Glasurit, one of the largest companies in the European coatings industry, takes place.	BASF acquisitions include the worldwide pharmaceutical business of UK-based Boots. Two years later, BASF rationalisation leads to the sale of its tapes business.	BASF acquires Degussa's construction chemicals business and the US catalyst manufacturer, Engelhard Corporation.

functional polymers for the automotive, oil, paper, packaging, textile, sanitary care, construction, coatings, and leather industries. BASF is also a major supplier of agricultural products and fine chemicals for the farming, food processing, human nutrition and personal care industries. In plant biotechnology, the company is developing plants that are less sensitive to drought or are more nutritious.

In addition, a BASF subsidiary explores and produces crude oil and natural gas. Together with Russian partner Gazprom it markets, distributes and trades natural gas in Europe.

RECENT DEVELOPMENTS

Recent acquisitions reflect a policy of investing in customer-oriented businesses driven by innovation and growth. In 2006, BASF acquired the construction chemicals business of Degussa AG, including 7,400 employees, production sites and sales centres in more than 50 countries, and a worldwide portfolio in excess of 40,000 products. Combining its own chemical expertise with Degussa's know-how in construction chemicals applications has enabled BASF to offer a greater range of innovative products, helping its customers to be more successful in the competitive construction sector.

Other recent acquisitions include: Engelhard Corporation, which has seen BASF become a leading supplier in the first growing market for catalysts; Johnson Polymer, which provides BASF with a range of water-based resins that complement its portfolio of high solids and UV resins for the coatings and paints industry; and the integration of Crop Design, a Belgian biotechnology company, into BASF's plant biotechnology activities.

The company is increasingly developing new products and services in partnership with key customers; more than £1 billion is invested annually in research and development, and BASF is among the top five

companies in Europe for patent applications. In the key emerging market of Asia Pacific BASF is positioning itself as a major chemical manufacturer; BASF has the ambitious target of generating 20 per cent of its global sales and earnings in the chemical business in Asia Pacific by 2010, with 70 per cent of Asian sales expected to come from local production. BASF inaugurated its new Verbund site in Nanjing, China in 2005 – the largest individual investment in BASF's 140-year history.

PROMOTION

BASF's brand positioning provides concrete support to the company's communications with investors and analysts as well as its other target groups. In 2004, BASF concurrently introduced a new corporate design and a new logo including the words 'The Chemical Company'. This clearly states what BASF is and what it wants to remain – the world's leading chemical company.

In Europe, where the company has been running corporate advertising since 2001, BASF has been presenting itself to a larger target group as an important part of society and a responsible partner, using the slogan 'Invisible Contribution. Visible Success'. The campaign focuses on customer needs and on the benefits provided by the company's products and services. Ads have appeared frequently in the national press in the UK and also on posters on the London Underground.

Since 2005, TV has played a growing part in the UK campaign. In addition to advertising in trade magazines, BASF produces a number of publications for customers, including plastics and coatings. BASF has been involved in a number of sponsorships over the years in education, the arts and the industries it supplies. For more than 30 years the company has been a sponsor of Manchester's Hallé Orchestra. BASF also sponsors the Energy gallery and the 2008 Science of Survival exhibition at the Science Museum in London.

BRAND VALUES

BASF's mission is to be of value to people – to create value for the company, its customers, shareholders, employees, and the countries in which it operates. BASF develops and maintains partnerships characterised by mutual trust and respect. BASF's corporate philosophy is based on the principle of sustainable development; key to this approach is taking accountability for balancing business development with environmental protection and social responsibility.

As a founding member of the United Nations' Global Compact initiative, and by subscribing to the Responsible Care initiative launched by the chemical industry, BASF has committed itself to steadfastly pursuing improvements in the realms of environmental standards, health and safety as well as customer satisfaction – economic considerations do not take priority over these issues. BASF also carries out partnership projects with public sector organisations and Non Governmental Organisations.

www.basf.com

Things you didn't know about BASF

BASF has developed a nanotechnology based finishing system that makes industrial textiles easier to clean. Particles of dirt can be rinsed off the nanostructured surface more easily with water. Also, awnings, sunshades and tents treated with Mincor® don't need to be washed.

Helped by customers and partners, BASF has built a house at Nottingham University to demonstrate how its raw materials can be used to create an energy efficient and affordable home.

CONICA, which has been part of the BASF's Construction Chemicals Division since 2006, is the world's leading supplier of synthetic sports surfaces. Examples include the Olympic Stadium in Rome and the famous blue running track at Berlin's Olympic Stadium where the next athletics World Championships will take place in 2009.

BDO Stoy Hayward

BDO Stoy Hayward employs 3,000 partners and staff operating from 15 business centres nationwide. It is part of BDO International, the world's fifth-largest accountancy network, with 30,000 people and more than 600 offices in over 100 countries. With a market-leading employment proposition and among the fastest growth in its sector, it was the first accountancy firm to be named Global Firm of the Year by Accountancy Age.

MARKET

In the UK, the accountancy market has traditionally been dominated by just four firms. These firms – PricewaterhouseCoopers, Deloitte, KPMG and Ernst & Young – currently audit all FTSE 100 companies, and the majority of the top 350.

This domination continues to be the subject of intense debate in the accountancy industry, with BDO Stoy Hayward at the forefront of the discussion. With the biggest international presence outside the Big Four, BDO Stoy Hayward argues that there are invisible barriers that restrict open

competition and choice for the largest audit assignments. Its response to a marketplace that is dominated by four firms is to keep drawing attention to its shortcomings. It speaks for change.

BDO Stoy Hayward prides itself on offering a credible alternative to the Big Four. It aims to bring together experts from different fields to form multi-disciplinary teams with a single focus: improving clients' business. It offers expertise and enthusiasm, along with one of the highest partner-to-staff ratios in the business, which means clients spend more time with the partner.

ACHIEVEMENTS

BDO Stoy Hayward is fast establishing itself as the firm that offers both clients and employees an alternative that is successful, relevant and refreshingly different. It now has the scale and scope to act for all but the

largest global companies. Recent clients include BT Global Services, Hammerson, HBOS, Orange Business Services and Randgold. The quality of its work has also been acknowledged within the profession with its win of the inaugural Accountancy Age Global Firm of the Year award. The judges commented that it "stood out by a mile".

Indeed, the firm has been recognised for its performance as an employer. In 2007 it became the only accountancy firm with a third successive listing in The Sunday Times 100 Best Companies to Work For survey, and was one of only two accountancy firms listed in the Best Workplaces UK 2007, published in the Financial Times. It was also named in The Times Top 50 Where Women Want To Work, and in The Times Top 100 Graduate Employers listing.

PRODUCT

Understanding clients' business sectors and markets is key to ensuring the best possible advice and quality of work. Accordingly, BDO

1903	1919	1952	1988	1994	2005
A F Stoy founds Stoy & Co.	R J Hayward joins the firm.	Originally based in the City of London, the firm moves to the West End to be closer to its client base.	The firm changes its name to Stoy Hayward.	The firm joins BDO International, the world's fifth-largest accountancy network, and changes its name to BDO Stoy Hayward.	BDO Stoy Hayward becomes the first firm outside the Big Four to audit a FTSE 100 company.

INSTANT ACCESS. WORKS FOR SAVINGS, SO WHY NOT ACCOUNTANCY?

Global accountancy firm of the year.*

BDO

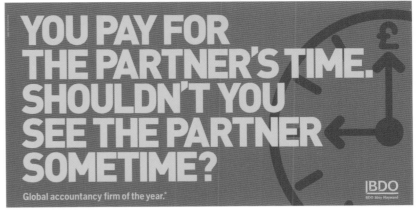

YOU PAY FOR THE PARTNER'S TIME. SHOULDN'T YOU SEE THE PARTNER SOMETIME?

Global accountancy firm of the year.*

BDO

Stoy Hayward continues to invest in building sector-specialist teams and now has groups focused on five key sectors: retail; financial services; technology, media & telecommunications; manufacturing; and real estate & construction.

In addition, the firm regularly operates in a wide range of other sectors, including natural resources and 'not for profit' organisations such as charities, education and registered social landlords.

The firm offers a full range of services, including business assurance, business restructuring, corporate finance and forensic accounting, as well as tax and investment management. It also offers market-leading services in specialist areas such as the Alternative Investment Market (AIM), IFRS conversion, Risk Assurance and Confiscation.

RECENT DEVELOPMENTS

BDO Stoy Hayward continues to gain market share from both the Big Four and mid-tier accountancy firms. In 2006/07 the firm's fee income increased by 15 per cent to reach £330 million.

The firm's sustained strong growth has led to it opening new offices in Gatwick and Cambridge and moving to new, larger offices in London and Manchester.

BDO Stoy Hayward remains market leader for new admissions to AIM, acting on 24 cases in 2006/07. Corporate Finance clients voted the firm M&A Accountancy Firm of the Year and AIM Accountant of the Year at the Growth Company Awards. It was also awarded Acquisition Monthly's AIM M&A Deal of the Year, 2007.

In October 2007 BDO Stoy Hayward added 70 tax professionals to its team when it acquired Chiltern, the UK's leading independent tax business, in a move that will create one of the most powerful tax offerings in the UK today.

PROMOTION

Creative, intelligent communications play an important role in building the BDO Stoy Hayward brand. Its award-winning thought leadership publication '33 Thoughts' and innovative approach to PR are excellent examples of this. BDO Stoy Hayward is bigger than most people think and, more importantly, offers a fresh way of doing business. Consequently, it has been working with one of London's top advertising agencies to raise awareness of its brand and demonstrate that it is 'the only credible alternative to the Big Four'.

The aim is to communicate one simple message – that when clients do business with BDO Stoy Hayward, they can be assured of an unrivalled client experience.

Strategically targeted campaigns have run throughout 2007, featuring bright, high-impact creative material with challenging statements such as: 'Don't want to be just another client? Don't go to just another accountancy firm' and 'You pay for the partner's time. Shouldn't you get to see the partner sometime?'. The strategy reinforces BDO Stoy Hayward's distinctly different approach, being bold and witty.

BRAND VALUES

'Being Successfully Different' is the vision underpinning the BDO Stoy Hayward brand. The firm is seen as 'high quality, straight-talking, pragmatic and human' and strives to be seen as 'the positive credible alternative' in the accountancy market. BDO Stoy Hayward strives to be the best, not the biggest.

For BDO Stoy Hayward, no two clients are the same, nor any two employees, and respecting people's differences is central to its values, which makes a tangible difference for its clients too.

www.bdo.co.uk

Things you didn't know about BDO Stoy Hayward

BDO Stoy Hayward offers employees six days a year for carrying out volunteer work.

BDO Stoy Hayward is one of the first professional services firms to commit to being carbon neutral.

BDO Stoy Hayward encourages its staff to give feedback on the firm by offering a charitable donation for every staff survey completed.

Ninety one per cent of BDO Stoy Hayward clients would recommend it to other companies.

BDO Stoy Hayward has more clients in the FTSE 350 than any other firm outside the Big Four.

2006	2007		2008
BDO Stoy Hayward becomes the fastest growing accountancy firm in the UK and the first firm to be named Global Firm of the Year by Accountancy Age.	BDO Stoy Hayward is named for the second year running in The Times Top 50 places Where Women Want to Work.	Also in 2007, new offices are opened in Cambridge and Gatwick.	BDO Stoy Hayward outgrows its existing London offices and moves to a landmark new building located at 55 Baker Street.

The British Market Research Bureau (BMRB) has been providing high quality research solutions for 75 years. It offers a range of approaches including bespoke proprietary research and consultancy, syndicated data and cost-effective omnibus research. BMRB is one of the leading market research agencies in the UK and a key operating company within the Millward Brown Group.

MARKET

Market research has seen a huge growth in demand in a number of key areas. The size of the UK research market has more than doubled in the last 10 years and according to the Market Research Society (MRS), was worth an estimated £1.3 billion in 2005. As one of the largest market research agencies in the UK, BMRB has been at the forefront of this growth.

ACHIEVEMENTS

BMRB's achievements run across all areas of the business, and in its commitment to quality, its staff, and its clients.

BMRB won two of the four BMRA Research Business Effectiveness Awards for 2005 – the award for Best Agency and the award for Quality & Service Excellence. BMRB was also shortlisted for the People Management award.

BMRB was one of the first market research companies to have professionally recognised training programmes for both research and operations executives.

Very high standards of client satisfaction are consistently achieved. In 2006, 96 per cent of clients gave the company an overall performance rating of 'excellent', 'very good' or 'good'.

PRODUCT

BMRB offers market-leading research services in:

Brand owner insight – Enlightenment harnesses the power of in-house and other data sources

and applies these to a range of applications. The service provides answers to all types of marketing questions, quickly and flexibly.

Employee and customer research – BMRB Stakeholder is a specialist unit dedicated to understanding customer loyalty and employee engagement. It helps organisations measure and respond to the needs of their customers, employees and other key stakeholders to improve their business performance.

Environmental and climate change research – BMRB offers a wealth of research resource and data on a wide range of issues relating to the environment. It conducts tailored qualitative and quantitative research amongst the general public, organisations and special interest groups.

Media research – BMRB Media works with the leading media owners and advertising agencies. It offers research expertise across all media and regularly provides insight into work relating to mixed media. BMRB aims to provide creative solutions and excellent client service for

1925	1933	1934	1939	1969	1987
The research department of JWT reported on its first survey – 'Report of Investigation on Pears Soap Consumers, United Kingdom'.	The British Market Research Bureau is set up, making it the longest established research agency in Britain.	One of the earliest and largest studies on newspaper readership for the Daily Herald is carried out.	BMRB becomes one of the first agencies to conduct major surveys for Government, including a survey for the Ministry of Food to monitor war-time rationing.	BMRB develops the Target Group Index (TGI) which has since become a standard trading currency for the UK media sector.	BMRB joins WPP Group plc.

media buyers, sellers, advertisers and regulators alike.

Omnibus surveys – Fast, accurate and cost effective, BMRB Omnibus is a leader in face-to-face, telephone, online and global omnibus surveys. Its broad portfolio of services offers flexible schedules and methodologies to suit wide-ranging research requirements.

Over 50s research – BMRB offers a range of research solutions for marketers targeting the over 50s as a consumer group, for policy makers measuring the impact of the over 50s on public policy and expenditure, and for employers realising the potential of the over 50s workforce.

Social policy and public sector research – BMRB Social Research is one of the largest providers of public policy research in the UK with a team of more than 70 dedicated social researchers. Its reputation for quality, technical excellence and creative solutions is second to none. BMRB regularly conducts prestigious national projects such as the British Crime Survey.

Sports research – BMRB Sport offers effective research solutions for all Sports sectors, from professional sports through to grassroots participation and active leisure. Its tools and techniques, designed to help the drive towards participation, are built around the principles of getting people to start, stay and succeed in sport. For the professional Sport sector, BMRB offers research to identify and grow revenue streams from media and sponsorship rights, and from the fan base.

Syndicated marketing and media surveys – TGI is the world's leading single-source measurement of consumers' product and brand usage, media consumption and attitudes. Originally developed in Britain by BMRB, TGI now operates in over 50 countries and is used by advertisers, media owners and agencies to provide worldwide consumer insight.

Travel & transport research – BMRB offers tailored research and insight for this diverse field. Its experience ranges from public policy research to commercial research for private travel operators and tourist boards.

RECENT DEVELOPMENTS

In 2006 BMRB launched new specialist areas of research including environmental and climate change; the over 50s; sports; and travel & transport. Each was established in response to emerging client needs.

BMRB was accredited ISO 20252 in April 2007. This new international standard sets a common level of quality for market research globally.

PROMOTION

BMRB uses a wide range of marketing communications tools to raise awareness and develop business for the products and services it specialises in.

BMRB's integrated marketing approach utilises advertising, PR, direct mail, website, email, delivering conference papers and sponsoring industry events. In addition, it regularly publishes a wide range of paper-based and online newsletters which focus on Social, TGI and Media research issues.

BMRB's findings and thinking are regularly published in the research and marketing trade press and in the national quality press. Coverage has been achieved in publications such as Research Magazine, Personnel Today, Human Resources, Marketing, Marketing Week, Brand Strategy, Campaign, The Times, FT, The Guardian, The Independent, The Telegraph and BBC Online.

BMRB's Centre for Excellence seminar programme plays an active role in helping clients better understand all aspects of the research

process. BMRB runs seminars and workshops for over 100 clients a year.

BRAND VALUES

By providing unimpeachable information, BMRB aims to empower clients to make better business decisions. An important contributory factor in maintaining BMRB's high standards is the quality of the company's staff training programmes – regarded as some of the best in the industry.

BMRB consciously avoids being a 'jack of all trades'. The company's established excellence in specific research sectors, reinforced by its comprehensive operational resources, enables it to be flexible and creative in meeting client needs. BMRB's core values are encapsulated in the words 'high quality tailored research solutions'.

www.bmrb.co.uk

Things you didn't know about BMRB

When BMRB launched TGI in 1969 it researched 25,000 respondents. By 2007 TGI had grown to more then 750,000 respondents annually worldwide.

Over the last five years BMRB has conducted more than 150,000 interviews for the British Crime Survey.

From 1969 to 1983 BMRB, backed by the music industry and the BBC, produced the Record Charts (the 'Top 20').

Jay K, lead singer of the band Jamiroquai, once worked as a research interviewer in BMRB's telephone unit in Ealing.

1997
It becomes the first to conduct Multi-Media Computer Aided Personal Interviewing (MM CAPI) nationally.

Also in 1997, BMRB conducts its first web-based research project – a readership survey for The Lancet.

2005
BMRB wins two of the four BMRA Research Business Effectiveness Awards for 2005.

2007
BMRB and Henley Centre HeadlightVision launch the Institute for Insight in the Public Services (IIPS), to share and promote global best practice on how public sector bodies can better connect with citizens.

bp

BP is one of the world's largest energy companies. Its distinctive products and services provide heat, light and mobility to millions of people around the globe. With a portfolio of master brands encompassing Aral, ARCO, ampm and Castrol, BP's brands are present in more than 100 countries, serving millions of customers every day.

MARKET

BP's specific areas of business include exploration for and production of crude oil and natural gas; refining and marketing of oil products; manufacturing and marketing of petrochemicals; and integrated supply and trading. BP is also an increasingly significant player in alternative energy and biofuels.

The relaunch of the BP brand in July 2000 proved to be a watershed in the company's history and that of the entire energy sector. Since unveiling its new 'Helios' mark, BP has

striven to establish itself as an environmentally-conscious brand, developing sustainable ways to meet the world's growing energy demands.

The success of the BP brand has not gone unnoticed even in the business to business sector, where the aviation, marine, bitumen and the liquefied petroleum gas businesses take pride of place and show commitment in the development of innovative and greener offers for their customers.

ACHIEVEMENTS

In the current climate of consumers' heightened awareness of environmental issues, brand leaders can be identified and recognised in terms of how they are responding to the climate change agenda.

In summer 2007, The Climate Group, jointly funded by Sky and Lippincott, undertook the Climate Conscious Consumer study. The aim was to track perceptions of how brands are performing on climate change. The BP brand

scored very highly in the US and the UK, ranking third and second respectively. The findings were reported on the Environment Leader daily news website.

PRODUCT

Today, people and businesses want the benefits of heat, light and mobility, but are often concerned about the consequences. BP has long been aware that it therefore needs to provide customers with alternatives that give them the benefits they want, with less environmental impact. The company continues to develop its portfolio of products based on this principle, with the simple aim of providing customers with a better quality of life.

One of BP Shipping's core values is 'Clean Seas' and together with BP Global LNG (Liquefied Natural Gas), it has set out to make the next generation of LNG ships world-leading in environmental performance. A ship

1901	**1909**	**1940s**	**1952**	**1954**	**1965**
Englishman William Knox D'Arcy obtains a concession from the Shah of Persia to explore for and exploit the oil resources of the country.	The Anglo-Persian Oil Company (as BP was first known) is formed.	After World War II, BP's sales, profits, capital expenditure and employment all rise to record levels as Europe is restructured.	The company commissions its first lubricating oils plant at Dunkirk.	BP Visco-Static, Europe's first multigrade oil, is brought onto the market.	BP finds the West Sole gas field – the first offshore hydrocarbons to be found in British waters.

has therefore been developed to incorporate a highly efficient dual fuel diesel electric propulsion system with the best available low emissions technology. This design solution has been shared with, and widely adopted by, the rest of the LNG shipping industry.

Still in the 'Clean Seas' arena, BP Marine together with Kittiwake Developments formed a joint venture known as Krystallon. Its main business is to supply eco-friendly, exhaust emissions control solutions to the marine industry.

The Krystallon Seawater Scrubber, which uses pollution abatement technology, is a recent innovation. It is the only marine exhaust gas scrubbing system in commercial operation today. The data from the Krystallon operational scrubber unit confirms over 95 per cent sulphur oxide gas removal and 80 per cent particulate removal, which marks a significant reduction in ship emissions and subsequent improvement in air quality.

RECENT DEVELOPMENTS

In the past year, BP launched its Carbon Footprint Toolkit (CFT), a free educational resource for teachers of 11-16 year-olds. This aims to provide information and activities to enhance understanding of carbon emissions and impacts, choices for reduction and alternative energy supplies. The resource was developed in consultation with teachers as well as experts at BP.

Through the CFT, BP has established thought leadership around climate change and carbon reduction, responding to the needs of teachers and building on innovative workshops developed within the employee-led Schools Link programme. In another significant development, BP's UK LPG (Liquefied Petroleum Gas) business recently established relationships with both Homebase and Argos, creating strategic collaborations that will build BP's brand presence. This is seen as a significant endorsement to the strength of the BP brand and its ability to partner with two other major brands in the UK.

PROMOTION

BP brands, each with their own unique heritage and history, are recognised and respected around the world. Together, they make BP the force it is today. BP is continually building its brands through investment and an innovative approach to brand management and positioning.

The Aral name remains one of the leading German retail brands, a byword for outstanding products and customer service on forecourts across the country.

BP's investment in consumer and B2B advertising and sponsorships for Castrol demonstrates the brand's continuing performance, especially in motor sport racing and sponsorship.

ARCO is the largest volume supplier of retail gasoline on the US West Coast. Alongside Arco fuels stands BP's franchised forecourt retail brand, ampm, which has been a household name in the US for more than 20 years.

BRAND VALUES

In all it says and does, BP aims to be performance driven, innovative, progressive and green. Performance driven means setting global standards of performance in every area, from protecting the environment to increasing growth and delivering greater satisfaction for customers and employees.

Being innovative means using the creative know-how of BP's people, combined with cutting-edge technology, to develop breakthrough solutions to business challenges and the needs of BP's customers.

Progressive means BP is always looking for new and better ways to do things. In touch with the needs of its employees, customers and local communities, BP aims always to be accessible, open and transparent.

Lastly, green means demonstrating environmental leadership. It also means overcoming the trade-off between providing access to heat, light and mobility and protecting the environment.

In summary, all BP employees aim to bring to life these brand values in their day-to-day work.

www.bp.com

Things you didn't know about BP

BP's aviation business, Air BP, was launched in 1926 and now supplies aviation fuels at 1,150 locations in more than 75 countries around the world.

BP's Global LPG (Liquefied Petroleum Gas) business unit has more than 10 million bottles in circulation in Europe alone.

BP's international marine business delivers half a million 18-litre pails of lubricants each year in more than 800 ports.

BP's Aromatics & Acetyls business uses cutting-edge technology to manufacture essential raw materials. One in every three polyester shirts or blouses worn today globally is produced from BP's PTA (Purified Terephthalic Acid).

1975	1990s	2000	2005
BP pumps the first oil from the North Sea's UK sector ashore after purchasing the Forties field – a development financed by a bank loan of £370 million.	BP merges with US giant Amoco, and the acquisitions of ARCO, Burmah Castrol and Veba Oil turn the British oil company into one of the world's largest energy companies.	The BP brand is relaunched with the unveiling of a new 'Helios' brand mark.	BP Alternative Energy is launched, a new business dedicated to the development and wholesale marketing and trading of low-carbon power.

British Gas Business has been supplying energy to businesses for the last 13 years as a separate unit and now has over 900,000 UK customers. It is the leading supplier of gas and electricity to business users in the UK and is dedicated to the needs of small and medium-sized enterprises (SMEs) through to industrial and commercial businesses. It is the first to offer account managers for all customers.

MARKET

British Gas Business operates in both the SME and Industrial and Commercial (I&C) UK energy markets, across which there are significant differences. The SME market has followed trends set by the domestic market, with the energy industry becoming ever more competitive since deregulation began in 1992. Currently SME customers are largely supplied by key domestic utility providers including Scottish Power, Powergen, npower, EDF and Scottish and Southern as well as smaller independents.

In contrast, the I&C market sees specialists taking a large part of the market share by volume with brands such as Gaz de France, Shell Gas Direct, British Energy and Elf Business Energy having high profiles in the market. All contracts are given bespoke prices on a fixed term contract basis – some for as long as five years.

Increases in wholesale energy prices over the past two years have impacted domestic and SME energy users, causing an increase in online switching websites and increased competition in the market. As wholesale energy prices began to decrease, British Gas was the first major energy supplier to lower prices in 2007 both for domestic and business customers.

Another key market for British Gas Business is the provision of related services for business, including insurance and energy compliance products.

ACHIEVEMENTS

With a share of more than 20 per cent, British Gas Business is the leader in the small business market – traditionally the brand's heartland. In recent years, it has also increased its share in the middle market and industrial and commercial markets.

Despite many challenges during the period of wholesale energy price increases, British Gas Business has since grown, investing in and implementing a new billing system to improve service for customers. In addition, to ensure customer service is delivered to a high standard British Gas Business believes in investing in its employees to develop a healthy workforce; for example, employees have the opportunity to take part in voluntary community schemes where they can work for charities or to be part of the work football teams. Through a flexible benefits scheme employees are also offered private medical and dental cover plus the option of discounted gym membership.

British Gas Business' commitment to identifying potential and providing career opportunities for its people within a supportive culture has resulted in it ranking in the top 10 Best Workplaces UK 2007

1948	1986	1994	1997	1998	2000
The Gas Act is introduced creating a nationalised gas industry throughout England, Scotland and Wales – the organisation 'The Gas Board' is formed.	Competition opens up for large gas customers who use over 25,000 therms of gas per year, and then, six years later, for gas customers using over 2,500 therms per year.	The Contract Trading division is established (later called Business Gas) in March after a British Gas restructure.	British Gas is separated into Centrica and BG plc. Business Gas transfers to Centrica within the British Gas Trading division.	In September Business Gas enters the commercial electricity market.	The number of non-domestic electricity customers reaches 100,000. In addition, the Utilities Act now defines business customers based on their activity, rather than usage.

index, published in the Financial Times, for the second year running – the third consecutive year that it has made the top 50.

Furthermore, in 2006 British Gas Business won the BBC Health Works Challenge for the Midlands before going on to win the Royal Society for Prevention of Accidents (ROSPA) Silver Award in 2007, for Health & Safety Practice.

PRODUCT

British Gas Business has a workforce of more than 2,000 people, all dedicated to providing business customers with the energy products and service they need – from arranging new connections through to offering account-managed support.

The company has been supplying gas to businesses for generations, but now also supplies electricity to half a million business customers.

In addition to the statutory requirements, British Gas Business offers the option of 100 per cent Green Electricity – provided from fully renewable sources and was recently named the greenest UK major energy supplier by the WWF.

British Gas Business is also spearheading the first dedicated online business insurance comparison service for small firms, Insurance-for-Business, in response to a growing frustration among Britain's SMEs at the lack of flexible insurance solutions.

Research has revealed that while more than half of all SMEs want to purchase their business insurance over the internet, the absence of a bespoke service has seen only 15 per cent buy online (Source: Finaccord 2006). British Gas Business' service aims to change this situation by providing a fast, easy route to a wide choice of business insurance from some of the UK's most trusted insurers.

RECENT DEVELOPMENTS

British Gas Business has recently rolled out a new look and feel in keeping with the parent brand, to raise the profile of its business energy expertise. In addition, as a result of customer research, British Gas Business has launched account management for all SME customers over the past year to offer dedicated personalised support to customers.

A key concern for all energy customers is receiving an accurate bill.

In response to issues with inaccurate meter readings British Gas Business is now the leading provider of Smart Meters to its business customers. The Smart Meters send automated readings and also help monitor and track usage. This is especially useful for larger I&C customers who can then identify ways to save energy.

British Gas New Energy was launched in 2007, a dedicated business unit committed to educating, engaging and enabling British Gas customers to reduce the impact of their energy use on their customers – an especially important issue for business customers.

PROMOTION

The TV advertising for the British Gas brand impacts business and domestic customers alike. The 'animated flame' concept has been used in advertising since 2005 and has become an effective creative property to make British Gas advertising more memorable. A more tailored approach is taken for communications to business customers, reflecting the specific messages for this audience. Targeted and timely campaigns inform SME customers about energy issues and ways to save energy, prompted through online and direct marketing channels.

Developing relationships with key partners such as the British Hospitality Association and Federation of Builders helps British Gas Business to reach key SME customers, as does attendance at events such as Business Startup and The Restaurant Show as well as sponsorship of the Southern Football League.

The I&C energy market requires a different approach; getting to the key decision maker is a tougher task with gate-keepers, boardrooms and complex business structures to contend with. Accurate data and stand-out communications are essential to secure success. Communications need to remain in the purchaser's mind for a long time, ready to be recalled when fixed term contracts come up for renewal.

British Gas Business has followed the approach of high-impact communications and detailed personalisation where possible to achieve its aims. In 2007, a 40 per cent response rate was achieved from sending customers a

jar of jelly beans with the challenge of guessing how many beans were in the jar. The aim was to increase awareness of the end to estimated readings through new metering technology.

BRAND VALUES

British Gas Business places its people at the heart of its brand promise to customers, that 'Your business is our business'. The personality of the brand grew from the internal values that British Gas Business people of all levels developed themselves in focus groups, demonstrating a commitment to delivering consistent levels of customer experiences across all touch-points.

British Gas Business aims to be approachable and attentive to the needs of business customers while being committed to resolving issues so its customers can get on with running their business. Being committed demonstrates the brand's desire to get things right first time, while being enterprising reflects an entrepreneurial spirit and drive to make real improvements for business customers.

www.britishgasbusiness.co.uk

Things you didn't know about British Gas Business

British Gas Business' biggest customer uses enough gas per year to supply the domestic gas for the whole of Oxford.

British Gas Business supplies electricity to more than half a million customers.

In 2006, Centrica, British Gas Business' parent company, had the lowest carbon emissions amongst the main suppliers.

British Gas Business has been used in a Government report about Health, Work and Wellbeing as a case study of best practice.

2001	2002	2007	
B2B (trading as British Gas and Business Gas) acquires Enron Direct Limited for £96.4 million with a portfolio of 160,000 commercial electricity customers.	Electricity Direct is acquired for £63 million with a portfolio of 97,000 commercial electricity customers.	British Gas Business is named in the top 10 of the Best Workplace in the UK 2007 index, published in the Financial Times, for the second year running – the third consecutive year that it has made the top 50.	The British Gas Business brand is revitalised to put the emphasis on business expertise, and all business customers are given their own account manager.

031

British Gypsum

British Gypsum is a major authority in the UK construction industry and the country's leading manufacturer and supplier of gypsum-based plastering and drylining solutions. With a long history of providing innovative, cost-effective and reliable products that meet the demands of the construction industry, the company is renowned for its pioneering work in training and product development, as well as its forward-thinking strategy on sustainable development.

MARKET

British Gypsum is the market leader in the supply of interior building solutions for the residential, commercial and RMI (refurbishment, maintenance and improvement) sectors of the construction industry, and has used its substantial expertise to develop the UK's leading range of wall, wall lining, floor, ceiling and encasement systems.

Five major manufacturing plants in Barrow-upon-Soar (Leicestershire), East Leake (Leicestershire), Kirkby Thore (Cumbria), Robertsbridge (East Sussex) and Sherburn-in-Elmet (North Yorkshire) provide nationwide manufacturing and distribution capabilities, serving the needs of a diverse range of customers and influencers, from specifiers and architects, contractors and housebuilders, to specialist distributors, builders merchants and DIY outlets.

ACHIEVEMENTS

In 2006, British Gypsum was named Best Overall Supplier by Travis Perkins and Sustainability Supplier of the Year by AMEC. In presenting the AMEC award for the company's work on Gateshead's Queen Elizabeth Hospital, AMEC's managing director said the project "demonstrated the kind of environmental results that can be achieved through good design, careful specification of products and British Gypsum's innovative Plasterboard Recycling Service".

This strong reputation stems from the company's determination to bring innovative, sustainable products to the country's building projects. British Gypsum pioneered the introduction of lightweight, fast-track building solutions in the UK and has had a huge impact on the residential and commercial built environment. Prestigious projects, including the O2 Arena, Emirates Stadium, St Pancras station, and Putney Wharf, rely on British Gypsum to deliver comfortable living environments though the provision of high performance internal lining systems.

The company's training and testing facilities reflect its market-leading status. Its Drywall Academy is a centre of excellence for training, with NVQ accreditation and Construction Industry Training Board recognition. Around 6,000 people pass through its three purpose-built training centres each year, gaining specialist knowledge in all aspects of drylining. As well as equipping contractors, organisations and its own employees with the latest industry skills, British Gypsum has been pioneering merchant training for over 30 years.

In addition, British Gypsum's UKAS-approved testing laboratories are the best-equipped and most advanced drywall testing facilities in Europe. Here, more than 10,000 tests and substantiation reports underpin the performance of drylining products and systems across the industry.

PRODUCT

British Gypsum offers a range of more than 700 products, sold under five individual brands: Gyproc plasterboard, Thistle plaster, Gypframe metal, Glasroc specialist board and Arteco ceiling products. In each area, the company is constantly reviewing, improving and adding to its products to ensure it has the most comprehensive and innovative offering available.

Customers benefit from a complete package of goods and services that includes

1917	1964	1967	1972	1975	1978
The British Plaster Board company is founded.	Gypsum interests are amalgamated to form British Gypsum.	British Gypsum opens its first dedicated training facility.	The White Book is first published.	British Gypsum launches the first performance plasterboard.	British Gypsum introduces metal framing into drylining systems.

on-site technical supervision and the SpecSure lifetime system warranty. Designed to deliver peace of mind, SpecSure guarantees systems are built from the highest-quality components, rigorously tested to provide guaranteed acoustic, fire, impact and thermal performance to meet even the most demanding of building requirements.

Supported by its Drywall Academy, British Gypsum provides the most comprehensive technical and training support package in the industry. From initial project design and planning through to site installation and beyond, specialist teams of technical experts deliver quality technical advice everyday.

The company's service even extends to waste collection and recycling. In 2001, it invested considerable funds in launching its Plasterboard Recycling Service, marking a major innovation for an industry faced with escalating waste costs. Now an established commercial venture, the scheme collects waste from construction sites and delivers it to one of two dedicated, cutting-edge recycling plants. Here, raw materials are obtained that can be fed back into the manufacturing process without affecting quality.

RECENT DEVELOPMENTS

Sustainability and environmental considerations are also given real emphasis in British Gypsum's extensive Corporate Social Responsibility programme. The company is committed to minimising its impact on natural resources and promoting sustainable development by delivering on its responsibilities to the environment, the economy and society.

Contributing to the company's success in the 2006 Travis Perkins and AMEC awards, the programme has also earned British Gypsum the prestigious Taylor Woodrow Sustainability Award 2007. The company was also shortlisted for both the 2007 WRAP and Building Commitment to the Environment Awards.

British Gypsum's products and systems are continually evolving. Recent successful launches include Glasroc Rigidur super-

All together covered

Only high quality branded products that have been designed and tested to work together will give you drylining system performance that's guaranteed.

That means total peace of mind with SpecSure™ - the lifetime system warranty from British Gypsum.

www.british-gypsum.com/specsure

British Gypsum
PURE INNOVATION

GYPROC
PLASTERBOARD PRODUCTS

THISTLE
PLASTER PRODUCTS

GYPFRAME
METAL PRODUCTS

GLASROC
SPECIALIST BOARD PRODUCTS

ARTECO
CEILING PRODUCTS

impact-resistant board, part of the GypWall EXTREME system for high-traffic public areas; Gyproc SoundCoat, an innovative sealer providing superior acoustic performance; and Gyproc ProMix LITE, a lightweight, ready-mixed cement for faster jointing.

Major investments have also been made in the company's manufacturing plants at East Leake and Sherburn-in-Elmet. In June 2007, £120 million was spent on significantly increasing capacity for both plaster and plasterboard products, ensuring it will continue to stay on top of rising demand. The two plants are recognised as among the most advanced in the world and the investment has been hailed as a world-class example of best practice in business planning.

PROMOTION

The strength of British Gypsum's brand lies in the close partnerships the company establishes with clients, building owners, designers, merchants and contractors. An important part of this is its commitment to making comprehensive, practical information readily available to the construction industry.

The company's website alone receives 40,000 visits a month, with all brochures, product data sheets and even the company's renowned White Book and Site Book available to download. Further development in 2008 will see the website become an even more useful resource.

The White Book is seen as the industry's leading publication on drylining and often referred to as the specifier's bible, while the

Site Book gives valuable guidance on site use and installation. An in-house design team also produces technical guides tailored to specific construction sectors.

Continuing its Corporate Social Responsibility strategy, British Gypsum sponsors CRASH, the construction industry's charity for the homeless. The company donates funds, provides materials to build shelters and encourages employees to take part in local projects.

BRAND VALUES

British Gypsum's success is grounded in a set of clearly defined guidelines: Professional commitment, Respect for others, Integrity, Loyalty, Solidarity.

www.british-gypsum.com

Things you didn't know about British Gypsum

Every month, British Gypsum delivers enough plasterboard, laid end to end, to stretch from London to Sydney.

It would take the water from four Olympic-size swimming pools to mix the amount of plaster delivered by British Gypsum every week.

Every day British Gypsum delivers enough bagged plaster to make a pile 35 times the height of Canary Wharf Tower.

British Gypsum is part of Saint-Gobain, the largest manufacturer of plasterboard and plaster in the world.

The Drywall Academy advice line receives over 10,000 enquiries every month and is one of the busiest in the construction industry.

1991	2001	2007	2008
The UK's largest plaster mining and manufacturing facility is built at Barrow-upon-Soar, Leicestershire.	British Gypsum introduces a Plasterboard Recycling Service for its customers.	British Gypsum invests £120 million in two new manufacturing plants.	Development of the brand's website takes place to provide a more comprehensive resource.

BSI Group is a global independent professional business services organisation that inspires confidence and delivers assurance to customers with standards-based solutions. The Group's key offerings are: the development and sale of private, national and international standards; second and third-party management systems assessment and certification; testing and certification of products and services; performance management software solutions; and training services.

MARKET

BSI works with clients operating in a myriad of sectors, including communications, banking, engineering, electronics, food & drink, agriculture and consumer goods. In order to compete and inspire their customers' trust, BSI's clients – which include 75 per cent of FTSE 100 companies, 42 per cent of Fortune 500 companies as well as 42 per cent of companies listed on the Hang Seng – rely on industry benchmarking and quality assurance, and the BSI Kitemark® is seen as one of the most trustworthy marks to be gained. BSI is one of the world's leading providers of standards-based solutions, covering every aspect of the modern economy.

ACHIEVEMENTS

Founded in 1901, BSI Group today employs over 2,250 staff and generated a turnover of

£163.9 million in 2006. It services clients in 110 countries, and assists nations such as Albania, Russia, Serbia and Sierra Leone in developing and improving their emerging standardisation infrastructures.

The organisation produces an average of 2,700 standards per year and has recently published the world's first standard for business continuity management, BS 25999.

BSI British Standards has won a number of recent awards including an IVCA Clarion Award in 2006 for its promotion of PAS 78, a standard that ensures anyone commissioning a website makes it accessible to disabled people. BSI's Kitemark® has also been recognised in 2008 as a Business Superbrand in its own right.

BSI remains at the forefront of the international standards industry, leading the international standards committee on

nanotechnology; pioneering new guidelines on information security, risk management and sustainability; and assisting in the development of the only internationally recognised food safety management standard.

The ISO 9000 quality series, now adopted by over 890,000 organisations in 170 countries, was developed from British Standard BS 5750 first published in 1979 and is now recognised as the world's most successful standard. Furthermore, the most widely accepted environmental management systems standard, ISO 14001, was derived from BS 7750 and has been implemented in 140 countries.

PRODUCT

BSI operates globally through three divsions: BSI British Standards, BSI Management Systems and BSI Product Services.

1901	1903	1929	1953	1979	1992
BSI Group is founded as the Engineering Standards Committee (ESC). One of the first standards to be published is to reduce the number of sizes of tramway rails.	The Kitemark® is first registered as a trademark.	The ESC is awarded a Royal Charter and in 1931, the name British Standards Institution (BSI) is adopted.	In the post-war era, more demand for consumer standardisation work leads to the introduction of the Kitemark® for domestic products.	BS 5750, now known as ISO 9001, is introduced to help companies build quality and safety into the way they work. The Certification mark is also introduced.	BSI publishes the world's first environmental management standard, BS 7750, now known as ISO 14001.

BSI British Standards develops standardisation solutions to meet the needs of UK business. It works with businesses, consumers and the Government to represent UK interests and to make sure that British, European and international standards are useful, relevant and authoritative. BSI British Standards' products and services help organisations to successfully implement best practice, manage business-critical decisions and achieve operational excellence.

BSI Management Systems is one of the world's largest certification bodies: over 60,000 certified locations, clients in more than 100 countries and market leader in the UK and North America. The division provides assessment, certification, verification and training services in management disciplines including: Business Continuity, Environment, Food Safety, Health & Safety, Information Security, Integrated Management, Quality and Social Responsibility. Its award-winning Entropy Software™ provides auditable solutions to improve environmental, social and economic performance.

BSI Product Services is best known for the Kitemark® which was the UK's first product quality mark. The division provides product and services testing and certification to ensure that vital safety and performance requirements are met – from vehicle bodywork repair to fire extinguishers, from gas appliances to medical devices. BSI Product Services provides CE marking under 17 European Directives for companies wishing to trade in the EU.

RECENT DEVELOPMENTS

BSI Group's website was relaunched in 2007 with full ecommerce capabilities, including all 40,000 standards and publications now available to purchase online.

In 2007 BSI was awarded UKAS accreditation for its BS 8555 STEMS scheme, which enables organisations to implement an environmental management system, leading to full ISO 14001 recognition. In 2006 BSI was one of the first organisations to be accredited to ISO 22000, the latest food safety management systems standard.

A major step for BSI is its partnership with the Carbon Trust and Defra to develop a standard methodology for the measurement of the embodied greenhouse gases in products and services, with nine companies, including Coca-Coca and Cadbury Schweppes, piloting the draft standard, PAS 2050.

In 2007 BSI and Thatcham developed PAS 125, a specification for vehicle bodywork repair, with the ensuing Thatcham BSI Kitemark® scheme providing independent certification that a bodyshop is competent to safely repair vehicles in accordance with the standard. Another automotive sector development is the Kitemark® scheme for Garage Services which ensures that the standards of PAS 80 are met and maintained for the servicing and repair of vehicles.

In 2007 BSI introduced BS 8901, the world's first standard on sustainable event management. Trialled at six locations including the Manchester International Festival and Live Earth, it sets out requirements for planning and managing sustainable events.

PROMOTION

Few organisations have a stronger claim than BSI Group to the assertion that it raises standards worldwide and for this reason it has chosen 'raising standards worldwide™' as its strapline, which was deployed in 2006.

In July 2002 a single BSI brand was created and the organisation

now has a consistent and clear visual identity, with all BSI staff working to maintain the standard.

BSI's marketing focuses on achieving the long term goal of a coherent global brand identity. Public relations plays a key role, as does BSI's business magazine, Business Standards, with a readership of 101,000 reaching into the business community.

To reinforce the brand internally, BSI's brand identity website – rebuilt in 2008 – is a crucial tool, making the corporate guidelines easily accessible to staff and suppliers.

BRAND VALUES

BSI Group's core brand values are integrity, innovation and independence. They are the foundation of the BSI brand, supporting the organisation as it strives towards its vision of inspiring confidence and delivering assurance to all customers through standards-based solutions.

BSI continually strives to deliver its brand values, with the aim of building a powerful, globally recognised brand, satisfying the needs of all stakeholders.

www.bsigroup.com

2002	2006	2007	
KPMG's ISO registration business in North America is acquired, making BSI Group the largest certification body in the region.	BSI acquires German certification company NIS ZERT, UK and Canadian-based software solutions company Entropy International Ltd and Australia's Benchmark Certification Pty Ltd.	BSI publishes the world's first standard for business continuity management certification, BS 25999-2, and BS 8901 for managing events sustainably.	

Things you didn't know about BSI

A 2006 survey carried out by GfK NOP showed that 88 per cent of the UK adult population trust the Kitemark®.

The original BSI committee met for the first time on the day Queen Victoria died – 22nd January 1901.

BSI Management Systems UK is the world's first carbon neutral certification body.

BT is a world-leading provider of communications solutions and services, operating in 170 countries across the globe. The company's principal activities include networked IT services, local, national and international telecommunications services, and higher-value broadband and internet products and services. BT is well positioned to become the UK's first truly converged provider of information, communications and networking services and is a major force in the digital networked economy.

MARKET

BT operates in a thriving, multi-trillion pound industry that spans the whole world. In recent years the global communications market has been focused on convergence, whereby the boundaries between telcos, IT companies, software businesses, hardware manufacturers and broadcasters have become intertwined to create a new communications industry – an industry driven by the relentless evolution of technology and insatiable customer demand for innovative communications solutions.

ACHIEVEMENTS

BT has successfully transformed itself in recent years. It has evolved from being a supplier of telephony services to become a leading provider of innovative communications products, services and solutions. Its business customers range from multinational corporations to SMEs and start-ups.

More than 80 per cent of the FTSE 100 and 40 per cent of the largest Fortune Top 50 companies rely on BT for networking, applications and system integration.

Organisations such as the National Health Service, the Post Office, Nestlé, Fiat, Microsoft®, Philips, Unilever and the Bavarian National Government are working with BT to maximise the power of networked IT and communications services.

BT has been a driving force behind the success of 'Broadband Britain'. Thanks to the company's investment, nearly every home in Britain now has access to broadband.

In September 2007, BT was recognised, for the seventh year running, as the world's top telecommunications company in the Dow Jones Sustainability Index (DJSI).

In 2007, Business in the Community (BITC), the business-led charity group, recognised BT's highly active approach to corporate social responsibility in its National Awards for Excellence. In the highly prized Impact on

Society Award category, BT was named as Company of the Year.

In addition, BT has been granted a Royal Warrant to supply communications, broadband and network services for Her Majesty The Queen. This took effect from 1st January 2007 and has been approved for use by BT for the next five years.

PRODUCT

BT provides a wide range of world-class communications solutions for all types of business organisation – from sole trader start-ups to multi-site global enterprises. The company's vision is to provide customers with access to all of their applications and information, wherever they are, on their choice of device, whilst utilising the best network available.

1984	1991	2003	2005	2006	2007
BT is privatised making it the only state-owned telecommunications company to be privatised in Europe.	British Telecom is restructured and relaunches as BT.	BT unveils its current corporate identity and brand values, reflecting the aspirations of a technologically innovative future.	Following the Telecommunications Strategic Review (TSR), BT signs legally-binding undertakings with Ofcom to help create a better regulatory framework.	Openreach launches and is responsible for managing the UK access network on behalf of the telecommunications industry.	BT begins the next wave of its transformation as it evolves into a customer-centric, software-driven 21st century services organisation.

To meet the needs of its business customers, traditional products such as calls, analogue/digital lines and private circuits are combined with products and services such as networking and network management, broadband, mobility, CRM, applications management and hosting as well as desktop services.

Specifically, BT is pioneering the take-up of public wireless broadband in the UK. BT Openzone enables customers on the move to surf the web, check emails and download documents at more than 8,500 'hotspots' in the UK, and now over 30,000 sites across the globe.

In the last 12 months BT has launched a number of unique and innovative products and services aimed at smaller businesses. This portfolio includes BT's IT Manager service and BT Tradespace, a social networking site designed to help businesses interact with customers as well as each other.

The company has also launched Office Anywhere, a breakthrough service that gives users the functions of a Windows PC, but in a smartphone small enough to fit in the pocket.

In January 2007, BT unveiled a WiFi version of its award-winning Fusion phone. BT Corporate Fusion allows customers to roam between WiFi and mobile networks, enabling them to benefit from all the value and convenience advantages of Fusion.

RECENT DEVELOPMENTS

In recent years, BT has transformed itself from a narrowband company to a broadband one. Now it has embarked on the next stage of its transformation that will be just as important and equally radical. BT is moving from being a hardware-based business into becoming a software-driven company.

This means delivering new software services for customers, instantly, at the push of a button rather than through a process of screwdrivers, rewiring and customer

visits. This will dramatically increase the speed at which BT can design new services and deliver them to its customers.

Furthermore, at the end of 2006, BT made communications history with the transfer of the first customer lines to its 21st Century Network (21CN), the world's most advanced next generation network.

PROMOTION

In 2007, BT launched a new television and online advertising campaign aimed at SMEs. The campaign, led by renowned UK TV chef and entrepreneur Gordon Ramsay, is based on the insight that smaller businesses want to focus on their core business and the things they love about what they do, rather than get distracted by IT. This is expressed by the campaign idea that BT is here to help you, the customer, 'do what you do best'.

The first ad aired on 1st May 2007, featuring Ramsay in one of his London businesses, Restaurant Gordon Ramsay. In the ad, the chaotic results of what happens when Ramsay becomes distracted by IT are reflected. Instead of concentrating on what he does best – running his kitchen – he is sorting out his IT, at the expense of his business.

In sponsorship, BT has become title sponsor of 'BT Team Ellen' – a new sailing team headed up by legendary sailor, Ellen MacArthur. The sponsorship agreement means that Ellen has become the ambassador for BT's worldwide corporate social responsibility programme.

BT Global Services' new campaign positions BT as the thought leader and the partner of choice for networked IT services across the globe. It demonstrates to a senior executive audience that BT understands the big issues that are of concern to them in their business, and gives an uplift to the brand.

The Bigger Thinking campaign is centred on

www.biggerthinking.com and incorporates television, print and posters across Europe, the US, India and China.

BRAND VALUES

BT's corporate identity defines the kind of company it is today – and the one it needs to be in the future. Central to that identity is a commitment to create ways to help customers thrive in a changing world. To do this, BT focuses on 'living' its brand values which are as follows: Trustworthy – doing what it says it will; Helpful – working as one team; Inspiring – creating new possibilities; Straightforward – making things clear; Heart – believing in what it does.

The BT strapline – Bringing it all together – aims to convey leadership in the way in which BT enables global business customers to profit from convergence.

www.bt.com

Things you didn't know about BT

BT is the number one conferencing provider in Europe with three quarters of the FTSE companies using its services.

BT equipment powers 1,400 trading floors across 51 countries with more than 60,000 users. Ninety per cent of traders on the New York Stock exchange use BT's voice trading technology.

BT is delivering the largest RFID (radio frequency identification) product tagging project in the world for the retailer Marks & Spencer.

BT supplies the CCTV security to Arsenal's 60,000 capacity Emirates Stadium.

BT Tower is a global media hub, handling an average of 90,000 hours of UK and international broadcast content every day.

CARBON TRUST

The Carbon Trust is the UK's leading authority on carbon reduction. Set up by the Government in 2001 as an independent company, it works with thousands of UK businesses, including more than 50 per cent of the FTSE 100, and 143 public sector bodies. Its mission is to accelerate the move to a low carbon economy.

MARKET

The UK's direct emissions of CO_2 are 560 million tonnes (Mt) a year – 40 per cent of which are created by business and the public sector. The Carbon Trust works with both of these to help them reach the Government's target to reduce overall UK emissions by at least 60 per cent by 2050.

In fact, the Carbon Trust is defined by this mission to accelerate the move to a low carbon economy. Its 'not-for-dividend' status means that any funds generated are reinvested in projects to meet the Carbon Trust's mission.

ACHIEVEMENTS

Recognising that businesses are motivated by commercial benefits, the Carbon Trust strives to offer solutions that deliver both carbon and cost savings to business and the public sector.

In 2006/07 alone, the Carbon Trust helped its customers to identify annual savings of 4.6-5.4 $MtCO_2$ and annual cost savings worth £485-£543 million. The carbon savings achieved since the Carbon Trust was set up in 2001 now total 10.8 $MtCO_2$.

In addition to driving low carbon action, the Carbon Trust has also recently been ranked as a top non-profit organisation coming fourth overall in Henley Management Centre's UK Thought Leadership Index 2007.

PRODUCT

To achieve its mission, the Carbon Trust works in five complementary business areas: Insights, Solutions, Innovations, Enterprises and Investments. The Carbon Trust

fundamentally believes that all these things are required to realise a low carbon economy.

'Insights' explains the issues and opportunities surrounding climate change and carbon reduction, developing low carbon strategies that engage Government, business and the public sector. It aims to increase understanding of the issues and their impact through strategic analysis of these issues, in-depth reports and technical publications, along with seminars and training events.

'Solutions' delivers carbon reduction by working with business and the public sector to identify carbon emissions, review their business strategy and practically find ways of reducing their carbon footprint in the short term.

'Innovations' helps develop commercially promising low carbon technologies through partnerships, funding, expert advice and large-scale demonstrations. This includes the Incubator scheme, which helps early-stage, low carbon technology companies attract commercial investment. It also recognises innovative development in carbon reduction,

with the Carbon Trust Innovation Awards, which attract more than 200 major entries.

'Enterprises' creates high growth, low carbon businesses by identifying opportunities and bringing together key skills and resources. It aims to unlock valuable, low carbon business opportunities by providing seed funding and commercial and business development expertise.

Finally, 'Investments' is one of the leading backers of early stage UK clean energy technology businesses. Its analysis of technology trends and market drivers gives the Carbon Trust a unique capacity to assess investment opportunities.

RECENT DEVELOPMENTS

Having restructured its business into the five areas, the Carbon Trust redefined its brand values, leading to the review and launch of a dynamic new corporate identity. In March 2007 it launched a Carbon Reduction Labelling Initiative to encourage companies to measure the carbon footprint of individual products and demonstrate a commitment to reduce that

2001	2002		2004	2005	
The Carbon Trust is established.	The Carbon Trust's offices in Scotland, Wales and Northern Ireland open.	Also in 2002, the Carbon Trust makes its first Venture Capital Investment.	The Carbon Trust Incubator scheme is launched to help early stage, low carbon technology companies attract commercial investment.	Carbon Trust Enterprises is established, with the aim of encouraging entrepreneurialism to unlock low carbon markets.	Also in 2005, the Marine Energy Challenge is completed, resulting in the launch of a new Marine Energy accelerator focusing on bringing the sector down the cost curve.

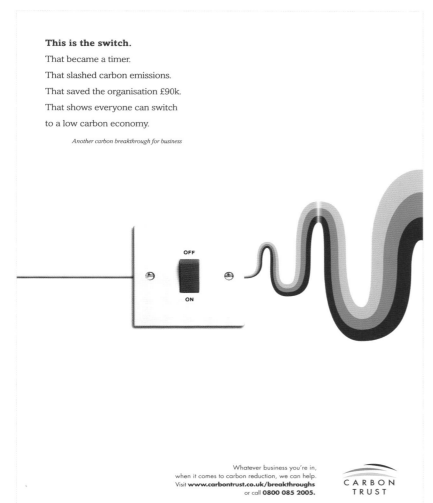

This is the switch.
That became a timer.
That slashed carbon emissions.
That saved the organisation £90k.
That shows everyone can switch
to a low carbon economy.

Another carbon breakthrough for business

Whatever business you're in,
when it comes to carbon reduction, we can help.
Visit **www.carbontrust.co.uk/breakthroughs**
or call **0800 085 2005.**

CARBON TRUST

The Carbon Trust is funded by the Department for Environment, Food and Rural Affairs, the Department for Business, Enterprise and Regulatory Reform, the Scottish Government, the Welsh Assembly Government and Invest Northern Ireland.

This is the sea.
That is a clean source of energy.
That could provide a fifth of our electricity.
That needs new technology.
That the Carbon Trust is accelerating.
To turn the tide towards a low carbon economy.

Another carbon breakthrough for business

Whatever business you're in,
when it comes to carbon reduction, we can help.
Visit **www.carbontrust.co.uk/breakthroughs**
or call **0800 085 2005.**

CARBON TRUST

The Carbon Trust is funded by the Department for Environment, Food and Rural Affairs, the Department for Business, Enterprise and Regulatory Reform, the Scottish Government, the Welsh Assembly Government and Invest Northern Ireland.

carbon footprint over the following two years. The Carbon Trust, in partnership with Defra, is now co-sponsoring the development of Product Carbon Footprinting Methodology into a public standard lead through BSI, piloted with Walkers Snackfoods, Boots and innocent drinks.

In September 2007, the Carbon Trust announced nine leading companies that will make up a second wave of partners to pilot the Carbon Footprinting Standard. These include Cadbury Schweppes, Coca-Cola, Müller Dairy and HBOS.

PROMOTION
The Carbon Trust's communication strategy spans the use of advertising, PR, direct mail, its website and electronic direct mail, annual reports and publications, events and seminars including EU briefings, and workshops on subjects such as labelling, footprinting and carbon management.

The strategy is based on the belief that carbon reduction requires two fundamental changes – reducing the amount of energy we use, and reducing the amount of carbon in the energy we use. Its recent 'Breakthroughs' advertising campaign launched in 2007, showcases real-life case studies aimed at inspiring organisations to embrace carbon reduction by demonstrating how small actions can have a large positive impact on their business. It also highlights the Carbon Trust's leading role in supporting innovative low carbon technology development, that delivers bottom line benefits to UK business. The Carbon Trust is positioned as the calm, authoritative voice in this vital but crowded sector where trust is key.

Recent communications tracking shows the Carbon Trust is the most favourably regarded brand within the carbon reduction sector, has the highest awareness and, of those who are familiar with it, 80 per cent of people were found to be prepared to recommend the Carbon Trust to others.

BRAND VALUES
The Carbon Trust has four values that it strives to embrace in everything it does.

Firstly, the Carbon Trust is objective – with so much noise and opinion in the sector, it's crucial that it weighs up the options to provide reassurance that the organisation has the right knowledge to make informed decisions. Secondly, it is collaborative – it works with organisations of all sizes on the measurement and reduction of carbon. Thirdly, it is creative – it aims to inspire organisations by thinking laterally about carbon reduction. Finally, it is straightforward – by providing simple, step-by-step approaches it makes it easy to get involved.

www.carbontrust.co.uk

Things you didn't know about Carbon Trust

The Carbon Trust has already helped to save 10.8 million tonnes of carbon dioxide ($MtCO_2$) since it was set up in 2001.

The Carbon Trust is the only Government-backed organisation in the world that funds the development of low carbon technology from R&D right the way through to commercial viability.

In 2006/07, more than 36,000 Carbon Trust energy efficiency stickers were requested by UK organisations.

2006
The Carbon Trust Research Accelerator launches, to research and develop the commercialisation of promising low carbon technologies.

Also in 2006, the Carbon Trust wins the Grand Prix at the B2B Marketing Awards for Best Integrated Campaign – placing carbon reduction on the business agenda.

2007
The Carbon Reduction Labelling Initiative is launched – pilot companies include PepsiCo, Boots and innocent.

The Carbon Trust's Customer Centre is recognised as the largest carbon advice centre for business in Europe.

Advert images, this page, left to right: Jason Tozer, Corbis

CBS OUTDOOR

CBS Outdoor has some of the most exciting and captivating advertising canvas in the UK. It is the market leader in transport advertising, providing an effective way of talking to the increasingly valuable and growing numbers of consumers on the move. Its innovative digital offering is changing the face of poster advertising, broadcasting full HD moving images where copy can be instantaneously changed and campaigns planned by time of day.

MARKET

The UK advertising market was worth £9.8 billion in 2007 and Outdoor advertising took a 10 per cent share. Posters and the internet were the only two advertising media delivering revenue growth in the UK in 2007.

CBS Outdoor is number two in the UK Outdoor market with 23 per cent share. JC Decaux also has 23 per cent share while the largest player in the UK in revenue terms is Clear Channel at 26 per cent. Both Clear Channel and JC Decaux's portfolios are predominately roadside posters.

ACHIEVEMENTS

In 2006 CBS Outdoor was awarded the largest outdoor advertising contract in the world – the London Underground – for 8.5 years. Worth

more than £1.2 billion and coveted by all of the world's main outdoor contractors, 31,000 advertising sites are being upgraded over two years with an unprecedented level of investment from CBS Outdoor.

CBS Outdoor has pioneered and is installing three of the most innovative digital products in advertising – Digital Escalator Panels, LCDs and Cross-Track Projection (XTP). Its network of 2,000 screens will make it the largest in the world.

CBS Outdoor was short-listed by Campaign magazine for media brand of the year in 2007. Furthermore, Yell.com's digital screen bus campaign was awarded a D&AD Yellow Pencil in 2007 – the first time a bus campaign has received this prestigious creative award.

PRODUCT

The Outdoor offering comprises static and digital poster sites on buses, the London Underground and the UK's train and tram networks. Outdoor's generic benefit of being a broadcast media, reaching an affluent, growing young audience is particularly true of CBS Outdoor's portfolio.

Bus advertising is unique in that it is the most seen media out of home and has a strong town centre presence. Like the Underground, it is often welcomed by consumers and is seen as relevant. On average people see bus advertising on five different occasions each day, making it a high frequency medium (Source: Q-Media).

The London Underground is an advertising environment like no other, being central to the nation's capital. The high dwell time and captive audience means long exposure to advertising messages. 6-sheet posters (a small poster site) offer the advertiser the opportunity to target discretely and create flexible bespoke packages in high pedestrian areas, whilst larger 48-sheet posters across the platforms offer brand stature and an average of three minutes exposure time.

The real value of CBS Outdoor's products is delivered through the audience who consume them. We are all spending more and more time out and about – now 70 per cent of our waking hours – and this trend is predicted to continue (Source: BBC

1994	1995	2001	2005	2006	2007
London transport advertising moves from the public to private sector when the contract is awarded to American backed TDI.	All UK bus advertising is privatised and consolidated into TDI.	TDI is bought and rebranded to Viacom Outdoor.	The first digital escalator panels are installed at Tottenham Court Road Underground station.	Viacom Outdoor is awarded the £1.2 billion contract to sell and run the advertising on the London Underground until 2015.	Viacom Outdoor rebrands to CBS Outdoor and the first LCDs are launched in Charing Cross and Canary Wharf in March – 105 are installed by the end of the year. XTP is successfully trialled and roll-out begins.

Daily Life Survey). Alongside this, as cities and towns become less car friendly, people are spending a greater amount of time on buses, trams and other transport systems. Outdoor advertising captures these consumers on the move like no other UK advertising media.

RECENT DEVELOPMENTS

Escalator Panels are advertising sites that run up and down the escalators in nearly every London Underground station on the network. By the end of 2007 CBS Outdoor had installed new Digital Escalator Panels (DEPs), which allow HD quality moving imagery, alongside escalators in 11 stations with a further seven stations planned for 2008. This new technology – only available with CBS Outdoor – was named the number one innovation by Campaign magazine in 2006 and when travellers on London Underground were asked to comment on the screens, 87 per cent said that their presence 'brightened and improved their journey' (Source: Clark Chapman Research).

CBS Outdoor has developed another world first this year with a new dry posting technique for putting up posters. This new system eliminates the need for wet glue, ensuring an enhanced advertising display.

After an extensive safety trial, London Underground has given CBS Outdoor the go ahead to roll out its digital cross-track

projection (XTP) across more than 20 central London stations in 2008. These screens enable full HD moving imagery to be shown a few feet away from where commuters wait on the platforms.

PROMOTION

CBS Outdoor has two key external audiences – marketing departments and their various media and advertising agencies. Its 200 plus sales team is supported by an ongoing communication strategy which aims to position the brand as the number one media brand for capturing and captivating consumers on the move. Motivating and engaging its internal sales team is therefore also a key objective of the marketing and communications plan.

In order to increase the familiarity and appeal of its new DEPs amongst the creative community, a competition to develop a compelling campaign which best utilised the unique and new features of the media was run. The winning Shelter campaign went on to win an industry award. This activity was deemed a success as the DEPs were sold out throughout 2007.

In November 2007, CBS Outdoor launched a dedicated website – cbsoutdoor-alive.co.uk – to critical acclaim. It received 3,500 visits in the first two weeks from 2,750

unique visitors. On average, people spent four minutes on the site and viewed six pages.

A key part of CBS Outdoor's bus strategy is to help advertisers better understand how effective the media is and how people consume and relate to it. In 2007, a groundbreaking piece of research – The Road to Enlightenment – took on this brief. It demonstrated the relationship people have with buses and bus advertising and the value they place on the medium. The research was communicated to over 1,000 advertisers and agencies at a bespoke conference and presentation road show in autumn 2007.

CBS Outdoor's 6-sheet Underground product is flexible and highly effective for precision targeting. In 2007 a microsite was developed to show advertisers these benefits and to position CBS Outdoor as the media who knows London and its various inhabitants best.

BRAND VALUES

The core business values of CBS Outdoor are to be smart, straight, brave, positive, proud, generous and to get involved.

www.cbsoutdoor.co.uk

Things you didn't know about CBS Outdoor

Every two weeks more than 200,000 posters are changed by CBS Outdoor across the UK on buses, trams, London Underground and the national rail network.

A third of all the time Londoners spend exposed to advertising messages is with posters on the Underground.

Buses carrying CBS Outdoor advertising cover 3.6 million miles every day.

Leslie Moonves, CBS Corporations CEO, has been named Variety's Showman of the Year and Entertainment Weekly's Most Powerful Man in Hollywood.

A UTC Fire & Security Company

Chubb, which has a history spanning 180 years, is the leading nationwide provider of security and fire safety solutions to businesses and industry. It supplies systems and services to most of the FTSE 100 companies as well as the highest levels of Government, defence and banking companies. Each year Chubb performs 110,000 security systems site inspections and services over four million fire extinguishers.

MARKET
Chubb is one of the most respected brand names in the fire safety and security solutions market, which is highly fragmented and fiercely competitive. The company's strengths are underpinned by a global infrastructure, a highly skilled and experienced workforce, a diverse range of quality products and services and a reputation for service excellence.

Chubb protects premises, property and assets throughout the UK and worldwide, operating across four continents.

ACHIEVEMENTS
From inventing the Detector Lock in 1818, to launching one of the first dedicated CCTV monitoring centres in 1999, Chubb's rich history of innovation continues today. For instance, Chubb was one of the first national security installers to adopt EN Standards for the installation of monitored intruder and hold-up alarm systems when British Standards were phased out in 2005. Also in 2007, Chubb was awarded a Business Commitment to the Environment Award for its groundbreaking extinguisher recycling programme, which processes more than 500,000 units every year.

Chubb is also entrusted to protect some of the world's most treasured and prestigious sites, such as Westminster Abbey, Alnwick Castle (the filming location of Harry Potter's school Hogwarts), Diamond Synchrotron (the largest scientific facility recently built in the UK) and the British Museum.

PRODUCT
Chubb's main product offerings include Electronic Security, Monitoring and Response Services, Fire Protection, Fire Detection and Fire Suppression Systems. Chubb's ability to integrate its products and services into tailored, comprehensive solutions, makes it uniquely positioned to meet a broad range of customer requirements.

By combining in-house design expertise with components sourced from some of the world's leading technology suppliers, Chubb is able to remain at the cutting-edge of system design and service innovation.

1818	1835	1870s	1945	1997	2000
Charles and Jeremiah Chubb respond to the increasing demand for greater security by inventing the original secure lock mechanism, patented as the Detector Lock.	The Chubb brothers patent the burglar-resistant safe.	A Time Lock mechanism is developed for protecting vault and safe doors. Although the designs have since been refined, the basic principles of security and quality have remained the same.	Chubb expands its operations overseas and extends its product range into fire protection.	Chubb is sold to Williams plc.	In August, Chubb's Lock Security Group is acquired by Assa Abloy, a Swedish-based lock manufacturer.

Enhanced.

Get Integrated Security Management from Chubb.

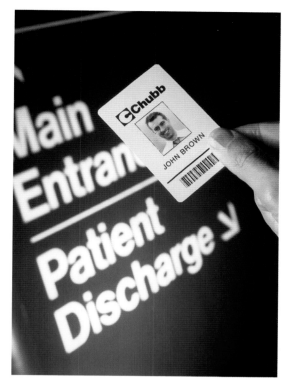

RECENT DEVELOPMENTS

Chubb's Remote Video Response (RVR) service is at the forefront of remote CCTV monitoring. The service remotely monitors CCTV video images from sites over IP networks and provides specialist security protection for large, open and vulnerable sites.

With the advent of Chubb's AFx system, integrated security is no longer only specified for large public sector organisations, such as the Ministry of Defence. More and more Chubb customers are choosing to integrate their security requirements onto a single platform in order to benefit from improved cost efficiencies, greater control and increased flexibility.

The Chubb ControlMaster1000 fire detection system, launched in 2007, has the potential to integrate with building systems and CCTV and is showcased at the Schools for the Future project at the Building Research Establishment. The system design was based on the Chubb Resonance fire detection system, which protects the Eiffel Tower.

Web-based fire risk assessment and fire safety training complement Chubb's traditional range of fire protection and fire detection services.

PROMOTION

Chubb is positioned as the UK's leading brand for security and fire protection. Chubb not only provides bespoke solutions for businesses of all types and sizes, but also commits to keeping customers informed of any legislative changes that could affect the security or fire systems they are operating.

This includes running educational seminars and publishing informative guides to support communities across the UK. In addition, since 2003 Chubb has sponsored the Scouts Fire Safety Badge to help educate children about fire safety issues.

BRAND VALUES

The Chubb brand is one of the most recognised and most valued security and fire brands in the world. Throughout its history, the company has demonstrated an ability to perform in new sectors and to incorporate new technologies in order to provide the most advanced and cost effective solutions. Trust, integrity and strength are Chubb's core brand values. With the backing of its parent

company, United Technologies Corporation (UTC), the Chubb brand is set to get even stronger with further investment in local service delivery, product innovation and people development.

Chubb is a national name – delivering at a local level – committed to service excellence.

www.chubb.co.uk

Things you didn't know about Chubb

In UK prisons, the phrase, 'Chubbing-up for the night' is a commonly used euphemism for 'locking-up for the night'.

The reputation of the Chubb brand has led to it being used as the generic term for security mortice locks, regardless of who the actual manufacturer is.

Chubb is the only national security company able to offer customers the complete security service including installation, maintenance, monitoring and response services.

The Chubb Keyholding service responds to more than 300,000 alarm activations each year.

More than 50,000 Scouts have passed their Fire Safety Badge since 2003.

The Chubb logo was originally designed to represent the front of a mortice lock.

	2003	2005	2008
In November, Chubb de-merges from Williams plc to become Chubb plc.	In July Chubb plc is acquired by United Technologies Corporation (UTC).	In April, UTC acquires Kidde PLC, forming UTC Fire & Security, the number two global player in the fire safety industry.	UTC Fire & Security employs more than 43,000 people in 30 countries, with a family of leading global brands including Kidde, Lenel and Chubb.

CIMA, the Chartered Institute of Management Accountants, is a membership body which offers an internationally recognised professional qualification in management accountancy. Its headquarters are in London but the organisation has more than 158,000 members and students in 161 nations around the world.

MARKET

CIMA's vision is to have its members driving the world's successful organisations. Most accountancy bodies are concerned with preparing students for a career with a professional accountancy firm. CIMA offers the only international professional qualification to focus solely on the development of financially trained business managers. Management accountancy is much more than just number crunching.

The qualification produces versatile professionals who have been assessed and can apply their business skills across the organisation. Management accountants have the skills to communicate complex financial information to non-financial people and the knowledge and experience to drive business success with a focus on future, rather than past performance. The strong threads of business governance, ethics and management which run through the CIMA syllabus put members in a position where they are a highly attractive proposition for companies, not-for-profit and public sector organisations alike.

ACHIEVEMENTS

CIMA's reputation as a guardian of accounting excellence continues to grow. The institute provides support to some of the world's leading employers. Study topics are reviewed every four years to ensure that the syllabus reflects the latest business developments and employer needs. CIMA is committed to upholding the highest ethical and professional standards to maintain public confidence in management accountancy. The institute has its own code of ethics and all members are

required to take part in a programme of continuing professional development (CPD).

Proof of the institute's success is reflected in the quality of the employment its members achieve across the world. More than a third of CIMA members are currently in some form of senior management positions (35 per cent), 14 per cent are financial controllers and another 14 per cent are finance directors. Approximately seven per cent have risen to the position of chief executive officer, managing director or some other kind of directorship. In the UK, 62 per cent of members are employed by organisations with an annual turnover of £50 million or more (Source: CIMA Member Survey 2006). Across the rest of the global membership, this figure is 52 per cent. This means that the majority

The CIMA difference:
our relevance to business

of its members are already in positions where they can make a significant impact on the business world. CIMA has strong evidence that this figure will continue to rise.

PRODUCT

When CIMA students begin their studies, they are embarking on a partnership that often continues throughout their working lives. The syllabus covers a wide range of topics including financial and non-financial analysis, risk management, information management, project management and the development of business strategy. This

1919	1975	1986	1995	2002	2006
The Institute of Cost and Works Accountants is founded, its objectives being to provide the range of information needed to plan and manage modern business.	The institute is granted a Royal Charter.	The institute changes its name to the Chartered Institute of Management Accountants, recognising the importance and commercial relevance of management accountants.	CIMA's members are given the right to use the title, Chartered Management Accountant.	Because of its growth, the institute relocates to its current global headquarters in central London.	CIMA opens an office in Shanghai.

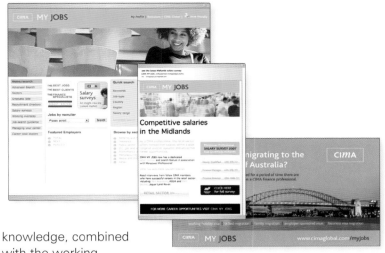

the vision to be different

knowledge, combined with the working experience passed finalists are required to attain before they fully qualify, provides them with all the key links to career success.

Once CIMA passed finalists have shown that they have the appropriate business experience to become fully qualified members of the institute, their journey continues. Under CPD requirements, all members must ensure that they keep up-to-speed with relevant developments in the business world.

CIMA also offers students and members an extensive range of learning resources to help their career development. Management accounting books, brochures and CDs are provided by CIMA Publishing while CIMA Courses and Conferences offers an extensive programme of financial and business management seminars.

RECENT DEVELOPMENTS
CIMA's assertion that it offers a syllabus that is most relevant to the business community has been supported by independent research. In July 2007, the University of Bath School of Management, ranked as one of the top 50 European Business Schools in the FT European Business Schools Ranking, published a study which compared the syllabi of nine leading international accountancy bodies. The findings concluded that CIMA is best for business and outlined the unique

CIMA and Land Rover. In business together.

CIMA, the Chartered Institute of Management Accountants, delivers forward looking, all-terrain, high-performing individuals who drive success in business.

Let CIMA drive success in your organisation.

I chose CIMA. Land Rover chose me.

'CIMA trained people like me go beyond accountancy providing analysis, decision support, value creation and risk management. CIMA is the most relevant professional accountancy qualification for business...'

Colin Mannell, Pricing Analyst, Land Rover

Let CIMA drive success in your organisation by texting your email address to +44 7786 200 151 or go to www.choosecima.com/landrover

combination of theoretical, practical and applied knowledge that defines the 'CIMA difference'.

Another of CIMA's core aims is to be recognised as a benchmark for best practice in management accounting. 2007 saw the launch of the CIMA Centre of Excellence at the University of Bath School of Management. The centre carries out independent research into best practice in the development of financial management. The results will enable employers to identify practical ways to drive their finance functions forward and help shape strategies to meet developments in the rapidly changing global marketplace.

In 2007 CIMA began a World Bank funded project in Bangladesh to help strengthen the capabilities of the Institute of Cost and Management Accountants of Bangladesh (ICMAB). Following a fact-finding mission, CIMA presented a series of recommendations to the World Bank, Bangladesh Ministry of Commerce and the ICMAB. The project will provide a model for CIMA to collaborate on other World Bank projects in developing countries.

PROMOTION
In September 2007, CIMA reasserted its role as the finance qualification for business with the launch of its first global corporate advertising campaign. The institute collaborated with companies including Land Rover, Tesco, Fujitsu, Ford and the Department for Work and Pensions to highlight how CIMA works with organisations to train and support key employees throughout their careers. The campaign continues into 2008.

Financial Management, the institute's monthly magazine, was relaunched in September 2007 with a fresh new look and a revised editorial focus on the science of management accounting. Copies of the magazine are sent free to members and by subscription to other interested parties. The magazine is considered one of the key members' benefits and an authoritative voice on financial management issues. CIMA's views are regularly reported in the trade and national media with press 'hits' generating an advertising equivalent value of around £2.5 million per annum.

CIMA also produces marketing literature to promote specific courses, seminars and

events and an online newsletter, Insight, which has a monthly circulation of 120,000. The CIMA website is another powerful communications platform – an average of 270,000 people visit the site each month. In addition, it was voted 2007 Website of the Year by readers of PQ magazine, the monthly magazine for part-qualified accountants.

BRAND VALUES
CIMA is positioned as the qualification for business with a management accountancy focus. It is driven by five core values: customer-focused, professional, open, accountable and innovative. These values aim to ensure a consistent company culture that is supported by all CIMA employees.

CIMA has also identified a purpose, vision and mission to enhance its sense of direction. The institute's purpose is to strive for the ever-greater employability of its members. Its vision is to see CIMA members driving the world's most successful companies and its mission is to be the first choice for employers in the qualification and development of professional accountants in business.

www.cimaglobal.com

Things you didn't know about CIMA

The first president of CIMA was Lord Leverhulme, the grandson of William Hesketh Lever, founder of Lever Bros (now Unilever).

The institute's current president, Gordon Grant, is the youngest ever elected CIMA council member and the youngest president for over 50 years; he is now 44.

Leading CIMA members include Andrew Higginson, head of finance and strategy at Tesco, Douglas Flint, chief financial officer at HSBC and Hanif Lalani, chief financial officer at BT.

In 2007 CIMA qualified its 70,000th member.

CNN is the world's leading global 24-hour news network, delivered across a range of multimedia platforms including television, mobile phones and the internet. Launched in 1985, the channel's output comprises its trademark breaking news, business news, sports news, current affairs and analysis, documentaries and feature programming. CNN viewers are global citizens; mostly business decision makers and opinion leaders, educated, well travelled and with high personal income.

MARKET

Since CNN pioneered the genre of 24-hour news, the pan-regional news market has expanded to include approximately 100 news channels worldwide. CNN has remained at the forefront of this increasingly competitive market, warding off competition from domestic and pan-regional news services with its growing international newsgathering operation and intricate network of regionalised services and affiliates.

According to the European Media and Marketing Survey (EMS) 2007, CNN International is the market leader for advertisers wanting to reach an upscale, elite audience as news consumption adapts to the digital age. The survey revealed that the channel was leading all international news channels in all measurements in the EMS Select demographic; CNN's reach is 47.6 per cent on a monthly basis (compared with Euronews at 35.7 per cent and BBC World's 35.9 per cent).

CNN continues to attract a range of high profile advertisers with its cross-platform ad sales offering, one of the most comprehensive and innovative in the industry. Online is currently the fastest-growing driver of the ad sales business, drawing major clients such as Lexus, Philips, Allianz and Ericsson.

Building on its expertise in this area, 2007 saw the launch of CNN's Tourism Advertising Solutions & Knowledge (TASK) Group to offer clients best of breed advice, information and intelligence to enhance their brand building efforts.

Breaking Fmr. Pakistan PM Benazir Bhutto assassinated

ACHIEVEMENTS

In 1980 CNN launched as a single US network available to 1.7 million homes. Twenty-seven years later, CNN's 22 branded networks and services are available to more than two billion people in over 200 countries and territories worldwide, distributed across a range of platforms including mobile and IPTV, over and above the landmark television service and international website, CNN.com.

CNN has become synonymous around the globe with breaking news and as a visual history book for the world. As world stories hit the headlines, CNN has been there: Tiananmen Square, the 11th September terrorist attacks and the ensuing war against terror in Afghanistan, the Asian tsunami, the July 2005 London bombings, Saddam Hussein's trial and 2006 execution, and in 2007, Benazir Bhutto's fateful return to Pakistan, to name a few.

CNN has evolved beyond television to become one of the most digitally integrated channels in the world. With an eye on changing consumer trends, CNN embraces

1980	1985	1989	1995	1997	1999
CNN launches on 1st June as a single US network; the brainchild of media entrepreneur Ted Turner, it becomes the first round-the-clock news channel.	CNN International launches, along with live 24-hour transmission to Europe.	CNN becomes available worldwide, 24 hours a day, with transmission on a Soviet satellite to Africa, the Middle East, the Indian subcontinent and South East Asia.	CNN.com, the world's first major news website, is launched. This is followed by the all-encompassing international edition.	CNN launches a regionalisation strategy with the guiding philosophy, "Global reach, local touch".	CNN Mobile launches, the first mobile telephone news and information service available globally with targeted regional content.

Group 4 Securicor

G4S plc
The Manor, Manor Royal,
Crawley, West Sussex,
RH10 9UN. UK.

Telephone: +44 (0)1293 554 400
Fax: +44 (0)1293 554 500
Email: info@g4s.com
www.g4s.com

Crawley, 22 July 2008

Dear colleague,

G4S plc has been named as one of the UK's leading business brands in the Business Superbrands 2008 list, for the second year running. The announcement followed a robust selection process, incorporating the views of an independent and voluntary council of experts and over 1500 business professionals surveyed by the market research agency YouGov.

Business Superbrands, operated by the Superbrands organisation, is in its eighth year and has become a key barometer on the performance of brands across a wide variety of industry sectors.

G4S has invested significant resources developing its brand identity and promoting the company as the world's leading supplier of security solutions. G4S has enviable brand awareness amongst the global business community, who have a real affinity with our brand and core values. For a brand that has only been in existence for just over two years, this is a remarkable achievement.

This award recognises the hard work and commitment that everyone at G4S has devoted to developing the brand. It recognises the strength of G4S' brand and expertise across a diverse portfolio of products and services.

Please find your personal copy of the Business Superbrands Yearbook 2008 enclosed. If you need any further information about Business Superbrands, please contact Group Communications.

Kind regards,

Karen Groenenboom
Communications Manager
G4S plc

G4S plc
Registered Office:
The Manor, Manor Royal, Crawley,
West Sussex RH10 9UN.
Registered in England No. 4992207

Directors:
Alf Duch-Pedersen (Chairman)
Lord Condon QPM (Deputy Chairman)
Nick Buckles (Chief Executive)
Trevor Dighton
Grahame Gibson
Mark Elliott
Thorleif Krarup
Bo Lerenius
Mark Seligman
Secretary: Peter David

the range of emerging, non-linear distribution outlets to maximise its presence across all platforms. Recent years have seen CNN content and archive footage completely reformatted for use across new platforms and devices – short-form video content is now an integral feature of CNN.com and CNN Mobile, as well as being available on third party IPTV and video-on-demand outlets.

CNN's user-generated content initiative, I-Report, has garnered more than 50,000 submissions from 189 countries and territories around the world since its 2006 launch. Images, video and text based eye-witness accounts from a network of 'citizen journalists' add a deeper, more personal perspective to many of the stories unfolding on CNN. Defining moments have included the 2006 coup in Thailand and 2007 unrests in Myanmar. When national media and internet outlets were shut down, I-Reports on CNN ensured that images and developments from those countries continued to reach the rest of the world.

PRODUCT

CNN's global news group currently consists of nine international networks and services, five international partnerships and joint ventures as well as eight US-based services. Available in six languages, the channel's joint ventures include CNN-IBN, CNN Turk, CNN+ in Spain and Japan's CNNj, as well as a number of websites, CNN.co.jp in Japan and CNNenEspanol.com.

While breaking news remains CNN's trademark, its feature programming line up caters to a wide range of audiences, covering business, sport, lifestyle and entertainment, compelling documentaries and special landmark programming. Throughout the year, CNN's best known faces, including Richard Quest and Hala Gorani, front regular shows such as CNN Business Traveller, Art of Life and Inside the Middle East. Special

documentaries in 2007 included God's Warriors, presented by CNN's chief international correspondent, Christiane Amanpour and Planet in Peril, presented by CNN's Anderson Cooper and Dr Sanjay Gupta as well as Discovery Channel's Jeff Corwin.

RECENT DEVELOPMENTS

The network has continued to consolidate its position as a market leader by integrating its content across a range of platforms. 2007 saw the channel go live across non-linear outlets such as Joost, YouTube, Jalipo and Vingo TV, and the relaunch of CNN Mobile, the network's comprehensive, free delivery service to handsets. In July, the network also unveiled its redesigned website, CNN.com, which now incorporates video, text, still pictures, maps and user-generated content within a single story page.

CNN is currently in the process of investing in its biggest ever expansion in its newsgathering operations. Plans include several new bureaux and correspondents worldwide, a regional news gathering hub in the Untied Arab Emirates and investment in its in-house wire operations. CNN's virtual hub in Second Life (opened in November 2007) provides further opportunities to gather user-generated content and interact directly with users.

PROMOTION

Since launch the CNN logo has been one of the world's most instantly recognised brands and is promoted via select marketing opportunities and partnerships.

CNN is the leading television news provider for 'global citizens'. These include world and opinion leaders and business decision makers, and are often hugely successful – affluent, intelligent and well travelled – although their definitions of success go beyond status or material possessions.

BRAND VALUES

For more than 27 years CNN has stood by the news values of accuracy, impartiality, integrity, credibility and speed.

The network's commitment to digital integration also ensures that its audiences get access to CNN 'whenever, wherever and however'.

Core brand values are reflected in the network positioning messages: Be the first to know; Live from anywhere; Quoted everywhere; Essential for business.

www.cnn.com/international

2006	2007		
CNN launches its Citizen Journalism initiative, I-Report.	CNN Mobile is relaunched and CNN.com is redesigned to incorporate video, text and images within the storytelling page.	Also in 2007, CNN launches across major IPTV and VOD outlets including YouTube, Joost and Jalipo and opens a virtual hub in Second Life.	In addition, CNN announces the largest investment in its international newsgathering resources in its 27-year history.

conqueror

Celebrating its 120th anniversary in 2008, Conqueror is an internationally recognised symbol of quality in external business communications. Constantly striving to deliver innovation combined with unparalleled quality, Conqueror is recognised as the gold standard for business stationery. With brand awareness levels at over 80 per cent in the UK, Conqueror successfully extends into applications such as brochures, reports, promotional materials and packaging in 120 countries around the world.

MARKET

Creating cut through in a world of message overload is more challenging than ever but Conqueror successfully conveys differentiation in busy business environments and can both stand alone or integrate effectively with other, electronic messaging mediums.

The Conqueror range is regularly updated to reflect trends in fashion and contemporary styling, as well as environmental and technological trends. Tangible and distinctive, its visual impact and tactile qualities can convey style and creativity as well as professionalism and a bold corporate image.

ACHIEVEMENTS

Conqueror is one of the few paper brands requested by name and although it remains most synonymous with quality business stationery, an extensive variety of modern day usages continue to demonstrate the wide-ranging solutions that Conqueror can provide.

Throughout its 120-year history, Conqueror has pre-empted the demands of the market

and embraced change. In doing so it has moved successfully from the era of pen and ink, through to today's sophisticated world of multiple print technologies and digital communications, where businesses are continually challenged by environmental pressures.

Best-in-category performance in recent years has confirmed Conqueror's status as one of the best known and most favoured brands of paper. This is frequently proven and substantiated through blind and branded tests, in which the brand is consistently chosen as the best quality and overall preferred. As the first CarbonNeutral® fine paper brand to be launched in Europe, and also only using pulp originated from FSC certified sources, Conqueror offers environmental credentials without compromising on quality.

PRODUCT

All Conqueror ranges are driven by trends and developments in technology, the environment and fashion. From multi-functional, environmentally friendly products with guaranteed performance for the very latest of print processes to its fashion-influenced ranges, Conqueror products have been found to achieve standout.

Now fully FSC certified and CarbonNeutral® accredited, the extensive Conqueror range is grouped into five sub brands: Conqueror Smooth/Satin, described as 'fresh and contemporary'; Conqueror Concept/Effects, 'futuristic and trend setting'; Conqueror Digital, 'high performance and developed for digital printing technology'; Conqueror Connoisseur, 'luxurious and classic'; and Conqueror Texture, 'traditional and tactile'.

1888	1945	1960s	1990	1991	1993
Conqueror paper first rolls off the paper machine at Wiggins Teape.	Changes in the production of Conqueror are developed, as well as quality control and specialised colour matching.	Conqueror continues to develop and grow its export business.	Arjowiggins Appleton group is formed from the merger of Wiggins Teape with the French paper manufacturer Arjomari and the US manufacturer, Appleton Papers.	A recycled option is added to the range for the first time.	The brand logo is changed to a horseman representing William the Conqueror alongside the Conqueror name.

Through its selection of colours, finishes, textures and watermarks, designed to be innovative and contemporary and available in a range of co-ordinated papers, boards and envelopes, Conqueror aims to guarantee the look and feel of effortless style and professionalism and 'ultimate interest' as well as impact, suitable for a wide range of applications.

As environmental pressures increase for businesses in the UK, Conqueror can also offer companies a medium to send positive messages to customers by reflecting a commitment to addressing global warming.

RECENT DEVELOPMENTS

In the last five years, Conqueror has endeavoured to continually develop and evolve its positioning, range and product offering in order to ensure maximum relevance within an ever-changing market place.

2003 saw Conqueror launch a specific collection of products into the Office and Retail channel, focusing on home-based as well as small and medium sized businesses. Two years later, the brand updated its range with new, patented Multi Technology products that work, uniquely, across both traditional and digital print processes. In addition, three new iridescent shades added to the Concept/Effects range meant that it achieved 30 per cent year-on-year growth versus 2004.

PROMOTION

Conqueror has successfully developed a sustained 'push-pull' marketing strategy that focuses on distribution partners, printers,

designers and end-users. Driven by applications and with a strong emphasis on brand awareness and brand building, global communications aim to deliver a consistent image and clear, targeted messages that are tailored to these key audiences.

Since its 2004 multi-million pound television and press campaign targeting the 'e-generation' of 25-35 year-old business users, Conqueror has continued to develop specially tailored promotions to its audiences announcing the various launch activities that have taken place. With a particular focus on direct mail to ensure its customers experience the touch, feel and quality of Conqueror, 2007 saw successful campaigns promoting Conqueror's full range of applications.

Most recently the launch of the Blank Sheet Project marked the announcement that Conqueror was to become the first CarbonNeutral® fine paper brand in Europe, while also using only pulp sourced from FSC certified sources. Aimed at SMEs, CEOs, CSR directors, existing customers and printers, the campaign used a range of marketing tools incorporating direct mail, online and press advertising to encourage businesses to share their ideas about the easily achievable steps that can be taken to help reduce carbon emissions.

BRAND VALUES

Conqueror provides a high quality range of distinctive papers, which is recognised globally for its suitability for both professional and creative communications. The value of the Conqueror brand lies in its quality, versatility, wide choice and availability as well

as its strong environmental credentials and reliable technical performance. Conqueror aims to deliver ultimate impact for image conscious businesses, as well as providing complete paper solutions to those businesses that use environmentally sound products as an integral part of their company culture.

Constant development and testing ensures that Conqueror continues to meet the performance demands of both traditional printing processes and the latest digital technologies, while inspiring creativity through a range of contemporary and versatile products.

www.conqueror.com

Things you didn't know about Conqueror

If all the paper that Conqueror made within one week were in the format of 100g A4 sheets, and laid end to end, it would stretch twice around the world.

Today, there are some 600 different line items available within the Conqueror range with users spanning Royalty and huge corporates to one-man businesses the world over.

In response to growing environmental concerns, Arjowiggins has committed to a significant investment of more than 500,000 euros in the brand's environmental credentials and over the last two years the company has reduced carbon emissions by five per cent.

Arjowiggins has calculated that if all companies switched to using Conqueror paper, UK businesses alone could save over 23,000 tonnes of CO_2 each year, which is equivalent to the annual emissions of almost 4,200 households.

2001		2004	2007
A new, contemporary, stylised logo and identity based on the Conqueror name is launched.	Also in 2001, iridescent papers are launched into the Conqueror Concept/Effects range.	Conqueror Digital Multi Technology is introduced as the only fine paper that is printable on offset and digital presses.	Conqueror becomes the first CarbonNeutral® fine paper brand in Europe, while also only using pulp sourced from FSC certified sources across the entire range.

corus

Corus is Europe's second largest steel producer with annual revenues of over £10 billion and crude steel production of about 20 million tonnes. Combining global expertise with local customer service, Corus offers value, reliability and innovation. The Corus brand represents a mark of quality, loyalty and strength. Corporate responsibility is integral to the way Corus does business and the objective is to be world-class. Corus is a subsidiary of Tata Steel.

The strongest relationships are built on trust

Safety
Our health and safety standards apply equally to contractors and Corus employees. A safe workplace: not without you.

The Corus Way
Value in steel

Take responsibility; act responsibly

Safety
Sharing good practice and learning from mistakes can help prevent incidents at Corus. That means we all have a duty to speak out. Intervene. To keep each other safe. A safe workplace: not without you.

The Corus Way
Value in steel

MARKET

Corus is a leading supplier to some of the world's most demanding markets, including construction, automotive, packaging, rail and engineering. Through its technical excellence, process capabilities and market understanding, Corus helps its customers to achieve results. It aims to provide the right solution, on time, supported by the right advice.

The company has major facilities in the UK, the Netherlands, Germany, France, Norway and Belgium as well as a global network of sales offices and service centres.

ACHIEVEMENTS

In 2006, Corus became the premier sponsor of British Triathlon. The sponsorship of this young but rapidly growing sport aims to develop strong future athletes at all levels including children, disabled and elite.

At a grassroots level, Corus is supporting a number of community-based initiatives, including a nationwide programme to develop triathlon for school age children, called Corus Kids of Steel. The sponsorship has also created a new series of televised elite events for the UK known as the Corus Elite Series.

Triathlon embodies the performance culture values of Corus. Dedication, focus and the desire to win are some of the attributes intrinsic to success in Corus. It also sees triathlon as an opportunity to demonstrate its commitment to the health, safety and well-being of its employees and their local communities by encouraging involvement and participation in triathlon and in sport.

PRODUCT

Corus manufactures, processes and distributes many steel products for a range of demanding applications, as well as providing design, technology and consultancy services.

For example, a wide range of construction products and services are available for the world's most impressive buildings. This includes structural sections, plates, floor decking and cladding products used in building structures, as well as a range of products used in building interiors, such as ceiling systems and partitions.

Strip steels, in coated and uncoated form, are supplied to markets such as automotive, domestic appliances, engineering and metal goods. Packaging steels are used for food, drink and aerosol containers, as well as for promotional and speciality packaging. Tubular products range from precision tubing for engineering applications to large diameter pipes for oil and gas transportation.

Other products include electrical steels for the generation, transmission and distribution of electrical power, railway products and services, plates, wire rod, special sections and bar and billet for engineering industries.

1999	2005	2006		2007	2008
Corus is created through the merger of two strong brands in the steel industry, British Steel and Koninklijke Hoogovens in the Netherlands.	'The Corus Way' is launched to inspire employees and involve them in Continuous Improvement.	The Corus brand evolves to reflect its new positioning of 'Value in steel'. The aim is for a more sophisticated, assured and refined look and feel.	In autumn 2006 Corus becomes the premier sponsor of British Triathlon.	In April Corus becomes part of Tata Steel but retains its name and identity.	The brand's new vision and strategy are revealed; 'The Corus Way' evolves to embed the values of the new performance culture.

RECENT DEVELOPMENTS

In April 2007, Corus became part of Tata Steel, combining a high quality growth platform in Asia with a leading presence in Europe. As the world's sixth largest and second most global steel producer, with a combined presence in nearly 50 countries, Tata Steel – including Corus – has 84,000 employees across five continents and, in 2007, a crude steel production capacity of 27 million tonnes.

PROMOTION

The name Corus was initially chosen for its distinctive, fresh, modern and easily recognisable qualities. It also conveys the idea that all the operations within Corus have different strengths but are more powerful when their voices join together.

Following the initial brand launch advertising campaign in 2000, promoting 'the future in metal' in international newspapers, Corus has concentrated its promotional activity on media relations as the main vehicle for its corporate messages. The company has also invested significant effort in ensuring that its internal communications are fully aligned to Company strategy and that all Corus employees are engaged in The Corus Way and Continuous Improvement. The communications effectiveness is routinely measured to ensure that employees understand the corporate messages.

At the same time, market promotional activity has been targeted at key market sectors, such as construction, automotive, packaging, rail and energy. Corus exhibits all over the world at targeted exhibitions and sponsors young designers through student award programmes.

BRAND VALUES

The essence of the Corus brand is about creating a performance culture, which will help achieve the ambition of profitability and growth while inspiring employees and customers. Corus has values to support its strategic business objectives which include aspiration, trust, openness, respect and integrity.

The Corus brand offering is about being perceived as an innovative and inspiring solutions provider helping its customers to realise their projects, ideas and dreams. Corus looks at its business from the customer's perspective to ensure that innovation and development are driven by what customers actually need. This translates to a differentiated and specialised product mix, better lead times, and unrivalled quality and efficiency.

www.corusgroup.com

Things you didn't know about Corus

Steel is 100 per cent recyclable and maintains its strength and durability no matter how many times it is recycled. More than 40 per cent of the world's production of 'new' steel is made from recycled steel without any loss of quality.

Corus is a major partner in ULCOS (Ultra-Low CO_2 Steelmaking) – a European project researching technologies that could bring about a step change reduction in CO_2 emissions from the steelmaking process in the medium to long term.

Corus is helping the healthcare sector to control bacteria such as MRSA, through its anti-bacterial pre-finished steels product range.

In 2008, Corus will be staging the world renowned Corus Chess Tournament for the 70th time. This event provides opportunities for community participation in games as well as a grand masters tournament.

COSTAIN

Costain is one of the UK's best-known construction and engineering companies, undertaking some of the world's largest and most challenging construction projects. It works in a wide range of sectors, including water, highways, health, education, nuclear, rail, retail, marine, and oil & gas.

MARKET

Construction is one of the largest and most important industries in the UK. Providing housing, infrastructure, employment and being a key indicator of economic health, the UK construction industry has been growing for the past 10 years thanks to low interest rates and good employment levels (Source: MBD).

The construction sector is extremely broad, but principally consists of five areas: house building, infrastructure, industrial construction, commercial construction and building materials. By value, the most significant sector is commercial work, followed by house building and together, these account for around 45 per cent of total construction output (Source: KeyNote).

ACHIEVEMENTS

Following a strategic review of the business initiated by chief executive Andrew Wyllie, appointed in 2005, Costain has been refocused around its 'Being Number One' strategy to develop market-leading positions in targeted market sectors of water, highways, health, education, nuclear, rail,

retail, marine and oil & gas. The company is now seeing benefits accruing from this strategy, which aims to adopt a greater focus in fewer areas of operation, enabling Costain to commit more resources to the areas where it believes it can build competitive advantage and market leadership.

The strategy is now bearing fruit and a set of positive results for the six months ended June 2007 showed that Costain has delivered profits before tax of £8 million and, for the first time in 15 years, the Group announced that it will pay a dividend to shareholders.

Costain has a quality order book of £1.6 billion, plus preferred bidder positions in excess of £0.5 billion. The turnaround from a

£62 million loss in 2006 has been driven by strong performance in civil engineering, which accounts for 80 per cent of the order book.

Costain has further strengthened its balance sheet with a rights issue as part of a major refinancing package to provide greater financial power to deliver on future objectives. It has raised £60 million in additional equity from shareholders.

PRODUCT

Costain's primary markets include water, health, roads, rail and education.

The Building Sectors, which encompass Health, Education, Retail and Developers,

1865	1933	1939-45	1951	1971	2007
Richard Costain, a 26 year-old jobbing builder from the Isle of Man founds a construction business in Liverpool.	Costain floats as a public company, with a share capital of £600,000.	The company plays an active role in the war effort, with wartime work including 26 aerodromes, part of the Mulberry Harbours, munitions factories and 15,000 post-war prefabricated Airey houses.	Costain builds the Skylon and Dome of Discovery for the Festival of Britain.	Costain becomes the first UK contractor to win the Queen's Award for Export Achievement.	Costain announces intention to pay dividend to shareholders for the first time in 15 years.

undertake complex projects throughout the UK. Costain takes pride in the relationships it has developed within the construction community and seeks to deliver value and quality through innovation and technical excellence.

Costain has established itself as a leader in the Asset Management market. This work involves clients who want long term, expert, building and maintenance care for their valuable assets. Costain has won most of this business in the water sector, in which it has a strong reputation, recently delivering £600 million of capital work to UK water companies, comprising 700 separate projects. It has won long term contracts with companies including Thames Water as well as a £750 million contract for Southern Water.

In addition, Costain Oil, Gas & Process is an international process engineering contractor, delivering safe, cost-effective solutions for investments in the worldwide energy and process sectors.

RECENT DEVELOPMENTS

For 140 years Costain has been at the forefront of UK and international construction. In the mid 1920s, Costain built thousands of houses throughout South East England and in 1935, Costain built 11 miles of the Trans-Iranian Railway, seven tunnels and two viaducts in isolated mountainous terrain.

More recently, the company's portfolio includes prestigious engineering projects, including The Thames Barrier, the new headquarters for the Met Office and the Tsing Ma Suspension Bridge in Hong Kong – the world's longest combined road and rail bridge.

Costain was also jointly responsible for the redevelopment of St Pancras into the new UK terminus for Eurostar, as well as completing the Stratford tunnels for the Channel Tunnel Rail Link, along with the redevelopment of Kings Cross Underground Station for London Underground.

Another significant contract is the £22.5 million project to upgrade the Grade 1 listed St Martin-in-the-Fields Church, in Trafalgar Square.

In the roads sector, Costain has won a major contract to improve the M1 motorway – the company's largest road contract to date – and has recently submitted its bid for the Private Finance Initiative (PFI) project to extend the M25, valued at £1.5 billion. This is the largest single PFI road scheme in the UK.

PROMOTION

As part of a wide-ranging brand awareness programme for 2008, Costain is ensuring that every Costain site and employee portrays a consistent brand image. To this end, Costain has produced two branding books, one aimed at employees, the other at customers, focusing on the values of the company and some of its major projects.

More generally, Costain promotes itself in a variety of ways, using national and international trade fairs and events, as well as advertising in key technical titles, and business-facing newspapers such as the FT.

Costain also uses its news magazine, Blueprint, as a means of raising awareness of current projects and new developments. Another of Costain's promotional channels, Building Awareness, performs an important social role, raising young people's awareness of the construction industry through direct involvement and partnership with schools.

BRAND VALUES

While the 'Being Number One' mission statement drives Costain forward, the company also maintains a clear set of brand values.

The key element underpinning Costain's brand is a desire to be relationship driven. In pursuit of this, Costain's vision is to be the leader in the delivery of sustainable engineering and construction solutions. Its mission is to embark on a path of business excellence involving innovation, initiative, teamwork and high levels of technical and managerial skills.

The Costain brand itself can be dissected into six key values: customer focused; open & honest; safe & environmentally aware; team players; accountable; and improving continuously – with the aim of making Costain the natural choice.

www.costain.com

Things you didn't know about Costain

Costain created the largest and deepest hole ever made in London clay during construction of the Aldersgate office complex.

Costain completed Hong Kong's first cross-harbour tunnel in 1972 – a 1,850 metre steel-immersed tube tunnel.

More than 10,500 drawings were needed to design the £232 million Dubai Dry Dock.

Specialist pre-cast concrete sleepers were produced by Costain for the rail track through the Channel Tunnel and for rail networks both in the UK and overseas.

>DATAMONITOR

Datamonitor is a market leader in the business information industry, providing business professionals across key sectors with data, analysis and forecasting tools on a one-stop online platform – helping 6,000 of the world's largest companies profit from better, more timely decisions. Datamonitor's research covers six major industry sectors: automotive and logistics; consumer and retail; energy and utilities; financial services; healthcare; and technology.

    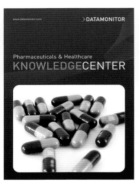 

MARKET

Reliable business information continues to be an essential tool for companies. Demand has been spurred by consolidation and globalisation across industries and the blurring of traditional business boundaries. Strong market and competitor intelligence play a fundamental role in helping businesses make winning decisions.

Datamonitor has moulded its offering to meet the needs of the changing business world. While many business information providers maintain a narrow focus, specialising in data or analysis for one particular industry, Datamonitor is unique in offering a 'total' solution for clients with both data and analysis from an industry-specific and cross-industry perspective. No other provider equals Datamonitor's breadth of industry coverage and depth of analytical insight.

ACHIEVEMENTS

The Datamonitor brand has achieved outstanding growth over its 19-year history. Starting as a five-man operation, the company developed quickly into today's global organisation of 1,500 employees with sales of US$250 million and double digit rates of growth.

This growth has been accelerated by the acquisition of a number of businesses that complement Datamonitor's core offering, including Ovum, Butler Group, Verdict

Research and Life Science Analytics. Such acquisitions, along with impressive organic growth, have fuelled the company's international expansion. In 2007 Datamonitor was acquired by Informa plc, enabling both companies to benefit and extend their global brand around the world. Today, Datamonitor operates globally with offices in London, New York, Seoul, Melbourne, Hong Kong, Chicago, Tokyo, Sydney and Hyderabad.

The Datamonitor brand continues to achieve global recognition through extensive press coverage. During 2007, the Datamonitor Group appeared in the press on average 870 times per month, with frequent mentions in the FT, Wall Street Journal, Forbes, Sydney Morning Herald and the Shanghai Daily, along with press mentions via news agencies such as Reuters, Bloomberg, the Associated Press (US), Press Association (UK) and Dow Jones. Brand visibility is maintained through regular appearances on broadcast channels such as BBC, Bloomberg TV and Sky News, enabling Datamonitor to build upon its reputation for providing

1989	**1993**	**1995**	**1997**	**1999**	**2000**
Datamonitor is founded by Mike Danson.	The first online delivery platform for Datamonitor products is launched.	Datamonitor opens its New York office. In addition, Datamonitor's primary website www.datamonitor.com is launched.	Datamonitor's first service-orientated offering is launched. Rebranding also takes place with the help of branding consultancy Interbrand, resulting in a new visual identity and new core values.	Datamonitor opens offices in Frankfurt and Hong Kong.	Datamonitor floats on the London Stock Exchange. In addition, branding consultancy Hicklin Slade & Partners develops the distinctive Datamonitor orange arrow.

insightful and independent opinion and research to both the business and journalist communities.

PRODUCT

Datamonitor's research is available to subscribers through its premium Knowledge Center service – a one-stop online platform with in-built time-saving functionality. Twelve Knowledge Centers span six key industries, each consolidating Datamonitor's information into separate interfaces. In total they provide millions of data points, thousands of pages of analysis and daily news and comment articles. Users can easily search, clip, extract and share this information.

For non-subscription clients the Research Store – Datamonitor's online shop – provides the ability to purchase individual research products. With a full historical library of products available to access immediately, this comprehensive source of information can specifically address strategic issues. Each product presents a detailed analysis of a particular market, issue or trend.

For clients with specific research needs, Datamonitor provides custom consulting services. These typically take the form of market entry analysis, product evaluations, end-user research, market forecasting or scenario planning projects. Subscribers can also submit questions to 'ask the analyst' through Datamonitor's Knowledge Center and benefit from a timely response from their independent team of in-house analysts.

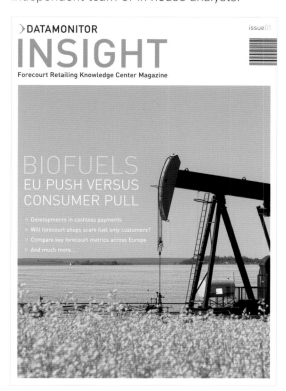

RECENT DEVELOPMENTS

In 2007 Datamonitor continued to invest in its technology platform, and has rolled out updated versions of its Knowledge Centers. Acquisitions by the Datamonitor Group have contributed to the launch of a number of new Knowledge Centers including a Telecoms and a CIO Knowledge Center.

All Knowledge Centers benefit from new features including increased content, improved display and navigation as well as enhanced visual style. Customers can also benefit from the newly launched Research Alerts, which provide the ability to set up customised email notifications as soon as relevant material becomes available.

PROMOTION

Datamonitor employs a strict house style when it comes to representation of the brand in promotional campaigns. The company's in-house marketing team ensure the brand's visual identity, based around the corporate orange and blue, together with its brand values, are consistently communicated.

Datamonitor's promotional strategy spans a variety of different media. Whilst emphasis is placed upon targeted email campaigns, flash presentations and marketing microsites to promote the company's services, Datamonitor still employs a fully integrated approach across both advertising and direct mail channels. The ever popular 'INSIGHT' magazines provide a different approach to showcase to clients the value and expertise available in-house. Furthermore, selected speaking and promotional appearances at conferences and exhibitions serve to maintain and raise the profile of Datamonitor's brand alongside fellow opinion formers.

BRAND VALUES

Datamonitor is committed to three core brand values: quality data, expert analysis and innovative delivery.

Quality data is guaranteed by the standard research process that is strictly adhered to by Datamonitor's dedicated research teams.

Expert analysis is provided by a skill base made up of multilingual, professional people from diverse backgrounds, including corporate finance, management consultancy, and graduates from the world's leading business schools.

Innovative delivery is the brand value associated with Datamonitor's cutting-edge online delivery platform, the Knowledge Center – a brand new concept in business information provision.

In addition to the three external brand values, in 2007 Datamonitor launched its five internal brand values which it felt were represented and embodied by employees: Exceptional People, Intellectual Excellence, Commercial Focus, Client Commitment and Execute Well. It is on these foundations that the Datamonitor brand continues to grow.

www.datamonitor.com

Things you didn't know about Datamonitor

During Datamonitor's 19-year history, the company has grown from a base of five people to employ 1,500 people today.

Information from a 2007 Datamonitor report on Germany's renewable energy market was used in a recent report for the New Zealand Government's Ministry of Economic Development, exploring the use of renewable energy as a means to combat climate change.

Datamonitor's first ever published report covered the topic of the UK Frozen Food industry.

2002	2004	2006	2007
ComputerWire is acquired and offices open in Tokyo and San Francisco.	Datamonitor acquires Productscan Online and eBenchmarkers. The following year, Butler Group and Verdict Research are acquired.	Datamonitor launches Knowledge Centers, a new delivery platform for subscribers. An office in Hyderabad is also opened and Datamonitor acquires Ovum and Life Science Analytics (MedTRACK).	Datamonitor opens a new office in Chicago and Informa plc acquires Datamonitor.

A Passion to Perform.

Deutsche Bank

Deutsche Bank is a leading global investment bank with a strong and profitable private clients franchise and provides a full range of financial services to corporate, institutional, high net worth and retail clients in all of the world's major markets.

MARKET

Deutsche Bank continues to build on its competitive edge in investment banking, reinforcing the leading market position of its Corporate & Investment Bank while expanding businesses that deliver stable earnings streams. Deutsche Bank is one of the most diverse global platforms in the financial services industry, with a major presence in Europe, the Americas, Asia Pacific and the Emerging Markets.

Deutsche Bank has long been recognised as a leader in intellectual-capital businesses, delivering high quality solutions for its clients. The Bank's investment banking arm has one of the world's most powerful sales and trading franchises and is the only bank to combine market leadership in commodity, credit, equity, foreign exchange and interest rate derivatives. Deutsche Bank continues to grow its global corporate finance platform with a strong European presence and a growing platform in the Americas and Asia. Importantly, stable businesses such as cash management and trade finance continue to thrive at Deutsche Bank.

Deutsche Bank is also one of the world's leading asset managers. It has significant positions in both institutional and retail asset management and is a leading mutual fund provider both in the US and Europe. The Bank's retail business has been enhanced by acquisitions in Germany – Berliner Bank and norisbank – and by new branches in Poland. Furthermore, the acquisition of Tilney Group in the UK and partnerships in China and Vietnam, have expanded the global wealth management offering.

Deutsche Bank is well positioned to take advantage of some of the trends

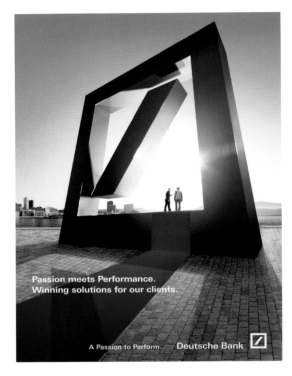

Passion meets Performance.
Winning solutions for our clients.

A Passion to Perform.   Deutsche Bank

In every market, we speak one language: Our clients'.

At Deutsche Bank, all that we do is dedicated to helping our clients make the most of their business opportunities. Achieving this demands performance, innovation and understanding on a level only possible thanks to the dedication and diversity of our people.

This is reflected in our commitment to supporting the broadest range of individuals and ideas – people with the insight, expertise and willingness to go further for our clients when it matters most. They speak the language of success and our clients are the winners.

Deutsche Bank is proud to sponsor the Women in European Business London Conference.

www.weblondon.db.com

Women in European Business

Women in European Business Conference 2007
'Taking ownership of your career'.
Thursday, 21 June 2007

A Passion to Perform.   Deutsche Bank

that are shaping the banking environment: globalisation; capital markets growth; and global assets growth.

ACHIEVEMENTS

Deutsche Bank continues to win accolades for its performance across all product disciplines. In the Euromoney Awards for Excellence 2007, Deutsche Bank won 31 prizes, including Best Credit Derivatives House and Best Foreign Exchange House. As well as M&A, debt and equity awards, Deutsche Bank was also named Best Cash Management House in both Western Europe and Asia. In the Americas, Deutsche Bank won six awards, including Best Risk Management and Best Foreign Exchange House.

Deutsche Bank was also successful in Global Finance magazine's awards and was named Best Investment Bank in Europe and in Germany.

PRODUCT

Deutsche Bank is one of the most global of banks and offers its clients a broad range of banking products and services.

The Private Clients and Asset Management Division comprises three areas: Private and Business Clients, Private Wealth Management and Asset Management. Private and Business Clients provides private clients with an all-round service extending from daily banking offers to holistic investment advisory and tailored financial solutions. Private Wealth

1870	1872	1917	1926	1970s	2007
Deutsche Bank is founded in Berlin to support the internationalisation of business and to promote and facilitate trade relations between Germany, other European countries, and overseas markets.	The first international branches open, in Yokohama and Shanghai, and trade relations begin with the Americas. The following year the first London branch opens.	Deutsche Bank M&A transactions begin.	Deutsche Bank arranges the merger of Daimler and Benz; takes on advisory roles for BP in a major UK deal; and advises on and finances the £2.6 billion London Underground Financing.	Deutsche Bank pushes ahead with the globalisation of its business: Deutsche Bank Luxembourg S.A. is founded and offices open in Moscow, Tokyo, Paris and New York.	The Bank now offers financial services in 76 countries throughout the world with more than 78,000 employees.

Management caters to the specific needs of high net worth clients, their families and select institutions worldwide. Asset Management combines asset management for institutional clients and private investors. As a global provider, it offers customised products in equities, bonds and real estate.

The Corporate and Investment Bank (CIB) comprises two areas: Global Markets and Global Banking.

Global Markets handles all origination, trading, sales and research in cash equities, derivatives, foreign exchange, bonds, structured products and securitisations and thereby occupies a leading position in international foreign exchange, fixed-income and equities trading as well as in derivatives.

Global Banking comprises the Global Cash Management, Global Trade Finance and Trust & Securities Services business divisions and handles all aspects of corporate finance, advises corporations on M&A and divestments, and provides support with IPOs and capital market transactions.

RECENT DEVELOPMENTS

Deutsche Bank is in the middle of the third phase of its management agenda: leveraging the global platform for accelerated growth. This involves maintaining cost, risk, capital and regulatory discipline; further growth of stable businesses; continued organic growth with selected acquisitions; and the build up of the Bank's competitive edge in its Corporate & Investment Bank.

Deutsche Bank is well placed to take advantage of some of the trends that are shaping the business environment of tomorrow: globalisation; climate change; the continued growth of the capital markets; and global asset growth. The Bank has positioned itself well for the increasing globalisation of business with a strategy of regional business diversification underpinned by an envied global network. Deutsche Bank's leadership in investment banking and culture of strong risk management enables it to exploit the growth of the capital markets.

Passion: Exceptional talent.
Performance: Exceptional support.

A Passion to Perform. Deutsche Bank

PROMOTION

Deutsche Bank's communication initiatives leverage its strong and globally renowned brand icon, the global symbol for 'growth in a stable environment' that was designed by the graphic artist Anton Stankowski and was first introduced in 1974.

The global brand communications concept puts the Deutsche Bank brand icon centre stage in conveying the corporate messages. Introduced in March 2005, the 'Winning with the Logo' concept gives the logo a physical presence, becoming Deutsche Bank's tangible face for effective and globally aligned communication of its winning corporate story. The campaign visuals convey Deutsche Bank's enhanced brand image, depicting leadership, global performance and client-orientated delivery. Each execution reflects a different interpretation of the Deutsche Bank logo to a very specific market.

The communication is targeted at people with a modern mindset, a can-do, achievement-oriented attitude. To ensure impact and brand alignment of its communications initiatives, Deutsche Bank regularly monitors progress of brand-related key performance indicators.

Deutsche Bank is highly aware of its role as a corporate citizen and aims to go far beyond the provision of financial resources alone. For many decades Deutsche Bank has been a dedicated patron of the arts and culture, and has supported community development projects and educational programmes. The bank's Corporate Volunteering programme encourages its staff members to become an active part of their community. The goal of the Bank's initiatives is always to enable individuals to push their limits, to discover their talents and to realise their full potential.

The bank's foundations and charitable institutions play a key role, firmly anchoring its Corporate Social Responsibility (CSR) activities around the world. With a global CSR budget of 85.2 million euros (in 2006), 5.7 million euros is dedicated to the UK. Projects have included numerous volunteer programmes in disadvantaged areas of London, working closely with more than 65 non-profit partner organisations. In addition, the bank owns the world's largest corporate contemporary art collection and uses its knowledge of business

and the arts to support new creative businesses, encourage art appreciation and mobilise art and culture to contribute to sustainable and healthy communities.

Through its social investing efforts, Deutsche Bank brings professional expertise and commercial approaches to addressing social needs. The bank currently manages about US$0.5 billion in socially motivated assets which are expected to grow to US$1 billion in the next 3-5 years. These assets are in the area of affordable housing, commercial real estate in distressed neighbourhoods, preservation of the environment, sustainable agriculture, as well as healthcare for the poor and microfinance.

BRAND VALUES

Deutsche Bank is a European global powerhouse dedicated to excellence, constantly challenging the status quo to deliver superior solutions to its demanding clients and superior value to its shareholders and people.

'A Passion to Perform.' applies not only to the Bank's relationships with its clients, but to every aspect of life at Deutsche Bank – it is the way Deutsche Bank does business.

www.db.com

Eddie Stobart

Eddie Stobart is a logistics company with national road, rail, inland waterway and deep sea coverage. Its reported turnover for the last financial year was circa £170 million with a fleet of over 950 trucks, 1,700 trailers, 27 depots, a port, 2.6 million sq ft of warehousing and 2,000 employees. During its 38-year existence, the company has steadily increased its market share and developed internationally, transporting a diverse range of products.

MARKET

The UK haulage industry is large but fragmented; 80 per cent of companies have less than 20 vehicles. The current trend in the industry is towards consolidation and rationalisation. Over the last few years Eddie Stobart has risen to fierce market challenges, for example the introduction of the working time directive, rising fuel costs, competition from overseas and a national shortage of skilled drivers.

The intense competition, changing conditions, pressure to reduce carbon footprint and cut supply chain costs, low margin and high level of investment required are typical characteristics of the haulage industry. Delivery lead times, especially to the national retailers, have reduced to 12 hours which has forced a high level of specialist equipment and systems. Eddie Stobart has a unique brand offering, symbolised by its commitment to provide a one stop solution to clients' distribution needs.

ACHIEVEMENTS

As an iconic British brand, almost every other famous brand in the UK will have been in the back of one of its vehicles at some point. Principally the company has built a reputation for running clean trucks, with smart drivers who arrive on time at their destination.

The naming of the trucks after girls caught the public's imagination, while the drivers' compulsory uniform turned the public's stereotypical image of a truck driver into that of a well dressed, disciplined professional. In addition, in response to public enquiries, the Stobart Members Club was established, with its extensive range of merchandise and members who come from all over the world.

Eddie Stobart's other achievements have been recognised through a number of high-profile awards, including Freight Achievement of 2007 at the National Rail Awards, which honoured the positive environmental impact of its move in to rail freight; Supplier of Excellence by the Institute of Transport Management; the PricewaterhouseCoopers Middle Market Award; and, perhaps its most prestigious to date, Haulier of the Year in the National Motor Transport Awards. Furthermore, in 2006, CEO Andrew Tinkler was recognised as the North West Director of the Year by the Institute of Directors (IoD).

1950s	1970s	1980	1988	1992	2001
Eddie Stobart establishes an agricultural contracting business in the Cumbrian fellside village of Hesket Newmarket.	To develop its transport and distribution interests, the business becomes incorporated as Eddie Stobart Ltd.	Re-location to a new depot in Carlisle takes place. The fleet of eight vehicles mainly consists of tippers, but soon evolves into more versatile articulated vehicles.	A second depot opens in Burton on Trent, with 50 vehicles and 450,000 sq ft of warehousing.	Eddie Stobart Ltd is voted Haulier of the Year by the Motor Transport Industry, testimony to its dedication and hard work in revolutionising the haulage industry.	A fleet of 900 vehicles operates from 27 depots, with a turnover of £130 million and 2,000 staff.

PRODUCT

Collection and delivery is the core function of Eddie Stobart; operating 365 days a year, a diverse range of products – from manufacturing to consumer goods – are transported throughout the UK and Europe. The company has vast experience in handling every type of consignment and load combination, offering a single or multi-drop option to and from any location. The service is supported by intermodal transport networks, an attractive pricing model, efficient vehicle planning and modern communication systems to ensure accurate tracking of vehicles and to maintain time-sensitive delivery schedules.

This is of particular importance in the refrigerated transport service, which offers next day delivery into Europe using state-of-the-art temperature controlled facilities.

The International fleet has significantly grown over the past decade, with vehicles operating cross-channel and throughout Europe. This diverse work is carried out by seasoned professionals with years of continental driving experience.

Storage and distribution is a fast moving, highly skilled discipline within the logistics industry. Eddie Stobart operates over 2.6 million sq ft of warehousing, strategically located throughout the UK and Europe, with a wide variety of storage options. 'Paperless' warehouses use a range of sophisticated bar-coding and tracking systems that can locate batches or individual pallets quickly.

Process management is an added-value service, which enables manufacturers to 'contract-out' all logistics related activities, allowing them to release resources to concentrate on their core business.

Stobart's rail freight service supports the Government legislation of lowering harmful emissions and promotes the switch from road to rail, which takes many wagons off the motorways in Britain.

RECENT DEVELOPMENTS

In August 2007, Eddie Stobart became listed on the London Stock Exchange after a £138 million merger with property fund Westbury. In a reverse take-over deal the new firm is known as the Stobart Group. Eddie Stobart's road transport, warehousing and rail freight operations, combined with Westbury's rail freight business and its port at Runcorn in Cheshire, will create a fully integrated logistics solution by offering road, rail and sea networks for customers and, potentially, an air freight business.

PROMOTION

The Eddie Stobart brand name has 95 per cent brand recognition throughout the UK and acts as a magnet for clients looking to contract out their distribution needs, however tough competition means that the company cannot afford to rest on its laurels.

The principal marketing channel used to promote the brand is the vehicles themselves, as they carry the distinctive livery and company contact details – an obvious approach to maximum exposure and to keeping advertising costs low.

Much of the company's promotional activity is to build brand awareness through trade publications, press releases, brand merchandising and sponsorship. Great publicity has come from its venture into motorsport. Stobart has its own rally team competing nationally and internationally –

with the likes of British star Matthew Wilson being the only British driver contesting the 2007 World Rally Championship – and for the last three years Stobart Motorsport has won the British Rally Championship. The company also continues to be a major sponsor of Carlisle United Football Club, an association of more than 13 years.

As well as its website, which has been designed to be of use to both customers and fans of the company, Eddie Stobart also produces a quarterly magazine to keep its clients and employees informed.

The company has won several high profile marketing awards over the years, including the SWOT Marketing Excellence and Marketeer of the Year awards.

BRAND VALUES

Eddie Stobart's vision is to offer a fully intermodal transport solution and to build strong partnerships with its customers and industry partners, to remove waste from the supply chain. Great importance is placed on keeping the brand fresh and exciting. In 2004, the company revealed a new corporate identity, heralding a bright new era. This rebranding has further enhanced the brand's identity and captures its core values of honesty, respect for people and the environment, and commitment to what it says it will deliver.

www.eddiestobart.co.uk

2004	2005	2006	2007
Eddie Stobart is acquired by WA Developments International. A major rebrand takes place involving changes to the distinctive truck livery, new uniforms and upgraded premises.	Eddie Stobart Ltd wins its first Tesco Distribution Centre contract.	Carlisle Airport is acquired and Stobart Air is formed. Stobart Rail is launched to offer a rail freight service. New central control at Warrington is built.	Eddie Stobart merges with The Westbury Property Fund in a £138 million deal to become the Stobart Group and is listed on the London Stock Exchange.

Things you didn't know about Eddie Stobart

All Eddie Stobart trucks parked in line would stretch in excess of 13 miles.

Twenty lorries today produce the same noise emissions as one 20-year-old lorry.

Stobart's vast Daventry warehouse complex covers 60 acres – equivalent to 20 Wembley Stadiums.

The fuel saving made by the Stobart train is equivalent to taking the entire Eddie Stobart fleet of vehicles off the road for 2.2 weeks every year.

All lorries are named by their drivers or lucky fans who can wait years for their chance to christen a truck.

ExCeL LONDON

ExCeL London has staged over 2,000 events since 2000. More than five million people from 200 countries worldwide have visited, experiencing everything from sporting events, gala dinners and religious festivals to award ceremonies, conferences and exhibitions. ExCeL London is home to eight of London's top 10 trade shows; two out of three of the UK's largest consumer shows; and hosts events for blue-chip corporate clients, government organisations and associations.

MARKET

ExCeL London is one of the UK's premier venues for exhibitions, events and conferences, a market currently worth £20 billion.

The venue operates across the sector, and markets itself as able to handle almost any event imaginable. Its two large halls, totalling 65,000 sq m, can be divided up or used in their entirety. ExCeL London also offers an additional 25,000 sq m of meeting space and is set in a 100-acre waterside campus, including over 30 bars and restaurants, six onsite hotels and a host of additional services.

ExCeL London works with the biggest names in the exhibition business, including Reed Exhibition Companies, CMPi, Haymarket, Emap, Clarion Events, IMIE and National Boat Shows. The Conference & Events Division, set up in 2004, has built a client list which includes Philips, Tesco, Rolls Royce, Barclays, Ernst & Young, Symantec, the NHS and AstraZeneca. It has also announced some major association wins including Gastro 2009 UEGW/WCOG London (12,000 delegates), Society of Stem Cell

Research (7,000 delegates), European Academy of Allergology and Clinical Immunology (8,000 delegates) and European Hematology Association (7,000 delegates).

ACHIEVEMENTS

ExCeL London has received many industry accolades over the years, and in 2007 was awarded Best Venue Support at the Exhibition News Awards, as well as Exhibition Venue of the Year at the Event Awards. The venue was also awarded Best Venue, Best Event Team and Outstanding Achievement at the 2007 Eventia Awards.

The venue has the additional accolade of being at the forefront of London's Thames Gateway regeneration, and will play host to six events and four paralympic events during the 2012 Olympic Games.

PRODUCT

ExCeL London is a £300 million international venue located on a 100-acre, waterside campus in Royal Victoria Dock. It is the largest and most versatile venue in London,

boasting 90,000 sq m of available multi-purpose space, compared to the 65,000 sq m offered by its nearest competitor.

The Platinum Conference Suite can stage conferences and dinners for between 400-1,100 delegates, whilst an additional 45 meeting rooms – many with dockside views – can cater for between 20-200 delegates. There are six onsite hotels, providing 1,500 bedrooms, ranging from budget to four star, 4,000 car parking spaces and three on-site DLR stations – linking to the Jubilee line. London City Airport, which is five minutes away from ExCeL London, offers over 200 flights a day, from more than 30 European destinations.

RECENT DEVELOPMENTS

ExCeL London is continually evolving and improving to ensure the visitor and event planner experience is of the highest standard. Recent developments include the installation of a new Materials Recycling Facility (MRF) onsite and colour coded bins for all events. The MRF is able to recycle paper,

1855		1950s	Mid 1960s	1981	1988
The Royal Victoria Dock site, on which ExCeL London now sits, is opened by Prince Albert as a working dock.	It becomes the first dock to take iron steam ships, and to use hydraulic cranes, handling shipments of tobacco, South American beef and produce from New Zealand.	Traffic through the Royal Dock reaches its peak.	Containerisation and other technological changes, together with a switch in Britain's trade following EEC membership, leads to a rapid decline.	The dock finally closes.	Architect Ray Moxley is approached by the Association of Exhibition Organisers (aeo) to locate and design a new exhibition and conference centre within the M25.

cardboard, plastic, wood and glass. The venue also installed the UK's largest and only commercial wormery. Food waste is collected from the kitchens and preparation areas and delivered to the wormery, where all types of food waste is naturally recycled into productive, nutrient rich soil.

Another improvement, for exhibitors, organisers and delegates, has been the installation of state-of-the-art fibre optic cabling with direct links to BT Tower, and 3G coverage. Technology is playing an increasing role in the events ExCeL London hosts, so it is vital that it remains cutting-edge in what it can provide.

Across the campus, a new Japanese restaurant has opened as well as an Italian restaurant, and a revamp of many boulevard retail units has taken place to widen the food and beverage offering further.

There are also plans to increase the venue's space, flexibility and functionality even further, as part of a seamless extension of the original building. Phase 2 intends to provide a greater sense of arrival at the east end of the venue, an increase in total event space from 65,000 sq m to just under 100,000 sq m. This will include a 5,000-seat semi-permanent auditorium, extra conference and meeting rooms, mezzanine casual dining, a production kitchen and additional underground parking. If built, Phase 2 would be completed in 2010. There are also possible plans for a leisure and entertainment district which would make full use of the waterside location and could include an additional hotel, bars, restaurants, spa, music club, tourist attraction, training academy for the local community and potentially a new casino.

PROMOTION

The marketing team targets two distinct audiences – the exhibitions industry and the conference & events market.

UK exhibition organisers are targeted via a variety of communication channels, including e-bulletins, sales literature, PR and the ExCeL London website. The venue also undertakes as much face-to-face marketing as possible, through organiser forums, corporate hospitality and Strategy Days with key organisers.

Unique to the exhibitions campaign is an award-winning marketing and PR support package, tailored for trade and consumer show organisers. Benefits comprise inclusion in 'what's on' materials, local PR, support with exhibitor days and familiarisation trips as well as contra-deals with local organisations (including the DLR, Canary Wharf, London City Airport and West Ham FC), London and UK wide partners (Tesco Clubcard and National Rail's 2 for 1 London) and media partners.

The conference and events marketing campaign targets both UK and international event planners and is very much focused on promoting the venue in the context of London, a key city in Europe. To this end, much of the international activity is executed in conjunction with Visit London where the destination and the venue are jointly promoted.

ExCeL London also exhibits at international shows and is involved with key industry bodies, hospitality events, speaking at industry seminar programmes and organising UK, European and US road shows, as well as press and client familiarisation trips. In 2007 the Conference & Events Team launched 'The Circle of Excellence', a forum which allows key event buyers to debate current and future trends and set best practice for the meetings and events industry.

BRAND VALUES

ExCeL London is more than an events venue. It's an organisation that promises its clients and staff 'space to perform'. This promise is underpinned by a commitment amongst staff to deliver the ultimate environment in which events can flourish; a blank canvas providing creative inspiration and flexibility; a meticulous approach to every aspect of a project; a caring attitude to the environment and to its neighbourhood.

www.excel-london.co.uk

Things you didn't know about ExCeL London

ExCeL London is a 2012 Olympic Games venue and will be hosting: boxing, wrestling, judo, Tae-kwon-do, weight lifting and table tennis, as well as five paralympic sports.

Will Young started his road to stardom at the Pop Idol auditions held at ExCeL London in 2002.

The test drive scene for the Batmobile in Batman Begins was filmed in the North Event Halls at ExCeL London.

As 007, Pierce Brosnan filmed the boat chase scene in the Royal Docks alongside ExCeL London in The World Is Not Enough.

1990	1994	2000	2008
A turning point is reached when the 100-acre Royal Victoria Dock site is found.	The London Docklands Development Corporation launches an international competition to appoint a preferred developer, which is won by the ExCeL London team.	ExCeL London opens in November, as one of Europe's largest regeneration projects.	Since opening, 2,000 events have been hosted and millions of visitors have passed through its doors.

Express

As the world's largest express transportation company, FedEx Express aims to provide fast and reliable delivery to more than 220 countries and territories worldwide. FedEx Express uses a global air-and-ground network to speed delivery of time-sensitive shipments, usually in one to two business days with the delivery time guaranteed. All 141,000 employees take on the FedEx Express commitment to make every customer experience outstanding.

MARKET

The UK market for express delivery services has increased, in value terms, by a cumulative 21 per cent to £4,691 million during the period 2003 to 2006, while annual growth rates fluctuated between six per cent and seven per cent (Source: MBD). In volume terms, nominal growth of 18 per cent took the number of packages delivered to 1,208.9 million in 2006 (Source: MBD).

Over the past year, FedEx Express has delivered solid financial performance despite increasingly challenging economic conditions in the US. Its results, which showed revenues of US$1,235 million for the financial year 2006/07, an increase of six per cent on the

previous year, benefited from the continued strong growth of its international express business and from its investments to expand its portfolio of service offerings, drive revenue growth and increase productivity.

ACHIEVEMENTS

Throughout its history, FedEx has amassed an impressive list of 'firsts'. Federal Express (as FedEx Express was formerly known) originated the Overnight Letter and was the first express transportation company dedicated to overnight package delivery, the first to offer next-day delivery by 10.30am, and the first to offer Saturday delivery. It was also the first express company to offer time-

definite service for freight and the first in the industry with money-back guarantees and free proof of delivery, services that now extend to its worldwide network.

This illustrious history has also resulted in many awards and honours. In 1990, Federal Express became the first company to win the Malcolm Baldrige National Quality Award in the service category. It also received ISO 9001 registration for all of its worldwide operations in 1994, making it the first global express transportation company to receive simultaneous system-wide certification. In 2006 FedEx Express was listed in Fortune magazine's 100 Best Places to Work and in the US, Black Enterprise magazine's 40 Best Companies for Diversity in 2007.

PRODUCT

FedEx Express offers time-definite, door-to-door, customs-cleared international delivery services and can deliver all kinds of time-sensitive shipments, from urgent medical supplies, last minute gifts and fragile scientific equipment, to bulky freight and dangerous goods.

1971	1973	1977	1983	1984	1989
Frederick W Smith buys the controlling interest in Arkansas Aviation Sales and identifies the difficulty in getting packages delivered quickly; the idea for Federal Express is born.	The company officially begins operations with the launch of 14 small aircraft from Memphis International Airport. It delivers 186 packages to 25 US cities on its first day.	Air cargo deregulation allows the use of larger aircraft (such as Boeing 727s and McDonnell-Douglas DC-10s), spurring the company's rapid growth.	Federal Express reports US$1 billion in revenues, making American business history as the first company to reach the landmark inside 10 years of start-up without mergers or acquisitions.	Intercontinental operations begin with service to Europe and Asia. The following year, Federal Express marks its first regularly scheduled flight to Europe.	With the acquisition of the Flying Tigers network, the company becomes the world's largest full-service, all-cargo airline.

Each shipment is scanned 17 times on average, to ensure that customers can track its precise location by email, on the internet or by telephone 24 hours a day. Whatever the urgency, size or weight of a shipment, FedEx Express aims to treat each package as if it were the only one being shipped that day.

The FedEx Express product range is consistently updated and tailored to improve the level of service to customers – for example: FedEx International Priority, which offers express delivery to over 220 countries for shipments up to 68kg per package; FedEx International Priority Freight, a dedicated service for bulk and heavy shipments of between 68kg and 1,000kg per item; FedEx International Priority DirectDistribution, which offers delivery from one origin to multiple consignees in one destination country; and the FedEx Dangerous Goods Service.

RECENT DEVELOPMENTS
Having acquired UK express company ANC Holdings Limited in December 2006, FedEx Express announced plans to rebrand ANC Express as FedEx UK in late 2007. The acquisition gives customers access to a broader range of shipping options, business and transportation services, under the FedEx brand. The full roll out of the new branding should be finished by the end of autumn 2008. By the end of the rebranding, 2,000 vehicles and 3,000 uniformed employees and contractors will carry the new Fedex UK livery.

In order to meet increased market demand for reliable express transportation services in the fastest-growing region in the UK, a dedicated direct flight between Manchester and the US was launched in August 2007. The flight has increased FedEx Express daily capacity on the important UK-to-US route by up to 50 per cent and from Europe to the US by up to 20 per cent.

In October 2007, a new feeder service from Newcastle International Airport direct to the FedEx European hub at Charles De Gaulle airport, Paris, was launched. The flight departs Newcastle International Airport daily Monday-Thursday and flies directly to Paris for onward connection to the FedEx Euro One network.

2007 also saw FedEx Express make strides in the fast-growing markets of Eastern Europe and China, acquiring Hungarian global service participant, Flying-Cargo Hungary Kft, and launching a next-business-day domestic express service in China. The domestic service in China, launched in June 2007, serves China's burgeoning market with next-business-day, time-definite delivery service to 19 cities and a day-definite service to more than 200 cities throughout the country.

PROMOTION
The expanded services in Newcastle and Manchester, launched by FedEx Express during 2007, have been supported by marketing communications including direct mail, outdoor advertising, local radio advertising and launch events.

More generally, one key focus of the FedEx Express marketing strategy in the UK has been centred on sports sponsorship. FedEx Express is the Official Sponsor and Express Courier of the European Rugby Cup (ERC) and the Official Logistics Partner of the Vodafone McLaren Mercedes Formula One team, where the FedEx logo is prominently displayed on the collar of the team drivers' overalls.

BRAND VALUES
The FedEx corporate strategy, or to FedEx Express employees the 'Purple Promise', is to 'Make Every FedEx Experience Outstanding'. The Purple Promise is the long term strategy for FedEx to further develop loyal relationships with its customers. The FedEx corporate values are: to value its people and to promote diversity; to provide service that puts customers at the heart of everything its does; to invent the services and technologies that improve the way people work and live; to manage operations, finances and services with honesty, efficiency and reliability; to champion safe and healthy environments; and to earn the respect and confidence of FedEx people, customers and investors every day.

www.fedex.com

Things you didn't know about FedEx Express

FedEx Express has the world's largest all-cargo air fleet – its planes have a total daily lift capacity of more than 26.5 million pounds.

In 2003, two custom-built transport containers housed two pandas during their 15-hour flight from China to Memphis Zoo in the US. Le Le, the male panda, and Ya Ya, the female panda, were the only cargo aboard a custom-painted FedEx MD-11 jet, which was renamed 'The FedEx PandaExpress' during the trans-Pacific journey.

In 2004 FedEx Express transported 504,000 bottles, or 630 tonnes, of Beaujolais Nouveau wine from Lyon-Saint-Exupery Airport to Japanese enthusiasts anticipating the annual uncorking on 18th November.

FedEx Express has been known to transport racing cars and even part of the Queen's art collection.

1994	1995	2000	2007
Federal Express officially adopts 'FedEx' as its primary brand, taking a cue from its customers who frequently refer to the company by the shortened name.	Federal Express obtains authority to serve China, becoming the sole US-based, all-cargo carrier with aviation rights to the country.	The company is renamed FedEx Express to reflect its position within the overall FedEx Corporation portfolio of services.	FedEx Express is the world's largest express transportation company, operating a fleet of 669 aircraft and a ground fleet of more than 44,500 motorised vehicles.

First
transforming travel

First, based in Aberdeen, is a world leader in public transport with revenues of over £5 billion a year. It employs 135,000 staff throughout the UK and North America and moves 2.5 billion passengers a year. First is a leader in safe, innovative, reliable and sustainable transport services – global in scale and local in approach.

MARKET

First is the UK's largest rail operator, with four passenger franchises – First Capital Connect, First Great Western, First ScotRail and First TransPennine Express – and one open access operator, First Hull Trains. Providing a balance of intercity, commuter and regional services, First operates a quarter of the UK passenger rail network, carrying almost 270 million passengers per year. It also operates the Croydon Tramlink network, transporting nearly 25 million passengers per year. The Group operates rail freight services through First GBRf.

First is the UK's largest bus operator, with a fleet of 9,000 buses carrying three million passengers every day in 40 major towns and cities. It holds an approximate 23 per cent share of the UK bus service market.

In the North American market, First has four operating divisions: Yellow School Buses (First Student); Transit Contracting and Management Services (First Transit); Vehicle Fleet Maintenance and Support Services (First Services); and intercity bus services (Greyhound). Headquartered in Cincinnati FirstGroup America Inc operates across the US and Canada.

ACHIEVEMENTS

First prides itself on innovation and investment, and continues to create a new standard of transport services across the UK.

It has invested heavily across all of its train companies to deliver passenger growth, better performance and increased capacity. First ScotRail was awarded Public Transport Operator of the Year in 2007 at the Scottish

Transport Awards and reduced delays by some 43 per cent. Following First's investment in a modern, high quality intercity fleet First TransPennine Express has benefited from improved operational performance and customer service. First's £200 million investment in the First Great Western fleet, stations and customer service, has resulted in much improved services for passengers. First Capital Connect moved to the new St Pancras Station in December 2007. Also in 2007, the company ran more trains on time than ever before.

First has invested over £200 million in new buses across the UK over the past three years which has resulted in greater passenger numbers in urban areas such as Glasgow, Manchester, Leeds, Bradford and Aberdeen. The company's operations in East London also topped Transport for London's league tables in 2007.

Meanwhile in North America, the acquisition of US firm, Laidlaw International

Inc in 2007, which includes the iconic Greyhound coach operation, makes First North America's leading school bus operator, running over 60,000 buses a day.

Across the Group, many awards have been won recently. These include the prestigious Tourism Transport Provider of the Year, awarded to First TransPennine Express. First's rail franchises all had notable successes at the National Rail Awards and First UK Bus dominated the UK Bus Driver of the Year Awards and the UK Bus Awards in 2007.

1995	1996	1997	1999	2003	2004
First Bus is born from the Grampian Regional Transport and Badgerline Group merger. The two companies merge to form FirstBus plc. The new company is listed on the Stock Exchange.	First acquires a 24.5 per cent holding in Great Western Holdings. The company operates the Great Western Trains franchise.	The name is changed to FirstGroup plc to reflect the growing interests of the business in rail and international.	The Group makes a significant entry into the North American transport market with the acquisitions of Bruce Transportation and Ryder Public Transportation. These acquisitions form FirstGroup America.	Through the acquisition of GB Railways First acquires GB Railfreight (First GBRf) and Hull Trains.	First is successful in winning the ScotRail bid. This franchise is now known as First ScotRail. It also began operating a new franchise – First TransPennine Express.

PRODUCT

First is divided into three principal divisions: UK Bus; UK Rail; and its North American business. UK Bus generates £1 billion per year in turnover, and runs a fleet of 9,000 buses. The company continues to invest in its fleet delivering an ever increasing number of high-quality, low-floor buses, that comply with EU IV emission standards.

UK Rail, which in 2006/07 generated a turnover of over £1.8 billion, is the market leader in the UK, running 4,500 train services per day, and carrying 270 million passengers per year. First has grown thanks to sustained investment and attention to customer service. Across all its rail companies, including First Hull Trains, which operate services from Hull to London, passenger numbers have increased.

Furthermore, in the rail freight business, First GBRf is a leading player in the UK, carrying two million letters every day for Royal Mail.

RECENT DEVELOPMENTS

While addressing environmental matters has been at the heart of First's strategy for many years, May 2007 saw it unveil its future Climate Change Strategy – the first of its kind in the surface public transport sector. First aims to reduce its carbon dioxide emissions by up to 25 per cent by 2020 throughout its UK bus and rail operations.

The targets will be achieved by improving the fuel efficiency of existing vehicles, purchasing higher efficiency vehicles, using alternative fuels and making operational improvements through driver training and in-cab technology.

Due to the continuing growth and development of First, the company is in the process of constructing its brand new global headquarters in Aberdeen, where the company was born. The new buildings will incorporate some of the latest advances in sustainable design and renewable energy sources.

In an age when 38.7 per cent of primary school children and 21 per cent of secondary school children get to school by car, these

green measures carry more resonance than ever (Source: raisingkids.co.uk). Indeed, 86 per cent of British parents would be willing to send their children to school in a dedicated US-style school bus (Source: raisingkids.co.uk). In response to these findings First has established the Yellow School Bus Commission, chaired by the Rt. Hon. David Blunkett MP, to examine the viability of the use of yellow school buses in the UK. First Student currently operates over 180 such buses across the UK, carrying more than 8,000 students every day.

PROMOTION

First has created a strong visual presence across all areas of its business. Its vehicles are the strongest representation of its brand, helping to establish First as the leader in public transport provision in the UK.

2007 saw First nominate Save the Children as its charity of choice in a partnership worth £1 million to the charity. First has committed to Save the Children's UK programmes, and the company's support will also be used to fill three new assistant programme directors' positions, who will work with local organisations in the UK to reach the children most in need. First trains and buses will feature Save the Children's logo and be seen by millions of passengers throughout the UK.

2007 also saw First host its inaugural 'First Monster Challenge', a 120km team duathlon (running and cycling) around the shores of Loch Ness. The successful event attracted several hundred competitors including a number of celebrities. First encouraged participants to raise money for

Save the Children. 'First Mini Monsters', a less strenuous version of the event, will be rolled out to various UK cities in 2008.

BRAND VALUES

First has a clear vision: to transform travel by providing public transport services that are safe, customer focused, professional and trustworthy, and committed to progressively improving.

It aims to be the 'best in class' in everything that it does, delivering the highest levels of safety and service, and constantly building on its reputation for innovation, investment and improvement. Safety is the number one priority for the Group, and it has created a culture of 'Safety First' throughout the business, following the launch of its Injury Prevention Programme (IPP). The message from First is, 'if you cannot do it safely, don't do it'.

www.firstgroup.com

Things you didn't know about First

First plants 1,500 new trees every year as part of its commitment to support biodiversity.

Fifty-seven per cent of First shareholders are employees.

First carries more than 2.5 billion passengers per year (or over 350 in the time it takes you to read these words).

More than one in five of all UK bus journeys are with First.

First was one of the first companies to sign the Government's Skills Pledge which is designed to improve adult learning. Training has become the cornerstone of First's employee strategy.

2006

First begins operating two new enlarged rail franchises, First Great Western and First Capital Connect.

First's award-winning articulated tram-like vehicle ftr is rolled out in York. The following year Leeds also implements the ftr, with Swansea soon to follow.

2007

First completes the acquisition of Laidlaw International Inc to become the leading transportation provider in North America.

First now employs 135,000 people globally and transports more than 2.5 billion passengers a year.

flybe.

Flybe was established in Jersey in 1979 and has grown to become Europe's largest regional airline with more bases and regional UK flights than any other airline. Flybe's 2007 acquisition of BA Connect has created a business flying eight million passengers in 2007, on 155 routes and generating more than £500 million in revenues.

MARKET

The boom in budget airlines over the past decade has lead to short-haul air travel becoming more popular. This has resulted in the market becoming highly competitive, with tight margins. However, it is a challenging market with increases in the price of oil, rising taxation on air travel, higher airport charges and pressure from environmental groups all factors likely to impact the aviation sector over the next decade.

ACHIEVEMENTS

Flybe has chalked up 28 years of continuous operations, evolving from its roots as Jersey European into a successful, innovative market leader within the low-cost airline industry. By flying from the UK regions, focusing on 'low-cost travel on your doorstep' and offering the country's only true low-cost business service, it has differentiated itself in the crowded airline marketplace.

The airline has also been highly successful in driving ancillary revenue, the key aim for any low-cost operator. It was the first airline in the world to charge for hold baggage and reward hand-baggage only passengers. Flybe has also become the in-flight sales market leader, taking a higher spend per passenger than any other short-haul scheduled airline.

Flybe is spearheading efforts to reduce the environmental impact of air travel. Investing more than US$2 billion in new aircraft since

2006, Flybe became the first airline to take delivery of the new Embraer 195. Its performance features include greater fuel efficiency and a reduction in noise levels. This 26-aircraft order, plus Flybe's order for the Bombardier Q400 aircraft, will give it one of the youngest and most environmentally sensitive fleets in the world, part of Flybe's drive to reduce fuel consumption by more than 50 per cent per seat by 2009.

In line with this commitment, 2007 saw Flybe become the first airline in the world to introduce an aircraft eco-labelling scheme. Passengers booking via the internet now receive a detailed breakdown of fuel consumption, carbon emissions and noise patterns, allowing them to contribute via Flybe to PURE, the Clean Planet Trust, appointed to operate carbon-offset schemes for Flybe passengers.

1979	1983	1991	1993	1993/94	2000
Jersey-based entrepreneur and successful businessman Jack Walker founds Jersey European.	The airline is taken over by the Walkersteel Group.	Jersey European gains its first London route from Guernsey to London Gatwick.	The Business Class Service is launched, making Jersey European the first domestic airline to offer two classes of service.	Jersey European wins the Best UK Regional Airline award at the Northern Ireland Travel and Tourism Awards.	Jersey European changes its name to British European, becoming Flybe two years later.

Low cost, but not at any cost.

flybe.com

The low fares, low emissions airline.

Flybe has recently won several awards including: Flight International's Best Management Team 2007 award; Best Airline Website in the UK at Wanderlust magazine's 2007 Travel Awards; and the Business Achievement Award at the Franco-British Business Awards 2007.

PRODUCT

Flybe operates services from 23 UK and 32 mainland European airports, with new routes to key commercial centres including Paris, Düsseldorf, Frankfurt and Milan. The airline's network is made up of 70 per cent domestic UK routes, 20 per cent business and 10 per cent leisure. Indeed, Flybe is the largest scheduled airline at Birmingham, Exeter, Norwich, Southampton, the Channel Islands and Belfast City.

For the business market, a key part of the airline's offering is Flybe Economy Plus. As well as free executive lounge access across the UK and Europe, this offers a range of

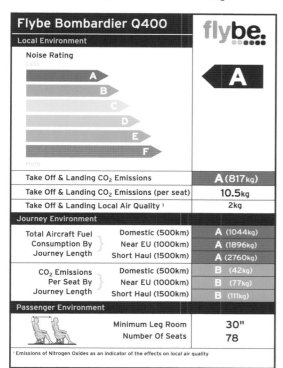

Flybe Bombardier Q400		flybe.
Local Environment		
Noise Rating		**A**
Less		
A		
B		
C		
D		
E		
F		
More		
Take Off & Landing CO$_2$ Emissions		A (817kg)
Take Off & Landing CO$_2$ Emissions (per seat)		10.5kg
Take Off & Landing Local Air Quality [1]		2kg
Journey Environment		
Total Aircraft Fuel Consumption By Journey Length	Domestic (500km)	A (1044kg)
	Near EU (1000km)	A (1896kg)
	Short Haul (1500km)	A (2760kg)
CO$_2$ Emissions Per Seat By Journey Length	Domestic (500km)	B (42kg)
	Near EU (1000km)	B (77kg)
	Short Haul (1500km)	B (111kg)
Passenger Environment		
	Minimum Leg Room	30"
	Number Of Seats	78

[1] Emissions of Nitrogen Oxides as an indicator of the effects on local air quality

other features such as: lower minimum check-in times; fully changeable tickets; dedicated check-in; and generous baggage allowance. The ongoing enhancement of Flybe Economy Plus means that customers now have access to many more executive lounges across the UK and Europe, many of which offer wireless internet access.

In addition to the airline, Flybe is a major player in Aviation Services, offering aircraft engineering not only for the Flybe fleet, but also third-party maintenance for clients that include British Airways. The business, which has won several industry accolades, employs more than 500 staff at its Exeter site, plus further line engineering teams across the UK and has recently invested £14 million in new hangar facilities in the South West.

RECENT DEVELOPMENTS

Flybe's acquisition of BA Connect has seen it become Europe's largest regional airline, with a network that has a unique balance between business and leisure passengers. Through its US$2 billion investment Flybe will increase its fleet to more than 80 Bombardier Q400 and Embraer 195 aircraft by 2010.

In 2007 Flybe announced its new frequent flyer programme, rewards4all, the UK's first low-cost customer loyalty scheme open to all passengers. The scheme provides all passengers with an automated programme that puts them in charge of their rewards. Customers can use their points for free flights or one year's free Executive Lounge access.

PROMOTION

In September 2007 Flybe launched a month-long advertising campaign to focus on the airline's brand positioning and key consumer benefits. The £1.5 million campaign ran across national and regional press, digital and email channels, with the primary objective of driving more people to its redesigned website and increasing flight sales. With the strapline

'Think Flybe, think… no compromises', it focused on the message of low-cost fares with high frequency schedules, high standard Business Traveller offerings, a high quality frequent flyer programme and its commitment to sustainable aviation. In addition, Flybe revealed a new-look website at flybe.com. Handled in-house by Flybe, the redesign sees the airline adopting a fresher, bolder look following the BA Connect acquisition.

Customer Relationship Marketing remains at the heart of Flybe's long term strategy to increase the lifetime loyalty of its customers. Flybe operates a highly segmented database and a communications strategy that is fast, bespoke and personalised.

Sponsorship is another important tool for Flybe and the airline has signed deals with four football clubs: Exeter City, Norwich City, Southampton and Inverness Caledonian Thistle.

BRAND VALUES

Flybe's brand is built on a vision to be modern, different, environmentally and socially responsible, transparent and customer-driven. Its contribution to regional economies, investments into local communities, advocacy for regional 'on your doorstep' services and strong regional heritage all feed into the identity of the brand. In addition, innovation and offering its customers a comprehensive wealth of services, is another key value.

www.flybe.com

Things you didn't know about Flybe

If all the tubs of Pringles sold on board in one year were stacked on top of each other, they would be 12 times higher than the world's tallest building, Taipei Tower, Taiwan.

Flybe could fill 15 Olympic-sized swimming pools with all the bottles of mineral water it sells in a year.

Flybe's aircraft fly a total of 44.4 million kilometres each year.

The fleet uses 1,800 aircraft tyres per year.

2003	**2005**	**2006**	**2007**
Flybe is voted Most Recommended UK Low Fares Airline by Holiday Which?	Flybe is voted Most Popular UK Domestic and France-bound Airline by Holiday Which?	Flybe becomes the first airline to offer online check-in to passengers carrying hand and hold baggage, along with functionality for online flight changes.	Flybe acquires BA Connect to become Europe's largest regional airline. Flybe also launches the UK's first low-cost frequent flyer programme, rewards4all, as well as the world's first airline eco-labelling scheme.

Group 4 Securicor

G4S, the international security solutions group, has a reputation for providing security solutions across the world. Its unrivalled geographic footprint and first hand experience of the key security issues in a broad range of markets means that it is uniquely placed to advise on identifying and managing risks. G4S provides a range of security solutions from manned security, risk management & consultancy, justice services, to cash & ATM network management.

MARKET

Over the past decade the global market for security solutions has developed substantially and is expected to continue growing year-on-year. Sustained growth is driven by the ongoing threat of global terrorism, new technology and greater customer awareness, fuelling demand for more integrated and sophisticated outsourced security solutions. G4S, listed on both the London and Copenhagen Stock Exchanges, is the global leader in providing security solutions, paving the way in new and emerging markets. Currently operating in over 110 countries, with more than 500,000 employees, it is the largest employer listed on the London Stock Exchange.

The group operates in two key sectors: Secure Solutions, with a £3,480.6 million turnover and Secure Logistics with an £873 million turnover (Fiscal Year 2006). Built on a broad range of specialist services, G4S

is able to offer complete secure solutions and fully outsourced cash management. This unique approach ensures a leading market position in many of the countries in which G4S operates. Its leading market position helps to attract driven, talented individuals – this strong leadership ethos boosting the continued growth and success of the brand.

ACHIEVEMENTS

G4S has a market value of £2.9 billion – its rating in the FTSE 100 index as of 24th December 2007 confirming its position as one of the UK's most valuable businesses.

G4S supports sustainable development, securing a reputation for initiating wide-ranging community support programmes. Its 'Investing in the Community' programme supports a range of health, welfare and community initiatives around the world, with

particular emphasis on new and emerging markets. The foundations of the programme are built around the brand credentials of giving something back to local communities – for instance, community tree-planting in Malawi and Gifts 4 Schools in Jamaica. These projects reaffirm G4S' focus on ethical responsibility towards employees, customers, suppliers, investors and communities.

Its launch of the G4S 4teen programme, to support aspiring young athletes from around the world, has also won many plaudits. Emerging markets have not been the sole beneficiary of G4S' community-led initiatives; the Group has also contributed substantially to UK sports development by teaming up with The British Judo Association to aid the development of the sport in the run up to the Olympic Games, to be held in London in 2012. The Group also joined forces

2004	2005		2006		
Group 4 Falck's security business merges with Securicor to create the world's second largest security provider, Group 4 Securicor – a combination of the two brands.	The G4S brand launches – an 18-month roll out to 110 countries and more than 400,000 staff.	Also in 2005, G4S' brand profile is heightened when it features in The Times '21st Century Stars: Group 4 Securicor' in May.	The G4S brand identity continues to be rolled out to all countries in the Group. By 31st December 98 per cent of the business has been successfully rebranded as G4S.	The 2006 Chairman of The Year award is presented to the Chairman of G4S, Alf Duch-Pedersen, by J-B International (Denmark).	Also in 2006, G4S secures Sponsorship of Skandia Team GBR.

with Skandia Team GBR in 2006, backing the British sailing team's quest for medals.

PRODUCT

G4S' services extend from secure solutions, such as manned security, event security, justice services, risk management & consultancy, to secure logistics. G4S is the world's leading provider of a range of secure logistics, including the transportation and management of cash & ATM networks and the fully outsourced management of cash centres. The brand offers these solutions to a wide range of markets, sectors and customers including governments, airports, financial institutions, retailers and major event venues, amongst others.

In addition it provides a comprehensive range of services that support the work of criminal justice and immigration agencies worldwide, employing more than 3,500 people in this growing sector across operations in the UK, the US, the

Netherlands, Israel and the Channel Islands. G4S monitors around 37,000 offenders daily.

RECENT DEVELOPMENTS

2007 was a pivotal year for G4S, beginning in January when two new US juvenile detention centres, in Florida and Georgia, were added to its ever-expanding criminal justice portfolio; and culminating in December when it formally cemented its credentials as a premier business by joining the FTSE 100 Index.

The intervening months saw G4S' Wackenhut Corporation in the US being named in Training magazine's Top 25 for 2007; G4S winning a major new contract to provide Electronic Monitoring (EM) equipment and services to the Department of Corrections in New Zealand, as a result of its wide-ranging international expertise managing EM programmes; and G4S being awarded Norway's largest security contract at Oslo airport, the most significant and vital security contract in Norway. In November 2007, G4S began working on a major defence contract, offering pre-deployment training for the British Army and marking a period of accelerated growth and development for the Group.

PROMOTION

G4S recently embarked upon an ambitious charity and sponsorship strategy designed to build the profile of the G4S brand worldwide, including community projects, G4S 4teen, an Employee Trust, and a Sponsorship Matching Programme. It is envisaged that wide-ranging sports sponsorship partnerships such as G4S 4teen, will provide

an international platform for G4S to engage with its employees and customers, whilst simultaneously raising awareness of the brand with a wider audience.

BRAND VALUES

G4S has six main pillars on which it operates: Expertise, Customer Focus, Best People, Integrity, Teamwork & Collaboration and Performance – each is championed by a designated member of the Group Executive Team. The Group's clear corporate vision, underpinned by these values, ensures that everyone understands the strategy of the organisation and their individual role in its delivery.

G4S uses these six defining pillars to maintain a close, open relationship with customers that engenders trust and is mutually beneficial to both organisations, developing and demonstrating its expertise through innovation and a leading edge approach to creating and delivering the right solution.

www.g4s.com

Things you didn't know about G4S

In October 2007 G4S became the world's first cash delivery firm to use SmartWater Technology in the UK.

G4S manages more than 30,000 ATMs across Europe and North America.

G4S provides embassy security in almost 40 countries.

G4S electronically monitors more than 37,000 offenders worldwide.

G4S employs more than 100,000 people in India. Between them, they speak over 30 different languages.

2007			
G4S Security Services (UK) wins the award for Best Integrated Security Solution at the 2006 Security Excellence Awards.	A Charity and Sponsorship strategy is implemented. It includes Community projects, partnering Skandia Team GBR, G4S 4teen project, an Employee Trust and a Sponsorship Matching Programme.	In June G4S hits the 500,000 employee mark.	In December G4S joins the FTSE 100.

GATWICK EXPRESS

Gatwick Express was established in 1984 and is the longest running dedicated airport service in the world. It carries approximately 14,000 passengers between Gatwick Airport and London's Victoria station throughout the day, with a non-stop journey time of 30 minutes and with trains departing every 15 minutes.

We're the fastest way to the airport.

(Nice to know when you've got a plane to catch.)

London Victoria to Gatwick Airport in 30 minutes¹, every 15 minutes. Visit www.gatwickexpress.com

GATWICK EXPRESS
— Anything else is a risk —

¹Average journey time.

MARKET

Gatwick Express will be owned by National Express Group until June 2008, when the franchise is going to Southern as part of the Department for Transport's Brighton Mainline Route Utilisation Strategy. Gatwick Express holds more than 70 per cent of the rail market between Gatwick Airport and central London.

ACHIEVEMENTS

Gatwick Express has the highest customer satisfaction levels of any train operating company in the UK. In the 2007 National Passenger Survey, Gatwick Express scored 94 per cent, an industry record and the seventh consecutive time over a four-year period that Gatwick Express has held the number one position.

Delivering excellent customer service is a constant challenge and the demands of customers are constantly evolving. Gatwick Express is always looking for innovative ways to improve the way in which staff interact with customers. To meet the needs of an increasingly sophisticated and customer-service focused market, Gatwick Express shifted its focus to providing flexible, positive and personal customer service. As a result, the innovative and award-winning 'Leading Lights' training programme was developed.

Designed as a training programme that proactively engages its workforce by using drama and theatrical elements to spark interest and maintain attention in trainees, Leading Lights helps frontline staff identify different types of customers so they can deliver exceptional service that meets the passenger's individual needs. The emphasis is on achieving targeted, long term change in day-to-day behaviour and performance.

Gatwick Express has the highest levels of employee satisfaction (as tracked in the National Express Group employee survey) across all Group companies, and in March 2006 Gatwick Express saw their satisfaction ratings increase to a record 85 per cent from 78 per cent.

Gatwick Express also plays an active role with the local community, supporting local schools and organisations through fundraising and donations. Gatwick Express is a family friendly company and has hosted school trips and youth groups to raise awareness of the importance of rail safety.

PRODUCT

Gatwick Express is a dedicated, non-stop, high speed rail-air link operating between central London and Gatwick Airport. The purpose built modern Juniper Class 460 trains, run from 3.30am–12.30am from London Victoria and from 4.35am–1.35am from Gatwick Airport.

Gatwick Express has its own dedicated platforms at Victoria station to allow passengers quick access on and off the trains. Similarly, the railway station at Gatwick Airport is at the heart of the South Terminal.

Gatwick Express Welcome Hosts are situated at the front of the platform to help customers with queries about the service and onward travel into London. In addition, Gatwick Express has installed flight departure boards on the platforms at Victoria to allow passengers to check the status of their departing flight.

Whether travelling for business or pleasure the emphasis is on comfort. Gatwick Express First Class interiors aim to provide a calming and spacious, air-conditioned environment for customers to make the most of their time whilst travelling to or from the airport.

Express Class includes modern, comfortable seating, air-conditioned surroundings and attentive staff, a full refreshment trolley service as well as room for luggage.

1936	1939	1955	Late 1950s	1980s
Gatwick Airport opens with one terminal, which is known as 'The Beehive' due to its distinctive cone shape.	The airport station is situated one mile south of the current station, and is used to service Gatwick Racecourse.	World War II sees the airport being used as a military base.	The airport is sold by Airports Limited to the state and a period of major development begins.	A new airport terminal is built and the Gatwick Racecourse station is developed into a dedicated airport station. The train link to Gatwick is limited, using dedicated carriages from part of another service.	The current station building is erected and business at Gatwick Airport expands rapidly.

RECENT DEVELOPMENTS

Gatwick Express was the first train operating company in the UK to utilise an e-ticketing solution to allow customers to book their tickets online. To support e-ticketing, Gatwick Express recently upgraded its website to simplify and speed up the booking process. Customers' personal details and favourite tickets can be securely retained, while customers that hold accounts can be notified of planned or unplanned disruptions on their date of travel.

PROMOTION

In order to reach its customer base, both in the UK and internationally, Gatwick Express uses press, outdoor and online communications to execute its promotional strategy.

In summer 2006, Gatwick Express launched a new advertising campaign specifically targeted at the time sensitive air traveller. A new strapline – 'Anything else is a risk' – was introduced, replacing the previous 'Timing is everything' line. The new strapline – still underpinned by the essence of 'certainty' of the Gatwick Express brand – takes a more competitive approach by referring indirectly to competitors between central London and the airport.

Key messages in the brand's advertising aim to reassure passengers and highlight the speed, the non-stop nature of the service, the frequency and strong customer service record.

Gatwick Express advertises in the inner London press to target the UK business and

Don't miss a minute

Breathtaking. Tower Bridge. 9.30pm June 3.

There's so much to see in London, why waste extra time getting to and from Gatwick Airport? Gatwick Express is the fastest way to and from Gatwick Airport from central London, with trains departing every 15 minutes and taking only 30 minutes non-stop from Victoria Station*.

Book online at www.gatwickexpress.com/londonplanner

GATWICK 'EXPRESS

——— Anything else is a risk ———

*Average journey times. See website for full timetable.

leisure audience, a strategy supported by online advertising at key times of the year on popular travel and business websites.

The majority of outdoor poster activity is concentrated at Gatwick Airport, Gatwick Airport station and Victoria station, aiming to reassure customers that they are making the right decision and to convert undecided travellers.

In October 2007, Gatwick Express won the Gold and Silver Awards at the CIMTIG (Chartered Institute of Marketing Travel Industry Group) Travel Advertising Awards for the best use of classified press advertising.

The focus for below-the-line activity is developing relationships with airlines at Gatwick Airport. For example, Gatwick Express is a partner of Virgin Atlantic's Flying Club programme; Silver and Gold members receive an allocation of First Class upgrades to use on Gatwick Express, which has proved to be extremely successful since its launch in 2003.

International travellers are targeted through airline partners; Gatwick Express has developed solid relationships with growth airlines, such as easyJet, GB Airways, Zoom, and Monarch, as a mechanism for reaching potential customers during the booking process or during their flight.

The current focus for Gatwick Express is on customer relationship marketing, with the objective of ensuring consistent and frequent communication with the customer base, providing news about promotions, new products and service enhancements.

Gatwick Express became the first train company to sell visitor Oyster cards onboard or at the ticket office in partnership with Transport for London (TfL). This new initiative was launched at a press conference at City Hall with the Mayor of London.

Gatwick Express also realises the potential of the ski and snowboard market which it is targeting through sponsorship of the

Time Out Ski & Snowboard Europe guide. This sponsorship is supported by concourse promotions at London Victoria station and online advertising on high profile ski websites as well as a 'four for two' promotional offer.

BRAND VALUES

Regardless of the passenger type there is a common belief that 'some journeys are simply more important than others'. It is acknowledged that there is heightened tension on a trip to the airport; for most air travellers, the consequences of a delay can be significant. Gatwick Express therefore, bases its brand promise on the certainty that passengers will arrive in a timely fashion.

This promise is broken down into the emotional and rational benefits of using the service. Rational benefits include the speed and frequency of the service, as well as its punctuality and reliability. Emotional benefits include the dedicated service, trust and reassurance, premium feel and the belief that the Gatwick Express is the 'official' way to and from the airport.

The Gatwick Express 'voice' that delivers these brand values in its advertising has been developed to represent that of an airline captain with wit and charm – someone who is confident, comfortable and unflappable.

www.gatwickexpress.com

Things you didn't know about Gatwick Express

Every year 1.6 million miles are travelled by Gatwick Express, the equivalent to over six times the distance to the moon.

Gatwick Express actively recruits multi-national and multi-lingual customer service staff to reflect an increasingly non-English speaking customer base. As a result, more than 35 languages are now spoken across the team. All employees who speak a foreign language are given name badges with flags to depict which languages they speak.

Each day, 14,000 passengers travel on Gatwick Express.

1984	1990s	2005	2008
The first dedicated Gatwick Express service is formed to provide a rail-air link to the airport.	Gatwick Airport continues to expand.	Gatwick Airport has 32 million passengers passing through it. This is expected to grow to 40 million by 2008.	Handover of the Gatwick Express franchise to Southern is due to take place – part of the Department for Transport's Brighton Mainline Route Utilisation Strategy.

GENERAL DYNAMICS
United Kingdom Limited

General Dynamics UK is a leading prime contractor and complex system of systems integrator working in partnership with the UK's Ministry of Defence (MoD) and other allies. With more than 1,600 highly skilled employees and over 40 years experience delivering complex systems, General Dynamics UK has the technical leadership, manufacturing expertise and prime contract management skills to deliver future network-enabled battlespace capabilities.

MARKET

General Dynamics UK works primarily in the UK defence industrial sector, with additional work in the Homeland Security and Resilience sector. Its principal UK customer is the MoD, with overseas success in the export markets including the Netherlands, Romania, and others in the near future.

Today, General Dynamics UK is the fourth largest UK defence company and the third largest defence prime contractor in the UK. It is part of the General Dynamics Corporation, one of the top six defence companies in the world with approximately 83,500 employees and reported 2007 revenues of US$27.2 billion.

As a prime system of systems integrator it takes leading products and technologies and performs the complex integration work required to enable their effective use at the system of systems level. This means that General Dynamics UK's market share is underpinned by a diverse supply chain, including a major contribution from SMEs.

ACHIEVEMENTS

General Dynamics UK has achieved significant growth on the back of major project successes since 2000 and has invested more than £14 million in facilities. Its workforce has more than tripled in size. Since 2002, nearly 1,000 new jobs have been created in Wales, adding over £30 million to the UK economy. In fact, every job created contributes on average £55,000 to the local economy.

General Dynamics UK takes its corporate responsibilities seriously and is very aware of the local communities in which it works, giving more than £500,000 in charitable contributions and sponsorships over the past few years. General Dynamics UK also actively supports several charities and benevolent funds associated with the military, including SSAFA (Soldiers, Sailors, Airmen and Families Association), the Army Benevolent Fund, and Combat Stress.

PRODUCT

General Dynamics UK is structured around four core business units: C4I (UK), Ground Systems, Mission Systems and Network Solutions.

C4I stands for Command, Control, Communications, Computing and Information. It is the integration of technology and networks that give commanders and politicians the vital information they need, when they need it.

General Dynamics UK's C4I business is successfully delivering Bowman to UK forces, giving them a decisive advantage. Bowman is a tactical communications system integrating digital voice and data technology to provide secure radio, telephone, intercom, situational awareness and tactical internet services. The programme includes the conversion of more than 12,000 platforms, including vehicles, helicopters, naval vessels, landing craft and fixed HQ buildings.

Ground Systems builds on the UK-based capability for armoured fighting vehicles and related sub-systems. The core activity within this business unit is associated with the development of solutions for the UK Future Rapid Effects System (FRES) programme.

The Mission Systems business unit delivers a family of integrated systems and avionics products, which provide airborne NEC and ISTAR capability for the UK MoD and export customers. Product families include military aircraft Mission Computers (such as the Future Lynx Tactical Processor), Surveillance and Intelligence Systems, safety critical Stores Management Systems, and ground-to-air and air-to-air tactical data networks. Current projects include TIEC (Tactical

1899	1952	1962	1990	1997	2000
The Electric Boat Corporation is established.	The Electric Boat Corporation becomes General Dynamics.	Computing Devices Company (CDC) is established in London to support an avionics project for the Anglo-Canadian Nimrod Mk1 maritime patrol aircraft.	The RAF use CDC's Real-Time Tactical Reconnaissance System in the Gulf War – the first world use of this technology.	General Dynamics Corporation acquires Computing Devices International.	CDC becomes General Dynamics UK, formed to support the UK MoD.

Information Exchange Capability) for the RAF and the Assessment Phase for LISTENER – the UK MoD requirement for a network to fuse multiple ISTAR sensor data in real time.

The Network Solutions team provides C4I solutions, like Bowman, for the export market. In addition, General Dynamics UK is a key partner in the Atlas Defence Infrastructure Information (DII) consortium through the Network Solutions business.

As a technology-independent prime system of systems integrator, General Dynamics UK is able to draw from the global marketplace, bringing together the best solutions for the UK Armed Forces and other allies. The extensive experience of its parent company – General Dynamics Corporation – aids in offering the right solutions to customers, at the appropriate technology and system readiness levels.

www.generaldynamics.uk.com

GENERAL DYNAMICS
United Kingdom Limited

RECENT DEVELOPMENTS

The British Army has successfully trialled the latest version of Bowman, developed by General Dynamics UK. The system is constantly evolving to respond to changes in experience on operations, evolving doctrine, updated requirements and advances in technology. The latest version, known as BCIP5, provides the Armed Forces with a highly robust, mobile tactical internet, which allows soldiers to pass data, messages and vital location information around the battlefield.

In addition, General Dynamics UK continues to develop the Defence Technology Centre in Data and Information Fusion (DIF DTC). This is a research consortium, led by General Dynamics UK in partnership with the MoD, industry and eight academic partners.

General Dynamics UK has developed a leading position in the British Army's future Armoured Fighting Vehicle (AFV) programme, FRES – the key element of a new medium force capability for the British Army. It is the largest ever Army programme with an acquisition value of around £16 billion, and through-life costs of £60 billion. It will also transform the UK industrial landscape in the AFV sector.

This builds on the Company's experience and facilities in the UK – integrating thousands of military vehicles for Bowman – as well as the track record of General Dynamics Corporation as the world's leading supplier of armoured fighting vehicles.

PROMOTION

General Dynamics UK works hard on reputation management using a variety of channels, including a comprehensive corporate responsibility programme.

As an integral part of General Dynamics UK, the Research Foundation exists to foster understanding of the evolving nature of technology and warfare, with particular emphasis on command and battlespace management.

The Research Foundation sponsors periodic conferences under the Whither Warfare title to promote debate of topical issues. These conferences attract defence chiefs, defence policy makers and industry, as well as acknowledged experts from academia, to present their views and to debate with an audience drawn from across the defence and technology community.

With a customer centric culture, the majority of promotional activities are centred around face-to-face communication, using advertising and promotion selectively. Long-standing relationships based on trust, and a firm belief that General Dynamics UK will deliver what it promises on time, every time, is key.

BRAND VALUES

Being dynamic – characterised by energy and effective action – is at the heart of General Dynamics UK. This manifests itself through five main aims:

To keep customers satisfied through maintaining close contact and understanding their needs; maintaining integrity throughout the Company; taking the right action at the right time and encouraging its people to take calculated risks, as well as being prepared to accept and learn from mistakes; working in partnership with other groups for the success of mutual goals and delivery of the best results; and valuing the contribution of others, recognising and appreciating different viewpoints.

www.generaldynamics.uk.com

Transforming technology into CAPABILITY
for the benefit of our customers

Want to join us? Find out more at
www.generaldynamics.uk.com

GENERAL DYNAMICS
United Kingdom Limited

Things you didn't know about General Dynamics UK

In Tactical Reconnaissance Systems, General Dynamics UK pioneered the move from celluloid film to digital video-based technology; allowing imagery to be interpreted in real/near real time in the cockpit.

General Dynamics UK is responsible for the conversion of more than 12,000 British Army vehicles to the state-of-the-art Bowman communications system. This conversion programme involves over 700 different designs in 100 types of vehicle, from Challenger tanks to Land Rovers.

2001
General Dynamics UK wins the Bowman contract from the UK MoD, worth £1.9 billion, followed in 2002 by the CIP information and data contract, bringing the total value of Bowman to £2.4 billion.

2005
General Dynamics UK reports turnover of more than £500 million.

2006
General Dynamics UK creates its Ground Systems division to focus on delivering the next generation of armoured fighting vehicles to the British Army.

2007
General Dynamics UK is selected to supply the TIEC capability to UK Tornado and Harrier fleets, continuing its role as a key avionics supplier to the RAF.

Harris®
World Class Decorating Products

Best known as a manufacturer of paintbrushes, family-owned LG Harris & Co supplies a broad range of decorating products, such as brushes, rollers and decorators' tools, into all of the UK DIY multiples, key trade outlets and more than 100 countries worldwide. Founded in 1928 and based in the Midlands, LG Harris & Co prides itself on high standards, utilising cutting-edge manufacturing technologies to bring innovative designs to market.

MARKET

The DIY multiples sector has continued to benefit from positive market conditions over the past 10 years, outperforming the overall retail sector with underlying growth of between 8-10 per cent per year between 2000-2003 (Source: British Home Enhancement Trade Association 2007), despite a number of negative influences including the global economic slowdown following 9/11. However, the UK economy, and consumer confidence and spending in particular, were affected by lower house price inflation and higher interest rates in 2004 and 2005. Consequently, the value of the DIY market declined slightly in 2005 to £7,595 million (Source: British Home Enhancement Trade Association 2007).

Despite the lower growth in the DIY market over the past two years, the market continues to be characterised by people wanting to make changes to their home environment, primarily driven by fashion. Within the decorating sundries sector of the DIY market, Harris has capitalised by launching a string of innovative decorating products designed to help consumers bring their inspirations to life.

The market value for decorating sundries is estimated at around £58.5 million, of which Harris's share in terms of turnover equates to approximately 60 per cent. Harris's turnover for the financial year ending 2007 was £35.2 million, up from £29.4 million the previous year, demonstrating a 20 per cent increase in sales.

ACHIEVEMENTS

From small beginnings in 1928, based in two Victorian houses in Birmingham, Harris today operates a British factory and headquarters based in Bromsgrove, as well as a wholly owned foreign enterprise in China, consisting of a three-site, 135,000 sq ft, £1 million plus factory investment.

A pioneering spirit has long infected all aspects of the Harris business, from new product development to innovative manufacturing techniques and marketing. In 1993 it launched its range of No Loss paint brushes as the world's first brush guaranteed against bristle loss whilst painting. It also developed dual moulding technology to bring soft-grip tool handles to the UK market.

Increasing costs of raw materials such as plastic and natural bristle have had to be carefully managed over the years by Harris, but new product designs have been introduced to reduce the plastic component requirements, and the manufacturing skills base has been broadened to include synthetic brushes. The business itself has diversified to include roller and frame production, as well as decorating tool manufacture. As a result of its success, Harris was voted as the UK's favourite supplier of decorating sundries by the British Hardware Federation in 2004 and MICA in 2007.

PRODUCT

Harris has a reputation for quality products and service. The current Harris range varies from the best traditional natural bristle paintbrushes to innovative Synthetic designs.

1928	1933	1947	1951	1961	1974
The Midland Trading Company is founded in Birmingham by LG Harris, buying and reselling paintbrushes.	The Midland Trading Company is renamed LG Harris & Co Ltd.	The business develops rapidly with the beginning of the DIY boom and a new 60 acre factory is built.	Harris begins its first national advertising campaign using cinema and press with the message, 'The bristles won't come out'.	The company is awarded the Royal Warrant by Her Majesty Queen Elizabeth II as the preferred manufacturer of paint brushes and decorators' tools to Royal Estates.	To accommodate the growing range of products, a new 100,000 sq ft warehouse and despatch department is built.

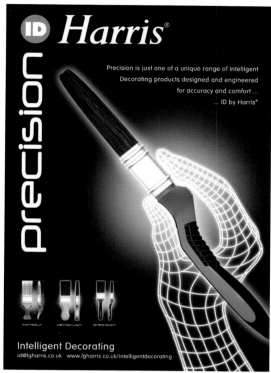

The 'Harris' product range represents the core of the portfolio's retail product offering. It comprises: brushes, rollers, tools and homeware products. This is supported by the 'T-Class' range, which is designed with professional decorators in mind. The 'Harris International' range has been built up over the years to meet the differing needs of global consumers. It largely comprises the core decorating product area of brushes, rollers and tools. These products exist to meet the needs of global customers who prefer different qualities in a product to those sold in the UK, such as different bristle mixes and lengths, handle materials and shapes. In supplying customers around the world, Harris aims to achieve 'global brand consistency with local product specificity'.

RECENT DEVELOPMENTS

The 'Harris ID' (Intelligent Decorating) range was launched in 2006 as a platform for new and innovative products designed specifically to make decorating easier.

The ID Contour and Precision brushes feature both unique curved handles, designed for comfort in use by left- or right-handed people, with an uninhibited line of sight for accuracy on edges and tight areas. The ID Flexibrush features a flexible cushion grip handle for comfort in use, while ID Vanquish is a roller with an ergonomically designed handle to be used with two hands, thus reducing fatigue, and an advanced fabric with a 2.25 inch core, which gives 50 per cent more coverage than standard products.

The past two years have seen Harris expand rapidly into export markets, with the development of a customer marketing platform that includes a bespoke range catalogue, and a global press and point of sale suite that can be rolled out across markets where required. Currently the range is being particularly well received in the Middle East, Scandinavia, the Philippines and Australia.

PROMOTION

Harris uses a comprehensive range of marketing communications tools to build awareness and drive demand for its products, both in the UK and in a global market.

Domestically, Harris's website – along with product-focused marketing campaigns timed to hit key decorating periods in the UK – have combined to help position the brand as a producer of world-class decorating products. The recent launch campaign for ID Vanquish, for example, communicates a single message, 'two hands are better than one'. The campaign used press, online, PR and viral environments using a simple but effective creative concept. In addition, Harris has recently added a sports sponsorship property by partnering with England Squash to build brand awareness through sponsoring the Inter County Championships and other brand carrying opportunities.

Internationally, Harris communicates to the retail trade through a select number of industry trade shows, combined with follow-up B2B campaigns, and targeted email-driven promotions.

BRAND VALUES

Harris is positioned as a producer of world-class decorating products. The company is proud of its Royal Warrant, which goes hand in hand with the high value placed on the company's heritage, especially since it remains family owned.

Harris is also committed to upholding the elements of its core brand values of experience, creativity, quality, desirable innovation and leadership, which have brought continuing success for the business.

www.lgharris.co.uk

Things you didn't know about Harris

The Harris range is currently sold across 103 countries worldwide.

Within the Harris brand portfolio there are more than 2,000 products.

Natural bristle comes from the Chinese hog and comes in both black and white varieties.

At one time in Harris's history, Harris planted and maintained its own forests (nearly 2,000 acres) in an effort to create its own raw material supply.

1990s	2003	2004	2006
The growth of the large DIY retailers heralds an unprecedented period of growth for Harris, which sees turnover triple in eight years.	Harris's first wholly owned Chinese facility opens, introducing twin manufacturing. The UK facility also grows in size and scope as a new £1.1 million, storage facility opens.	The T-Class brand is launched in the UK – products are specifically designed for the professional decorating market – while Harris begins rapid export expansion.	Harris's ID range is launched as a platform for new and innovative products designed specifically to make decorating easier.

Heathrow **express** ⊗

Serving the world's busiest international airport, Heathrow Express is one of the most successful high-speed rail-air links in the world. The service carries more than 16,000 passengers a day on the 15-minute journey between Heathrow Airport and central London.

MARKET

Every year, some 63 million passengers pass through Heathrow Airport. Compared to many other international airports, Heathrow has historically been one of the hardest to get to, with passengers travelling to and from London facing the choice of a long journey by tube, or risking traffic congestion by car or taxi.

Heathrow Express has tapped into a growing trend among world airports to offer a premium, dedicated and high-speed train service, giving passengers an easy, reliable and fast option for travelling between city centre and airport. It reaches the airport in just 15 minutes, compared to 40 minutes by London Underground, or 40-140 minutes by taxi.

Carrying more than five million passengers per year, Heathrow Express is one of the leading airport rail links in the world.

ACHIEVEMENTS

Since its launch in June 1998, Heathrow Express has gained market share over both the London Underground and taxi travel to the airport from central London, firmly establishing itself as a favoured route for both business and leisure passengers. The service removes approximately 3,000 journeys from the regional roads every day, and has made savings to the UK economy in terms of time, compared to the use of tube, taxi or bus, of over £444 million.

Heathrow Express has also eased congestion on London's roads with its Taxi Share scheme, introduced in 1998. Operated in conjunction with the Licensed Taxi Drivers Association, passengers can share a taxi on their onward journey from Paddington Station. The lower fares and shorter waiting times generated by the scheme allow 40-75 per cent more people to leave Paddington by taxi

during the morning peak hours. More than 668,000 travellers have shared a taxi so far, saving about 1,608,000 taxi miles and easing the pressure on London's morning rush hour.

Heathrow Express has won a host of awards, and been recognised internationally as one of the most successful airport rail services. Its marketing has attracted accolades, with its corporate identity and branding, developed by Wolff Olins, among the most comprehensive branding and design projects ever undertaken in transportation. This was recognised when the project became the 2000 Grand Prix Winner of the Design Business Awards.

Heathrow Express has worked hard to translate its customer service ethos into action and in September 2006 was judged to be the Customer Service Team of the Year at the National Customer Service Awards – the UK's most prestigious award for customer service.

1987	1991	1998	2001	2007	2008
Commissioned by the UK Government, the Heathrow Access Surface Study concludes that a main line rail link between Paddington and Heathrow would increase public transport most effectively.	The Heathrow Express Railways Act gives BAA the power to construct the Heathrow Express.	Heathrow Express is officially launched by the Prime Minister, Tony Blair.	Heathrow Express places an order for five new carriages, costing a total of £6.5 million.	In partnership with T-Mobile and Nomad Digital, a WiFi Hotspot service is introduced, allowing passengers uninterrupted 2Mps internet and email access throughout the entire journey, including the 6km tunnel.	A further Heathrow Express terminal is scheduled to open beneath the new Heathrow Terminal 5.

Trading standards have ruled that a sausage called the Welsh Dragon be renamed as it doesn't contain dragon.

You can get from central London to Heathrow in 15 minutes.

Amazing, isn't it? | Heathrow **express**

Trains leave from Paddington Station every 15 minutes. www.heathrowexpress.com

*Timetabled journey times for trains from London Paddington to Heathrow terminals 1, 2 and 3 (approx 8 minutes more to terminal 4) between 05.10 and 23.10.

In 2007, Heathrow Express secured a double first by topping the poll in the independent National Passenger Satisfaction Survey and achieving the highest score in the survey's eight-year history. Heathrow Express was announced as the nation's favourite rail service with a 96 per cent satisfaction rating.

PRODUCT

Heathrow Express is a dedicated, non-stop, high-speed rail-air link operating between Heathrow Airport and central London, departing every 15 minutes, with a journey time of 15 minutes. There are currently two dedicated stations at Heathrow: Heathrow Central (serving Terminals 1, 2 and 3) and Terminal 4, which is a further 6-8 minutes away.

One of the biggest milestones in the history of Heathrow Express will be the opening of Terminal 5 in March 2008 and its new station beneath the terminal.

Passengers will arrive at Heathrow Central, where Heathrow Express will stop for people to alight the train, before arriving in the heart of Terminal 5 eight minutes later. Passengers wishing to travel to Terminal 4 can change at Heathrow Central and then board the free inter-terminal rail transfer service.

The design of the Heathrow stations ensures that they offer customers swift, convenient access to the train service. The purpose-built trains, capable of travelling at 100mph, run daily, 365 days a year. The carriages are air-conditioned and have ergonomically designed seating, generous luggage areas and on-board TVs. There are also Quiet Zones on the trains where the use of mobile phones is prohibited and Express TV is not in use.

Heathrow Express is a member of Airport Express, a joint alliance between BAA plc and

National Express Group, which promotes and markets the Heathrow Express, Gatwick Express and Heathrow Connect rail services. The alliance brings together the sales and marketing activities of all three operations to create a single point of contact for airlines, travel trade agents and tour operators.

RECENT DEVELOPMENTS

Heathrow Express is an innovative media owner and is constantly looking for ways to give other businesses commercial access to its hard-to-reach business audience.

In January 2007, Heathrow Express launched the first ever 'motion picture videowall' advert in Europe. Four-hundred and fifty 'frames', each holding an individual printed image, were installed in the train tunnel walls, covering a total distance of 1,500ft. Seen from a train travelling at 70 miles per hour this created a 15-second moving image advert.

Heathrow Express has also enhanced its groundbreaking onboard TV service, Express TV. It was the first rail service in the UK to introduce onboard televisions at its launch in 1998. Created specifically to cater for the Heathrow Express passenger, it delivers a personalised news bulletin from BBC News 24 covering domestic, international and business news as well as entertainment clips, from the BBC show Top Gear and the Comedy Channel.

PROMOTION

Heathrow Express primarily uses press, outdoor and online to promote its service. The 2006/07 advertising campaign, 'Amazing, isn't it?', aimed to communicate the key benefits of the service to the business market, particularly within the UK. The objective was to encourage trial among prospective business passengers by focusing on the core business messages – speed, frequency, reliability and convenience.

The campaign was based around 'amazing' facts and included stories featuring in the current news agenda.

The company uses below-the-line media to target its audience, investing in customer relationship marketing to boost frequency of use amongst its most loyal customers, and developing marketing relationships with airlines at Heathrow Airport. Frequent travellers are the focus of joint initiatives run in conjunction with key airlines. For example,

Heathrow Express is a partner within the Virgin Atlantic Flying Club programme, whereby Silver and Gold members receive an allocation of First Class upgrades to use on Heathrow Express. This has proved extremely successful since its launch in July 2003, adding value to both brands. The partnership is communicated within membership packs, statements and email newsletters.

It also has sales agreements with various airlines, including bmi and GB Airways, which sell Heathrow Express tickets in-flight.

BRAND VALUES

Heathrow Express' key brand values are speed, frequency and certainty. Recent research has shown that these are the benefits of the service that are most recalled by customers.

For both business and leisure customers, Heathrow Express aims to provide the high levels of comfort and customer service that air travellers have come to expect.

However, different aspects of the brand's personality are highlighted for the business and consumer markets. For the business traveller, the brand is portrayed as fast, frequent, reliable and convenient. When speaking to the leisure market, the brand is reflected as not being overly formal or austere while being fast, reliable, convenient, approachable, and family friendly.

www.heathrowexpress.com

Things you didn't know about Heathrow Express

Every year, almost one million miles are travelled by Heathrow Express, the equivalent to almost four times the distance to the moon or 37 times around the world.

Since Heathrow Express was launched in June 1998, it has carried almost 47 million people.

There is a special Meeter/Greeter fare for those travelling to the airport to see friends and family off, or to meet them on arrival.

HISCOX

Hiscox is a leading specialist insurer covering a diverse portfolio of personal and commercial risks, that range from marine, terrorism, aerospace, technology, media and professional indemnity through to high value personal insurance, such as homes and contents, fine art, bloodstock and kidnap and ransom. With 100 years of underwriting heritage, Hiscox has more than 740 staff, with offices in 13 countries.

MARKET

Hiscox operates in the international insurance markets as well as local markets in Europe and the US. The Group has three main underwriting divisions, namely Hiscox Global Markets, Hiscox UK and Europe, and Hiscox International.

Hiscox Global Markets underwrites mainly internationally traded business in the

London Market – generally large or complex business which needs to be shared with other insurers or needs the international licences of Lloyd's. Meanwhile, Hiscox UK and Hiscox Europe offer a range of specialist insurance for professionals and business customers, as well as high net worth individuals. Hiscox International includes offshore operations in Bermuda and Guernsey as well as Hiscox USA.

ACHIEVEMENTS

In 2006, the Group controlled a gross premium income of £1,126.2 million with record pre-tax profits of £201.1 million.

Hiscox has received a wide range of awards in recent years. In 2006 it was recognised as British Insurance Awards Underwriter of the Year and was placed first for service in personal and commercial lines

of insurance business in the 2006 British Insurance Broker's Association survey, and in the top three for overall service satisfaction. It also won the Best Financial and Intelligent Innovation awards at the Direct Response Intelligence Awards.

In 2007 at the Insurance Times Awards it won both Personal Lines Insurer of the Year and Commercial Lines Insurer of the Year, as well as Lloyd's Syndicate of the Year. In addition, the Marketing Society Awards gave it the Best Brand Extension award and at the Data Strategy Awards it received the Best Use of Data for a Financial Product award.

Hiscox has also featured four times in The Sunday Times '100 Best Companies to Work For' survey.

As a world-leading insurer of fine art, Hiscox also promotes new artists through Hiscox Art Projects, a contemporary exhibition space

1938	1946	1967	1987	1993	1995
Ralph Hiscox joins the Roberts agency at Lloyd's and starts Syndicate 33, writing non-marine insurance.	Ralph Hiscox and the Roberts family form the Roberts & Hiscox partnership, as both managing agent and members agent.	Ralph Hiscox is elected chairman of Lloyd's. Robert Hiscox (his son) starts underwriting for Syndicate 33, specialising in fine art and personal accident insurance.	Hiscox Holdings Ltd is formed as a holding company for the group, with two major subsidiaries: Hiscox Syndicates Ltd as managing agent and Roberts & Hiscox Ltd as members agents.	Robert Hiscox serves as deputy chairman of Lloyd's during the years of 'Reconstruction and Renewal' (1993–1995), leading the introduction of corporate capital into Lloyd's.	The first overseas offices are opened in Munich and Paris.

situated in the London office. With free entry to the public, it provides artists with an opportunity to exhibit their talents; in 2006 the exhibition included work from five graduates from the prestigious Ecole Nationale Supérieure des Beaux-Arts in Paris. In 2007 work from Virginie Litzler, Lucy Orta, Katrina Palmer, Martina Schmuecker, Santiago Sierra and Jemima Burrill was featured.

Hiscox has established the Hiscox Foundation – a charity funded by an annual donation from Hiscox, which donates to deserving causes. It gives priority to any charity in which a member of staff is involved.

PRODUCT

Hiscox provides insurance for both individuals and businesses and underwrites a wide range of personal and business risks, often too complex or too large for other companies.

For individuals, services include insurance for homes and overseas property, fine art and collections, kidnap and ransom, bloodstock and personal accident and travel cover.

For businesses, Hiscox provides insurance for professional indemnity, directors and officers, employment practices liability, energy, aerospace, telecommunications and satellites, corporate protection, internet and email, fine art, hacker attacks, property, media liabilities, banks and specie, political risk, marine (including hull, cargo and liability), kidnap and ransom, personal accident and travel, terrorism and reinsurance.

RECENT DEVELOPMENTS

Hiscox is building its UK as well as international business in Europe and the US while retaining its focus on niche areas. With a growing mid to high net worth sector in the UK, Hiscox continues to expand its regional operations to offer a local service for household insurance as well as for commercial customers.

In addition, the company is rapidly expanding its web offering to enable both household and commercial customers to buy their insurance online.

PROMOTION

In 2005 Hiscox was barely known outside the City. As a result it moved to become the first specialist insurer to extend its brand by targeting mid- and high-net-worth consumers with a direct insurance offer.

Hiscox needed to launch not only a new consumer brand into a crowded and highly competitive market, but also a new product proposition. While differentiated from its broker-serviced proposition, the direct offer needed to reflect Hiscox's core values of extraordinary cover and a first-class service.

The marketing task was to build a quality brand and challenge target consumers to question whether standard insurance cover was appropriate for their needs.

In May 2006 Hiscox unveiled its first TV campaign. 'Superstitions' was a unique take on insurance advertising and featured a well-dressed man confidently ignoring typical signs of bad luck, including a road full of black cats, because he was protected by Hiscox.

The campaign drove both brand awareness and revenues up by more than 200 per cent. In doing so it also won four awards for campaign effectiveness including the prestigious Marketing Society Award for Best Brand Extension.

In August 2007 Hiscox sought to build on this success with the launch of the new 'Certainty' campaign. Once again the advertising challenges industry convention while encouraging consumers to confidently insure with Hiscox.

BRAND VALUES

Hiscox has a series of core values upon which the brand is developed, defined as: integrity; respect; courage; quality; and excellence in execution.

www.hiscox.com

1997	2000	2005	2006
Hiscox plc is admitted to full listing on the UK Stock Exchange.	Hiscox Online is launched as the first internet insurance site for owners of valuable homes.	Hiscox Bermuda opens in December to write a combination of worldwide reinsurance and Group retail business.	Hiscox increases consumer awareness with the launch of its first ever TV campaign. The first US office also opens.

Things you didn't know about Hiscox

Hiscox is the world's largest provider of specialist kidnap, detention and extortion insurance, with a market share of 60-70 per cent by premium income.

Hiscox was the sponsor of the Bermudian cricket team World Cup campaign in 2007.

Hiscox employees are eligible for a fully paid eight week sabbatical once they have worked for the company for 10 years.

INVESTORS IN PEOPLE

Investors in People enables organisations to maximise their potential through the continuous development of business improvement tools. By establishing a benchmark for world-class practice Investors in People matches what people can do and are motivated to do, with what is required. Designed to advance an organisation's performance through its workforce, Investors in People offers two directly linked leading business improvement tools, the Investors in People Standard and Profile.

MARKET

Investors in People is used by 48,000 organisations as a tool for performance improvement and managing change. Around 33,000 organisations, varying in size across both public and private sectors and employing some 6.7 million people, are currently recognised by Investors in People. In addition, a further 15,000, employing in the region of 900,000 people, are committed to the Investors in People Standard and are currently working towards recognition. Investors in People is committed to delivering continuous improvement to these and future organisations through the development of its business improvement tools that assist effective and adaptable people management and development.

As a performance enabling tool Investors in People has no direct UK competitors, although it operates in the marketplace of both standards and HR consultancy to provide tailored business solutions and to help organisations and staff to reach their full potential. Its distinctive emphasis on people and good practices complements

other quality standards in the marketplace, such as ISO 9000 and the Business Excellence Model.

ACHIEVEMENTS

Since its inception Investors in People has achieved acclaimed industry recognition, as demonstrated by the many thousands of organisations now working within its framework.

The Standard has been through three extensive reviews using best practice to challenge organisations to improve. In the past six years the marketing of Investors in People has focused on readdressing the perception that Investors in People is simply a training tool. The Standard has been

repositioned as a business improvement tool that delivers real bottom line benefits and challenges organisations to evaluate exactly what it achieves for them. In studies undertaken it was found that for 64 per cent of recognised employers, the Standard was either crucial or very influential in making significant changes.

PRODUCT

Adopted widely throughout the UK and internationally, the Investors in People Standard and Profile are flexible frameworks that organisations, regardless of size or sector, can work with. The Standard assists organisations to improve performance and realise objectives through the effective

1990	1991	1993	1995	1998	2000
Investors in People is created when The Employment Department is tasked with developing a national standard that sets out a level of good practice for training and development to achieve business goals.	The first 28 'Investor in People' organisations – both large and small – are celebrated at the formal launch of Investors in People on 16th October.	Investors in People UK is formed as a business-led, non-departmental public body. The following year the first Investors in People Week is launched.	The first review of the Standard is carried out and an operation is also established in Australia.	Five international pilot projects get underway.	The Ambassador programme is launched. Two years later the Profile framework is launched.

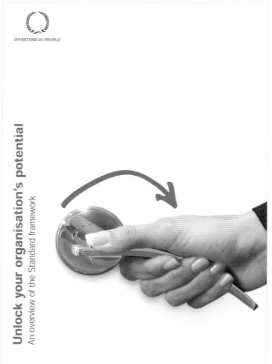

The Champions Programme and The Ambassadors Programme. Champions disseminate and share best practice with organisations of all sizes and within all interested sectors, engaging in additional promotional activity to extend understanding of the Standard and its benefits. A total of 36 organisations have now gained the prestigious status of Investors in People Champion.

Ambassadors promote and represent Investors in People through personal experiences and recommendations and strive to inspire other businesses and organisations. They take part in a series of high profile events and speaking platforms from a wide variety of sectors.

Investors in People carries out research that is focused on key topical business issues and is regarded as a credible voice in the media, enabling it to further develop and encourage organisations to adopt a 'business improvement through people' approach.

management and development of their greatest asset: their people. The adaptable framework ensures each organisation can achieve this in a way suited to their management style of working and individual requirements.

Investors in People helps businesses become more effective by developing and supporting best practice and by ensuring that they achieve the right return on investment, as well as challenging organisations to continually strive for improvement.

'Profile' builds on the breadth and depth of the Standard, but goes further to embrace a wider range of people management issues, exploring them in considerable depth. Through Profile, organisations can gain a deeper understanding of how they are performing against an extensive criteria. It allows organisations to continuously improve through taking an in-depth look at strengths and weaknesses and also benchmarks an organisation's performance against others. This allows organisations to prioritise targets and improve the performance of the business.

RECENT DEVELOPMENTS

A significant recent brand development was the launch, in November 2007, of Investors in People Interactive, a unique free

online support tool, built around five management practices that relate directly to the Investors in People criteria. Investors in People Interactive has been specifically designed to guide organisations through development activities in order that they can establish a clear understanding of their current strengths and prioritise areas that may require further development and input. This is achieved through using the tool's 'Diagnostic'. Everything in Investors in People Interactive revolves around the five key management practices – Strategic Planning, Effective Management, Developing People, Culture and Communication, and Managing Performance – directly linked to the Investors in People Standard.

PROMOTION

Investors in People's marketing strategy focuses on the promotion and positioning of the brand as a business improvement tool.

Investors in People carries out extensive direct mail and online campaigns that are targeted to different sectors, organisation size and business issues.

Investors in People thrives via word-of-mouth recommendation through trusted, respected sources and has two programmes recognising the value of advocacy:

BRAND VALUES

Investors in People aims to ensure that its brand is inspiring and energising. It is distinctive in the marketplace but straightforward, with a proven framework for delivering business improvement through people, which is universally applicable.

www.investorsinpeople.co.uk

Things you didn't know about Investors in People

Investors in People is eco-friendly as assessments against the Standard require no paperwork; they are conducted through a series of interviews.

Investors in People brings a wide range of benefits to businesses of all sizes. It's not so much that it's 'scalable', more that the principles and indictors on which it is built have been carefully developed so that they are universally relevant.

Investors in People operates in over 18 different languages; assessments have taken place in 70 countries illustrating that any organisation can be assessed, wherever it is in the world.

2004	2006	2007	
The Champions programme is launched and the revised Standard and Profile are launched.	Investors in People celebrates 15 years of improving business and the first organisation achieves the top score of all level fours when assessed against Profile.	Nine new organisations are awarded Investors in People Champion status. A further 10 organisations successfully retain their status for another three years.	Also in 2007, Investors in People Interactive, a free online support tool, is launched.

The Institute of Directors (IoD) is recognised as one of the UK's premier business membership organisations, for informing, supporting and inspiring the ambitions of individual directors, and setting the highest possible standards in business leadership and governance. The IoD has approximately 55,000 individual members, at director level, from across the business spectrum – from the largest public companies to the smallest private firms.

MARKET

Membership of the IoD is on an individual rather than corporate basis. Exclusively providing members with everything they need to be successful in business, including information and advice to give members a competitive advantage, voicing members' opinions to Government, providing knowledge through an extensive suite of conferences and professional development programmes, as well as providing free meeting space and networking opportunities in locations across the country. The brand's positioning is reflective of British business: incorporating past successes with innovation.

The majority of the IoD's members come from small and medium-sized enterprises (SMEs), reflecting the business demographic of the country as a whole. However, the organisation also has members on the boards of 92 per cent of firms listed on the FTSE 100.

ACHIEVEMENTS

In 2007 the IoD's efforts at maintaining and enhancing customer relationships, and therefore loyalty, with business customers were recognised. Successful in winning the Best Customer Relationship Campaign at the B2B Marketing Awards, several IoD projects were also nominated and short listed for marketing awards.

2007 also saw the IoD's publication, Director magazine, celebrate its diamond anniversary edition. For 60 years this publication has been an authoritative and highly regarded business journal. Circulated to all IoD members and to thousands of subscribers, it attracts high-

Lead don't follow

profile contributions and comment from business leaders around the world including Lord Conran, Sir Martin Sorrell, Sir Richard Branson and the late Anita Roddick.

The IoD's policy team is highly successful and influential in representing the views of members to Government and in providing comment on significant events in business, helping shape the business environment. Creating a dialogue with members, they ensure that they are advised of policy changes and Government comment.

The IoD Information & Advisory Services Team has also won a prestigious award, at the 2006 International Information Industry Awards, for the Best Team in a Business Environment. This award recognises strong team spirit, an innovative approach to team-working and the contribution they provide to the organisation and its members.

PRODUCT

The IoD provides an extensive, exclusive network for its members on a local and national level. Providing members with assistance at both a grassroots and strategic level, the IoD offers a wide range of products to enable its members to make connections, have direction, be inspired and achieve their ambitions.

Providing its members with opportunities to make connections that will benefit their business, this is often seen as one of the IoD's most important benefits. The Institute holds more than 1,000 events a year, on both a national and local level, from the traditional networking drinks receptions to interactive golf days and sporting dinners.

Its flagship event, the Annual Convention, has been held at the Royal Albert Hall since 1961. This inspirational event is the biggest

1903		1921	1950	1976	1987
WA Addinsell, the head of a family run accountancy firm, becomes the founding pioneer of the IoD.	Also in 1903, the first group of senior directors meet to form the first 'Council of the IoD', responding to concerns about the creation of new company legislation in 1900-1901.	The forerunner to Director magazine, entitled Advance, is launched.	The IoD holds its first annual conference, moving to the Royal Albert Hall in 1961.	The IoD moves to its current headquarters, 116 Pall Mall, London.	Margaret Thatcher addresses the IoD Annual Convention.

AMBITION REALISED INSPIRATION FOUND CONNECTIONS MADE

YOUR IoD DISCOVERED
www.iod.com/discover

and one of the most important business events in the UK, attracting high-profile speakers including Sir Ranulph Fiennes, Jacqueline Gold, Bill Gates, Gordon Brown and David Cameron.

Furthermore, the IoD one-day business conferences are designed to react swiftly to market trends and provide up-to-the-minute information on key business issues. Expert speakers from a range of organisations are selected to share their knowledge and experience. Topics include: Finance for SMEs; Maximising your Business Potential through the Internet; and Profit through Property.

As of February 2007 members have also been able to connect with each other online, using the IoD Business Directory. Hosted on iod.com, all members are encouraged to list their company's activities as a key part of their membership benefits.

The Institute also plays a key role in representing the views of its members to senior politicians and the media, ensuring that key issues facing IoD members in the current economic and political climate are discussed. The IoD strives to bring about change to improve business, not to support one particular political party.

Aimed at supporting emerging leaders, the IoD operates Young Directors Forums across the UK to provide opportunities for emerging leaders to develop their professional skills through workshops, events and mentoring and to network with likeminded individuals. The Forum is for tomorrow's leaders spanning all industry sectors, whether on a business or social level.

Taking its role as a centre for professional development very seriously, the IoD runs an extensive range of courses and development programmes, including the Diploma in Company Direction leading to Chartered Director status. These equip directors with the all-round skills, knowledge and

understanding needed to direct an organisation from a strategic perspective, whilst providing them with the flexibility to look after their business to ensure that they still progress professionally.

The IoD also offers members a complimentary information and advisory service and an extensive range of insightful publications and guidebooks to assist them in all parts of their business.

RECENT DEVELOPMENTS

Due to popular demand from its members, in 2007, the IoD reintroduced the Women as Leaders conference, to provide an insight into how to identify and develop tomorrow's female business leaders. Due to the success of this event the IoD will be focusing on the creation of a Women as Leaders Network in 2008.

Expanding its international footprint, the IoD is constantly growing its network of premises, most recently opening an office in Brussels. In addition the IoD is setting the international benchmark with its strong corporate governance model. Providing bespoke programmes at board level in countries including Abu Dhabi, Moscow and Ghana, the IoD is leading the way in best practice.

PROMOTION

The Institute promotes itself through a comprehensive range of media, keeping members and non-members abreast of major developments in the Institute's product portfolio.

Feedback from members inspired the IoD to initiate a refresh of the brand to more clearly communicate its values and services. Previously it had taken a standardised approach to member communications, but now aims to build a more personalised strategy, communicating and delivering a more

tailored approach and increasing engagement with its members. Member communication now highlights the variety of benefits and the unashamedly five star approach in a more holistic manner, positioning the organisation as the place where new and exciting ideas are shared, deals are done and ambitions are achieved.

The IoD is listening to its members and adapting accordingly. This will become more evident during 2008 as it maximises technological advances and increases its online marketing activity, consequently reducing the amount of direct mail each member receives. From the introduction of video casts and regular blogs from the IoD's director general, these developments are aimed at bringing members closer to the Institute and encouraging two-way communication between the IoD and its members. This trend will increase during 2008 with its ongoing development and redesign to deliver a more interactive members area online.

BRAND VALUES

The IoD knows that its members are its biggest asset; in fact, current brand guidelines focus on putting the Director before the Institute and this is reflected in the powerful and iconic IoD logo which features a larger D and smaller I. With this at the forefront of its thinking, the IoD is undergoing a design refresh to bring its communications up-to-date whilst still reflecting its core themes of Direction, Connection and Innovation.

www.iod.com

Things you didn't know about IoD

The IoD director general, Miles Templeman, previously led a wide range of consumer brands such as Daz, Ribena, Levi's, Boddingtons and Stella Artois.

The IoD has a vast international presence with branches, affiliates and associated bodies across the world, from France to New Zealand and the US.

The Institute's premises at 116 Pall Mall, London, were used for one of the scenes in the Batman film, The Dark Knight, due to be released in 2008.

1999	2001	2003	2007
The world's first independently accredited qualification for directors, Chartered Director, is launched.	IoD 123 is opened by Tony Blair. In addition, the Business Leaders Summits are introduced and www.iod.com goes live.	The IoD's commitment to business excellence expands globally with the launch of IoD International.	IoD launches its own channel on YouTube to promote its vidcasts.

JCB is the world's third largest manufacturer of construction equipment. It sells machines in 150 countries around the world. The company has 17 plants on four continents, employs more than 8,000 people and sold more than 55,000 machines in 2006. In 2007, the company manufactured more than 70,000 machines. JCB's range comprises 279 different models.

MARKET

JCB is the third largest manufacturer of earth moving and construction equipment in the world.

It is the biggest privately-owned company in the market and the premier manufacturer of construction equipment in Europe. The company's iconic Backhoe Loader – the machine that JCB is most famous for – is the clear leader in the world market.

In 2006, JCB achieved its business objective of achieving 10.4 per cent of the world market for construction equipment – no small task, considering there are more than 500 manufacturers in the industry.

ACHIEVEMENTS

JCB is one of Britain's biggest industrial success stories. In 2006 JCB had its most successful year ever by setting new records for pre-tax profits, turnover, machine sales and global market share. Pre-tax profits rose by 35 per cent to £149 million, turnover rose to a record of £1.75 billion, while machine sales rose to more than 55,000, up from 45,000 in 2005. This meant that JCB rose one place to become the world's third largest construction equipment manufacturer by volume.

Over its 62-year history, JCB has won more than 70 major awards for engineering excellence, exports, design, marketing, management and for its care for the environment. Among them are 21 Queen's Awards for Technology and Export Achievement. In 2007,

the company won three Queen's Awards for Enterprise in the International Trade Category.

The company invented one of the most recognisable pieces of heavy machinery, the 'digger', also known as a backhoe loader. This was first introduced by JCB in 1953. Since then it has become the brand leader virtually the world over and JCB's yellow machines are a familiar part of the landscape and language. The JCB name even appears in the Oxford English Dictionary and has become one of the world's best known brands.

Another major achievement was the introduction of the Loadall telescopic handler in 1977. This revolutionised aspects of the building industry, allowing bricks to be lifted in pallets instead of being carried in a hod by a labourer. JCB also developed the first –

and still the only – road-legal high-speed tractor, the Fastrac, winning numerous awards, including the Prince of Wales Award for Innovation in 1995.

PRODUCT

JCB manufactures 279 different machines and attachments, exporting 75 per cent of its UK-made products to 150 countries.

Its wide range includes: backhoe loaders; Loadall telescopic handlers; tracked and wheeled excavators; wheeled loading shovels; articulated dump trucks; rough terrain fork lifts; mini excavators; Robot skid steer loaders; JCB Vibromax compaction equipment; and the Teletruk forklift for the industrial sector.

In addition, for agricultural markets, the company produces a range of telescopic handlers and the unique Fastrac tractor, a range that was expanded in 2007 to include three machines in the new 7000 Series – the most significant tractor launch for JCB since the original Fastrac in 1990.

1945	1953	1979	1986	2000	2001
Joseph Cyril Bamford starts his business manufacturing a tipping trailer, made with a £1 welding set. He sold the product at the local market for £45.	The backhoe loader becomes the first product to carry the JCB logo. It is now universally known as a 'JCB'.	JCB begins its Indian operations with the opening of a plant in Ballabgarh to build backhoe loaders as part of a joint venture.	'JCB' enters the Collins English Dictionary as an eponymous noun, and the 100,000th backhoe loader rolls off the production line at Rocester.	US-manufactured machines are first produced in a new plant in Savannnah, Georgia. £1 million is raised by JCB employees for the NSPCC and matched by Sir Anthony.	Manufacturing of backhoe loaders begins at JCB's new plant in Saracoba, Sao Paulo, Brazil.

JCB continues to increase the proportion of major parts manufactured in-house. In 2004, JCB's own off-highway diesel engine, the JCB Dieselmax, went into production at a new plant in Derbyshire, following an investment of £80 million. The company already produces its own transmissions, axles, cabs, chassis, booms, hydraulic rams and excavator arms.

RECENT DEVELOPMENTS

2008 will prove to be an important year for JCB, with work due for completion on its £7 million JCB Attachments factory. The 120,000 sq ft facility is being built next to JCB's World Parts Centre in Uttoxeter, Staffordshire. The company is also proposing to relocate its Heavy Products plant, where heavy excavators are manufactured, to a new £40 million facility.

The past few years have been vital for JCB, marking the start of production of backhoe loaders and mini excavators at the company's newest manufacturing plant in Pudong, near Shanghai, China. Local production will ensure that the company is well positioned to take advantage of the massive potential of the Chinese construction equipment market.

JCB is also expanding in India, where it is the clear market leader and has been manufacturing backhoe loaders at a plant in Ballabgarh, near Delhi, since 1979. Two further factories have since been built in Pune, close to the port of Mumbai. A £15 million fabricated components plant began operating in 2005 and a second £12 million factory started manufacturing heavy excavators a year later.

PROMOTION

JCB has a rich heritage of striking promotional activities, with the company's founder, Joseph Cyril Bamford – known as Mr JCB – setting new standards in heavy equipment marketing.

As well as a tradition of award-winning advertising in the industry trade press, the company is also famous for its customer events featuring the JCB Dancing Diggers, in which backhoe loaders demonstrate the power and stability of their hydraulics by 'performing' synchronised stunts to music.

But perhaps the most breathtaking example of JCB's dynamic approach to marketing came in August 2006, when it broke the world land speed record for diesel-powered cars with the JCB Dieselmax car. The vehicle, developed in less than 12 months, was powered by two specially-modified versions of the JCB Dieselmax engine as it reached a speed of 350.092mph. The project received awards for Best PR Campaign and the Grand Prix for the UK's Best B2B Marketing Campaign at the UK B2B Marketing Awards in 2007.

BRAND VALUES

The 'DNA' of JCB's brand is hard work. Mr JCB's son, Sir Anthony Bamford, continues the standard set by his father, and the company's machines also work hard to meet the demands put on them by customers.

JCB has also always been known for its attention to detail. A JCB machine is seen as world-class, innovative, high performance, strong and stylish. The company is also renowned for the first class service delivered to its customers via its network of global dealers.

Being family-owned, JCB has a sense of community and pays particular attention to helping those who are underprivileged. JCB takes its philanthropic responsibilities seriously and as the company has grown, so has the level of support it is able to offer to less fortunate people around the world.

JCB's charitable roots go deep and, in the UK, the Bamford Foundation has existed since 1979. Its board meets regularly and distributes resources to organisations in the communities where JCB manufactures. The company has supported the NSPCC since 1986. It became JCB's nominated charity through the involvement of Lady Bamford, wife of JCB Chairman, Sir Anthony Bamford. JCB employees in the UK raised £1 million for the NSPCC through the Digging Deep appeal in 1999-2000 and Sir Anthony doubled that figure by donating a further £1 million.

In addition, JCB donated £1 million worth of equipment to aid the massive clear-up operation after the Asian Tsunami of December, 2004. JCB machines have also been used following earthquakes in Izmit, Turkey, in 1999, Gujarat, India, in 2001, and southern Peru, in 2007. JCB also donated £100,000 worth of machines to help with the clear-up operation in a region of the Philippines devastated by a typhoon in 2007.

www.jcb.co.uk

2004	2005	2006	2007
Production of the JCB Dieselmax diesel engine begins, and JCB donates £1 million worth of machines for relief work in devastated Asian Tsunami regions.	Production begins at JCB's £15 million fabricated components plant in Pune, India. JCB purchases compaction equipment manufacturer Vibromax, which becomes JCB Vibromax.	JCB opens its first plant in China and a second in Pune, India. The JCB Dieselmax car breaks the world land-speed record for a diesel-powered car – at 350.092mph.	JCB become the third largest construction equipment manufacturer in the world as it gains a 10.4 per cent share of the global market.

Things you didn't know about JCB

JCB takes pride in its logo. From 1960 the company fitted typewriters with special keys to accurately render the logo. Today all JCB computers have pre-set logos for faxes, letters and memos.

In 1958, Mr JCB bought 10 scooters with the number plates JCB1 to JCB10. JCB has also purchased registration plates for company cars, which are all white. JCB owns numbers 1-14 and 17-20, but JCB 15 and JCB 16 are still missing.

Since 1975, UK manufacturing employment has fallen from 7.7 million to under four million. In this time, JCB's workforce has doubled.

kall kwik
business design + print

Kall Kwik, one of the UK's leading providers of business design and print solutions, continues to evolve from its familiar high street presence for traditional copy and print to a wider and deeper consultative strategy and design approach. Offering a complete Design to Delivery™ (D2D) solution, services include creative design, direct mail, email services, large format poster print and corporate image development within its portfolio of full service marketing solutions.

MARKET

In the UK, more than £1 billion is spent every year on design, printing and copying services, generally described as the 'print on demand' sector; Kall Kwik is the biggest player, with a market share of seven per cent. It is a large and highly fragmented sector, with Kall Kwik competing against a wide range of other service providers, ranging from traditional small quick printers, to larger commercial printers, design and direct mail agencies as well as full service marketing agencies.

However, in another sense, Kall Kwik is unique – no other network player can consistently offer such a broad and integrated range of design and print-based solutions.

Adding value beyond just printing services is an important factor in this market, and is something that Kall Kwik has tapped into.

Research undertaken by Cap Ventures reveals that for every £1 spent on print, businesses normally spend at least £6 on the design and fulfilment of the printed material.

Marketing, sales, training and human resources departments are often the main clients of the sector, requiring corporate brochures, product and sales literature, direct mailers, email on demand, display materials, reports, training course manuals and presentations.

ACHIEVEMENTS

Kall Kwik's biggest achievement has been in making on-demand print equally accessible to small businesses and corporate users, providing complete marketing packages.

In a challenging and rapidly changing market, Kall Kwik has also achieved strong

growth through diversification – for example, its corporate brands team, which works in partnership with national corporate clients with dispersed locations to provide complete marketing solutions. Kall Kwik's success can also be attributed to its award-winning franchise-based business model, with Kall Kwik UK providing intensive marketing, training and operational support to its franchisees to ensure all services and products are delivered to a consistently high standard.

Kall Kwik UK has consistently been recognised as a leader in the franchise field, winning a host of awards, such as the British Franchise Association's (BFA) Franchisor of the Year award in 2005. Many of its franchisees have also won awards, such as Kall Kwik in Edinburgh winning BFA Franchisee of the Year and the Kall Kwik

1978	**1979**	**1999**	**2005**		**2007**
The company is founded by Moshe Gerstenhaber, who purchased the master franchise from the US Kwik Kopy organisation.	The first Kall Kwik opens in Pall Mall, London.	Kall Kwik UK is acquired by Adare Group, the leading provider of print, mailing and data management solutions throughout the UK and Ireland.	Kall Kwik UK is named as the British Franchise Association's Franchisor of the Year.	Also in 2005, Kall Kwik launches D2D and the first k design studio is opened in Winchester.	The 33rd k design studio is launched and the 154th Kall Kwik Centre is opened in Stockport.

franchise in Middlesbrough who were named Best in the World 2007 at the National Association of Printers' annual conference in Chicago. Kall Kwik is the first brand to be recognised within both the franchisor and franchisee categories.

Kall Kwik has also won accolades for the quality of its communications, winning Marketing magazine's Connections 2000 award for Best Use of an Intranet.

PRODUCT

Kall Kwik offers its business customers a complete range of print-based services for all of their communications needs. It describes this integrated service package as Design to Delivery™.

This service offers access to eight key product fields: design; direct mail; client service; expertise; oversize print; technology; print; and delivery. The strategy was developed in response to client requirements and market trends that highlight a gap in the marketplace for an accessible and single-source provider of design-led communications.

Kall Kwik has a rapidly expanding network of design agencies, employing over 250 designers. This is more than any other private sector company and reflects the business' ability to offer creative solutions.

Direct mail has always been a staple of Kall Kwik's offering, with locations able to manage the whole process, from co-ordinating a campaign to completion. As well as its creative design skills, Kall Kwik has the technology to offer digital personalisation and can improve targeting even more by sourcing targeted mailing lists.

Print services are at the heart of Kall Kwik, with the business committed to continuous innovation in the fast-changing and high-tech print sector. Careful pre-planning means that Kall Kwik can help choose the most cost-effective option from a wide range of techniques and processes, from on-demand digital, to litho print, personalised

Switch on to...
oversize print

Exhibitions ♀ Banners ♀ Signage
Advertising ♀ Display stands ♀ Posters

look the business™

kall kwik®
business design + print

communications and custom finishing. It can also produce jumbo-sized print for exhibitions, banners, signage, advertising, display stands and posters.

RECENT DEVELOPMENTS

Kall Kwik has recently supported franchisees who wish to develop a second income stream from high-end creative design. Today, there are more than 40 k designgroups in the UK and new k design studios are opening every month throughout 2008. The new k designgroups are structured as a confederation of local design studios, each with a shared approach to business design and common mantra of 'accessible creativity'.

Set up to offer an intimate local design service, but with all the resources of a national organisation, k designgroup's teams can take on a wide range of projects, including logo design, advertising, business branding, marketing, e-media, graphic design, and multimedia (including web design).

PROMOTION

Kall Kwik aims to produce proactive and well-targeted marketing, reflecting its ability to serve its clients' own marketing objectives.

As it is a franchise-based business, Kall Kwik's franchisees initiate promotion in support of individual locations, albeit in accordance with guidelines from Kall Kwik UK.

Direct mail is Kall Kwik's preferred promotional medium, with mailers, awareness cards and 'D2D' magazine distributed to clients and prospects. The business uses the Mtivity marketing asset management system to enable individual franchisees to select and personalise their marketing materials.

Kall Kwik also uses the internet to advertise its services, along with local and UK-wide promotion via traditional and new media routes to market.

The company also teams up with strategic alliance partners, such as Canon and Pitney Bowes, to undertake joint advertising to cut through to the business audience.

BRAND VALUES

The Kall Kwik brand personality is unpretentious and aims to be 'on the same wavelength' as its clients. It is professional, with a touch of design flair. The company has a vision to make Kall Kwik the leading and most innovative national branded design to delivery network, enabling B2B communications with continuous profitable sales growth.

Ultimately, Kall Kwik aims to satisfy the need to make B2B communications stand out in a crowded, competitive marketplace. This is expressed through the tagline 'look the business'.

www.kallkwik.co.uk

Things you didn't know about Kall Kwik

Kall Kwik was hired in the final episode of the 2007 BBC television series, The Apprentice, to undertake a design and print job that was 'make or break' for the candidates and will also take part in the 2008 series.

Kall Kwik arranged for its Putney operation in south west London to print the 'Feed Me Better' campaign petition that was handed to the UK Prime Minister by TV chef Jamie Oliver.

Kall Kwik employs over 250 designers across the group – more than any other private sector company.

KIMBERLY-CLARK PROFESSIONAL* is part of Kimberly-Clark Corporation, a leading global health and hygiene company employing more than 55,000 people worldwide. With operations in 37 countries, Kimberly-Clark's global brands are sold in more than 150 countries. Focusing on business needs, KIMBERLY-CLARK PROFESSIONAL* delivers leading health, hygiene, and productivity solutions for people in their work places or while they are away from home.

MARKET

The KIMBERLY-CLARK PROFESSIONAL* vision is to be the global leader in providing market changing, branded health, hygiene and productivity solutions. Its customers are in every 'Away from Home' market segment. From the industrial manufacturing site that needs wipers to clean machinery, to electronics industry laboratories wiping away lint, to bathrooms in busy offices, to the nurses' wash station on a busy hospital ward. Across the brand's product range, solutions are designed with the aim of making the user more productive, safer or cleaner in their work environment.

ACHIEVEMENTS

KIMBERLY-CLARK PROFESSIONAL* aims 'to improve the health, hygiene and well-being of people everywhere'. This has driven it to invent three major product categories: facial tissue, paper towels and folded toilet paper.

Applying the same imaginative thinking has led the brand to develop patented market leading technologies – such as its HYDROKNIT* Material and AIRFLEX* Fabric for its wiper and hand towel categories, which offers 'cost in use' benefits through improved performance. In 2000, its innovation was recognised with a Millenium Design Award for the Roll Control wiper dispenser which uses patented designs to allow users to control the quantity and cost of products used.

KIMBERLY-CLARK PROFESSIONAL* has been recognised for its environmental work and aims to become the most responsible business organisation it can be. Developments include purchasing over 250,000 tonnes of waste paper every year,

using recycled fibre in 88 per cent of the Professional business and recycling all internally generated waste at all its mills. In addition, Kimberly-Clark Corporation has been ranked number one in Personal Products in the Dow Jones Sustainability Index for three consecutive years.

KIMBERLY-CLARK PROFESSIONAL*, as part of the Kimberly-Clark Corporation, is also committed to responsible fibre procurement practices and sustainable use of natural resources. The Forestry Stewardship Council (FSC) now has a certification for recycled fibre products; all KIMBERLY-CLARK PROFESSIONAL* KLEENEX® Toilet Tissue products made from recycled fibre produced in its Flint mill are now FSC Certified.

PRODUCT

KIMBERLY-CLARK PROFESSIONAL* is well known in the marketplace as the provider of Europe's widest range of wiping, safety and washroom products.

Its range of limited use WYPALL*L Wipers offer absorbency and hygiene, ideal for use in areas such as restaurants or hospitals. Its extended use WYPALL*X Wipers offer high performance, specifically designed for the heavy demands of manufacturing or engineering environments where professionals take pride in getting their work done right first time.

Proprietary fabric development and garment design allow the KLEENGUARD* brand – which encompasses Apparel, Eye Wear, Respirators, and Industrial Gloves – to deliver the highest levels of protection whilst

1870s	1890s	1920s	1930s	1940s	1950s
Kimberly, Clark and Co. is founded in 1872 by John A Kimberly, Havilah Babcock, Charles B Clark, and Frank C Shattuck in Neenah, Wisconsin.	Toilet paper is first sold on a roll.	Kimberly-Clark introduces Kotex Sanitary Napkins and its disposable Cold Cream Towel – KLEENEX® Facial Tissue.	KIMBERLY-CLARK PROFESSIONAL* is established in the UK.	Kimberly-Clark introduces KIMWIPES* Wipers, the first delicate task wiper for labs and research.	Bathroom Tissue is first advertised on national television.

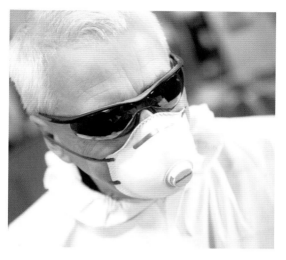

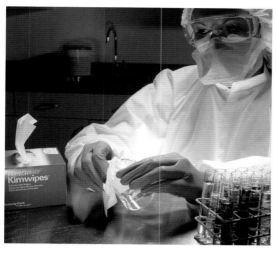

keeping workers comfortable. Under the KIMTECH* brand KIMBERLY-CLARK PROFESSIONAL* is a market leader in the Laboratory and Cleanroom channels with a unique Glove and Mask offering.

KIMBERLY-CLARK PROFESSIONAL* aims to continually set standards when it comes to the Washroom environment with innovations such as electronic towel, tissue and soap dispensers under development and a portfolio of world famous brands such as KLEENEX® and SCOTT®.

RECENT DEVELOPMENTS

Under its Global Business Plan, KIMBERLY-CLARK PROFESSIONAL* is evolving into a global business capable of serving customers to the same high standards worldwide. To enable this transformation, a new Global brand identity has been created.

The culmination of two years intensive international development, the new identity was launched simultaneously around the world in October 2007. The execution will be completed by the end of 2009.

The graphic identity, with refreshed logos and the use of contemporary curved elements, reflects the brands' transition, embodying closer working relationships with key customers and the provision of more complete solutions to the health, hygiene and productivity challenges they face in their businesses.

Every aspect of the KIMBERLY-CLARK PROFESSIONAL* parent brand and the six global product brands (KLEENEX®, SCOTT®, KIMCARE*, KLEENGUARD*, KIMTECH* and

WYPALL*) has been reviewed. The broad remit included every step from reviewing brand strategy, through graphic design of packaging, to marketing communications material, to signage and business stationery.

In doing so the programme ensures consistency of brand experience in every geography from Alaska to Zambia, across each business unit and across all media.

PROMOTION

The diversity of the KIMBERLY-CLARK PROFESSIONAL* offering means it comes to market through many channels and distributors. Solutions are promoted through sales teams to channel partners as well as marketing direct to end users.

The brand has a long history of pioneering marketing communications, starting with black and white advertising appearing in the colour supplements of the Sunday newspapers in the late 1970s and early 1980s.

In 1991, The Golden Service Awards were created by KIMBERLY-CLARK PROFESSIONAL* as part of a continuing programme to recognise and reward high standards in the cleaning industry. Known as 'The Oscars' of the cleaning industry, the programme now runs in Australia and New Zealand, South Korea, Italy, Belgium and the Netherlands.

By 1996, KIMBERLY-CLARK PROFESSIONAL* was heading into the digital-age launching the industry's first website, which has now grown to encompass over 70 country and language versions.

In 2005 KIMBERLY-CLARK PROFESSIONAL* joined forces with the Royal College of Nursing, the Infection Control Nursing Association and Nursing Standard magazine to tackle the growing issue of MRSA, launching the 'Wipe It Out' campaign to provide practical advice to health

professionals on hand hygiene. The resulting press coverage reached 16 million people.

In the same year, the brand conducted the largest market research study ever carried out in Europe on the attitudes to food hygiene among restaurant customers, helping to associate KIMBERLY-CLARK PROFESSIONAL* with food hygiene issues.

In 2006, its channel development programme was a finalist in the 'B2B Marketing Magazine' Awards.

BRAND VALUES

The KIMBERLY-CLARK PROFESSIONAL* brand promises to be 'Your indispensable business partner, delivering leading-edge health, hygiene and productivity solutions that provide tangible value every day, everywhere'.

This promise is delivered through five brand pillars: developing enduring partnerships built on business understanding and integrity; a unique and comprehensive portfolio of products and services; innovating with dynamic, insight-driven design solutions; high performing products and services preferred by choosers and users; and fulfilling the role of a dedicated, responsible global leader in the communities it serves.

The five brand pillars are delivered by a global team whose aim is to: create superior products; exceed expectations; encourage teamwork and care for others.

www.kcprofessional.com

Things you didn't know about KIMBERLY-CLARK PROFESSIONAL*

KIMBERLY-CLARK PROFESSIONAL* has the longest Hand Towel Roll on the market; at 304 metres, it is longer than the Eiffel Tower is tall.

Every day, 1.3 billion people use Kimberly-Clark products.

KIMBERLY-CLARK PROFESSIONAL* dispensers can be found in the most unusual places. For example, one has been spotted on the Machu Picchu train in Peru.

1970s	1980s	1990s	2000s
WYPALL* Wipers are introduced for industrial cleaning.	The KLEENGUARD* Safety Range is introduced and Bulk Pack Toilet Tissue is launched.	Kimberly-Clark celebrates its 125th anniversary and Kimberly-Clark and Scott Papers merge. Also, The Golden Service Awards are launched in the UK.	A global rebranding takes place, called the One Voice project.

LandSecurities

As the leading commercial real estate brand for more than 60 years, Land Securities has focused on delivering a customer offering which provides its occupiers with quality accommodation and high levels of customer service. Three signature qualities exemplify the Land Securities brand: expert – recognisably an expert in commercial real estate; progressive – genuinely changing in a changing world; and accessible – easy to talk to and do business with.

MARKET

Land Securities is the UK's leading Real Estate Investment Trust (REIT). Its national portfolio of commercial property, worth many billions of pounds, includes some of Britain's best-known retail outlets, including Leeds White Rose Centre and Gunwharf Quays in Portsmouth, as well as London landmarks such as the Piccadilly Lights and Westminster City Hall. Land Securities has a multibillion pound development programme with projects in Bristol, Cardiff, Leeds and Glasgow city centres as well as key sites in central London. It is also one of the leading names in property partnerships and through urban community development is involved in long term, large scale regeneration projects in the South East.

Leading competitors in the market are institutional investors such as Prudential Property Investments Management, Legal and General, Standard Life and Morley Fund Management, quoted competitors such as British Land and Hammerson, together with private commercial companies such as The Crown Estate and Grosvenor.

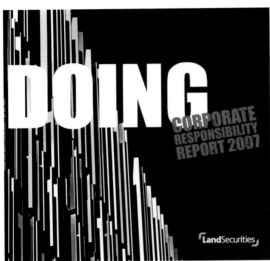

ACHIEVEMENTS

The Group's investment portfolio was valued at £15 billion at its half financial year on 30th September 2007, making it the world's third largest REIT.

The Group's achievements have again been recognised by the accolades it has received. These include the Estates Gazette Offices' Property Company of the Year 2007, the 2007 Property Week Property Company of the Year and the 2007 Property Week Developer of the Year. Also, the highly acclaimed Princesshay development in Exeter received the Supreme Gold award at the 2007 British Council of Shopping Centres (BCSC) Awards.

Land Securities is a member of the FTSE4Good and the Dow Jones Index, which acknowledges commitment to corporate responsibility, and in July 2007 it was the only British Company in the 2007 Sustainable Business 20 (SB20) List: The World's Top Sustainable Stocks. In its sixth year, the list consists of 20 public companies that are having an important impact on the creation of an environmentally sustainable society.

PRODUCT

Land Securities operates mainly in the £500 billion UK commercial property market and, measured by market capitalisation, represents 20 per cent of the UK quoted property sector. Its business model is diversified, focused on retail property, London offices and property outsourcing. In the core markets of retail property and London offices, the Group provides about 5.8 per cent and four per cent respectively of the market floorspace and it is recognisably the market leader in property outsourcing by number of contracts. Within its core market segments

1944	**1950**	**1968**	**1982**	**1987**	**1994**
Harold Samuel buys Land Securities Investment Trust Limited, which at this point owns three houses in Kensington together with some Government stock.	Shares purchased for 44p in 1945 are now worth £6.15. The following year, Associated London Properties is purchased for £2 million. This marks the first big take-over by the company.	In Britain's biggest property deal of its time, Land Securities takes over City Centre Properties, which has assets of £155 million.	The name of the company is changed from Land Securities Investment Trust Limited to Land Securities plc.	The total income of the Group exceeds £200 million and the portfolio valuation tops £3 billion.	Following the recession, the portfolio increases in value to more than £5 billion.

LandSecurities

Retail. Our retail destinations provide retailers with the thriving environments they need to increase footfall and sales, and consumers with a great shopping experience.

Land Securities' activities include property management, investment, development and the provision of property related services.

RECENT DEVELOPMENTS

In the past year, the Retail team completed a major regeneration project in the heart of Exeter. Combining the city's rich Roman heritage with new high quality design, Princesshay opened in September 2007 and offers a pedestrianised environment featuring a distinctive mix of independent and niche retailers along with nationwide chains in 65 retail units and 123 city centre apartments, alongside a new restaurant and café quarter which is focused around a new civic square.

The development at One New Change, in the heart of London's financial district, will open for business in 2010. The mixed use scheme will bring a long awaited retail focus to the area to the east of St Paul's Cathedral, accommodating 70 retailers on the lower three levels and a roof terrace on the sixth floor which will open up new views of the Cathedral and its surroundings.

The Land Securities Board completed a review of the structure of the business and announced in November 2007 the conclusion that, over the long term, the Group's component businesses, and shareholders, will benefit from separation, and proposes to demerge the Group into three specialist separately quoted entities.

This change will represent a continued evolution of the Land Securities business model. In 2004, the Group demonstrated its preference for a focused, sector-based approach by exiting industrial property and moving the group structure to one built around the Retail, London and Outsourcing sectors rather than the functions of asset management, development and outsourcing. Since this time, the Group has developed three specialised business divisions, which have seen strong growth and each of which has considerable scale and leadership positions within their respective peer groups.

PROMOTION

For the first time in 2007 the Group sponsored a major art exhibition, helping to bring Global Cities to the Turbine Hall of Tate Modern over the summer. The exhibition attracted more than 300,000 visitors, making it the most popular architecture exhibition ever presented in London. With more than half the world's population now living in urban areas, cities increasingly lie at the centre of public debate, cultural speculation and media attention. The exhibition acted as a platform for debate, both informally and through series of public programmes.

Group advertising in a combination of national and industry specific press helped to clearly establish Land Securities as a leader in terms of its commitment to corporate responsibility – and as a result downloads of the annual CR report from its website more than trebled.

The first ever campaign for the Retail business, featuring endorsements from a selection of retail occupiers, saw a significant uplift in the attribution of key brand values and good recognition levels of Land Securities' 'retail experience' strapline.

BRAND VALUES

Land Securities' brand values are: excellence – striving to achieve the very best; customer services – never forgetting that its customers are the source of its strength; innovation – new ideas inspiring the Group to new heights; integrity – people trust Land Securities; and respect for the individual – everyone has the power to help, to grow, to influence, to contribute.

These values are reinforced by the Group's Values into Action initiative which recognises and rewards employees and key stakeholders whose behaviour reflects the core values.

www.landsecurities.com

Things you didn't know about Land Securities

Lord Samuel, Land Securities' founder, coined the phrase 'Location, location, location'.

More than 300 million customer visits are made to its shopping centres each year.

Some of Land Securities' most recognisable landmarks are the Piccadilly Lights, New Scotland Yard, the Home Office and the Bullring, Birmingham.

Its property partnership arm, Land Securities Trillium currently provides accommodation for more than 455,000 people.

2000	2005	2006	2007
With the purchase of Trillium, Land Securities enters the new property outsourcing market. Pre-tax profits rise by 11.7 per cent to £327.7 million and the portfolio is valued at £7.5 billion.	Land Securities acquires Tops Estates – a quoted shopping centre company – and LxB, an out of town retail specialist. Its portfolio is valued at £14.5 billion.	Land Securities enters into a joint venture with the Mill Group. Secondary Market Infrastructure Fund is also acquired, marking the company's entry into the primary and secondary PPP markets.	Land Securities completes a review of its business structure and proposes to demerge the Group into three specialist separately quoted entities.

LG Electronics was established in 1958 and rapidly became a pioneer in the Korean consumer electronics market. Since then it has become a major global force with more than 82,000 employees working in 76 countries. It had projected worldwide sales of around US$44 billion for 2007.

MARKET

LG Electronics competes on a truly global scale, operating production and sales offices on every continent, with around 85 per cent of its sales coming from outside Korea. In 2006 North America was its biggest overseas market, accounting for 24 per cent of sales, with a further 19 per cent coming from Europe.

The company is active in a host of consumer facing and business electronics segments, but in the business to business sphere, LG is particularly strong in plasma display panels, with a 27 per cent share, and also in air conditioning, where it is market leader. It has also dominated the optical storage market – including re-writable CDs and DVDs – for the last eight years. In mobile communications, LG ranks fifth in global mobile handset sales and it is market leader in home cinema systems and DVD players.

ACHIEVEMENTS

LG has grown exponentially in recent years, recording an annual growth rate of 21 per cent since 2001. It is now the global leader in several key electronics categories and has recorded industry firsts, going back as far as the 1950s and 1960s, including Korea's first radios, black and white television sets and refrigerators.

More recently, LG pioneered the world's first fully touch sensitive mobile – the Prada phone by LG – which won Best Fashion Handset in trade magazines Mobile Choice and What Mobile. This was followed by the launch of the LG Viewty, which was the first mobile with 120 frames per second video functionality.

Additionally, the company brought to market the world's first 76 inch plasma TV, the first dual format HD and Blu-ray DVD player – the Super Multi Blue – and the first computer monitor with a contrast-ratio of 5000:1, as well as the fastest Blu-ray optical rewriter. It has also revolutionised washing machine design, with the first Steam washing machine, called the Steam Direct Drive, which uses 35 per cent less water and 21 per cent less energy than conventional washing machines.

The company is also at the forefront of home appliance networking, allowing appliances such as washing machines, air conditioning, televisions, refrigerators and cookers to be remotely controlled via computer.

LG has received numerous industry awards for its cutting-edge products and innovation. In 2007, it won three trophies at the European Imaging and Sound Association

(EISA) awards for three of its design-led home entertainment products. Its landmark Super Multi Blue player also won the title of Most Innovative Gadget of the Year at the first T3 Awards in 2007.

In 2006, LG's slim LCD monitor with f-Engine, won both the iF design award and the red dot design award. Meanwhile, LG's mobile handsets recently won the iF design award, red dot design award, and the President's Award for Good Design in Korea.

PRODUCT

The company is active in several key areas of the electronics market, principally digital appliances, digital displays, digital media and mobile communications. From washing machines and refrigerators, televisions to laptop computers, optical drives to air conditioning systems, and mobile phones to vacuum cleaners, LG's product range spans consumer and business to business sectors. In the B2B sphere, LG is perhaps best known for its air conditioning products, making

1958	1959	1960s	1978	1988	1991
Goldstar, the forerunner of LG Electronics, is established.	The company develops Korea's first radio.	Technological developments include Korea's first refrigerator, black and white TV, air conditioner and washing machine.	Exports surpass US$100 million – a first for Korea's electronics industry.	Production subsidiaries in the UK, Thailand, Mexico and Philippines are established.	Goldstar invests in Zenith Electronics Corp in the US and agrees to jointly develop HDTV.

super-slim indoor units under the Art Cool brand name, and heavy-duty industrial units for commercial use.

Its digital display products, such as plasma televisions and display screens, and also LCD televisions and computer screens, have further cemented LG's position as a leading partner to business clients. Notebook computers, wall mounted HD-ready projectors and satellite navigation systems also boost LG's credentials as a leading technology supplier to the business community.

RECENT DEVELOPMENTS

LG recently underlined its reputation as one of the world's leading innovators of LCD and plasma televisions, by unveiling a 100 inch LCD TV, which made it into the 2007 Guinness World Records Book. It is approximately 1.5 times bigger than the largest LCD TV (82 inches) currently available.

Apart from continual product innovation, LG has also undergone a radical shift in corporate strategy, recently launching a study by McKinsey Group to look at the perceptions and future direction of the brand. Underlying this is a strong commitment from LG to become a top three consumer electronics player by 2010.

Specifically, LG plans to double its sales volume, profit and shareholder benefit by 2010 with 30 per cent of its sales volume and 50 per cent of its profit being derived through products with high growth potential (based on sales performance), market leadership (based on market share) and contribution toward profit.

PROMOTION

To engage with customers around the world, and bring the brand to life, LG has implemented a programme of high-profile sponsorships. On a global scale, it has sponsored the International Cricket Council (ICC) since 2002. Additionally, the ICC World Cup in the West Indies in 2007 provided a major international stage to showcase the LG brand and connect with a global audience.

On the domestic level, LG's highest profile sponsorships are in the English Premier League. From the start of the

2006/07 football season, LG became the official supplier of mobile phones to Arsenal FC. It also became the official shirt sponsor of Fulham FC from the beginning of the 2007/08 season. In addition, for the last seven years, LG has sponsored British Gymnastics.

In 2007, LG launched its new giant LED screen in Piccadilly Circus. Through the innovative use of CGI, the new screen profiles some of London's greatest landmarks and shows some of LG's key products, incorporating clips of live HD content from the FA Premier League, profiling LG's key sporting partners – Fulham and Arsenal Football Clubs – alongside some key TV advertising clips.

LG has also entered into a partnership with Sky News to run a 24-hour news ticker across the bottom of the screen, streamed live over the internet, framing the day's headlines, sporting results and other vital public information, including travel news and weather.

The company also makes extensive use of above-the-line advertising to sell specific products, such as

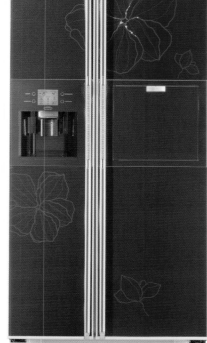

a recent £6 million ad campaign to back the launch of its Viewty mobile phone and its freeview Playback TV.

Shows and live events also play an important part in LG's marketing strategy, especially when it comes to connecting with business audiences. It also has a considerable presence at the world's premier electronics events, such as CES, IFA, 3GSM and the Ideal Home Show.

BRAND VALUES

LG has four cornerstone values – Trust, Innovation, People and Passion. These link into the central promise of the LG brand, which is 'to provide tangible innovations that enrich the lives of customers'. LG's products also carry this promise to the consumer, by aiming to be easy to use, reliable and simple in design, while delivering an enriching experience.

As well as these product benefits, LG also acts as a responsible and caring corporate citizen, building relationships with the local communities in which it works and striving to sustain the environments it operates within.

www.lge.co.uk

Things you didn't know about LG

LG launched the world's first internet-enabled refrigerator, in 2000.

The LG name evolved from 'Lucky Goldstar', the company's name prior to 1995, and from 'Goldstar' before that.

As well as telecommunications and electronics, LG is also active in chemicals, energy, finance and services.

1995
The company changes its name to LG Electronics and completes acquisition of Zenith Corp in the US.

1999
LG Electronics forms a joint venture with Philips, creating LG-Philips.

2002
LG introduces the world's first commercialised home networking system.

2007
LG has projected worldwide sales of around US$44 billion.

LLOYD'S

Lloyd's is not an insurance company, it is instead a market of independent businesses where many of the world's most skilled and experienced underwriters come together to insure and reinsure the world's toughest risks. Business comes into Lloyd's from over 200 countries and territories, and includes 92 per cent of FTSE 100 companies and 93 per cent of Dow Jones companies.

MARKET

In 2007 Lloyd's had the capacity to underwrite approximately £16.1 billion worth of business. Just under half of this is for UK listed and other corporate clients, but Lloyd's also underwrites significant amounts of business for the worldwide insurance industry, as well as private individuals.

The London insurance market is more than just Lloyd's alone. Of the world's 20 largest reinsurance groups, 18 have a physical presence in London. This is also the capital of the world's maritime insurance sector, accounting for two thirds of the global market.

But this is only part of the global picture. New competitor markets are on the rise, such as Bermuda, as well as other reinsurance markets in the US and Europe. All have to compete with alternative techniques for transferring risk, and deploying and redeploying capital, supported by an army of analysts and consultants.

Although Lloyd's has a record of tradition and expertise, it has to stay modern and offer a world-class service to remain competitive.

ACHIEVEMENTS

Lloyd's has been around for more than three centuries, helping communities and businesses to survive major world crises from the San Francisco earthquake of 1906 to the terrorist attacks of 9/11. During that time, many aspects of Lloyd's have changed, but its priorities and values have remained consistent.

Its incredible history and reputation mean that Lloyd's is a truly famous global insurance brand.

This reputation is largely earned through the expertise of some of the world's best underwriters and some of the most innovative insurance products available – on a daily basis. It's an offering that few can rival.

Lloyd's also has a global network with which few can compete, underwriting in more than 200 countries and territories around the

world. This global status, like its track record of paying valid claims when disasters strike, has been built up over the past 300 years.

Key to Lloyd's dependable reputation is its financial solidity. The market's ratings have recently been upgraded, with an 'A+' rating from the ratings agencies Standard & Poor's and Fitch, and a confirmed 'A' rating from A.M. Best.

PRODUCT

Like any market, Lloyd's brings together those with something to sell – underwriters who provide insurance coverage – with those who want to buy – brokers, working on behalf of their clients who are seeking insurance.

Lloyd's is structured as a society of corporate and individual members, who underwrite insurance in syndicates. The make-up of Lloyd's underwriting membership has gone through a major change; today most of the capital supporting underwriting in the Lloyd's market comes from corporate

1688	**1871**	**1887**	**1904**	**1906**
Edward Lloyd opens a coffee house in Tower Street, London. A clientele of ships' captains, merchants and ship owners quickly grows, with Lloyd's coffee house recognised as the place for obtaining marine insurance.	Lloyd's becomes incorporated by an Act of Parliament.	The first non-marine policies are underwritten at Lloyd's by Cuthbert Heath.	The first Lloyd's motor policy is issued, followed seven years later by the first aviation policy.	San Francisco earthquake claims are met by Lloyd's underwriters, establishing Lloyd's reputation in the US.

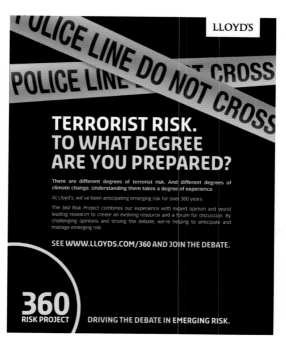

**TERRORIST RISK.
TO WHAT DEGREE
ARE YOU PREPARED?**

There are different degrees of terrorist risk. And different degrees of
climate change. Understanding them takes a degree of experience.

At Lloyd's, we've been anticipating emerging risk for over 300 years.

The 360 Risk Project combines our experience with expert opinion and world
leading research to create an evolving resource and a forum for discussion. By
challenging opinions and driving the debate, we're helping to anticipate and
manage emerging risk.

SEE WWW.LLOYDS.COM/360 AND JOIN THE DEBATE.

360 RISK PROJECT DRIVING THE DEBATE IN EMERGING RISK.

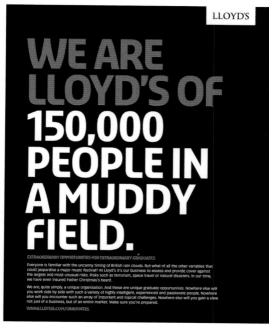

**WE ARE
LLOYD'S OF
150,000
PEOPLE IN
A MUDDY
FIELD.**

EXTRAORDINARY OPPORTUNITIES FOR EXTRAORDINARY GRADUATES

Everyone is familiar with the uncanny timing of British rain clouds. But what of all the other variables that
could jeopardise a major music festival? At Lloyd's it's our business to assess and provide cover against
the largest and most unusual risks. Risks such as terrorism, space travel or natural disasters. In our time,
we have even insured Father Christmas's beard.

We are, quite simply, a unique organisation. And these are unique graduate opportunities. Nowhere else will
you work side by side with such a variety of highly intelligent, experienced and passionate people. Nowhere
else will you encounter such an array of important and topical challenges. Nowhere else will you gain a view
not just of a business, but of an entire market. Make sure you're prepared.

WWW.LLOYDS.COM/GRADUATES

bodies, while private individuals, or 'Names' as they became known, supply only 10 per cent of the market's capital backing. Lloyd's unique capital structure, often referred to as the 'Chain of Security', aims to provide excellent financial security to policyholders and capital efficiency to its members.

A member or a group of members form a syndicate. A syndicate's underwriting is managed by a managing agent, who employs underwriters to accept or decline risk on behalf of members. There are 72 syndicates operating within Lloyd's, covering many speciality areas, including: marine; aviation; catastrophe; professional indemnity; and motor.

Businesses from all over the world can come to Lloyd's to find insurance, often for highly complex risks. There are 167 firms of brokers working at Lloyd's, many of whom specialise in particular risk categories.

Lloyd's underwriters are renowned for devising tailored, innovative solutions to complex risks. As a result, Lloyd's covers the world's most demanding and specialist risks – from insuring oil rigs, man-made structures and major sporting events through to new areas such as cyber-liability and terrorism.

RECENT DEVELOPMENTS
After two years of exceptional hurricane activity with the Asian tsunami and Hurricane Katrina devastating major regions in 2005, 2006 was exceptional for very different reasons. A lack of catastrophe activity meant that Lloyd's produced a strong profit.

These challenging times have proven that Lloyd's is now better prepared to manage the insurance cycle. Through a combination of underwriting for profit rather than market share, the use of state-of-the-art modelling tools, better availability and application of data, the flexibility, responsiveness, resilience and underlying financial strength of Lloyd's is greater than ever before.

In 2007 Lloyd's opened its new reinsurance company in Shanghai, which enables Lloyd's to underwrite onshore reinsurance business throughout China. It provides Chinese insurers with full access to the Lloyd's market and gives Lloyd's improved access to the rapidly developing Chinese reinsurance market.

PROMOTION
An important part of the promotion of Lloyd's is creating a high level of awareness of what Lloyd's is, how it works, what it stands for and what makes it different. In all of this,

Lloyd's speaks with the voice of a market leader – bold, confident and with flair.

Over the last year Lloyd's has launched two major campaigns to address key industry issues of emerging risk and talent.

Through the work of the 360 Risk Project Lloyd's is tapping into the concentrated expertise and knowledge within the Lloyd's market – combined with the views of experts from the insurance, business, political and academic worlds, to stimulate thought-provoking discussion about the changing nature of risk and how to best manage it in today's business environment. A growing body of quality collateral is being communicated to a wide audience via a predominantly online campaign using the FT, The Economist and insurance trade press.

The attraction, development and retention of talent are key issues facing the insurance industry today. In response to this Lloyd's has launched a graduate programme and is promoting it through a range of media, including its website, brochures, print and online advertisements, recruitment fair attendance and direct mail. Lloyd's is at the forefront of financial services and offers graduates a chance to begin their career at a cutting-edge organisation with a strong history and tradition.

BRAND VALUES
The Lloyd's brand is a massive asset, not just for the market itself, but for all the businesses associated with it. Today it is recognised all over the world as a leading global market which is able and trusted to take on some of the world's most complex risks.

It is a highly distinctive brand, known for its traditions, its unique way of doing business, and its ability to meet highly specialised requirements.

'Constant Originality' encapsulates the core idea behind the Lloyd's brand; 'Constant' conveys its good faith, security and reliability, whilst 'Originality' conveys creativity, individuality, authenticity and adaptability.

www.lloyds.com

Things you didn't know about Lloyd's

Lloyd's provides insurance for 88 per cent of the world's top banks and 86 per cent of the world's top airlines listed in the Fortune 500 companies.

In 2004 Lloyd's insured £27 million worth of jewellery worn by the stars at the Oscars.

Lloyd's offers hole-in-one insurance, protecting golf tournament organisers against the rare event of a player hitting such a shot and claiming the large prize offered for such an achievement.

1998
Government announces independent regulation of Lloyd's by the Financial Services Authority, effective from midnight on 30th November 2001.

2002
Lloyd's Members approve the proposals of the Chairman's Strategy Group – outlining major changes to transform Lloyd's into a modern, dynamic and attractive marketplace.

2005
In the aftermath of Hurricane Katrina, Lloyd's emerges with only a small market loss and reinforces its commitment to help rebuild a devastated region.

2007
Lloyd's opens an onshore operation in Shanghai, enabling it to access one of the fastest-developing economies.

MASSEY FERGUSON

A truly global brand, Massey Ferguson (MF) agricultural equipment can be seen working in virtually every country in the world. With a 160-year heritage of being at the forefront of farm machinery technology, MF continues to pioneer developments to improve farming efficiency worldwide. More than five million farmers rely on Massey Ferguson equipment to manage their land and grow their crops.

MARKET

As the largest brand within AGCO Corporation, a US$6 billion world leader in the design, manufacture and distribution of farm machinery, Massey Ferguson supplies a full range of equipment including tractors, harvesting machinery and implements to global markets. The MF red livery and 'Triple Triangle' emblem are an integral part of the rural landscape across all continents – from the mixed farming areas of Northern Europe to the wide open plains of the Americas and the tough conditions of Africa and the Middle East. Today, the MF Triple Triangle marque has the largest global tractor population of any brand in the farm machinery industry.

The world's growing population and economic expansion are increasing consumption of food and agricultural products. In addition, rising biofuel production is placing further demand on the world's grain supply and supporting growth in commodity prices. Markets for farm machinery are on the move and, with its global product range, Massey Ferguson is well placed to serve the needs of modern agriculture.

Backed by multimillion dollar investments in new product development, Massey Ferguson maintains a leading presence in every product sector it operates in every region of the world.

ACHIEVEMENTS

Massey Ferguson has always had a reputation for innovation, pioneering many new techniques that have helped shape modern mechanised agriculture. Among its

achievements are the development of the first commercially-viable self-propelled combine harvester, as well as the development of the three-point linkage system by inventor Harry Ferguson. Integrating tractor and implement as one unit, the system is now the industry standard.

More recently, Massey Ferguson was the first to harness the power of electronics and computer technology to create the world's first 'thinking tractor', which incorporated advanced features to automate and control

many of its functions. Drivers of the latest MF machines now operate from super-quiet, luxurious cabs with a whole array of electronic devices at their fingertips to boost productivity and efficiency while minimising fatigue. They can now even drive hands-free. MF machines can be equipped to use GPS satellite navigation to provide highly accurate automatic steering to within 2cm – day and night.

Massey Ferguson was also one of the pioneers of the technique known as 'precision

1847	1930s	1953	1958	1976	1986
Daniel Massey sets up a farm implement factory in Canada. Later, in 1891, Massey merges with farm machinery specialist Harris, forming Massey Harris.	Harry Ferguson produces his first tractor featuring the revolutionary three-point linkage system of implement control. Massey Harris develops a commercially-viable self-propelled combine harvester.	Massey-Harris-Ferguson is formed.	Massey-Harris-Ferguson is renamed and rebranded as Massey Ferguson.	193,300 tractors are produced at MF factories worldwide.	MF 3000 Series – the world's first 'thinking' tractor – is launched. Massey Ferguson also pioneers precision farming using GPS monitoring.

farming' which enhances efficiency and helps reduce environmental impacts. Here, GPS is employed in combine harvesters to help produce yield maps which enable farmers to track the amount of crop produced in each area of their field. The contours of the yield map – showing good areas and bad – provide information from which to make decisions about inputs such as seed, fertilisers and pesticides. This is all downloadable onto the farm's PC and used to plan and control tractor and implement operation.

In the last four years Massey Ferguson has won more accolades for its contribution to the advancement of farm machinery design than any other farm machinery manufacturer. These include four European Tractor of the Year awards, a Gold Medal for its 7260 combine harvester and, most recently, an award from the American Society of Agricultural and Biological Engineers for its Dyna-VT tractor transmission.

PRODUCT

As a global brand, Massey Ferguson offers products designed to fulfil the needs of widely differing market requirements, crops and conditions. Spearheading the comprehensive range are tractors, combine harvesters, balers, tillage and seeding implements, materials handling equipment and grounds care machinery.

Eighty-five models of tractor cater for the immense diversity of world farming. Extending from the ruggedly simple right through to high horsepower, high specification machines, the product line also includes specialist, utility and compact tractors for niche applications.

The range of combine harvesters is designed to tackle a huge variety of crops, from cereals to grass seed, maize and rice. MF balers – for hay, straw and silage – produce high-density square and round bales. The latest Massey Ferguson 2100 series Big Square balers are acknowledged as the best available anywhere in the world.

RECENT DEVELOPMENTS

2008 marks the 50th anniversary of the brand and the debut of the Triple Triangle marque. The anniversary commenced with the opening of new facilities at its Beauvais manufacturing operation in France, which builds four ranges of MF tractors. These include a state-of-the-art Training Centre, new Sales Offices, and the MF Technology Centre, to enhance the visitor experience at the site.

AGCO's Massey Ferguson Beauvais Facility, one of several around the world, is the largest farm machinery manufacturing plant in France and the largest that AGCO operates globally. Eighty five per cent of production is exported around the globe, making AGCO France's largest farm machinery exporter.

PROMOTION

With many new ideas and concepts to promote to the farming community, Massey Ferguson relied on the power of marketing from its earliest days. Today, as farm machinery technology accelerates even faster, informative promotional material and powerful demonstrations of equipment are a key element in reinforcing the brand's reputation for practical innovation and reliability.

In 2002, an MF 8280 tractor broke the world ploughing record, completing 251 hectares (602 acres) in 24 hours. A Massey Ferguson tractor is also the inspiration behind the logo that fronts the UK's Red Tractor food assurance programme.

Recent recognition for the MF brand's trade press advertising came in the UK's Farm Business Marketing Awards 2007. This included the overall award as the brand most trusted to deliver on the promises made in its advertising.

BRAND VALUES

When customers choose Massey Ferguson, they gain access to a comprehensive network of skilled local dealers around the world. Brand values rest on the twin pillars of 'the best products and the best back-up'. This is driven by quality engineering, industry-leading parts supply, top-level maintenance and service support – all designed to help farmers do what they do, even better.

www.masseyferguson.com

Things you didn't know about Massey Ferguson

To promote its launch onto world markets and as a demonstration of manoeuvrability, in 1956 Harry Ferguson drove one of his revolutionary TE20 tractors around the ballroom and down the steps of Claridge's Hotel in London.

Sir Edmund Hillary used Ferguson tractors in a 1,200-mile journey across Antarctica to reach the South Pole in 1958.

In 1985, 10 MF tractors were sent to Ethiopia as a result of funds raised by Band Aid. Each tractor had 'Love from Band Aid' painted across the bonnet.

A Massey Ferguson tractor is sold every five minutes.

1987	1994	2004	2008
Massey Ferguson becomes the best-selling agricultural tractor in the western world for the 25th consecutive year.	Massey Ferguson is purchased by AGCO Corporation.	Massey Ferguson's largest tractor, the MF 8480 is voted European Tractor of the Year. Subsequently Massey Ferguson branded machines win more awards than any other make of machine.	Massey Ferguson celebrates its 50th anniversary.

Michael Page
INTERNATIONAL

As a world-leader in the recruitment of qualified and skilled professionals for organisations across a broad spectrum of industries and professions, Michael Page International has been one of the fastest-growing brands in this increasingly competitive market. From a small London consultancy, it has grown to become a renowned international company based in 24 countries, with 144 offices and over 5,000 staff.

MARKET

Recruitment consultancies continue to play a vital role in keeping the wheels of industry turning, acting as the intermediary between companies and prospective candidates. Identifying and finding suitably qualified people for job vacancies, either for permanent or contract positions, is a highly valuable service for employers, and also for the appointees whose careers progress as a result.

The company has been quick to embrace the internet in a way that develops its business. With an increasing number of candidates seeking roles through websites, Michael Page International is committed to maintaining a leading presence in the online recruitment arena. While embracing technology, the company remains mindful that it is essentially a people-focused business and that building relationships with clients and candidates is essential to its success. It is this personal approach that has helped it maintain growth and gain a healthy slice of the worldwide multi-billion pound recruitment services market.

Its growth has been entirely organic, through a strategy of opening new offices around the world, as well as opening new disciplines in existing locations.

ACHIEVEMENTS

Michael Page International is one of the most widely recognised brands in the global professional recruitment industry – a strength which provides a competitive advantage in attracting clients, candidates and consultants.

Our shared values
make successful futures

It boasts a client base including all of the FTSE 100 Index and over 80 per cent of the companies included in the FTSE Eurotop 300 Index, serving their needs with a database of over 1.8 million candidates around the world.

Michael Page International can lay claim to a considerable number of industry 'firsts'. It was the first to set up an in-house consultant training programme and first to see the benefits of an international computerised applicant network. The company has continued to invest heavily in the development of IT systems, gaining recognition as the most innovative in the business.

A growing number of initiatives and awards are testament to its commitment to delivering quality. Michael Page International has been voted one of Britain's strongest Business Superbrands since 2000, was voted into The Sunday Times 100 Best Companies To Work For in 2005, 2006 and 2007, and was voted one of Britain's Top Employers in 2005 by the Guardian.

PRODUCT

The Michael Page International service is based on 'The 4C's' – consultants, candidates, clients and care – and it believes

1976	1985	1988	1997	2001	2007
Bill McGregor and Michael Page, who came from the oil and brewing industries respectively, establish Michael Page International in London.	Michael Page International opens its first overseas office in Australia and establishes Michael Page City, providing specialist services to banking and financial markets.	The company is admitted to the Stock Exchange, allowing further expansion, as an office opens in Germany.	www.michaelpage.co.uk, the first generation website, is launched.	Michael Page International opens in Tokyo in 2001, followed in 2003 by an office in Shanghai. In 2006 offices in Dublin, Johannesburg, Dubai, Mexico and Russia follow.	Accountancy Additions becomes Page Personnel Finance. Plans are announced for further expansion into Argentina, Turkey and Austria.

that professional consultants are the key to success. The Group's organic growth strategy ensures that meritocratic internal promotion is inherent, which encourages personal growth and tenure within the company. This is evidenced in the management of the company, where almost all of the current management are the result of internal promotion, ensuring consistency, continuity of culture and a service-led approach across the whole business.

To ensure that consultants are professional in the way they work, they are not paid by commission. The company believes that if you provide an honest and transparent service to candidates, a long term business relationship, built out of mutual respect, will be developed. Michael Page International has long realised that the creation of loyalty stems from an understanding of the candidate's career aspirations and then enabling them to realise their vision.

Candidates are attracted to the company's door by way of referral or via the website, creating a strong pool of talent which in turn attracts clients. Many of these candidates often go on to become clients and trusting business relationships develop.

Michael Page International sees its people as its most important asset, as they have played a key role in achieving an unrivalled level of market penetration and created a strong brand presence.

The company's breadth of experience is reflected in the 14 specialist divisions in which it is now structured. These comprise: Finance & Accounting, Banking, Legal, Marketing, Sales, Technology, Engineering & Manufacturing, Procurement & Supply Chain, Property & Construction, Human Resources, Retail, Secretarial, Hotel & Catering and Healthcare.

RECENT DEVELOPMENTS
The Michael Page International website is constantly developing to allow candidates to conduct faster, more detailed, accurate searches; giving a more satisfactory user experience. In the UK, 37 per cent of candidates register their CVs online, while 65 per cent receive interviews via an online application and these figures are increasing. On a global basis, there are 13 million page views, 1.6 million visitors, and 300,000 CV submissions made each month.

Page Personnel Finance, a sub-brand of Michael Page International, has recently been launched in the UK. With offices already established in Europe, Page

Personnel replaces the Accountancy Additions brand with the aim of providing a greater range of services covering several sectors focused on mid-level candidates. Page Personnel Human Resources, Secretarial and Office Support have also been launched.

Michael Page International has taken strides to ensure it plays a responsible role in the environment and wider community. Whilst it does not operate in a business sector which causes significant pollution, it recognises that it does have an impact on the environment and is keen to establish its green credentials and reduce its carbon footprint. As such, it is committed to making the workplace as energy efficient as possible.

Within its business it vigorously promotes a culture of diversity. Clients expect proposed candidates to have a healthy range of attitudes and characteristics that reflects fairly the society in which we live. To this end, it has its own internal diversity policy that is communicated to all employees.

Employees are also encouraged to be involved in local initiatives. In 2007, Graduate Programme participants were involved in painting and gardening at a local school in Chelsea and setting up a new community college in North London. In 2008, it will also give employees one working day off per year to get involved in voluntary/community work.

Following a hugely successful campaign for Breast Cancer Care in 2006, Michael Page International committed itself to raising £150,000 for Cancer Research UK in 2007. Staff members participated in a variety of sponsored events, including Race for Life and a Pro-Am Golf Tournament.

PROMOTION
The web is a vital tool in the recruitment industry. As well as online job search, the company produces mini-sites for individual disciplines and clients, with e-shots and banners to attract candidates constantly in demand.

Offline, press continues to play a key role in the range of marketing communications and the company remains one of the biggest recruitment advertisers.

Creating superior quality and creative content in its marketing communications is an important factor in promoting the company's principal objectives and providing strong support to the brand.

The company's global office network, which has established close relationships with local organisations, promotes the recruitment services of Michael Page International to a wide audience. This regional

presence underlies the company's extremely high level of local market penetration.

BRAND VALUES
The quality and expertise of its consultancy and support staff are the best expression of the brand values of Michael Page International. The company's policy is to recruit and train its staff to be the best in the business – to be passionate about their work and make the best matches possible between candidates and clients – and above all, to uphold the philosophy of 'The 4C's'. This philosophy is backed up by the key values of pride, resilience, passion, fun and teamwork; values, which have remained consistent over the past 31 years and are regarded as key to future success.

www.michaelpage.co.uk

Things you didn't know about Michael Page International

Michael Page International has been the largest recruitment advertiser in the Financial Times every year since 1992.

Every minute someone makes a job application on the Michael Page International website.

Throughout 2007/08 Michael Page International is aiming to raise over £150,000 for Cancer Research UK.

In 2003, Michael Page International was present in 16 countries. In four years it has increased its global presence by 50 per cent, today being located in 24 countries.

MINTEL

Mintel is a global supplier of consumer, media and market research. Its wide-ranging products provide valuable insights that have a direct impact on its clients' success. Mintel's leading analysts are world-renowned experts in areas as diverse as consumer goods, retail, financial services, leisure and social trends.

MARKET

The world of research is now unrecognisable compared to the market back in 1972 when Mintel was first established. As Mintel experienced a shift in its client base from research and development to marketing departments, clients started demanding so much more than simply pages of statistics. As a result Mintel provides innovative ideas and trend analysis, that help its clients hit upon that 'one big idea' that will set them apart from their competitors.

Market research has always formed the foundations of sustainable growth and profitability, making it a hugely exciting and challenging area to work in.

ACHIEVEMENTS

Mintel has been a Business Superbrand for over seven years and aims to remain consistently ahead of client demands and the competition.

Culturally, Mintel is very proud of the fact that the company has successfully retained the entrepreneurial family culture of its early days, despite growing its workforce to more than 500 full-time and 17,500 associated employees globally.

A comprehensive global people strategy has been implemented to cover every stage of the employee lifecycle. This involves hiring the best talent, investing in training to grow employees' skills across the group and an ongoing performance management scheme.

The company's commitment to environmental issues and charities continues. Mintel and its employees regularly organise events to raise money for charity, while the company's 'Green Team', set up in 2006, continues to promote an environmentally friendly work ethic.

PRODUCT

Mintel's product portfolio is the result of years of client feedback and the innate ability to sense exactly what the market needs.

Whether looking for the newest marmalade in Guatemala or the latest pizza sauce from the Philippines, the Mintel Global New Products Database (GNPD) monitors product innovation in the global consumer packaged goods market. With some 20,000 new products added every month, there are now more than one million launch records on Mintel GNPD. All this allows clients to be truly innovative, track their competitors and stay ahead of all industry developments in more than 50 countries.

Mintel Comperemedia allows clients to monitor print advertising as well as all communications sent to consumers' mailboxes and email inboxes each day. Mintel uses an extensive panel of households in both the US and Canada and covers sectors including telecommunications, finance and automotive.

1972	1997	1998	1999	2000	2001
Mintel is established in London, providing food and drink research in the UK.	Mintel Reports go online as Mintel becomes the first research supplier to provide instant internet access.	The US office opens in Chicago and Mintel GNPD goes online.	Mintel Comperemedia is launched in the US.	The Australian office opens in Sydney.	Mintel publishes the first European and US reports.

Mintel Menu Insights highlights those flavours, ingredients and food combinations that are the real big hitters on US restaurant menus, enabling clients to pre-empt what consumers will be looking to reproduce in their own kitchens.

Mintel Oxygen Reports is the new online delivery platform for Mintel's reports. It is a core element of the Mintel portfolio, focusing on enhanced content, insight and exclusive opinions from Mintel's authoritative analysts, updated daily. Mintel has recently commented on subjects as diverse as the rise of Botox and the recent sub-prime lending crisis.

Mintel Inspire provides clients with extensive research into the very latest global market and consumer trends, helping clients gain new perspectives and become inventive, original thinkers, so that they can create genuinely new business ideas.

For those looking to capitalise on grassroots trends, Mintel Research Consultancy provides bespoke research solutions for all information needs. This service can also source anything from the lip balm that curbs your appetite to the chocolate that moisturises your skin, and get it onto your desk in a timely fashion.

RECENT DEVELOPMENTS

Constant innovation and improvement underpin the streamlined structure and product portfolio offered by Mintel, as it recognises its clients' need to stay ahead in an increasingly competitive global market.

Within Mintel Oxygen Reports, Mintel has significantly expanded its exclusive consumer

research offering. This guarantees that clients make informed business decisions based on accurate, in-depth consumer analysis. In addition, reports now include a 'Brand Elements' section, giving clients a detailed look at a market's brand dynamics.

Mintel Inspire is the new comprehensive, global resource for trends, providing foresight into the very latest consumer behaviour patterns. Mintel Inspire was created in response to a need for a 'thought leadership tool', which through its intuitive interface provides inspiration for new concepts and product development.

Mintel GNPD IRIS populates product records in Western Europe and the US on Mintel GNPD with volume sales data from IRI so that clients can now accurately monitor the true performance of new launches.

The acquisition of Cosmetic Research in 2005 added to Mintel GNPD an in-depth and broad insight into the fiercely competitive high-end cosmetics market.

With Mintel Comperemedia's new email monitoring tool, clients gain a near 360° view of their competitors' marketing strategies.

PROMOTION

Media coverage is an integral part of Mintel's brand promotion and Mintel's research boasts daily coverage across all media. These include Bloomberg News, The Wall Street Journal, the FT and BBC News. Mintel has also formed successful affiliations with trade associations and industry bodies around the globe.

Passion for education is demonstrated by Mintel's sponsorship of the CIM awards and by the company's close relationship with the world's leading educational establishments,

which now rely on Mintel's information to tutor the business leaders of tomorrow.

BRAND VALUES

Mintel believes that every member of its team is a brand ambassador; every contact Mintel makes with a client should leave them with a consistent message of how Mintel can help them make informed business decisions.

Mintel's brand values have been condensed into one simple phrase: insight + impact. The company provides invaluable insight into its clients' markets, consumers and products, questioning the status quo and ultimately having a positive impact on the clients' profits.

The continuing support and loyalty of its clients, many of whom had their first Mintel experience while studying at university, is also an integral part of its branding success.

www.mintel.com

Things you didn't know about Mintel

The latest exclusive consumer research from Mintel has found that 44 per cent of British adults would now consider cosmetic surgery. What is more, the UK market for cosmetic surgery will this year become a billion-pound industry.

Results from Mintel GNPD show that at least one new consumer packaged goods product is launched somewhere in the world every two minutes.

In less than 10 years, Mintel Comperemedia has collected more than 4.7 million pieces of direct mail in the US.

Americans love to dip their food; Mintel Menu Insights shows more than 6,000 menu items include a sauce for dipping.

In the last year alone Mintel has been mentioned in the global print media no less than 10,000 times.

2004	2006	2007	2008
Mintel Menu Insights is launched.	Mintel Comperemedia launches its email panel.	Mintel Oxygen Reports platform and Mintel Inspire are launched. In addition, the Chinese office is opened in Shanghai.	Mintel's expert health and beauty research platform is launched.

One of the UK's best known energy brands, npower is also one of the youngest. Launched in 2000, npower faced a tough challenge to build a brand in an industry dominated by long-established competitors. However, it hasn't let youth stand in its way – quickly becoming a household name and a leading UK energy supplier.

MARKET

The liberalised UK energy industry is the most competitive in the world. Since deregulation in 1992, a raft of mergers and acquisitions has resulted in six major energy companies – all fiercely competing to supply gas and electricity to UK households and businesses. npower is a key player in this market, it has a customer base of 6.8 million residential customer accounts and is the second largest supplier to the business market.

As privatisation intended, customers have been the main beneficiaries of this competitive environment. UK energy prices are amongst the lowest in Europe and switching rates are high and rising – last year, for example, 30,000 more people switched each month than in 2005 (Source: Ofgem).

Businesses of all sizes are also expecting more from energy suppliers. Large business customers, who use significant levels of energy, want increasingly sophisticated levels of specialist support. Many companies have now started to purchase their energy on a flexible basis and, to help with this, the npower Optimisation Desk keeps them abreast of movements in the energy market. npower also offers a risk management service for 'flexible customers' to help them establish an energy price risk management strategy.

ACHIEVEMENTS

The strength and distinctive style of the npower brand has allowed it to consistently grow customer numbers and build market share. Today, npower is the UK's largest

electricity supplier and its customers include household names such as Marks & Spencer, Sainsbury's and Lloyds TSB. As well as being major customers, these big names bring the benefit of brand association – and npower has been quick to realise and act on this, especially when it became 'Official Energy Supplier' to Wembley Stadium, before the construction on the stadium had even begun.

npower matches power consumption at Wembley with renewable energy and is a leader in this field. It is the UK's largest wind farm operator and is planning to spend £100 million on new wind farm developments. Overall, npower is working to reduce its generation CO_2 intensity by a third by 2015, which will need a total investment of around £1.7 billion.

Domestically, npower also invests heavily in helping its customers save energy: over the last three years, npower has delivered 500,000 tonnes of annual carbon savings for its residential customers and, in 2008, npower will invest approximately £100 million in energy efficiency measures for its customers.

2000	2001	2003	2004	2005	2007
npower is launched – subsequently combining the former electricity and gas supply businesses of eight companies.	In partnership with Greenpeace, npower launches npower Juice – a pioneering new clean electricity product using identified renewable sources at no extra cost.	The creation of the npower Juice Fund is announced, designed to assist the development of projects in other renewable energy fields such as wave and tidal energy.	npower signs the world's biggest green energy deal with BT. The contract provides BT with the equivalent yearly energy needed for more than 210,000 homes.	npower wins two Hollis Awards – Best Sports Sponsorship and, in partnership with the Federation of Disability Sports, Best Grassroots Sponsorship.	The summer solstice on 21st June sees npower launch a one-stop-shop installation service for Solar PV (photovoltaic) panels in residential homes.

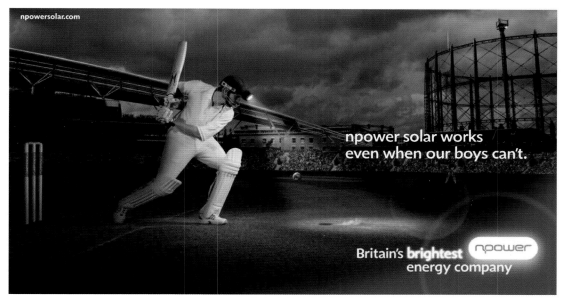

PRODUCT

In an industry as competitive as this, the maxim 'innovate or die' couldn't be more apt. Luckily, npower prides itself on creating innovative products which challenge the way the energy industry has always done things.

npower was the first to introduce a domestic green energy tariff at no extra cost. npower Juice, which has well over 50,000 customers, uses electricity from the UK's first offshore wind farm at North Hoyle. npower is now building its second offshore wind farm, Rhyl Flats, and together these wind farms will make enough clean, green electricity to meet the needs of more than 100,000 homes every year.

To help small and medium sized businesses go green, npower has created 'e3', a proposition which helps them to cut energy costs and shrink their carbon footprint. At the same time, to remind businesses about energy efficiency best practice, npower introduced 'The Big Switch Off' – a campaign to get companies to turn everything off during the August Bank Holiday.

Its not just in the green arena where npower has shaken things up: in 2007, npower introduced a tracker product. The first of its kind in the UK, it provided retail prices that more closely mirrored wholesale costs for those customers who want to manage their own risk.

RECENT DEVELOPMENTS

A major step for the npower brand is its groundbreaking, multi-million pound partnership with The National Trust. Announced in September 2007, npower supplies all its sites and helps the Trust neutralise its carbon footprint by installing energy efficiency and microgeneration measures at historic properties across the country. npower is also helping the Trust create a network of 'low carbon villages', where local communities can develop practical solutions. At the same time, a new domestic green tariff, National Trust Green Energy, will match usage with electricity from renewable sources and contribute to The National Trust Fund.

npower has also recently launched a central heating division, npower hometeam. Its aim is to offer a real, affordable alternative for people fed up with poor customer service and to bring a fresh approach to a stagnant market. npower has just taken on two hundred new hometeam employees and the division continues to grow rapidly.

PROMOTION

In 2007, npower introduced a new brand positioning as 'Britain's brightest energy company', to communicate its aim of engaging customers with exciting, bright ideas. This concept was brought to life through an iconic, national TV campaign (the first advert to feature footage from inside the completed Wembley Stadium). The ad showed fans streaming into Wembley and ended on a dramatic, night-time aerial shot of the floodlit stadium.

Around the same time, npower teamed up with Lenny Henry to take a lighter approach to saving energy and launched the search for the nation's top 100 light bulb jokes. It also

joined forces with Comic Relief to support Red Nose Day, and raised half a million pounds by giving £1 to Comic Relief for every person who called npower for a quote.

As well as Wembley and Comic Relief, npower has taken a challenger approach to its sponsorship of Test Cricket. npower was the first sponsor to designate a specific area of Test match grounds for children. It is adept at getting PR value from its sponsorship and during the huge success of England's Ashes victory it generated nearly £23 million worth of media coverage. It has also played a key role in widening interest in cricket beyond traditional audiences. For example, in 2006, npower created the concept of Urban Cricket – the equivalent of 'jumpers for goalposts'. Its objective was simple: to put 60,000 cricket kits into the hands of 7-12 year olds across the UK.

BRAND VALUES

In everything it does, npower strives to bring its 'personal, rewarding and forward-thinking' brand values to life and live up to its claim of being Britain's brightest energy company.

www.npower.com

Things you didn't know about npower

Macmillan Cancer Support has been npower's corporate charity since 2004, and the partnership is now valued at £1.9 million to Macmillan.

npower is listed in The Times Where Women Want to Work Top 50 and The Times Top 100 Graduate Employers.

npower was awarded Platinum status in the Business in the Community (BITC) CR Index in 2007.

npower was the first company in the world to 'starvertise' – by buying stars to form a constellation of its logo.

Black n' Red

Black n' Red was first produced in 1964 as a 'quarter bound' book with a black cover and a red cloth spine. In 1984 the brand was relaunched in its current casebound format and a wide range of sizes and formats followed to meet the broader needs of the business professional. Oxford Black n' Red is now the UK's leading business notebook.

MARKET

The target market for Oxford Black n' Red is business people between 25-60 who pride themselves on their professionalism. The brand is a staple of the office stationery cupboard for companies, offering a range of value for money, high quality notebooks. The brand prides itself on being suitable for use by a wide range of companies and individuals – from taxi offices and on-site surveyors to chief executives. This universal appeal is attributed to the robust nature and high quality of the product.

Oxford Black n' Red notebooks are available through both retail outlets (high street and grocery) and the office products channel including wholesale and contract stationers. More recently there has been a huge growth in the ecommerce channel, both by current distributors and new suppliers entering this arena.

Oxford Black n' Red is the outright brand leader in its sector with an 80 per cent share of the branded manuscript book market, which has an estimated total (brand and own label) market value of £19 million at manufacturer selling price (Source: MPA 2005).

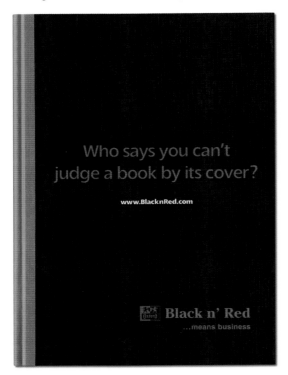

ACHIEVEMENTS

In 2005 Oxford Black n' Red won the Brand Awareness Award at the industry Oscars, the BOSS Awards. This was followed in 2006 by Oxford Black n' Red being awarded a commendation at the Campaign Media Awards for its integrated advertising campaign. The high level of competition in the category reinforced the level of achievement for Oxford Black n' Red in terms of the effective and creative use of a relatively small media budget to drive sales through the office products channel and major retail customers.

PRODUCT

Attention to detail is a key attribute of Oxford Black n' Red products. All books (including recycled) are made with smooth, premium quality 90gsm paper, reducing show-through and allowing the user to write on both sides of the page – even with a fountain pen. The paper also resists yellowing which helps maintain the quality of archived notes.

All books include metric conversion tables as standard, while the classic A4 and A5 hardback casebound books also feature a range of maps and travel information.

In addition, the range includes a hardback wirebound calculator book, which has a full function, solar powered calculator built into the inside cover, as well as books with polypropylene covers, 'smart ruling' for the 'organised note-taker' and the recently added recycled variant.

1964	1984	1989	1991	1996	2002
Spicers launches a 'quarter bound' book with a black cover and red cloth spine.	Black n' Red is relaunched in its current casebound format.	A hardback wirebound variant is introduced.	A soft cover range is launched, taking Black n' Red into the notepad market.	DS Smith, owner of Spicers, purchases John Dickinson Stationery and Black n' Red becomes a John Dickinson brand as Spicers refocuses on wholesaling.	Paper in Black n' Red products is upgraded to premium 90gsm. A wirebound polypropylene variant is launched with an elastic closure strap.

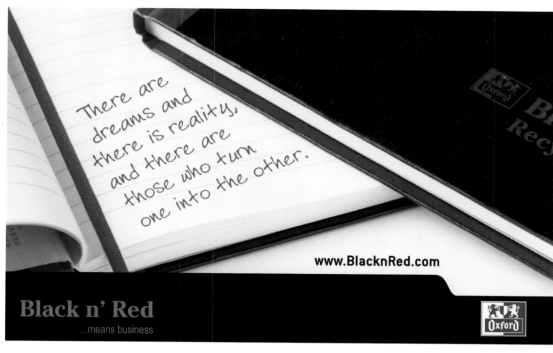

RECENT DEVELOPMENTS

Due to a dramatic increase in the demand for eco-friendly office products, in 2006 the first Oxford Black n' Red Recycled book was launched by John Dickinson – an environmentally friendly version of the iconic notebook that remains faithful to the original. Following the success of this single product, an additional five new Oxford Black n' Red Recycled lines have been added: A4 hardback and polypropylene wirebound books, as well as A5 hardback wirebound, polypropylene wirebound and casebound books.

The brand is innovating further to ensure that the covers of its polypropylene notebooks are also as environmentally friendly as possible. The paper stock has also been improved to achieve a better whiteness without the need for chlorine-based bleaches.

Most recently the brand has introduced a range of diaries designed with the professional's organisational needs in mind – easy to use with a unique page layout which has been specially developed to help manage and plan time more effectively. Oxford Black n' Red diaries also feature Quicknotes™, a planning tool which is useful for prioritising tasks or setting personal reminders. The diaries feature a full colour map section, reference information and address book as well as perforated page corners and ribbon markers to ensure that the current week can be accessed quickly and easily.

PROMOTION

Oxford Black n' Red launched a major media campaign in May 2006 in The Times. It also ran across City A.M., the trade and PA press, such as Executive PA and OS Magazine, as well as numerous online sites – such as Telegraph.co.uk, The Guardian Unlimited and The Times online. Oxford Black n' Red also became the sole sponsor of the Alex cartoon strip in the business section of The Telegraph and even went mobile, with fans downloading their daily dose of Alex's wry wit direct to their mobile phones for free.

The campaign aimed to inspire and attract the attention of PAs, office workers and city professionals who might be looking to buy a notebook, whether it be for themselves or for the office.

The Oxford Black n' Red brand marketing programme has also included bi-monthly mailers with strong consumer promotions, and sales force sampling.

Online consumer attitude magazine surveys and exhibition questionnaires are used for new product development and promotional strategy.

More recently the 2007 press advertisements continued to reflect the style and professionalism of the brand, featuring striking, hand written quotations such as 'Excellence is not an act but a habit' and 'Success is preparation meeting opportunity' which were designed to provoke thought and express humour with Oxford Black n' Red's target audience.

BRAND VALUES

Fundamentally, loyalty to the product is built on its functionality and heritage. It is a high quality product but offers value for money, durability, reliability and dependability.

Oxford Black n' Red is 'the classic notebook for serious professionals'.

www.blacknred.com

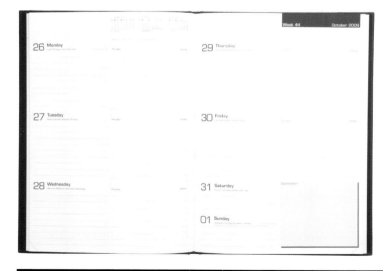

2004	2005	2006	2007
The Black n' Red digital writing solution is created (now part of an exclusive range under the Oxford Easybook brand) in partnership with Anoto and Nokia.	Half-sheets on wirebound products and peelable stickers on casebound books are introduced to effectively promote product features at point of sale.	Black n' Red becomes a range in the Oxford portfolio following the purchase of John Dickinson by Groupe Hamelin in 2005. Recycled variants are launched under Oxford Black n' Red.	Oxford Black n' Red returns to consumer media with a high profile press campaign. Oxford Black n' Red Diaries are launched for the 2008 calendar year.

Things you didn't know about Oxford Black n' Red

The brand has been seen on TV in programmes ranging from Coronation Street and Emmerdale to The Apprentice and Newsnight.

Though its heartland is the UK market, Oxford Black n' Red launched in the US in 2003.

In 2004, Irish singer/songwriter David Kitt released an album entitled 'Black and Red Notebook' – a name inspired by the Black n' Red books he used while song-writing.

Quality - this time - next time - every time

As the UK market leader in high-quality accommodation solutions, Portakabin aims to provide peace of mind for its customers. Portakabin provides added value services such as data communications and security systems, to ensure that the working environment is of the highest standard. Its Customer Charter, pioneering warranty package and broad product range ensure that Portakabin is able to provide value added flexible solutions.

MARKET

A member of the Shepherd Group, Portakabin is part of one of the leading private family owned businesses in the UK. With turnover in excess of £600 million, the Group's operations cover construction and engineering, manufacturing and property development in national and international markets.

The Portakabin Group is divided into a number of divisions that allow customers from a variety of market sectors to choose to hire or buy a quality working environment. Portakabin employs more than 1,300 people throughout the UK and continental Europe. This well-established infrastructure allows it to fulfil its commitment to providing a rapid response and a comprehensive support service.

Already market leader in the UK, Portakabin is a multinational organisation and is actively pursuing a European development programme through the expansion of its network of hire centres. Portakabin offers one of the widest and most comprehensive ranges of modular building solutions from its businesses across the UK, Ireland, France, Belgium and the Netherlands.

ACHIEVEMENTS

Portakabin is proud of its track record in delivering buildings on time and on budget, particularly when its statistics are compared to the construction industry average of only 63 per cent of projects being delivered on time and just 49 per cent on budget (Source: Research carried out by BCIS on behalf of the Royal Institute of Chartered Surveyors Construction Faculty Sept 2004). Portakabin, however, has delivered 99.6 per cent of its buildings on time and on budget, based on orders from January 2004 to April 2007.

Portakabin has earned ISO 9001:2000 quality management systems standard, awarded for everything from office procedures right through to its zero tolerance manufacturing process.

PRODUCT

Having originally conceived his idea of a relocatable building in the 1940s, Portakabin founder Donald Shepherd developed the concept, beginning production of the first Portakabin building in 1961. Today, as market leader and pioneer in the development of relocatable and modular accommodation, Portakabin produces some of the most sophisticated building solutions available.

Designed and manufactured at the 250,000 sq m Portakabin site in York, solutions are offered for a wide range of uses, from office space, marketing suites and classrooms to surgeries and clinics, toilets and showers as well as storage facilities.

The broad Portakabin product range includes modular buildings such as: Ultima and Ultima Vision, which can accommodate

1961	**1965**	**1980**	**1991**	**1992**	**1998**
Portakabin launches its original site accommodation building, the PK16. Success leads to the formation of Portakabin Ltd and registration of the trademark in 1963.	Portaloo is launched, providing mobile toilet and shower facilities.	After receiving the Queen's Award for Export Achievement in 1978, Portakabin is awarded a British Board of Agrément certificate – the first for a building module system.	Portakabin earns the BS 5750 quality system certification; this is the forerunner to ISO 9001:2000 quality management systems standard.	Portakabin recieves the Queen's Award for Technological Achievement.	Lilliput Nursery from Portakabin becomes the first and only modular building to be awarded Millennium Product status by the Design Council.

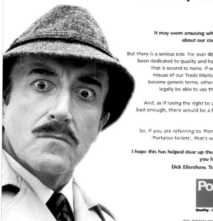

Unlike Richard Henry Sellers, we would like to keep our name.

It may seem amusing when we make a drama about our company's Trade Marks.

But there is a serious side. For over 40 years, Portakabin has been dedicated to quality and has earned a reputation that is second to none. If we never contested the misuse of our Trade Marks and allowed them to become generic terms, other manufacturers would legally be able to use them for their products.

And, as if losing the right to our own name wasn't bad enough, there would be a heavier price to pay in lost sales and jobs.

So, if you are referring to 'Portakabin buildings' or 'Portaloo toilets', that's what they have to be.

I hope this has helped clear up the situation, and thank you for your co-operation.
Dick Ellershaw, Trade Marks Manager

Portakabin
Quality - this time - next time - every time

between one and 1,000 people within individual offices or large open-plan spaces; Portakabin Solus, which offers up to 30 sq m of office space with improved aesthetics, including larger windows and doors; and Titan, the largest single modular building in Europe that can be sited with minimal groundwork required. Portakabin also provides a range of classroom and nursery products, such as the Lilliput Children's Centres, which are delivered complete with nappy-changing rooms, junior toilet facilities, vibrant colours and wipe-clean surfaces.

RECENT DEVELOPMENTS
Portakabin has recently become the first in the industry to introduce the 'On time, on

budget' promise. This means that if the company fails to meet a client's contracted start date, it will provide a week's free hire for every day that it is late on a hire contract or an additional six months' warranty on the building on a sales contract.

In addition, Portakabin has introduced the 'Lead Time Leadership Initiative', whereby its customers can choose any one of 42 building solutions and have them built and delivered within just 15 working days.

Portakabin is the first modular building supplier to offer a suite of biometric site access management solutions for relocatable buildings. This means that a range of state-of-the-art biometrics equipment can be fitted and supplied with the building. This can include retina scanning, managed access or fingerprint recognition as well as more conventional systems such as the barcode swipe-card.

Portakabin is also making strides with regard to sustainability. With a 17 per cent year-on-year reduction in carbon emissions, over 60 per cent of waste recycled, a 50 per cent reduction in the cost of waste sent to landfill over the past three years, as well as product development that includes the introduction of the new Titan Solar building; the Portakabin Group takes its responsibility to the environment seriously.

PROMOTION
Portakabin wanted to communicate the real meaning of what it provides, which is 'peace of mind for its customers'. It therefore developed an advertising campaign with peace of mind as the main message. The creative output, known as 'the couple in bed', was used across continental Europe and

managed to generate a higher brand awareness than competitors' advertising, while using only a fraction of their budget. The UK version adapted for its target market, known as the 'man on the beach', communicated the same message in a different way. More recently Portakabin has moved to promoting its 'On time, on budget' promise as its main differentiator.

Protecting the Portakabin trademark is extremely important to the company and as part of that strategy, Portakabin developed a campaign targeted specifically at journalists and editors to help them use the trademark correctly.

BRAND VALUES
The essence of the Portakabin brand is to provide peace of mind for its customers across Europe, through quality buildings and services.

www.portakabin.co.uk

Things you didn't know about Portakabin

Portakabin uses 5,000 tonnes of steel every month to produce its buildings.

Since 1998 Portakabin has built more than 120 Lilliput Nurseries and Children's Centres.

Yorkon, a subsidiary of Portakabin, manufactures Tesco Express stores. Yorkon has also manufactured restaurants for Pizza Hut and 200 restaurants for McDonald's.

Since the launch of its warranty package in January 2004, Portakabin has sold 2,000 buildings and only 0.17 per cent of customers have made a claim.

Portakabin was first to market with a solar powered relocatable building – Titan Solar.

On time, on budget... our promise

Big words. Big back-up.

When it comes to meeting those tight deadlines, you need a supplier that can deliver. The Royal Institute of Chartered Surveyors has reported that only 63% of traditional building projects are completed on time and only 49% to the agreed contract sum.*

Last year, 99.6% of Portakabin buildings were delivered on time and on budget

In fact, we are the only modular building provider to commit to delivering your buildings on time and on budget. And it's a promise we back up. Whether you hire or buy, if we fail to meet your contract start date, we'll give you **a week's free hire for every day we're late** or **an additional six months' warranty** on your new building.

Call us now and discover why a Portakabin solution means complete peace of mind

If you would like to ensure that your building arrives on time and on budget, call in today on 0845 355 0350 (Hire) or 0845 200 1111 (Sales). Or alternatively, visit us online at www.portacharter.co.uk

*Source: Research carried out by RICS on behalf of Royal Institute of Chartered Surveyors Construction Faculty - September 2004.
**Based on Portakabin order analysis for 2005.
Terms and Conditions apply. A copy is available on request.
Portakabin are registered trade marks.

Portakabin
Quality - this time - next time - every time

2000	2004	2005	2007
Portakabin expands its service with building access, air conditioning and furniture hire businesses. Titan – the largest single modular building in Europe – is also launched.	Portakabin becomes the first and only modular manufacturer to launch a Customer Charter, and to offer five-year product and 20-year structural warranties.	Titan Building System is launched, allowing more flexibility. This is followed in 2006 by Ultima Vision, a contemporary building for hire, designed for greater productivity.	Portakabin launches glazed Titan – featuring a fully glazed wall – Titan Solar, with solar powered capability, and a suite of biometric site access management solutions.

Portakabin is a registered trademark

prontaprint

trusted to deliver, every time.

Prontaprint has maintained its position at the forefront of the corporate print-on-demand market by delivering distinctive design and print solutions, underpinned by a commitment to first class customer service. It has grown to become the largest and best-known brand in the business.

MARKET

In an age where design and print technology is rapidly developing, the business print world demands the very latest digital know-how the minute it hits the market.

Prontaprint is exploiting its commercial design and print expertise, concentrating on tailored communications for business clients – and the number of centres with turnover in excess of £1 million is growing rapidly.

Prontaprint is committed to taking a completely client-focused role to ensure that the network is in a strong position to capitalise on major changes within the B2B market. Understanding clients' businesses is crucial to satisfying a greater proportion of their needs. Delivering exceptional standards of client care and relationship management are key to the total service offering.

In recent years, clients have increased in-house capabilities, becoming digitally enabled and web-smart. In response, Prontaprint has repositioned to offer an enhanced range of services to business. This enhanced range comprises design, print, display, direct mail and finishing services.

ACHIEVEMENTS

Established over 35 years ago, Prontaprint has a fully integrated European network of more than 170 digitally linked centres across the UK and Ireland and employs over 1,100 people with an annual turnover nearing £50 million.

The company is a founder member of the British Franchise Association (BFA) and played a crucial role in establishing a regulatory body for the Franchise industry. It remains a strong supporter of the BFA

and was appointed to the board in 2005. Prontaprint is also a former winner of the prestigious BFA Franchisor of the Year award.

It is also affiliated to the British Print Industry Federation, the British Association of Printers and Copy Centres, the Institute of Printers and XPLOR International (the Electronic Document Systems Association).

Furthermore, it was the first national print-on-demand network to sign a formalised licensing agreement with the Copyright Licensing Agency. This allows licensed copying of specified material within agreed limits. Prontaprint is therefore able to offer clients advice on copyright issues and help protect businesses from potential copyright infringements.

In 2007, Prontaprint won a prestigious Franchise Marketing award for the work it had done repositioning the brand to appeal to higher value business clients; the Best Overall Marketing Campaign award was judged by a panel of experts from the Franchising Industry and the Chartered Institute of Marketing (CIM).

PRODUCT

Prontaprint offers a comprehensive portfolio of business communication solutions to businesses of all sizes including design, print, display, direct mail and finishing services.

Its centres feature the latest design, black and white and colour high volume digital print equipment alongside traditional print capabilities.

1971	1973	1980s	1990s	2000s	2008
The first Prontaprint centre is opened in Newcastle-upon-Tyne, aiming to overcome the high prices, large minimum orders and long lead times associated with traditional commercial printers.	Following the signing of the first Franchise Agreement, the Prontaprint business model goes from strength to strength.	The company continues to expand widely across the UK, as well as into international markets.	Prontaprint focuses heavily on the B2B print-on-demand sector.	Prontaprint is now the largest design and print network in the UK and Ireland and repositions to consolidate its place at the forefront of the corporate print-on-demand market.	Prontaprint is currently rolling out a new brand positioning, following an investment of over £3 million and almost two years of research into the market, brand development and training.

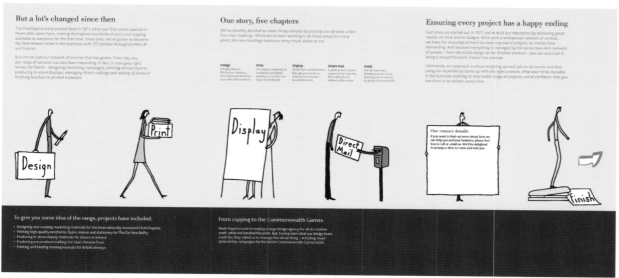

The company is committed to an ongoing programme of investment in the latest digital technology to improve and develop its products and services. This allows clients to order what they require, whenever they require it, reduces the need to hold stock, minimises wastage and requires less up-front investment.

With most documents now produced digitally, clients' original designs can be easily enhanced, updated, and amended. Work can also be securely stored electronically at Prontaprint centres, where it can be easily accessed.

Prontaprint's direct mail service focuses heavily on the use of variable data printing. This new service enables images and text to be totally customised to the recipient. This service, offering one-to-one marketing solutions, underpins Prontaprint's consultancy approach to servicing clients.

The versatile nature of the Prontaprint digital network means that material can be supplied to one centre and sent out digitally across the network to be produced at different centres simultaneously, simplifying distribution and increasing capacity and efficiency. This not only saves the client time and money with reduced wastage and storage costs but also improves competitive advantage by enabling clients to respond to market opportunities quickly.

RECENT DEVELOPMENTS

Proud of its heritage, Prontaprint remains focused on consistently evolving the brand to meet changing client needs in the commercial design and print market.

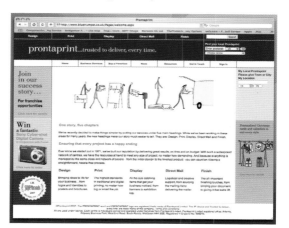

With a corporate client base including British Airways, NEXT, Hush Puppies and Dixons, Prontaprint is rolling out a new brand positioning to develop this market further with an investment of over £3 million following almost two years of research.

The new brand positioning was initially piloted at seven Prontaprint centres across the country, chosen to represent a cross section of the print market in terms of size, offer and service. The six-month trial delivered a sales growth seven times higher than the rest of the network.

The roll out includes a new corporate identity, learning and training for Franchisees and their staff and enhanced business services. A powerful new positioning statement – 'trusted to deliver, every time.' – has been introduced, alongside the strong use of illustration and a warm aubergine corporate colour, reinforcing the human face of the brand.

PROMOTION

Prontaprint has been transformed from a high street print and copy shop into a key player in the B2B print-on-demand sector, through continual investment in the development and promotion of its brand on a local, national and international level.

It has maintained its market leading position through a sustained and structured approach to business planning, sales and marketing strategy at both macro and micro levels.

Marketing activity is based on extensive client feedback and market research. Independent in-depth surveys of existing, lapsed and potential customers help to identify changing factors of importance among small, medium and large businesses when buying print and related products and services.

Results provide Franchisees with a greater understanding of buyer behaviour as well as identifying new market opportunities.

Prontaprint believes that consistent and regular external sales and marketing activity is central to the ongoing profitable growth of each centre. This activity is focused on the acquisition, retention and development of business clients.

It also provides Franchisees with a wide range of central sales and marketing tools and resources to enable them to grow their businesses locally coupled with external sales support.

BRAND VALUES

Prontaprint has four key brand values – Close, Connected, Can-do, Collaborative.

'Close' focuses on building long term relationships with clients on a one-to-one level. This is achieved through close contact with clients and close understanding of their needs.

'Connected' refers to Prontaprint's network of talented and experienced people as well as the use of technology. Prontaprint harnesses these connections, aiming to ensure clients get the best results with their business communications on time, every time.

'Can-do' reflects the business culture of getting things done. Whatever the job, large or small, Prontaprint aims to go the 'extra mile' ensuring it is 'trusted to deliver, every time.'

Finally, 'Collaborative' reflects that talking to clients is the start of a two-way conversation, rather than a one-way sales pitch. By working in partnership with clients and each other, Prontaprint consistently guarantees distinctive design and print solutions.

www.prontaprint.com

Rentokil

From humble beginnings 80 years ago, Rentokil has grown to become one of the UK's most recognised brands and the leading pest control company in the world, operating in 44 countries and employing over 5,000 people to work with more than 300,000 customers. In 2006 Rentokil generated global sales of £280 million – a 33 per cent increase since 2005 – as demand for its expert pest control services and international expansion continued apace.

MARKET

Rentokil provides expertise in pest control services around the world. It is not only present in many countries, but can also claim to have leading positions in many of those markets. Being an international company, it has real depth and breadth of experience it can call upon to find solutions for its clients, wherever they may be.

Around the world Rentokil manages many different types of pest and operates in many different cultures. For example, in America and Australia, termites are a major part of the pest control landscape; in Australia, termites cause more damage to property than storms, fire or floods. As climate temperatures change, Rentokil expects termites to move across Europe: expect them to arrive in Paris soon and be in Brussels by 2012.

In Africa, Rentokil helps to protect vital crops from tobacco beetles, while in many countries around the world it fumigates against mosquitoes, to act against the associated health risks. In Asia Pacific, snakes and large spiders are part of the pest control business.

While Rentokil has a significant presence in the residential market, more than 80 per cent of Rentokil's worldwide sales are to commercial customers, whose typical sector focus is: pharmaceutical, food processing, food retail, leisure and industrial.

ACHIEVEMENTS

Since 1941, Rentokil has had its very own research and development team. Using their expertise, they have formulated and developed effective products and processes for the pest control business.

Over the years, Rentokil has provided services to remove pigeons from Buckingham

Palace and beetles from Westminster Hall. In Ireland, the company protected 'The Taking of Christ' – a priceless painting by Caravaggio – which following its discovery, was found to be infested by biscuit beetle.

In 1946, Rentokil removed a rat infestation from Reykjavik after it was estimated that 80 per cent of the 4,845 properties were infested with rats. After three treatments, 87 per cent of infested properties were declared free of rats; the Mayor of Reykjavik wrote to Rentokil in praise. Ten years later, the company cleared rats from Bahrain in the Persian Gulf. A complete laboratory was shipped to the Middle East and after five

1927	1939	1940	1941	1957	1964
The British Ratin Co. Ltd – soon to be Rentokil – is incorporated following the discovery of Ratin, a strain of bacteria lethal to rodents.	Rentokil's reputation grows fast as it steps in to protect the nation's dwindling wartime food stores from pests.	The company begins to offer insect control services.	The first Rentokil Laboratories are established for the company's own research and development.	Rentokil's Woodworm and Dry Rot divisions are established.	A Royal Warrant for woodworm and dry rot control is granted to Rentokil.

about their pest control programmes, PestNetOnline was the first remote reporting service, becoming a market-leading offer.

PROMOTION
The internet is a vital tool in Rentokil's global promotion strategy, building relationships with its business customers. To this end, Rentokil recently launched a new global online hub, from which new local websites can be accessed. The sites feature a host of vital information and support tools for customers, even down to a section on the lifecycles of persistent pests.

Rentokil also uses directories and direct mail to boost its brand awareness, and has recently given a greater push behind public relations activities. The company is also implementing a new CRM system across its markets.

BRAND VALUES
Rentokil believes that its customers should be free to focus on what is important to them, without the worry of pest and hygiene issues.

As a pest control specialist with 80 years' experience, Rentokil provides front line professional expertise in a straight-forward and reassuring manner, aiming to give residents and businesses peace of mind by protecting them from pest, hygiene and financial risks.

www.rentokil.com

months, the rat population was reduced by an estimated 90 per cent.

Rentokil continues to expand its geographical spread, having recently launched in the Balkans. In 1932 Rentokil's turnover stood at £10,000, by 1966 this had grown to £5 million and in 2006 the company topped £280 million. It is now listed on the Dow Jones Sustainability Index World (DJSI World) and its European equivalent (DJSI STOXX).

PRODUCT
Following the 1927 discovery of Ratin – a poison deadly to rodents – Rentokil was formed to meet demand for a trusted service that would remove the problem of pests from specific locations such as food processing facilities, hotels, museums, retailers, restaurants, offices, pharmaceutical plants and the home.

Today, Rentokil offers services to control a range of more than 250 pests, including cockroaches, flies, bedbugs, rats, ants, mice, beetles, pigeons, moles, rabbits, squirrels, wasps, bees and more.

Its pest control technicians have a crucial role in the protection of public health and hygiene. Dealing with pest problems quickly and effectively is paramount, and Rentokil attributes much of its success over the past 80 years to its expert technicians.

A full range of DIY products for homeowners is offered for sale via large national and independent local hardware stores. They cater for the residential market where jobs have increased by 42 per cent year to date (YTD), an increase in the UK YTD business value of 13 per cent.

RECENT DEVELOPMENTS
In 2006 Rentokil launched the first Mouse Radar, and it has recently been upgraded with the ability to send an alert to a customer's or technician's computer on activation. Dubbed 'the world's smartest mouse trap', it led Rentokil to win the 2006 PETA Proggy Award for Best Humane Wildlife Innovation. A 21st century rodent unit, it uses infrared motion sensor technology to capture the pest, before delivering a burst of CO_2 to quickly and humanely kill the rodent.

Rentokil is currently working to upgrade PestNetOnline, its exclusive online extranet reporting system available only to registered Rentokil customers. Principally aimed at customers in the food and catering sector who require very high levels of reporting

Things you didn't know about Rentokil

The first reported appearance of brown rats in Western Europe was in Copenhagen in 1716. It was however to be nearly 200 years before major developments in systematic rodent control took place – once again in Denmark.

Rentokil provides surveys free of charge, but the average cost of treating a mouse infestation in London is £200-£250.

The new Wembley Stadium and the Oval cricket ground are amongst the many famous venues and buildings to use Rentokil to prevent pests from becoming a problem.

When the Ministry of Works discovered mice in the House of Commons' kitchen, Rentokil surveyed the whole of the Palace of Westminster and arranged for 750 trays of mice bait to be laid down.

In Europe, customers tend to want to have the problem removed without actually seeing the pest. In China and other parts of the world, customers expect to see the pests that have been removed.

1967	**1969**	**1972**	**2007**
Buckingham Palace is treated for moth and pigeon problems.	Rentokil Group Ltd is listed on the Stock Exchange with one of the largest new share issues the City had seen.	Rentokil's Pest Control Division profits top £1 million.	Rentokil celebrates its 80th anniversary.

RIBA

As the voice of architecture in the UK, the Royal Institute of British Architects (RIBA) champions good design to Government, the public and the construction industry. It believes that everyday life can and must be improved through better designed buildings and communities, and that the architect's role is crucial. RIBA Enterprises, the RIBA's principal commercial arm, is the leading information provider to the UK construction industry.

MARKET
The founding mission of the RIBA, 'to advance architecture by demonstrating public benefit and promoting excellence in the profession', remains true, but today's sustainability agenda has transformed the design and construction of buildings. It is RIBA members who will be designing much of the future, and the Institute is helping them meet challenges facing the profession and the construction industry – such as the well-voiced need for energy saving in new buildings, and the threat to design quality caused by the dash for high-volume contractor-led projects.

Through the work of its members, the RIBA provides focused guidance on the principles, tools and techniques necessary to design and build low-carbon buildings and to advise clients on what is possible, and the Institute constantly champions the need to bring good design 'upstream' in the procurement process. The RIBA also validates architecture courses around the world with schools producing future generations of architects.

ACHIEVEMENTS
The Institute's voice is being heard more strongly than ever. The RIBA's recent 'mid-term report', following its 2005 Manifesto for Architecture, showed that the Government has adopted no fewer than 14 of the Institute's 21 recommendations for good design to be valued economically, socially and environmentally. Success can be seen with reform of the planning system which reflected the RIBA's demands to protect and encourage the best designs, improve the speed and efficiency of the planning process, and deliver more sustainable buildings. While its members are behind the creation of some of the UK's most daring and brilliant architecture, the RIBA is also keeping up the pressure on the Government, challenging them to improve the design of the everyday – schools, hospitals and other public buildings.

Supporting the work of the Institute, a recent reorganisation of RIBA offices nationwide has refocused it to exert even greater influence on local government on the need for design quality.

PRODUCT
Although new well-known landmarks such as the British Airways London Eye, the Eden Project and the Gateshead Millennium Bridge are all creations of RIBA members, most of what the RIBA does is not about big design statements. It is about raising the standards of the buildings and spaces everywhere by supporting the designers of everyday necessities. RIBA Client Services offers a range of services to help clients commission the right architect for their project and the RIBA Competitions Office is dedicated to helping clients run competitions to select architects for their project. Clients are also

1834	1837	1863	1931	1934	1996
The Institute of British Architects is founded.	The Royal Charter is bestowed upon the Institute.	The first formal (but voluntary) exams in architecture by appointment of a board of examiners are introduced by the RIBA.	The RIBA is instrumental in establishing the Architects' Registration Act – the first UK register of practicing architects.	The RIBA moves to its Art Deco headquarters at Portland Place, London.	The RIBA Stirling Prize is inaugurated.

benefiting from the RIBA Client Design Advisor scheme, which provides independent, expert advisors to guide clients through the, often complex, public sector procurement process.

Within the 'Enterprises' portfolio and under the RIBA brand is a thriving publishing and bookselling business. Through its National Building Specification (NBS) sub-brand, RIBA Enterprises supports the technical side of architecture. As well as being the de facto specification system for buildings in the UK, NBS also provides access to technical and regulatory information and publishes the UK Building Regulations on behalf of the Government. Its RIBA Product Selector offers a range of advertising options that provide the interface between product manufacturers, the architectural community and construction professionals. RIBA Bookshops provide one of the largest selections of both UK and international titles covering architecture, the built environment and design.

RECENT DEVELOPMENTS

The London 2012 Games offer a potential showcase for the highest design quality the UK has to offer, as well as an opportunity for architects to contribute to the event and its legacy. The RIBA is working closely with the Olympic Delivery Authority, and through networking events, it has enabled many small innovative practices to meet and present to the main procuring authorities, making it possible for some to secure places on the shortlist of suppliers.

In order to help improve the business effectiveness and customer service of architects' practices, the Institute launched its RIBA Chartered Practice scheme – a client-focused accreditation scheme for architectural practices – in July 2007. The scheme was initiated in response to clients' requirements for quality assurance, increased public and Government pressure for consumer protection, and architects seeking increased promotional and technical support from the RIBA.

PROMOTION

The RIBA brand is driven through its press activity and public relations as well as its lobbying of Government. In addition, its network of members plays a vital role in developing the brand. The RIBA works collaboratively with bodies such as the Construction Industry Council, Institution of Civil Engineers, and Royal Town Planning Institute, and on the consumer front, with shows including Grand Designs Live.

The RIBA Trust, the Institute's cultural arm, partners with other organisations to help promote interest in architecture. Recently the Trust worked with the BBC and produced web content for the TV programme How We Built Britain. Through talks, exhibitions and an education programme, the RIBA Trust works to widen public awareness of good architecture.

The RIBA president, who stands for two years, acts as the spokesperson for the

Institute to the media, representing the RIBA when talking to Government, and at industry and public focused events.

BRAND VALUES

The brand is crystallised in the letters 'RIBA', which represent architecture's gold standard, and which are valued by RIBA members and the public alike. The RIBA aims to be responsive to its stakeholders and audiences; to be influential through its advocacy and campaigning; to be bold as it addresses 21st century challenges of design and construction; and to add value to society through the work of its members. In all that it does, it aims to inspire trust, demonstrate competence and show leadership.

www.architecture.com

Things you didn't know about RIBA

Every year some 20,000 students emerge from schools of architecture, both in the UK and worldwide, whose courses have been validated by the RIBA.

In 1983 the RIBA presented its first Design for Energy Efficiency award, to a gas service depot in Manchester.

Throughout the 1990s the RIBA lobbied Government to recognise the importance of listing post-war buildings, resulting in a change in legislation.

Two sisters, Ethel Mary Charles and Bessie Ada Charles, were the first female members of the RIBA. Ethel was elected in 1898, her sister a few years later.

1997	2004	2005	2007
The US chapter of RIBA is launched in recognition of the 700 plus RIBA members who are at work across the US.	The V&A+RIBA Architecture Partnership is launched at the Victoria and Albert Museum.	RIBApix – the online image database of the RIBA British Architectural Library – is launched.	Sunand Prasad is elected RIBA president.

Royal Mail

Every person in the UK, at home and at work, is a Royal Mail customer – making the company unique. The reach of Royal Mail's network makes it a brand that touches everyone. Royal Mail covers the entire UK population – that is greater penetration than any other media channel, including TV, the internet, mobile and landline phones.

MARKET

The postal market in the UK has undergone a complete transformation in the past few years, with full market liberalisation introduced in January 2006. Today Royal Mail faces its biggest challenge, working in a competitive marketplace yet continuing to offer its universal one-price-anywhere service. It has already completed the biggest turnaround in corporate history, to annual profits, from losses of £600 million a year five years ago.

With nearly 175,000 staff, Royal Mail handles more than 82 million letters and packages every day, with recent growth in the goods distribution markets heavily influenced by the huge increase in online trading.

ACHIEVEMENTS

Royal Mail is one of the world's largest international carriers, carrying 900 million items a year destined for more than 240 countries.

Its focus is on quality. First Class service remains at target levels, with 93 per cent of First Class stamped letters arriving the day after posting. Royal Mail's Special Delivery service provides time-critical deliveries by 9am and 1pm with 99 per cent arriving by the guaranteed time (Source: Royal Mail Track and Trace April 2007).

Royal Mail Group's corporate social responsibility policies have been commended by industry and peer awards. Most recently, Royal Mail Group was recognised for the work it is doing to reduce its impact on the environment and the integrated approach it is taking to carbon management. This was

recognised by the Chartered Institute of Logistics and Transport when they gave Royal Mail Group the European Award for Excellence in the Environmental Improvement category. In addition, Royal Mail Group was recognised at the National Payroll Giving Awards, and was the winner of Pay Magazine's Best Payroll Giving Award.

In 2007, Royal Mail's website won best B2B website at the NMA Effectiveness Awards. In addition, its Contact magazine won Best-Designed B2B Magazines at the MDA Awards and also won an award for the Most Effective B2B Title at the APA Awards in November 2007 for the second year running.

Furthermore, Royal Mail received a Direct Marketing Association Bronze ECHO award for the Special Delivery 'Stop Lateness' direct marketing campaign in the Business and Consumer Services category. The ECHOs are the Oscars of direct marketing and a much sought-after industry honour.

PRODUCT

Royal Mail is the custodian of an immensely powerful human network, derived from the reach it has, not only geographically – 99.9 per cent of all households – but also emotionally – the trust placed in the postman.

1635	1840	1883	1924	1968	1974
Charles I allows the public to use his Royal Mail for the first time. Postage is paid by the recipient.	Uniform postage is introduced with the Penny Black; any item, sent anywhere for a penny, paid in advance by the sender.	Postmen are introduced.	The first commemorative Special Stamp is issued.	The first Second Class letter is sent.	Postcodes are designated for all UK addresses.

As a result of Royal Mail's unique universal service offering, anywhere in the UK is accessible for one price. Royal Mail's First Class service delivers items sent in the UK the next working day with Second Class deliveries made in two days.

Royal Mail's business mail services allow bulk mailers to send thousands or even millions of items with significant savings on standard rates. Royal Mail's products don't just start and end with the physical mail, it also offers a range of end-to-end logistics services, data and media services to help businesses find, grow and keep their customers.

RECENT DEVELOPMENTS

Royal Mail has always been at the forefront of innovation; for example, in 2004 it introduced one of the world's first digital stamps, SmartStamp, which enables customers to buy personalised postage from the internet and print directly on to the envelope.

In 2007, several new products were launched including Personalised Integrated Media in partnership with Sony DADC. This concept was a winner at the 2007 UK Mail Innovation Awards. It fuses traditional postal communications with digital media, enabling advertisers to personalise communications for their customers by using individual information on content-rich and interactive CDs.

E-Redelivery, also launched in 2007, gives customers the added option to arrange their

redelivery via Royal Mail's website. This self-serve solution takes account of the need to pay additional charges for items where customs charges or postage is owed. E-Redelivery has delivered proven and measurable benefits to mail users.

The Carbon Neutral Door to Door scheme was also introduced in 2007. This scheme – the first of its kind in the UK – is part of Royal Mail's programme to encourage customers to adopt Responsible Mail principles. Royal Mail's Carbon Neutral Door to Door scheme makes it easier for companies to reduce the carbon footprint of their mailing by giving advice on sustainable production, such as recyclable paper, biodegradable inks and paper finishes, as well ensuring effective campaign targeting in order to minimise waste. After carbon impact has been minimised in line with scheme standards, Royal Mail calculates the remaining CO_2 emissions generated by the mail campaign and pays to offset through schemes such as the Woodland Trust's Carbon Plus, which plants native trees in the UK.

Royal Mail's long running and award-winning Special Stamp programme celebrates British identity, history, culture and achievements throughout the UK and the world. Stamps celebrating the Beatles and the conclusion of the Harry Potter books have been the most successful stamp issues of the last decade. Royal Mail also commissioned

Lord Snowdon to create a new portrait of the Queen and Prince Philip for their Diamond Wedding stamps.

PROMOTION

Two innovative campaigns to demonstrate the power of direct mail were launched in autumn 2007. Under the umbrella theme of 'D loves E' (meaning direct mail complements electronic communications), contacts received a direct mail pack designed to look like a computer desktop with instructions on how to fold it to make an origami man, 'Mr Complete'. The aim was to entice them to visit their own personalised microsite. Once online, an animated Mr Complete demonstrated the benefits of integrating direct mail with their digital advertising. In the second campaign, 'Touching Brands', Royal Mail targeted major advertisers with a letter made from chocolate, demonstrating how direct mail can be used powerfully to engage customers' five senses and develop emotional attachment to the brand.

BRAND VALUES

Royal Mail aims to help the nation thrive and grow, by connecting businesses with their customers and people with people. Its brand values are Expert, Proud, Together, Trustworthy and Hungry.

www.royalmail.com

Things you didn't know about Royal Mail

Each working day Royal Mail collects items directly from its 113,000 post boxes, 14,300 Post Office® branches and from some 87,000 businesses.

More than 200 million First Class Christmas stamps are printed every year.

Royal Mail delivered 600,000 pre-ordered copies of the sixth Harry Potter book during one Monday morning in July 2007.

During 2007, Royal Mail delivered 18 billion items.

1993	2004	2006	2007
Self adhesive stamps are introduced.	SmartStamp is launched.	The UK postal market is fully liberalised – only the second in Europe. Changes in pricing are made to take into account size as well as weight.	E-Redelivery, Royal Mail Tracked, Responsible Mail and Online Business Account are introduced.

Ryman
stationery EST. 1893

Ryman is currently undergoing a rapid transformation from a 90-store operation to a nationwide chain of 250 shops. Having purchased nearly 150 Partners and Stationery Box stores, which are currently being re-branded, Ryman is building the only national chain of specialist high street stationers. Turnover for the group is estimated at around £140 million, with substantial growth also being driven in online sales.

MARKET

Ryman is the only specialist commercial and family stationery retailer operating in the high street. Others tend to compete in the wider personal, home and student sector, selling games, books, CDs, magazines and other non-stationery items. However, in the face of this diversification, Ryman has continued to build on more than 100 years of service and a long-standing reputation as the UK's stationery specialist.

Ryman has always been innovative in this marketplace, including being the first to open a self service stationery outlet. Today Ryman is competing in an extremely competitive market, further intensified by direct mail companies such as Viking and out of town superstores such as Staples.

However, much of Ryman's success can be attributed to the specialist products stocked, the breadth of services offered in-store and a professional, knowledgeable and highly trained customer service team.

According to Key Note research, the UK market for personal and office stationery is worth around £3 billion, made up primarily

of core products such as paper and board, writing instruments, filing and storage solutions.

However, the stationery market is constantly changing and Ryman has reacted and adapted to factors influencing this market such as changes in the way we work and the tools we need to do so. Many predicted that the IT revolution and rise of the so-called 'paperless office' would torpedo demand for paper, pens and traditional office supplies. But, despite the growth of electronic information storage and trading, there seems to be as much demand for stationery as ever.

In addition, the computer-based office has led to a surge in demand for consumables

such as ink jet cartridges, paper and storage devices, such as USB Memory sticks, CDs and DVDs. These are now available in a wide variety of options to suit a proliferation of PC and printer led uses.

With identity theft growing at a current rate of 165 per cent a year and costing over £1.3 billion a year, the business has seen a significant increase in sales of shredders.

Other factors keeping the sector buoyant include more students in higher education, lower unemployment and increasing numbers of people working from home.

Technological advances have also increased Ryman's scope of operations. Electronic developments – such as multi-function machines and mobile phones – are

1893	1960s	1995	1996	2001	2007
Ryman is founded in by Henry J Ryman, with the first store opening on Great Portland Street, London, where one of its major London stores still stands today. The first week's takings are £50.	Up until this point, the store chain is family owned.	Ryman is acquired by Chancerealm Ltd, in which Theo Paphitis is the controlling shareholder.	The Ryman direct mail order catalogue is launched, followed by Ryman.co.uk ecommerce website in 1998.	Ryman purchases Partners the Stationers, comprising 86 stores.	Ryman purchases 61 Stationery Box stores.

now areas of significant growth. However, this has further increased the number of Ryman's competitors which include retailers such as Currys.digital and Argos.

ACHIEVEMENTS

Ryman has managed to grow and prosper in a particularly difficult market. The high street has been under pressure from out of town shopping, mail order and, more recently, ecommerce. Furthermore, the market for paper products has been hit by high prices and IT-related uncertainty.

Given that background, Ryman is an impressive performer, with compound growth since 1995 of 80 per cent. Today, the business boasts a turnover of more than £140 million. The secret of its success has been to invest in the key areas of its business – its people, information technology as well as the warehouse and distribution function.

It has also continually invested in updating and improving its stores and diversified into new product areas – such as new electronic developments – to react to changes in market conditions. A significant achievement in its sector was to become the first stationery retailer to sell mobile phones. An important element of its success in putting service and product knowledge at the top of the agenda has been a policy of investing in people and promoting from within.

PRODUCT

Ryman sells a wide range of office supplies – from writing equipment, paper, filing and storage solutions, to high-tech items such as mobile phones, printers and multi-function machines. It sells a full range of products needed to support most office machinery, including print cartridges, discs and storage devices. It also sells office furniture encompassing desks, chairs, workstations and filing cabinets. Ryman has always been at the forefront of stationery innovation bringing colour to what is traditionally a very conservative area, often being the first to introduce products such as box files, ring binders and filing cabinets in a variety of shades.

As a specialist stationer, Ryman carries products not often found in a generalist stationery retailer. Furthermore, products are available with grades and sizings to suit specific needs. New product innovations are

quickly embraced and Ryman strives to be ahead of the competition in all areas.

Ryman offers a full business service in a number of stores for photocopying, binding, laminating and faxing. Self service photocopying both in black and white and in colour are also available.

As well as its physical retail outlets, Ryman also sells these products via its website, www.ryman.co.uk, a mail order catalogue, Ryman Direct, and an office supplies directory, covering thousands of extra lines.

RECENT DEVELOPMENTS

Having grown the chain to around 250 shops, Ryman is now a fully national business. It has achieved this by opening new stores and acquiring competitors' stores, enabling both significant short term growth and long term sustainability through reduced competition. The product range has been aligned across the chain to ensure that the Ryman own-brand products become even more competitive through increased distribution and the enhanced buying power of the group that will ensure greater value to the consumer.

The newly acquired stores also have a large range of products for family use, rather than the business customer alone. This has increased the group's target audience, allowing range extensions to previously non-core ranges such as Artist Materials, Card Making and Craft. It will also ensure that the key seasonal peaks for the business at 'back to school and college' and Christmas become even more significant.

PROMOTION

Ryman's promotional strategy is a combination of consistently offering value for money coupled with excellent service through ongoing multi-saver offers and regular price-led promotional activity. A typical Ryman promotion lasts between four to five weeks; however, key selling times

such as 'back to college' will last between eight to nine weeks.

National and regional press advertising is used to promote the new technology ranges such as mobile phones and the Ryman telemarketing team maintain contact with its large database of customers.

BRAND VALUES

The Ryman brand values are quality, value, reliability and service. These have been developed and nurtured over 100 years and Ryman is an acknowledged specialist in its field.

These values have enabled Ryman to build and retain a loyal customer base. It is proud of its record for investing in its people, training them to be able to deliver a high standard of service, backed by expert knowledge of the range of products and their applications.

www.ryman.co.uk

Things you didn't know about Ryman

Ryman sells 100 million sheets of paper and two million pens every year. That's enough ink to draw along the length of the Great Wall of China almost 300 times.

At present there are 12 members of staff who have been with Ryman for over 25 years, 20 members of staff who have celebrated at least 20 years' service and 52 members of staff who have been with Ryman for more than 15 years. One member of staff has been with the business for 50 years.

Ryman sells over 80 different own-brand cartridges and stores have a cartridge recycling point.

The Samsung Group is now one of the largest global corporations. From its beginnings in South Korea, it now operates worldwide across a multitude of sectors as diverse as finance, chemicals and heavy industry. At the forefront of this well known brand is Samsung Electronics, a subsidiary of the wider Samsung Group and currently one of the world's most dynamic and successful organisations.

PRODUCT

Samsung is divided into several different affiliated companies, with Samsung Electronics the best known and most profitable. It manufactures a wide range of products, including audio/visual, computer-related and telecommunication products, as well as home appliances and various components.

RECENT DEVELOPMENTS

2007 was a significant year for Samsung in terms of innovation. Its continued investment in research and development has long been a hallmark of the company. This focus, involving a research and development investment in 2007 of almost US$7 billion, is centred in 42 research facilities located around the world. It is the aim of some 36,000 researchers to ensure that Samsung remains at the cutting-edge of innovation.

MARKET

Over the last decade, Samsung Electronics has morphed from a small-scale manufacturer with a little known brand into one of the world's strongest and most powerful technology companies.

Boasting a vast product portfolio, Samsung's success can be largely attributed to its strength in three areas – memory chips, liquid crystal displays (LCDs) and handheld telephones. Samsung is a leader in all of these spaces, commanding an 18 per cent share of the thin-film transistor (TFT) market and a 12.6 per cent share of the mobile handset market, as well as being a market-leading producer of three types of memory – DRAM, SRAM and flash memory.

ACHIEVEMENTS

Samsung has evolved into a group of companies spanning multiple industries with widespread success. Coherently structured, streamlined, globally-focused but responsive to the needs of local markets, Samsung Electronics delivered consolidated sales of around US$100 billion in 2007.

Following its achievement in previous years, Samsung has continued to gain recognition and its innovative products have won almost 100 influential design awards in 2007. For example, the prestigious International Forum Design (iF) organisation bestowed 26 iF design awards on Samsung products in 2007. In addition, Samsung received four EISA (European Imaging and Sound Association) awards.

1938	1950s	1960s		1970s	1990s
Samsung General Store is opened in North Kyungsang Province, Korea.	Samsung becomes a producer of basic commodities such as sugar and wool.	Samsung expands overseas and is one of the first Korean companies to do so.	Also in the 1960s, the company penetrates the communications sector, successfully establishing a newspaper and broadcasting company.	The foundations for the present day Samsung are laid. Investment grows its strengths in the semiconductor, information and telecommunications industries.	Significant change in relation to Samsung's approach to management takes place.

The fruits of Samsung's research and development process resulted in a number of world firsts in design and technical innovation during 2007. The launch of the G800 mobile phone saw Samsung introduce the world's first five megapixel camera phone with 3x optical zoom, and a Xenon flash to enable close-ups and exceptional photo detail without sacrificing design for functionality.

Innovation is not exclusive to mobile phone handsets. Other developments include the arrival of the P2 MP3 player, which was ranked among the Top 10 Gadgets of the Year 2007 in Time Magazine as well as the world's first ultra mobile PC, the Q1. Samsung also launched its designer range of home appliances, combining strong design with leading-edge technology – namely the Refrigerator J-Series and Oven J-Series, conceived by Jasper Morrison, one of today's most influential industrial designers.

PROMOTION
Research and development, alongside product design, have yielded dramatic results for Samsung in recent years. However, the company

development has been supported and assisted by an aggressive marketing campaign. Six years ago, Samsung pledged to re-position its brand, aligning itself with premium, cutting-edge products. The policy has brought results; according to an influential survey of the world's most valuable brands by BusinessWeek and Interbrand, Samsung is now ranked at position 21, with a value of US$16.85 billion, increased from US$3.2 billion in 1999, making Samsung the most valuable Consumer Electronics brand in the world.

Sponsorship has played a significant role in increasing the visibility of Samsung's brand. Its sponsorships cover a diverse range of sporting clubs and events across the world, including Chelsea Football Club and Samsung Super League. Furthermore, Samsung has been an official sponsor of the Olympic Games since 1997. The Beijing Olympic Games in 2008 are expected to be the climax of the company's efforts of the last 10 years. Samsung has also collaborated with the European Olympic Committees (EOC) in launching the Youth Anti-Obesity programme. In addition, Samsung partners with Pink Ribbon charities in nine

European countries, to promote greater awareness of breast cancer.

BRAND VALUES
The Samsung brand is based around core values of technology, design and innovation and is associated with premium, cutting-edge global brands, such as Microsoft®, Audi, adidas, Twentieth Century Fox and Universal Music Group. All alliances involve the development of joint products or use existing Samsung technology to complement the partners' offerings.

www.samsung.co.uk

Things you didn't know about Samsung

Samsung launched the world's first 3D-enabled plasma HDTVs in 2008, following the debut of 3D-enabled DLP in 2007.

Collaborations between Samsung and some of the world's leading designers have included prestigious partnerships with Bang & Olufsen, Giorgio Armani and, in 2007, Jasper Morrison.

Samsung is the world's number one manufacturer of AMOLED (Active-Matrix Organic Light Emitting Diode) displays.

Samsung launched the world's first designer Refrigerator and Oven – the J-Series in 2007.

As the world's first producer of ultra mobile PCs, Samsung presented the HSDPA-enabled Q1 ultra – the next generation of Q1 – in 2007.

1993	2000	2006	2008
Chairman Kun-Hee Lee's introduction of 'New Management' acknowledges the need to transform the company in order to keep pace with a rapidly changing global economy.	A 'Digital Management' approach is adopted to ensure that Samsung maintains a leading position in the Information Age.	World firsts include the launch of an 82 inch full HDTV TFT-LCD, and a 10 mega pixel 8GB HDD cameraphone.	The Olympic Games in Beijing offer Samsung a prime sponsorship opportunity.

SKANSKA

As part of one of the world's largest construction groups, Skanska UK is a construction service business operating under two clear business streams – Construction and Infrastructure. Its business model is to integrate its core disciplines to deliver project solutions in its chosen market areas. By integrating all disciplines and working together with its clients, partners and supply chain, the company's aim is to make a difference to the way construction is normally delivered.

MARKET

Skanska is a multinational construction and development company headquartered in Sweden. Skanska was founded in 1887 as Aktiebolaget Skånska Cementgjuteriet manufacturing concrete products. It quickly diversified into a construction company and within 10 years the company received its first international order – which happened to be in Leeds.

The company played an important role in building up Sweden's infrastructure including roads, power plants, offices and housing.

Growth in Sweden was followed by international expansion. In the mid 1950s Skånska Cementgjuteriet made a major move into international markets, entering South America, Africa, Asia and, in 1971, the US market. The company was listed on the Stockholm Stock Exchange in 1965 and in 1984 the name 'Skanska', already in general use internationally, became the Group's official name.

During the latter part of the 1990s and early 2000s, Skanska embarked on its most expansive phase ever and sales doubled in only a few years. While the major portion of this growth was organic, a string of successful acquisitions also paved the way for Skanska's growth into a global company. One of these acquisitions, in November 2000, was the construction arm of Kvaerner –

a Norwegian conglomerate – which has become today's Skanska UK.

Skanska is a local player in many countries. Primary markets are the Nordic region, the UK, US, Central Europe and Latin America. The Group's operations are based on local business units, which have good knowledge of their respective markets, customers and suppliers. These local units are backed by Skanska's common values, procedures, financial strength and Group-wide experience. Skanska is thereby both a local construction company with global strength and an international builder with strong local roots.

Skanska's mission is to develop, build and maintain the physical environment for living, working and travelling. Skanska's aim is to be a leader in the markets in which it operates.

ACHIEVEMENTS

Skanska UK undertakes over £1.3 billion of work each year and prides itself on being able to draw on a combination of the best in British engineering with the best in Swedish innovation and design. All operating units have certification to the management systems ISO 14001, ISO 9001 and OHSAS 18001 and work strictly in accordance with the Skanska Code of Conduct.

Skanska has worked on a wide range of notable contracts. In London, a few recent examples include 30 St Mary Axe (the Gherkin), Moorhouse, Palestra on London's Southbank and the latest edition to its portfolio – Heron Tower.

Skanska has undertaken more infrastructure projects for the Channel Tunnel Rail Link than

1887	1897	1927	1965	2000	2008
Aktiebolaget Skånska Cementgjuteriet, later renamed Skanska, is founded by Rudolf Fredrik Berg.	Great Britain's National Telephone Company places Skanska's first international order; over 100km of hollow concrete blocks are supplied to hold telephone cables.	Sweden's first asphalt-paved road is constructed in Borlänge in central Sweden – a milestone in Skanska's role in building Sweden's infrastructure.	Skanska is listed on the Stockholm Stock Exchange.	Skanska enters the UK construction market by acquiring Kvaerner's Construction business, which had previously been part of the Trafalgar House Group.	Current projects include: Heron Tower; M1 Junctions 6a-10 widening works; National Grid's North London gas mains replacement programme; and the UK's first Building Schools for the Future (BSF) project, in Bristol.

any other contractor and is currently carrying out major civil engineering works for the new Docklands Light Railway extension to Stratford, which is expected to play a key role in transport plans for the 2012 games.

Skanska is a UK leader in the development and operation of Privately Financed Initiatives (PFI) and is currently undertaking the UK's largest hospital development – Barts and The London. The company is also one of the largest providers of utilities and infrastructure services in the UK.

During 2007, Skanska's progress in sustainable development was recognised and rewarded by numerous independent organisations. Its many accreditations and awards included Sustainable Contractor of the Year for the second year running.

PRODUCT

Skanska UK is a leading PFI provider. From the successful completion of the country's first PFI scheme in the late 1980s when it built the Queen Elizabeth II Bridge on the M25 crossing the Thames, Skanska's portfolio is now in excess of £3 billion, covering Healthcare, Custodial, Education, Transportation and Defence.

Complex civil engineering projects are often involved in developing and improving Britain's physical environment for living, working and travelling. The need to improve the infrastructure of our roads, railways and utilities has lead to upgrades that draw upon a wide range of expertise and experience. Skanska combines civil engineering and utilities expertise with its specialist businesses to provide total solutions to its clients.

In the market of commercial construction, Skanska UK's capability and experience, encompassing the entire scope of construction, is unique. Skanska offers its clients more than just a traditional construction service.

RECENT DEVELOPMENTS

Skanska UK employs over 5,500 people, placing them at the heart of its business. The company operates across design,

construction, civil engineering, integrated projects, piling, steel decking, mechanical, electrical and facilities services, utilities, infrastructure services and ceilings as well as decorative plasterwork units. The company operates throughout the UK, integrating the skills of its operating units in a collaborative style in order to provide a construction service to its clients that delivers real benefits.

PROMOTION

Skanska's approach to brand promotion in the UK could be described as a 'little bit different'. While the company does occasionally promote its services and skills in the traditional way with advertising and exhibitions, this is secondary to the way in which the company prefers to be seen and recognised.

At Skanska, it's much more about being truly recognised for the way it lives up to its brand values. This is by the performance and behaviour of its people – Skanska people are 'team players who care and want to make a difference to the way construction is delivered' – creating projects that its staff, clients, partners, and the communities in which it works are proud of.

Every office and major Skanska construction site in the UK is planned using a bespoke approach to meet the needs of its teams, partners, and clients – creating a 'shop window' for the company's visual brand identity.

Skanska is extremely proud of its third party recognition, which it considers a true measure of the value and performance of the company and the brand. In the last few years, Skanska has received over 100 external awards not only for the projects it has constructed, but for key areas of its performance including Health and Safety, the Environment and Sustainability. In 2007, Skanska received the prestigious accolade of Most Considerate Contractor. Furthermore, Skanska is extremely proud of its Business Superbrands 2008 status.

BRAND VALUES

Skanska's key responsibility is to develop and maintain an economically sound and prosperous business. It is committed to the countries, communities and environments in which it operates, as well as its employees and business partners.

Skanska stands for technical know-how and competence combined with an understanding of its customers' needs. The ability to apply these skills to new areas enables it to produce the innovation that its customers demand. Skanska aims to develop, build and maintain the physical environment for living, working and travelling, and to be the client's first choice in construction related services and project development.

www.skanska.co.uk

Things you didn't know about Skanska

Miniland London at LEGOLAND Windsor, was built with the help of Skanska.

Skanska is the only Swedish contractor in the UK.

More than 56,000 people work for Skanska worldwide.

In December 2006, Skanska acquired McNicholas plc and became one of the largest providers of utilities and infrastructure services in the UK.

Snap-on.

Founded in 1920, Snap-on is a leading global innovator, manufacturer and distributor of tools, diagnostics and equipment solutions for professional users. Product lines include hand and power tools, tool storage, diagnostics software, information and management systems and workshop equipment.

MARKET

Snap-on has more than 85 years of one-to-one relationships with professional tool users. The company sells its products and services in more than 150 countries in North and South America, Europe and Asia. Consistently delivering high value-added products and services, its customers include automotive workshops and their technicians, manufacturers, users in aerospace, commercial aviation, the marine industry, construction, agriculture, mining, oil and gas industries, together with military forces worldwide.

Snap-on tools are used in a wide range of industries around the world – from servicing cars in dealerships to motor sport, including Formula One and from the maintenance of the jet engine to use in the oil fields in the Arabian Gulf.

ACHIEVEMENTS

In the UK Snap-on received the coveted 2007 Frost & Sullivan Technicians' Choice Award in all four major product categories – hand tools, power tools, diagnostics and tool storage. Snap-on was recognised by this diagnostics survey as the clear market leader for automotive hand-held scan tools. It also led the competition in all categories explored, including Best Quality, Most Innovative, Best Retailer Customer Experience and Overall Best Brand.

Snap-on is one of the longest serving members of the British Franchise Association, the self-regulating governing body for the UK's £10 billion franchising industry. Most recently the company was acclaimed as the top UK franchise by winning the Association's 2007 Franchisor of the Year award.

PRODUCT

Snap-on's products and brand command enduring allegiance. The products often become treasured objects for virtually every type of professional tool user. With a focus on innovation and quality, Snap-on's designers and engineers, whether working on the latest screwdriver design or vehicle diagnostics software development, are continuously looking for ways to improve the company's products and customer efficiency. The company currently holds 2,000 active and pending patents.

One of the company's most recent innovations has been a revolutionary new ratchet with Dual80™ technology. A ratchet is not only one of the most constant components of the technician's toolkit but also one which takes the most stress. Building on its successful sealed head design Snap-on has now developed a twin pawl technology which makes this ratchet one of the smoothest and strongest ratchets in the world today.

1918	1920	1945	1959	1965	1978
Snap-on co-founder Joe Johnson develops the interchangeable socket set.	The Snap-on Wrench Company is formed.	Salesmen for the company start carrying inventory.	Joe Johnson retires.	Snap-on forms its UK subsidiary, Snap-on Tools Ltd.	Snap-on Tools Corporation lists on the New York Stock Exchange.

In 2007 the company celebrated its 1,000th UK MODIS™ sale. MODIS is a complete premium price handheld diagnostic solution, which helps the technician pinpoint and diagnose problems on today's complex vehicles. In 1985 cars with engine management systems made one calculation per second. Even the most basic car today calculates at a rate of a million times a second. Snap-on is at the forefront of this technology and products such as MODIS™ maintain this technology-led ascendancy.

RECENT DEVELOPMENTS

Snap-on is driving for even faster customer responsiveness and is strengthening internal processes to advance its competitive position and increase sales and earnings. Its Rapid Continuous Improvement (RCI) process has been adopted throughout the organisation. The process focuses on four principles – safety, quality, delivery and cost.

These four principles will help drive profitable growth and financial performance. Snap-on's enhanced long-range planning process facilitates growth through internal development, growth of its customer base – particularly in the emerging markets – and a continuous stream of innovative new products.

The company recently acquired ProQuest Business Solutions, a world leader in electronic parts catalogues. Renamed Snap-on Business Solutions (SBS) its products transform complex technical data for parts catalogues into easily accessed electronic information for the world's automotive, power equipment and power sports manufacturers and their dealer networks. SBS also provides warranty management systems and analytics to help vehicle dealerships manage and track performance.

PROMOTION

The one-to-one relationship that Snap-on franchisees have with customers is the primary way that the quality of Snap-on is sold. Snap-on franchisees pay weekly visits to customers, to keep them up-to-date on

new products and services. They also handle warranty repair and replacement when necessary and provide affordable programmes for technicians to build their tool kits and their capabilities. The values of the brand have been handed down from generation to generation.

Snap-on's brand is also visibly associated with motor sports, most notably Formula One, MotoGP, World and British Superbikes and the World Rally Championship. The company's staff spend time with some of the best racing teams in the world to understand exactly what they need from tools and equipment under extreme race conditions. Snap-on monitors how products perform at the track to consistently enhance the quality, durability, and performance of the tools for the professional tool user. The company is continually developing new motor racing themed products in tool storage, hand tools and power tools, inexorably linking the modern vehicle technician to the pinnacle of his profession.

BRAND VALUES

The word 'Snap-on' aims to conjure up images of quality, service, and innovation as well as conveying superior workmanship. There is a distinct pride of ownership among customers who use Snap-on products. The essence of the Snap-on brand can be boiled down to seven key attributes: high-quality products, exceptional service, innovation, expertise, premium price, productivity, and leadership.

www.snapon.com

Things you didn't know about Snap-on

In 1918 Snap-on co-founder Joe Johnson pioneered the interchangeable socket set for professional mechanics, using the slogan 'Five do the Work of Fifty'.

As part of the 1941 Lend-Lease programme, quantities of Snap-on products arrived in the UK to support the World War II war effort. One of these tools was a tappet adjuster for use on the Supermarine Spitfire's Merlin engine.

The longest tool Snap-on ever made was a square drive extension wrench, which was used in a nuclear reactor. The wrench was 25 feet long and always had to float upright in water.

Snap-on tools accompany most of the US voyages into space and were most conspicuously used as part of the Apollo space programme.

1992	2005	2007	
Snap-on acquires the Sun Electric Corporation.	Snap-on customers donate more than £35,000 to its UK Guissa Quid campaign for The Prostate Cancer Charity.	Guissa Quid raises more than £53,000 for The Prostate Cancer Charity.	Also in 2007 Snap-on wins the UK Franchisor of the Year award.

The **Banker**

The Banker, part of the Financial Times group, is the premier magazine for the world's investment, retail and commercial banking sectors. Established over 80 years ago The Banker has sought to stimulate and inform, offering an unrivalled combination of authoritative news, features, surveys and interviews.

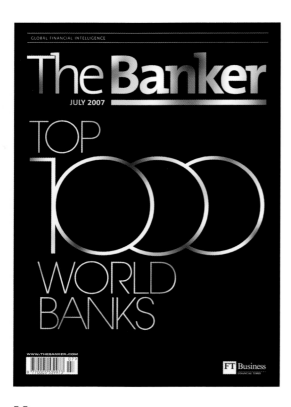

MARKET

The Banker was established in 1926 and is the leading global publication for both banks and companies alike.

Covering Central & Eastern Europe, Western Europe, Asia, the Americas, the Middle East and Africa, the combination of relevant features, surveys and other in-depth contributions has made this title one of the most respected among global financial media. The magazine has been cited as essential reading for leading CEOs, CFOs, corporate treasurers and central bank governors. The Banker has an ABC audited circulation of more than 28,000 and with an average of three readers per copy, reaches an audience of over 90,000 of the world's most influential finance professionals.

ACHIEVEMENTS

The Banker prides itself on providing high quality, relevant content across the global banking arena.

Its rankings and awards are respected as industry benchmarks. Its 2007 Bank of the Year Awards highlighted winners in a record 143 countries and its Top 1000 World Banks 2007 is the definitive ranking of its type. Over the past few years the Top 1000 has tracked the rise of banks from the emerging markets.

Every year an elite group of world leaders and top bankers are interviewed in the magazine giving a precious insight into key financial and economic trends.

PRODUCT

The Banker is a monthly publication and content is available both in printed form and online at TheBanker.com. It is read by senior level decision makers in financial institutions, corporations, investment management firms and central banks in more than 190 countries.

1926	1937	1946	1950s	1970	1990s
The Banker is established by Brendan Bracken.	Bracken ceases his editorial reign.	Various articles in The Banker address post war financial issues.	The Banker deals with issues of post war expansion.	The first worldwide ranking of banks is published, covering 300 banks. In later years, the ranking will go on to cover the top 1000 world banks.	The Banker includes a specific section on technology issues facing banks.

The Banker's journalists travel all over the globe to provide relevant and detailed content with regular features covering capital markets, retail banking, FX and derivatives, cash and securities services and technology. Popular articles include the Bracken column, a think tank named after the magazine's founder Brendan Bracken; Viewpoint, commentary by industry leaders; Karina's Kolumn, interviews with the people that shape the world of international finance and politics; and RegRage, looking at how the next piece of legislation will affect you.

The Banker publishes the following awards, listings and rankings throughout the year: Bank of the Year Awards, Deals of the Year, Investment Banking Awards, Technology Awards and Top 1000 World Banks.

The annual Top 1000 World Banks ranking forms part of the July edition of The Banker and is internationally recognised as the leading guide to the global strength of banks. It ranks the world's top banks by tier one capital as well as by assets and a range of other measures.

RECENT DEVELOPMENTS

The Banker has recently launched its Leadership Series, assembling thought leaders and opinion formers to participate in a series of debates organised around agenda setting themes. Readers can keep in touch with this agenda via the medium of their choice, either streaming video, podcasts or print.

PROMOTION

The Banker is based upon more than 80 years of global expertise and remains a leading brand due to an effective positioning and marketing communications strategy.

The marketing strategy is centered around delivering high quality content in an innovative and audience appropriate way, using an integrated marketing strategy and the full range of communications tools. The recent launch of The Banker Leadership Series, for example, sees leading industry figures get involved in a series of debates on agenda setting content which can be consumed in the reader's preferred medium.

The Banker is also distributed at the annual meetings of the World Economic Forum, the International Monetary Fund/World Bank, the African Development Bank, Asian Development Bank, European Bank for Reconstruction and Development, Inter-American Development Bank and The Institute of International Finance.

BRAND VALUES

The Banker has clear brand values and goals: to remain prestigious, pioneering and thought provoking.

Since its launch The Banker has remained a leading product that is innovative, informative, reliable and well respected – and by effective brand management, it intends to stay that way. The Banker has constant input from key industry figures and its journalists travel the globe to ensure it delivers compelling and relevant content.

As part of the Financial Times group, The Banker is committed to the community and supports a wide range of charities which in 2007 included: Community Service Volunteers, Children's Safety Education Foundation, UNICEF, Unicorn Theatre, Crisis and Ray of Sunshine.

www.thebanker.com

Things you didn't know about The Banker

The Banker's founder, Brendan Bracken, went on to be a minister during Sir Winston Churchill's wartime Government.

The first issue of The Banker cost one shilling and profiled Montagu Norman, the then governor of the Bank of England.

The Banker is read in over 190 countries including some of the smallest in the world such as Nauru and San Marino.

1996
Bill Gates praises the success of The Banker.

2001
The Banker discusses the potential impact of the euro.

2003
Brian Caplen begins editing The Banker.

2007
The Banker reports the rise of the emerging markets, especially Brazil, Russia, India and China.

The Daily Telegraph

The Daily Telegraph delivers quality journalism six days a week and is the biggest selling broadsheet newspaper in the UK. Noted for its outstanding coverage of news, both home and overseas, the stand-alone broadsheet business section is highly respected in the city and the wider business community. The newspaper's appearance is defined by its sophisticated use of traditional typography and strong photographs.

MARKET

The combined circulation of UK national daily newspapers in September 2007 was 10.9 million, of which the four qualities account for 2.16 million per day on average. The Daily Telegraph takes 41.2 per cent circulation share of the quality market, 237,000 copies ahead of The Times. According to ABC figures for September 2007, The Daily Telegraph achieved an audited average daily circulation figure of 890,973. Furthermore, the average daily readership stands at 2,167,000 adults (Source: NRS July 2006 to June 2007, Mon-Sat).

ACHIEVEMENTS

Telegraph Media Group (TMG) was awarded the title of Best Online Consumer Publisher in the Association of Online Publishers' (AOP) 2007 awards, for leading the field in applying the strengths of traditional publishing to digital platforms. TMG was nominated for a total of 11 awards, more than any other publisher.

Furthermore, The Daily Telegraph has been voted the Personal Finance Newspaper of the Year at the 2007 Bradford & Bingley Personal Finance Media Awards. Your Money, the Telegraph's personal finance section, was praised for its combination of excellent news delivery, presentation and objectivity. Faith Archer, deputy personal finance editor, was also named the Personal Finance Consumer Mortgage Writer of the Year.

PRODUCT

The Daily Telegraph's separate, dedicated Business section is recognised for its accurate, bold and insightful coverage and

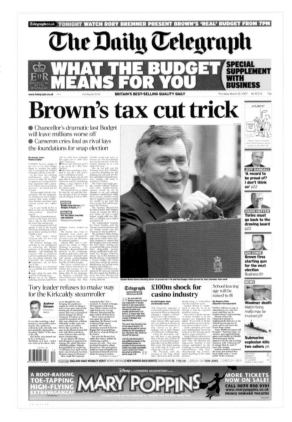

boasts an award-winning team of journalists including Jeff Randall, Ambrose Evans-Pritchard, Christopher Hope, Edmund Conway, Ian Cowie, Richard Fletcher, Alistair Osborne and Russell Hotten. Damian Reece is group executive for business across all three Telegraph titles (The Daily Telegraph, The Sunday Telegraph and Telegraph.co.uk). In addition, the newspapers and website regularly feature contributions from leading business figures.

In the summer of 2006 The Daily Telegraph Business section's 'Fair Trials for British Business' campaign provoked 7,500 signatures of support, while in 2007 its campaign for an EU Referendum has resulted in more than 110,000 readers signing up, indicating once again that Telegraph campaigns resonate strongly in the consciousness of its readers.

When Gordon Brown delivered his final Budget as Chancellor of the Exchequer on

1855	1862	1897	1947	1987	1992
The first Daily Telegraph & Courier is published, having been founded as a vehicle for its proprietor, Colonel Sleigh, to wage a vendetta against the Duke of Cambridge and his conduct in the Crimea War.	The Daily Telegraph's championing of charitable causes sees the newspaper raising £6,000 for starving cotton workers in Lancashire.	A young Winston Churchill reports from the North West Frontier for the Telegraph.	In April Telegraph sales exceed one million.	The Telegraph moves from Fleet Street to the Isle of Dogs.	The Telegraph leaves the Isle of Dogs for Canary Wharf.

21st March 2007 the Telegraph's editorial team were on hand to provide up-to-the-minute coverage, comment and insight into what the latest round of tax and spending changes really meant.

The Telegraph's multi-platform approach allowed its readers to get the latest Budget news and reaction online as it happened. This exclusive content included breaking news throughout the day, audio reaction from Roger Bootle at 2.45pm, a downloadable Budget edition of TelegraphPM at 3pm, a Budget calculator – to help readers find out how it affected them – went live at 4pm, and at 5.30pm Damian Reece presented reaction to the Chancellor's speech in a special Budget Business Show.

Following Budget day, comprehensive analysis appeared in a special 16-page Budget edition of the Business section as well as additional content on Telegraph.co.uk. One of the highlights on Telegraph.co.uk was the exclusive video of Rory Bremner's 'Real Budget Speech', featuring the popular satirist as Gordon Brown delivering his no-nonsense take on the day's revelations.

The Telegraph is committed to providing the latest Business news and expert analysis from the City and around the world in print, online, via video or podcast or direct to mobile devices in an ever-evolving and engaging way.

One of the most popular features of The Daily Telegraph Business has long been its Alex cartoon. A stalwart of the Business section since his creators joined the Telegraph in 1992, Alex is held in great affection amongst the business community. Much more than a cartoon, Alex comments on the wheeling and dealing of the business world, winning awards and accolades for his creators.

In 2007 Alex was brought to life on stage in London, with Robert Bathurst in the title role. In an acclaimed performance, Alex is ingeniously recreated with a supporting cast of animated characters from the cartoon, appearing alongside him.

RECENT DEVELOPMENTS

As a result of The Daily Telegraph's success in integrating newspaper and online news publishing, the Telegraph's multimedia production has flourished. 2007 saw the launch of Telegraph TV News Now, an online news programme featuring some of the Telegraph's biggest talents including Jeff Randall, Andrew Pierce, Sarah Crompton and Henry Winter. Telegraph TV is updated throughout the day, offering news, business, sport and entertainment features on-demand.

The Telegraph's current affairs programming is complemented by a suite of feature-based video services reflecting its editorial strengths from Travel and Motoring to Fashion and the Arts. One of the most successful and established Telegraph TV programmes is The Business Show. Presented by Damian Reece and Sunday Telegraph deputy editor, Dan Roberts, The Business Show provides a concise, daily business bulletin featuring the latest City news alongside company and market reports and interviews with industries' biggest names.

It's not just coverage of big business that the Telegraph is renowned for; providing support to small businesses and helping readers with their personal finances are also high on its agenda. Telegraph.co.uk's Your Money website is dedicated to providing essential information, advice and services to readers from financial comparisons to Liz Dolan's agony aunt-style consumer advice column. The Telegraph Business Club features case studies, master-classes, events and a host of services covering strategy, personnel, finance, technology and operations to help entrepreneurs and SME professionals succeed.

PROMOTION

The Daily Telegraph ran a successful campaign in 2007 promoting its Budget coverage with online advertising to drive users to Telegraph.co.uk.

The campaign not only promoted Telegraph.co.uk's live budget coverage and in-depth analysis the following day, but also, through rich media advertising, the online video of Rory Bremner's Real Budget Speech.

The campaign combined display advertising on the finance channels of sites including Yahoo!, MSN and AOL, PPC search marketing and viral seeding of Rory Bremner's Real Budget Speech.

As a result, Telegraph.co.uk was the most visited newspaper website for budget coverage on Budget Day. The campaign generated six per cent uplift in copy sales for the 16-page Budget special in The Daily Telegraph the following day – demonstrating how both web and newspaper coverage can work successfully in tandem.

BRAND VALUES

The Daily Telegraph brand values are accuracy, honesty, integrity, quality and heritage.

Its brand personality is intelligent, British, trusted, good humoured, authoritative and engaging.

www.telegraph.co.uk

1994
The Electronic Telegraph becomes the first British newspaper to launch an internet presence.

2004
The Barclay Brothers buy the Telegraph Group.

2005
The Daily Telegraph relaunches with a stand-alone broadsheet Business section and a separate compact Sport section. It also becomes the first British newspaper to have a daily podcast.

2006
The Group rebrands to become Telegraph Media Group and moves from Canary Wharf into state-of-the-art offices on Buckingham Palace Road, London.

The Open University

The Open University (OU) is the university of choice for busy professionals, allowing them to study without disruption to their careers. Some 70 per cent of students remain in paid work throughout their study, benefiting from applying their knowledge and skills immediately to their career. The OU's UK students have voted it top for overall student satisfaction in all three National Student Surveys to date, endorsing the OU's unrivalled flexibility, quality and support.

MARKET

In creating the new Department for Innovation, Universities and Skills, the Government is recognising the need for 'greater and more sustained engagement between universities, colleges and employers in training, skill development and innovation'. The Open University and the OU Business School (OUBS) work with thousands of organisations to promote professional and management skills that deliver business results. With its range of business, management and vocational courses as well as renowned flexible learning methods, the OU is increasingly front of mind when companies of all sizes are looking at staff development programmes that are cost-effective without compromising on quality.

Whether public, private or not-for-profit, organisations today are challenged by the rapid pace of change, advances in technology and the impact of global competition. The Open University is well-placed to help businesses respond to these challenges. In particular, the OU's capability for scale and reach makes it the obvious partner for organisations with multi-site locations in the UK and beyond. Wherever employees are based, an organisation can be confident that the same quality of teaching and support will be delivered. A growing number of employers are looking to recruit staff direct from sixth forms and colleges – Open University courses and qualifications can be offered to these young people, giving them the twin benefits of starting a career

and getting a degree. Similarly, staff with potential who may not have had formal education beyond GCSE level could also benefit from OU study.

Outside the UK, the University continues to build partnerships with businesses and higher education institutions across the world – a reflection of the increasingly globalised nature of modern business.

ACHIEVEMENTS

Less than four decades since its launch in 1969, The Open University is widely respected as one of the finest teaching universities in the world. Its students give the OU an overall satisfaction rating higher than any other university's in the annual National Student Survey – an accolade the OU has achieved for the past three years.

The OU Business School (OUBS) is among the largest business schools in Europe and among the largest MBA providers in the world. The OUBS is also one of an elite group of business schools that have been triple accredited by AMBA, AACSB International and EQUIS.

1966	1967	1969	1971	1973	1983
Labour's manifesto for the 1966 General Election contained a commitment to establish the University of the Air.	Detailed work on planning the University begins after the election, which Labour wins.	The Open University is formally opened.	The first students begin work on the first of the University's courses.	The University's first degree ceremony is held.	The OU Business School is opened.

One of the key factors in the OU's reputation for teaching is its internationally-renowned research. Open University researchers work closely with industry to meet research and development needs and with government and public services to help to develop and explore the impact of new policies and practices.

The explosion of new media means that it is possible to reach and engage students, to bring learners and teachers together, in previously unimagined ways. The OU remains at the cutting-edge in harnessing new technologies that will enable it to deliver the very best learning experience to a potentially worldwide audience.

Underpinning its major role in developing best practice in higher education, the University is one of only two in the UK to have been awarded the leadership of four nationally important Centres for Excellence in Teaching and Learning; the project has attracted funding of £12 million over a five-year period.

Outside the UK, The Open University is the only British university dedicated to delivering learning inside Africa. Whether it is training teachers, supporting curriculum development, developing future leaders, improving the use of ICT in classrooms or simply helping a child come to terms with the loss of their parents from HIV/Aids, The Open University pursues a strategy in Africa to help build capacity.

PRODUCT

The Open University's portfolio features supported open learning courses at all levels of higher education – from Openings introductory programmes to postgraduate masters and doctorate programmes. More than 580 courses are offered in subjects including arts and humanities; business and management; computing, education; engineering, environment; health and social care; information technology; law; mathematics; modern languages; science; social sciences; and technology.

The University is also adding to its range of foundation degrees, which are targeted

at those in work who are seeking formal recognition for vocationally-focused learning.

Furthermore, the OU's new Centre for Professional Learning Development Services offers tailored courses to develop key capabilities including leadership skills, change management and managing people. The Centre can also work in partnership with organisations to develop and deliver in-house programmes based on the OU's proven materials and methods. The OU's academic Credit Rating Service can assign a credit value to professional bodies, employers and other organisations seeking recognition for their own programmes and courses.

RECENT DEVELOPMENTS

In 2006 The Open University launched OpenLearn, a website providing free worldwide access to educational resources. In its first year, OpenLearn was used by more than one million learners and educators across the globe.

This was followed in 2007 by the launch of a partnership between the OU and the Royal College of Nursing, created to initiate imaginative development and change in healthcare education and practice.

PROMOTION

The University promotes its provision across a wide range of media channels – television, radio, posters, exhibitions, national and specialist press, relationship marketing and,

The first thing you'll learn is:
Every course is a unique adventure.

increasingly, digital platforms. The OU's unique partnership with the BBC is also key. Popular programmes such as Coast, Child of Our Time and, most recently, Nature of Britain are a vital part of the OU's awareness raising activity in addition to bringing learning to life for the BBC's viewing public.

BRAND VALUES

The Open University retains an ambition to continue to break down social and economic barriers to make higher education as accessible as possible. The development of an increasingly comprehensive and diverse range of courses that make lifelong learning relevant to everyone, whatever their previous experience or ambition, is part of this intent.

It stands for being innovative, international, democratic and inclusive, and is driven by a goal to achieve ever-higher standards of academic excellence and achievement for all its students.

www.open.ac.uk

Things you didn't know about The Open University

Over 67 per cent of FTSE 100 companies have sponsored – or sponsor – their staff on OU courses.

Almost three-quarters of OU students are aged under 44.

Professional bodies recognise many OU modules and qualifications.

Thirty-five per cent of all part-time undergraduate students in the UK are studying with The Open University.

1987	1998		2006
Student numbers exceed 100,000 for the first time.	The 25th anniversary of the first degree ceremony and the conferment of the University's 200,000th graduate are celebrated.	Also in 1998, student numbers reach 200,000 for the first time.	OpenLearn, which provides free access worldwide to educational resources, is launched.

Travis Perkins

Travis Perkins is a leading brand in the builders' merchant market. A supplier to one of the largest UK industries – building and construction – Travis Perkins continues to follow a successful growth strategy of acquisition and organic investment. The company supplies more than 160,000 product lines to trade professionals and self-builders including general building materials, timber, plumbing and heating, kitchens, bathrooms, landscaping materials and tool hire.

MARKET

In 2006, the UK building and plumbers' merchants market was worth an estimated £13.5 billion (Source: AMA Research June 2007), covering heavyside materials such as cement, bricks, timber and gravel, and lightside materials including bathrooms, plumbing and heating, tools and tool hire.

The Travis Perkins group currently has over 1,080 branches across the UK and employs more than 16,000 people nationwide. It has a 10 per cent share of the DIY and builders' merchants market. Travis Perkins' main competitors in the builders' merchant market include Build Center, Howdens, Jewson, Plumb Center, and Screwfix.

ACHIEVEMENTS

For 210 years Travis Perkins has been at the forefront of UK building supplies. Throughout its history, Travis Perkins has pre-empted the demands of the industries it supplies and has built its business by developing and acquiring specialist merchants to strengthen its offering.

The company is dedicated to creating services that help improve efficiency for customers. This was demonstrated clearly in June 2007 when it opened a new branch exclusively for Luminus Group, a social housing provider in Huntingdon.

The branch stocks the materials required by tradesmen in Luminus' maintenance division, who carry out repairs in over 7,000 homes, and for Luminus Suregas, which serves 22,000 homes. This type of service is also offered to a number of other social housing groups and local authorities throughout the country.

Travis Perkins is committed to the communities in which it operates. Its current '1,000 projects, 1,000 places, 1,000 days' initiative is a nationwide scheme through which Travis Perkins' staff donate their time to projects that benefit local communities and charities. Since the initiative was launched in 2006, many projects have been completed, including the production of a raised vegetable garden for Ridgeway School for the Disabled in Bedford, offering easy access from wheelchair height.

Travis Perkins has been recognised throughout its history for best business practice. In 2004, it was awarded FSC and PEFC Chain of Custody Certification in recognition of the strong commitment shown by the company to using responsibly managed timber resources. Furthermore, in January 2007, Travis Perkins won the Strategic Planning Society's Best Objectives and Strategy by a FTSE 250 Company award, due to its evaluation, discussion and presentation of its strategy in its 2005 Annual Report.

Travis Perkins, in partnership with The Wrekin Housing Trust, won the Procurement and Technology Improving Performance award at The British Building Maintenance Awards in November 2006. The partnership was rewarded for its innovative changes to procurement practices and the creation of a digital superstore, resulting in efficiency savings for the Trust of more than £300,000 in the first year. It also improved tenant satisfaction with 94 per cent of tenants satisfied with the Trust's repairs and maintenance services.

1899
Travis & Arnold forms as a partnership and opens a number of branches in the Midlands as a merchant of timber and other wood products.

1970
Travis & Arnold begins more than a decade of substantial acquisitions, including Brown & Son of Chelmsford, Ellis & Everard Building Supplies, and Kennedys.

1988
Travis & Arnold merges with Sandell Perkins to become Travis Perkins plc.

1999
Travis Perkins acquires Keyline Builders Merchants with its 101 branches and £300 million turnover. A further 38 branches are added to the network with the acquisition of Sharpe & Fisher.

PRODUCT

The Travis Perkins group has six operating brands: Travis Perkins' builders' merchant brand sells all the materials needed for a full house build and has a network of over 570 branches; Keyline has 76 branches and specialises in heavy building materials, civils and drainage products; City Plumbing Supplies specialises in plumbing and heating materials, covering 180 branches; with 34 branches, CCF is dedicated to dry lining, partitioning, insulation, ceilings and fire protection; Wickes operates 183 stores for serious DIY customers and tradesmen; and Benchmarx, a specialist kitchens and joinery business, is the newest addition to the Travis Perkins group, operating from 22 branches.

Trademate, Travis Perkins' transactional website, allows account customers to order products online, collect from branch and manage their invoices. Other services include: Tool Hire, which delivers tools to site in four hours; an estimating service that helps customers to accurately cost a job; delivery to site; and kitchen and bathroom design services.

RECENT DEVELOPMENTS

Travis Perkins is firmly focused on providing sustainable solutions to its customers. With around 27 per cent of the UK's carbon emissions coming directly from the home, Travis Perkins has been looking continuously for new technologies to help the building industry reduce this volume.

In July 2007, Travis Perkins opened its first renewable energy centre in Chelmsford. The branch has working displays and demonstrations, including solar energy systems and ground source heat pumps. Specialist staff are also able to provide advice and help specify the right products for each job.

Over the past year, additional Travis Perkins branches have been opened, extending coverage in Cumbria, Kent, Leicestershire, Lancashire, Lincolnshire and Wales.

The specialist kitchens and joinery brand Benchmarx was established in 2006; this is a one-stop-shop for kitchens, joinery, doors and flooring. Following its successful launch in London and the South East, Travis Perkins will be looking to replicate the model in other areas of the country in 2008.

PROMOTION

Although the internet has become an important part of its promotion strategy, Travis Perkins recognises that the majority of its customer base is not office based. Therefore, more traditional forms of marketing are used to maintain awareness of products and services.

Customer focused marketing includes targeted direct mail with relevant offers and information. All branches are supported with brochures, price lists, point of sale material and offers. Travis Perkins stays in touch with the relevant trade press through providing a news feed and holding media events. In addition, new branches benefit from public relations

campaigns targeting local media, advertising, open days at the branch and direct mail.

Sponsorship and community activities play a key part in ensuring the brand maintains a local presence. With headquarters in Northampton, Travis Perkins has been the sponsor of local club Northampton Saints Rugby Club since 2001. The brand is highly visible to all visitors at the ground and is prominently displayed on the kit.

BRAND VALUES

Travis Perkins has built its business foundations on listening to its customers and keeping in touch with them. Travis Perkins is committed to offering its customers an honest, reliable service and product range, where staff are knowledgeable and offer a personal service. The branch staff are the key to Travis Perkins' success, with many of them building lasting relationships with their customers over many years.

www.travisperkins.co.uk

Things you didn't know about Travis Perkins

Travis Perkins' Dartmouth store is built on the site of an old prison.

When the floods hit Yorkshire in June 2007, Keyline Morley delivered more than 300 tonnes of grit sand in bulk bags, to use as flood defences, in just a few days.

CCF, owned by Travis Perkins, supplies a third of all office ceiling tiles in the UK.

The Pimlico branch of Travis Perkins is the UK's oldest Timber merchant, having been trading on the original site since 1844.

2001
Travis Perkins opens its 500th branch in Preston. The following year Travis Perkins acquires City Plumbing Supplies Limited and Commercial Ceiling Factors (CCF).

2003
Further acquisitions – of Jayhard (53 branches) and B&G (12 branches) – reinforce Travis Perkins' presence in the supply and distribution of plumbing and heating materials.

2004
Travis Perkins achieves Chain of Custody accreditation for all of its timber-supplying branches – more than any other national merchant.

2005
Travis Perkins Group acquires 176 Wickes Home Improvement stores. The following year, Travis Perkins Group opens its 1,000th branch in Hatfield.

WARWICK
BUSINESS SCHOOL

Warwick Business School (WBS) is a leading 'thought-developer' and innovator, in the top one per cent of global business schools. Its students come from over 120 countries to learn at undergraduate, masters, MBA and PhD level. WBS educates and develops global citizens, and promotes new knowledge to benefit business and society, through its executive education and applied research. WBS is consistently top-rated for teaching quality and research.

MARKET

There are more than 5,000 business schools across the world, aiming to develop the next generation of business leaders. Warwick Business School is one of the largest in Europe and ranks in the top one per cent worldwide. As the largest department of the University of Warwick, WBS aims to offer its students both excellent facilities and a prestigious reputation.

A high quality business education is valued by employers and employees alike; employers can gain competitive advantage by recruiting and developing talent with knowledge and critical thinking skills, while individuals can gain new options for career progression, both sideways and upwards. With literally thousands of schools offering MBAs worldwide, the business school market is incredibly competitive. To be a success, and to attract successful people, needs a respected brand. WBS was the first

Changing lives, challenging minds
Global business education □ Graduates □ Consultants □ Research □ Executive Education
www.wbs.ac.uk

among fewer than 30 schools to be endorsed by all three international business school accreditation schemes.

WBS academics work to produce world-leading research in all fields of management. With recognised research leaders across disciplines as diverse as pensions, industrial dispute resolution, business strategy, customer service, enterprise, corporate social responsibility, sports management, public sector governance, sales marketing, and energy policy, people go to WBS to explore grounded, well researched ideas that work in the real world. WBS research and expert opinion is valuable, sometimes crucial, to the success of corporations, not-for-profit organisations, Government and society.

ACHIEVEMENTS

WBS has achieved a global reputation for excellence in just 40 years. It has one of the broadest subject bases and most highly regarded faculty of any business school in the world. In the last national assessment of University research output, WBS achieved the highest five star accolade, placing it as one of the top three research business schools in the UK. These research credentials are fundamental to its culture and differentiate it from teaching colleges or commercial training companies. WBS has been awarded more Economic and Social Research Council (ESRC) funding for students for 2006-2008 than any other UK business school.

The performance of its degree programmes continues to excel. Its undergraduate

1965	1981	1986	1989	1997	1999
The University of Warwick is founded by Royal Charter. Two years later, WBS is created as the School of Industrial and Business Studies, with five staff, 24 students and three courses.	The Warwick MBA brand is launched.	The Warwick MBA by distance learning launches.	WBS achieves five star rating for research excellence.	On its 30th anniversary, WBS has 3,160 students, 263 staff, and turnover of £12.4 million.	WBS becomes the first business school in the world to hold accreditation from all three global management education bodies: AMBA, EQUIS and AACSB.

programme is consistently ranked in the top five business and management degrees in the UK; WBS was also ranked 10 out of 10 for job prospects in The Guardian University Guide 2008.

In addition, its portfolio of masters courses provides highly specialised learning in areas of business that are increasingly important in the search for sustainable competitive advantage.

More than 20 years of combined learning experience enable WBS to deliver the Warwick MBA to over 2,400 experienced managers each year, wherever they are in the world.

Furthermore, its long-standing commitment to work across the private, public and voluntary sectors created the Warwick MPA – the first MBA for the public sector in the UK.

Warwick Business School's reputation means WBS graduates are highly sought after by business leaders and can be found in senior positions around the world. Its expertise is clear from its diverse list of clients and sponsors, including Accenture, AT Kearney, The Bank of England, Barclays, BP, British Antarctic Survey, The Cabinet Office, Capgemini, Deutsche Post, Experian, GlaxoSmithKline, Grant Thornton, IBM, Islamic Bank of Britain, Johnson & Johnson, JPMorgan, Nestlé, PepsiCo, Procter & Gamble, SABMiller, Siemens, UBS Investment Bank, Unilever and Vodafone.

PRODUCT
Warwick Business School has something to offer individuals at every stage of their career. It offers a range of business and management undergraduate degrees; nine specialist masters courses; a generalist MSc in Management; the popular and flexible Warwick MBA, as well as its public sector equivalent, the Warwick MPA; and one of the world's most respected PhD programmes. For corporate clients and individuals, it also offers a range of diplomas, short courses and customised programmes.

WBS consults with industry to keep its programmes fresh, relevant and accessible. The fact that many graduates return for further study at WBS later in their career demonstrates its effective blend of academic research with the practicalities of the workplace. Learning by sharing experience and insight is key to the student experience at WBS. Alumni members, which number 21,000 in total, have cited the combination of a highly intelligent and internationally diverse cohort as being a major benefit of their learning experience as well as their future careers.

RECENT DEVELOPMENTS
WBS celebrated its 40th anniversary in 2007. It has grown from offering three courses to 26, and now has more than 7,000 students enrolled, with a turnover of £36.3 million. The course portfolio continues to expand and diversify, with a recent contract to customise delivery of the Warwick MBA for a major multinational solutions provider, as well as new courses in the pipeline.

WBS has recently established a Fund for Academic Excellence to invest in future leaders, faculty, and its learning environment. Since August 2003, the fund has helped to support many students, recruit 16 new

professors, and expand facilities, with a £9 million building recently completed and £17 million earmarked for further development. WBS recognises that to retain competitive advantage, it is essential to continue to gain funding for growth.

PROMOTION
WBS maintains a solid global presence with a range of below- and above-the-line segmented international marketing. Its 'extremely usable' website (according to the independent survey, WebWorks 2007 Study by CarringtonCrisp) attracts in the region of 2,500 visitors a day and is an essential platform for communicating. However, for many people its brochures are still an important channel, providing tangible evidence in a knowledge-based sector.

WBS is no stranger to using creative channels, having used airport advertising, taxis, and sports events sponsorship to attract attention. But, ultimately, its graduates are its best adverts and its best advocates.

BRAND VALUES
WBS has simple core values: excellence in all it does, nurturing fresh-thinking in staff and students, ensuring a positive impact from the ideas it creates, and continuing to be international in outlook and approach. From these foundations WBS aims to continue to challenge minds, change lives, and create tomorrow's leaders.

www.wbs.ac.uk

Things you didn't know about Warwick Business School

Every FTSE100 company employs a WBS graduate.

WBS academics have written more than 120 books in the last five years and over 600 papers in the last 12 months.

WBS has 172 academic and teaching staff, supported by a team of management and administrative staff.

2000	2003	2006	2007
The 2,000th student graduates from the Warwick MBA by distance learning.	The Guardian survey of top employers rates WBS graduates as the most employable in the UK.	The Times Good University Guide rates WBS as the best overall undergraduate business education provider in the UK.	WBS is 40 years old, has 7,000 students, 357 staff, turnover of £36.3 million and 26 courses.

WEBER SHANDWICK

Advocacy starts here.

Weber Shandwick is one of the world's leading PR and creative ideas agencies. Its roots in the UK go back to the early 1970s, and in its newest incarnation Weber Shandwick celebrated its sixth anniversary in 2007. Part of The Interpublic Group of marketing companies, the agency puts its creative talent, communications expertise and specialist teams to work for some of the biggest companies and most innovative brands in the UK and around the world.

MARKET

The UK public relations market is growing in size and diversity, with an estimated 50,000 people now working in the industry, in-house and in consultancies. It is also growing in terms of spend, with many companies and organisations switching marketing resources from traditional advertising to PR, digital and other marketing disciplines.

The key growth areas for public relations are healthcare, digital, corporate responsibility,

multi-cultural communications, technology, and corporate reputation.

The consultancy sector varies from one-man bands to UK-only agencies and international players. Weber Shandwick is the UK's largest consultancy, employing around 350 people in the UK and some 2,000 internationally in a network of offices and specialist consulting groups. Internationally, Weber Shandwick has 84 owned offices in 40 countries, as well as affiliates that expand the network to more than 132 offices in 82 countries.

ACHIEVEMENTS

In 2007, Weber Shandwick won praise from peers across the world when it was recognised by The Holmes Report as European Consultancy of the Year and Best Agency to Work For, while PRWeek called Weber Shandwick "the PR industry's leading blue-chip firm" and rated it top for delivery of overall client satisfaction.

Weber Shandwick has now won the prestigious United Nations Grand Award for Outstanding Achievement in Public Relations for three years running. In 2007 the award was given to 'Say Condom Freely', a public health campaign to promote condom use and awareness in India.

The agency won dozens of other industry accolades for client work during 2006/07, including multiple awards for KFC's 'Face from Space' campaign, where the London team created the world's first logo visible from space as part of a global brand relaunch.

High-profile assignments have included helping the Russian city of Sochi to win the bid for the 2014 Olympic and Paralympic Winter Games; building a tree office and hosting Microsoft®'s prestigious media event at the British Library to launch Windows Vista; enlisting Lily Allen as the face of Braun's Satin Hair styling range; carpeting London's Millennium Bridge with money to

1974	1987	1998	2000	2001	2007
Shandwick International is founded in London with a single client and a global vision.	The Weber Group is founded in Cambridge, Massachusetts as a communications agency for emerging technology companies. In less than a decade it goes on to become a top 10 PR firm.	Shandwick is acquired by The Interpublic Group.	Shandwick merges with The Weber Group.	BSMG Worldwide merges with Weber Shandwick.	Weber Shandwick continues to win awards and is recognised for its work across the European market, earning the title of The Holmes Report's Pan-European Consultancy of the Year 2006/07.

launch Mastercard's PayPass cashless payment system; launching Samsung's Youth Anti-Obesity Programme with the European Olympic Committee; helping A1GP with initiatives to reduce its environmental footprint; and managing the UK's digital television switchover.

PRODUCT

Weber Shandwick is a full service public relations agency. Its policy of recruiting the best media and PR professionals means it now has some of the strongest teams of senior ex-journalists and communications specialists in the business.

In the UK Weber Shandwick has six specialist practice teams in technology PR, healthcare PR, financial communications, corporate communications, consumer marketing and public affairs. The UK business employs around 350 people across offices in London, Manchester, Leeds, Glasgow, Edinburgh, Aberdeen, Inverness and Belfast. Weber Shandwick also has an office in Dublin and an affiliate agency in Cardiff.

Globally the company is part of the extensive global IPG network with a strong PR presence across the US, Europe, Asia-Pacific and in the future economic giants of China, India, Russia and Brazil.

RECENT DEVELOPMENTS

During 2007 Weber Shandwick's focus shifted to advocacy, and investing in new ways to create, identify and harness the power of advocates for clients' brands, causes, products, and services.

Weber Shandwick's corporate responsibility and sustainability practice has been rebranded as Planet 2050, and is helping clients to prepare for the challenges of a planet under social and environmental stress, from strategy, stakeholder engagement and benchmarking, to marcoms and media relations. The agency's London office

achieved the environmental standard ISO 14001 during 2007, as part of a move towards being a more sustainable business.

The digital team was rebranded as Screengrab, a pan-European virtual team that ensures interactive, social and emerging media are seamlessly integrated into all client campaigns. The agency also launched a partnership with Radian6 Technologies to provide clients with social media intelligence.

SLAM, Weber Shandwick's creative lifestyle boutique, celebrated its first birthday and the opening of a new office in Manchester, while MCC (Multi-Cultural Communications) was launched in March 2007 to advise clients on reaching UK ethnic groups. MCC's research project exploring ethnic minority attitudes towards marketing and brands showed its appearance is timely: three-quarters of Asian and Black people and half of Chinese people in the UK feel mainstream brand marketing has little or no relevance to them.

In the past year Weber Shandwick has strengthened its sports PR and sponsorship offering, handling high-profile assignments such as Tokyo's bid for the 2016 Olympic Games, and promoting Exxon Mobil's motorsports sponsorship programme.

PROMOTION

In May 2007, Weber Shandwick launched its new 'Advocacy starts here' positioning, illustrating its shift in focus to communications programmes that forge emotional bonds and higher levels of involvement with stakeholders. This has underpinned the work of Weber Shandwick's strategic marketing team across all marketing platforms during the past year.

Weber Shandwick's investment in its specialist offering has also led to a number of high-profile new hires and internal promotions, including a new head of sport, a new creative director and a new head of UK public sector campaigns.

BRAND VALUES

Weber Shandwick is about ideas, creativity, passion and commitment. It has a pool of specialist talent and strong European and international networks. Its clients are among the top brands, companies and organisations in the UK and around the world.

Weber Shandwick makes a significant investment every year in staff learning and development to ensure the consultancy continues to develop added-value services and to deliver real business results for its clients.

www.webershandwick.co.uk

Things you didn't know about Weber Shandwick

Weber Shandwick has created an employee volunteering scheme in partnership with The Media Trust to help small charities with pro bono work worth thousands of pounds.

The agency works closely with sister companies McCann Erickson (advertising), FutureBrand (branding consultancy), Jack Morton (event management) and Octagon (sports marketing); it is currently working alongside sister sports marketing agency, Octagon, to promote the London 2012 Olympics.

UK & Ireland CEO Colin Byrne launched his blog on public affairs and PR, Byrne Baby Byrne, in March 2007. It was named as one of the top 50 blogs for business by The Times.

Weber Shandwick is one of the biggest graduate recruiters in the UK public relations industry.

Yellow Pages™

Yellow Pages directories are published by Yell, a leading international directories business whose UK brands also include Yell.com, Yellow Pages 118 24 7 and Business Pages, which list approximately two million businesses between them. Last year, 28 million copies of the Yellow Pages were delivered to homes and businesses across the UK, helping to make it the UK's most used classified directory (Source: Saville Rossiter Base 2006/07).

MARKET

Yell is the biggest player in the £4 billion UK classified advertising market (Source: The Advertising Association 2006). This highly competitive market consists of a range of media, including printed directories, search engines, 118 directory services, magazines and local and national newspapers.

ACHIEVEMENTS

Since Yellow Pages was first published in the UK in 1966, the directory has become a part of everyday life, delivering results for both consumers and advertisers. With the expansion and diversification of the brand in the past decade into Yell.com and Yellow Pages 118 24 7, Yell has maintained its position as the UK's best-loved directory service and has continued to build on its reputation for quality.

The award-winning directory enquiries service from Yellow Pages

In 2007, Yellow Pages 118 24 7, the directory enquiry service from Yellow Pages, beat its rivals to become a 'Top Five' UK brand for customer satisfaction, in an annual consumer survey across key business sectors. The directory enquiry service came fourth – behind Waitrose, Asda and Amazon – in an analysis of consumer perceptions of more than 35 organisations, part of the annual CompariSat benchmarking study. Furthermore, for the third year in a row, the 118 24 7 call centre won the Best UK 118 Service in 2006.

Yell is very aware of environmental and social issues and of its impact on the wider community.

In April 2007, Yell won a second Queen's Award for Enterprise, acknowledging the sustainable approach at the heart of its business. A large part of this decision was based on the Yellow Woods Challenge, Yell's flagship environmental campaign for schools, run in partnership with the Woodland Trust and local authorities across the UK. School children collect old Yellow Pages directories for recycling, with the chance to win a cash prize for their school.

The past year has been hugely exciting for this fun and educational campaign as it beat its target to involve one million school children and recycle one million directories.

Yell now works with 99 per cent of local councils to facilitate the recycling of old Yellow Pages directories.

In addition, Yellow Pages has been lead sponsor of Marie Curie Cancer Care's Great Daffodil Appeal since 1999 and in 2007 helped the charity to hit a milestone fundraising target of £20 million. In the past three years, Yellow Pages has also worked with the charity

1966	1973	1979	1993	1996	2001
Yell's first Yellow Pages directory appears, bound into the standard Brighton telephone directory.	Yellow Pages is rolled out across the UK.	Yellow Pages becomes a registered trademark.	Talking Pages is launched.	Yell.co.uk is launched, later to be replaced by Yell.com in 2000.	Full colour advertising is launched nationally in Yellow Pages. In addition, Yellow Pages Insurance Guide is launched.

to extend the campaign into schools with Mini Pots of Care, which has involved more than 730,000 youngsters to date.

PRODUCT

Yellow Pages is the UK's most used classified advertising directory with nearly one billion uses per year (Source: Saville Rossiter Base 2006/07). In 2007, 104 editions were printed across the UK; 95 per cent of UK adults have a Yellow Pages directory at home and 84 per cent use it (Source: Saville Rossiter Base 2006/07).

From Alexander Technique to Cake Makers & Decorations, from Tree Work to Veterinary Surgeons, the classifications aim to ensure users can find the business they want easily. In fact, nearly seven out of every ten 'look-ups' result in a business being contacted and more than half (57 per cent) of contacts result in a purchase (Source: Saville Rossiter Base 2006/07).

Yell.com, Yell's online directory service, is the UK's local search engine and a major online advertising medium for UK businesses. It offers more than two million

UK business listings, including 203,000 searchable advertisers (June 2007), and can be accessed via the website and on web-enabled mobile phones, with both a JAVA™ application and browse (WAP) services.

Yell.com also provides several useful features such as zoom-enabled maps, driving and walking directions, and a personal Yell.com address book to keep a record of regularly used businesses.

Yellow Pages 118 24 7 has also seen a period of significant growth, with its UK based call centres building further on its reputation for quality service. It offers a classified business directory service, as well as opening hours, store locations, delivery and payment information for its advertisers.

RECENT DEVELOPMENTS

Yell is constantly looking at new and innovative ways to improve and enhance Yellow Pages, as well as extending into new areas to stay at the top of the increasingly competitive classified advertising market.

In 2007, Yell teamed up with Visit Britain to produce six pages of specialist regional 'Great Days Out' information in the front of 88 regional Yellow Pages, to ensure that the content continues to be relevant and informative to consumers. The new information, which details attractions and events that are close to home or up to two hours away, is being rolled out in directories throughout 2008.

For the 13 London directories, Visit London has also provided six pages of specialist 'Discover London' content and Transport for London has supplied 16 pages of London travel guide content, covering everything from information on the congestion charge to local bus maps and cycle routes.

January 2007 saw the enhancement of Yell.com mobile, an in-depth local information service, offering phone numbers, addresses, maps and directions for more than two million UK businesses, shops and services, sent directly to a mobile for free (the Yell.com mobile service is free from Yell, but standard network charges apply). This new service

gives consumers the power of Yellow Pages, and more, in the palm of their hand whenever they want it.

The continuing success of Yellow Pages 118 24 7 in 2007 has led to expansion of the service through the opening of a new call centre in Newport, Wales.

PROMOTION

In 2007, a new integrated campaign – Here's to the people behind the numbers™ – was launched for Yellow Pages and Yellow Pages 118 24 7. It supports Yell's mission to champion and celebrate the people whose skills, ingenuity and passion make up big and small businesses across the UK, through using real Yell advertisers in the campaign.

In addition, Yell is sponsoring network films on Channel 4, including those across E4, More 4, Film4, online and Movie Rush.

BRAND VALUES

The Yellow Pages family of brands are built on their reputation for accessibility, trustworthiness and warmth, underpinned with a commitment to champion enterprise.

www.yellgroup.com

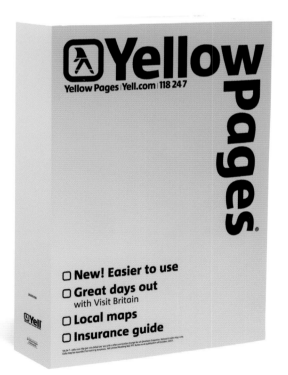

2003

Yellow Pages 118 24 7 is launched.

2006

Yellow Pages 118 24 7 wins five awards at the International Directory Assistance Awards – including Best UK 118 Service, for the third year running.

Also in 2006, TFL travel guide is launched across London Yellow Pages directories.

2007

Enhanced Yell.com mobile is launched and Yellow Pages 118 24 7 opens its second call centre, which could see the creation of more than 250 jobs, phased over the next four years.

The Yellow Pages 118 24 7 phone service. Calls cost 14p per minute billed by the second with a 69p connection charge for all Directory Enquiries. Network costs may vary. Calls may be recorded for training purposes. Yell Limited, Reading, RG1 7PT. Rates correct at time of publication, February 2008.

Charities Supported by the Business Superbrands

On the pages that follow you will find details of some of the charities supported by the Business Superbrands featured in this publication.

Brake, the road safety charity
www.brake.org.uk
www.roadsafetyweek.org
Tel: 01484 559909
Registered Charity No: 1093244

Every day, nine people are killed on UK roads and nine times as many are seriously injured. Many of those whose lives are tragically cut short are young – road crashes are the biggest killer of 15-24 year-olds. Brake is a national charity dedicated to preventing road death and injury and caring for people bereaved or injured in road crashes. Our work includes educating different road users – from children and their parents, to young people learning to drive, to professional drivers – through resources, training and events. We co-ordinate National Road Safety Week and provide free community training on different road safety topics, including family road safety and young driver safety, through the FedEx & Brake Road Safety Academy. Our BrakeCare division is the national provider of support for road crash victims – helping families whose lives have been devastated by a sudden death or serious injury.

Supported by: FedEx Express

Cancer Research UK
www.cancerresearchuk.org
Tel: 020 7242 0200
Registered Charity No: 1089464

Cancer Research UK is the world's leading independent organisation dedicated to cancer research. We carry out scientific research to help prevent, diagnose and treat cancer, and we ensure that our findings are used to improve the lives of all cancer patients.

We have discovered new ways of treating cancer that together have saved hundreds of thousands of lives across the world and we work in partnership with others to achieve the greatest impact in the global fight against cancer.

We help people to understand cancer by providing life-changing information to patients, their families and friends, and we run cancer awareness campaigns to help people reduce their risk of the disease.

One in three of us will get cancer at some point in our lives. Our ground-breaking work, funded almost entirely by the general public, will ensure that millions more people survive.

Together we will beat cancer.

Supported by: G4S, Hiscox, Michael Page International and Superbrands (UK) Ltd

ChildLine
www.childline.org.uk
ChildLine Helpline: 0800 1111
Registered Charity No: 216401

ChildLine, a service provided by NSPCC, is the free and confidential 24-hour helpline for children in trouble or danger across the UK. Trained volunteer counsellors comfort, advise and protect children and young people who may feel they have nowhere else to turn.

Since it was launched in 1986, ChildLine has saved children's lives, found refuge for children in danger on the streets, and given hope to thousands of children who believed no one else cared for them. ChildLine has now counselled over two million children and young people.

Children call ChildLine about a wide range of problems, but the most common problems are abuse (both sexual and physical), bullying, serious family tensions, worries about friends' welfare and teenage pregnancy.

Supported by: BT, G4S and Hiscox

BBC Children in Need
www.bbc.co.uk/pudsey
Freephone: 0845 733 2233
Registered Charity No: 802052

BBC Children in Need helps disadvantaged children and young people in the UK. Some have experienced domestic violence, neglect, homelessness or sexual abuse, and others have suffered from chronic illness, or have had to learn to deal with profound disabilities from a very young age.

Many organisations supported by the charity aim to create a lasting impact on children's lives. Some offer low achieving children from areas of deprivation a chance to develop their educational skills and ambitions and others create opportunities for young people who are homeless or socially excluded, to enable them to move forward and secure a fulfilling future.

The charity offers grants to voluntary groups, community groups and registered charities around the UK that focus on improving children's lives. Grants are targeted on the areas of greatest need and money is allocated geographically to ensure that children in all corners of the UK receive a fair share of what is raised.

Supported by: BT

COMIC RELIEF

Comic Relief
www.comicrelief.com
Tel: 020 7820 5555
Registered Charity No: 326568

Comic Relief was launched from the Safawa refugee camp in Sudan, on Christmas Day 1985, in response to crippling famine in Africa. The aim was to take a fresh and fun approach to fundraising and, through events like Red Nose Day, inspire those who hadn't previously been interested in charity to get involved. Since then there have been 11 Red Nose Days and four Sport Reliefs, raising over £450 million. Red Nose Day 2007 raised more than £67 million.

Comic Relief has worked with some of the biggest names in entertainment, sport and business and tackles some of the biggest issues facing people across the world. Their work ranges from supporting projects that help children who are living rough in India to community programmes helping the elderly across the UK. A number of high profile partnerships have brought in millions of pounds to help reach these aims but the biggest group of supporters remains schools, with over 60 per cent taking part in Red Nose Day 2007.

Supported by: BT

Community Network
www.community-network.org
Tel: 020 7923 5250
Registered Charity No: 1000011

Community Network provides a telephone conference call service to other charities and not-for-profit organisations. As the pioneers of social telephony, the emphasis is on creating opportunities for social inclusion, breaking down the isolation many people suffer through age, frailty, mobility, location, transport or caring responsibilities. Community Network creates 'virtual' communities of interest using user-friendly, affordable, accessible technology – no special equipment is required, just a phone.

Working in partnership with other agencies, including local government, Community Network has developed projects such as: FriendshipLink, 'bringing' friends to your home by phone; FaithLink, allowing people to 'attend' religious services from their homes; telephone group book clubs; and 'respite care' groups for carers.

Supported by: BT

Coram
www.coram.org.uk
Tel: 020 7520 0300
Registered Charity No: 312278

Coram, was founded in 1739 when Thomas Coram established the Foundling Hospital, to care for abandoned babies dying on the streets of London. Over 250 years later, the streets of London are still as dangerous for many children and young people, all too many of whom are growing up without the support of a loving home. Coram develops and promotes best practice in the care of vulnerable children and their families. We work with over 6,000 children, young people and their families each year, transforming their lives through practical help and support. We build self-esteem and well-being, preparing children and young people for a fulfilling adult life.

Services include adoption for some of the most vulnerable children; a Parents' Centre, which provides education and training; support and life skills training for care leavers and young people at risk; and family support programmes, both in the community and through schools.

Supported by: Lloyd's

CRASH
www.crash.org.uk
Tel: 020 8742 0717
Registered Charity No: 1054107

CRASH is the construction and property industry charity for the homeless. It harnesses the skills, products, talents and goodwill of the industry to improve buildings and premises for voluntary agencies working with homeless people, throughout the UK.

CRASH is a unique example of a corporate sector coming together on a charitable basis to tackle homelessness. Companies from the industry provide us with their materials and professional expertise. The charity's key aim is to provide a decent, well-designed environment in the certain knowledge that bright, smart surroundings go a long way to help develop the self esteem and self worth of some very vulnerable individuals in our society.

Supported by: British Gypsum

DESIGN MUSEUM

Design Museum
www.designmuseum.org
Tel: 0870 833 9955
Registered Charity No: 800630

The Design Museum is the world's leading museum devoted to contemporary design in every form from furniture to graphics, and architecture to industrial design. It demonstrates both the richness of the creativity to be found in all forms of design, and its importance. The Design Museum's mission is to celebrate, entertain, and inform.

Twenty-five years ago, Terence Conran established the forerunner of the Design Museum, the Boilerhouse, in the basement of the Victoria and Albert Museum (V&A) in London. As planned, the Boilerhouse quickly outgrew the V&A and in 1989 it moved on to become the Design Museum, in an architecturally striking transformation of a Thameside warehouse near Tower Bridge. Since then it has emerged as an institution with international status and significance, playing a vital role in making design and architecture a part of the cultural agenda.

Supported by: Deutsche Bank

Dreams Come True
www.dctc.org.uk
Tel: 01730 815000
Registered Charity No: 800248

Dreams Come True was established 20 years ago with the aim of helping to fulfil the dreams of children with terminal and serious illnesses. The charity now fulfils a dream a day for children and young people aged 2-21 with conditions such as leukaemia, cystic fibrosis and muscular dystrophy.

The dreams are as varied as a child's imagination and recent dreams have included feeding sea lions from a boat, having a helicopter ride and meeting the pop group Keane.

Since the charity was founded, over 3,500 children have experienced their dream becoming a reality. With further support, Dreams Come True can help many more children.

Supported by: Mintel

Fairbridge
www.fairbridge.org.uk
Tel: 020 7902 1119
Registered Charity No: 206807

Based in 15 of the most disadvantaged areas in England, Scotland and Wales, Fairbridge supports young people aged 13-25 who are not in education, employment or training – giving them the motivation, confidence and skills they need to change their lives.

We encourage young people by offering them a unique combination of personal support and opportunity: opportunity in the form of a wide range of challenging and structured courses; support in the form a tailor-made action plan for each young person. And we do this in a safe environment that challenges negative behaviour and recognises achievement.

Supported by: Deutsche Bank

FareShare
www.fareshare.org.uk
Tel: 020 7394 2468
Registered Charity No: 1100051

FareShare is the national charity working to relieve food poverty, by providing quality surplus food from the food industry to a network of over 400 community organisations supporting disadvantaged people in the community.

Alongside making food more accessible to help improve the health and well-being of over 20,000 of the UK's most disadvantaged individuals, FareShare also provides education and training around the essential life skills of safe food preparation and nutrition, through the charity's Eat Well Programme, in preparation for vulnerable people leading more independent lives.

Last year, 2,000 tonnes of food were saved from being sent to landfill, helping to reduce CO_2 emissions by 13,000 tonnes and contributing towards 3.3 million meals. In addition, 250 work and volunteer placements were created – by receiving FareShare's food – and £5 million was saved by the community organisations FareShare supports, allowing greater investment into the other support services they provide.

Supported by: Deutsche Bank

FARM-Africa
www.farmafrica.org.uk
Tel: 020 7430 0440
Registered Charity No: 326901

Eighty six per cent of Africa's people are smallholder farmers and livestock-keepers who depend on the food they grow and the animals they keep to survive. Forty six per cent exist on less than 50 pence a day.

FARM-Africa works with these families and communities to build their assets through agricultural production. We help them to develop livelihoods free from poverty through sustainable activities that generate regular income.

For example, dairy goat farmers in FARM-Africa's Meru project in Kenya have increased their annual income from US$93 to US$995. With our support, they have also formed a co-operative for milk production and are now supplying supermarkets in Nairobi. They use the income to improve their homes, send their children to school and purchase vital healthcare.

Activities like these offer real and lasting solutions to African poverty.

Supported by: Lloyd's

International Osteoporosis Foundation
www.iofbonehealth.org
Tel: 0041 22 994 0100

The International Osteoporosis Foundation (IOF) is the largest global non-governmental organisation dedicated to the prevention, diagnosis and treatment of osteoporosis.

The vision of IOF is a world without osteoporotic fractures. IOF's mission is to increase awareness and understanding of osteoporosis, to motivate people to take action to prevent, diagnose and treat osteoporosis, and to support national osteoporosis societies in order to maximise their effectiveness.

The IOF, registered as a not-for-profit, non-governmental foundation in Switzerland, functions as a global alliance of patient, medical and research societies, scientists, healthcare professionals, and international companies concerned about bone health.

Supported by: Weber Shandwick

Kidscape
www.kidscape.org.uk
Tel: 020 7730 3300
Registered Charity No: 326864

Kidscape is committed to keeping children safe from abuse. Kidscape is the first charity in the UK established specifically to prevent bullying and child sexual abuse. Kidscape believes that protecting children from harm is key.

Kidscape works UK-wide to provide individuals and organisations with practical skills and the resources necessary to keep children safe from harm. The Kidscape staff equip vulnerable children with practical non-threatening knowledge and skills to keep themselves safe and reduce the likelihood of future harm.

Kidscape works with children and young people under 16 years old, their parents/carers, and those who work with them.

Kidscape offers: a helpline offering support and advice to parents of bullied children; booklets, literature, posters, training guides, educational videos on bullying, child protection,

and parenting; a National Comprehensive Training Programme for schools on anti-bullying, child safety and behaviour management issues; and assertiveness sessions for children who are bullied.

Supported by: Eddie Stobart

Leicester Hospitals Charity
www.uhl-tr.nhs.uk/fundraising
Tel: 0800 389 1321
Registered Charity No: 1056804

Leicester Hospitals Charity is a registered charity which raises funds to support Leicester General Hospital, Glenfield and Leicester Royal Infirmary.

More than one million patients are treated in Leicester's hospitals each year. Please support us and help us to provide them with the best care and facilities we can.

All money raised is spent on making our wards more comfortable, buying state-of-the-art equipment and funding vital research projects.

Supported by: British Gas Business

WE ARE MACMILLAN. CANCER SUPPORT

Macmillan Cancer Support
www.macmillan.org.uk
Tel: 0808 808 2020
Registered Charity No: 261017

Macmillan Cancer Support works to improve the lives of people affected by cancer and provides practical, medical, emotional and financial support, pushing for better cancer care.

We offer a source of support, helping with all the things people affected by cancer want and need, and are a force for change, pushing for better cancer care.

Macmillan Cancer Support takes into account not just the medical needs of people affected by cancer but the social, emotional and practical impact cancer can have. We are there for people from the moment they suspect they have cancer, and for their families too.

We deliver our own services and work with other partners to develop new ones. Our largest partner is the NHS but there are others in the public, voluntary and private sectors of care too.

Supported by: ExCeL London, Hiscox and npower

Make-A-Wish Foundation® UK
www.make-a-wish.org.uk
Tel: 01276 405060
Registered Charity No: 295672

Make-A-Wish Foundation UK grants magical wishes of children and young people fighting life-threatening illnesses.

Make-A-Wish has no cures to offer and all too often some of our endings are sad, but during desperate times when there seems to be no hope, Make-A-Wish steps in to provide positive and uplifting relief. Most of all, a wish granted brings a time of magic and joy, for the special children and families that we serve. Over 4,700 special wishes have been granted since 1986.

Supported by: Flybe

Marie Curie Cancer Care
www.mariecurie.org.uk
Tel: 0800 716 146
Registered Charity No: 207994

Marie Curie Cancer Care provides free high quality nursing to give terminally ill people the choice of dying at home, supported by their families.

Every day 410 people will die of cancer in the UK. Most want to be cared for in their own homes, close to the people and things they love. This year Marie Curie Cancer Care will care for more than 27,000 people. But for every family that we help there are always others that we can't. We want to reach all of these families – making choice a reality for them all.

Supported by: Hiscox and Yellow Pages

MENCAP
Understanding learning disability

Mencap
www.mencap.org.uk
Tel: 020 7454 0454
Registered Charity No: 222377

Mencap is the UK's leading learning disability charity. Our services in housing, education and employment support thousands of people with a learning disability across England, Wales and Northern Ireland. Through our work in the community, we support thousands more to speak up for themselves and their rights, gain confidence and take part in the activities that really interest them.

Our vision is of a world where everyone with a learning disability has an equal right to choice, opportunity and respect, with the support they need.

We know that there is still a long way to go before people with a learning disability, their families and carers are given the recognition that they deserve. We are ambitious for our future and the future of all those that we support – together we can achieve a lot.

Supported by: Travis Perkins

MHA
www.mha.org.uk
Tel: 01332 296200
Registered Charity No: 1083995

MHA is a charity providing care homes, housing and support services for older people throughout Britain. Our mission is 'to improve the quality of life for older people, inspired by Christian concern' and our services are open to all in need.

Established 65 years ago, MHA now delivers a range of services to over 12,500 individuals. MHA serve approximately 3,000 older people in residential, nursing and specialist dementia care homes; 1,500 older people in sheltered housing and housing with care; and 8,000 older people in community projects.

Our services are delivered by 4,000 dedicated staff and a further 5,000 committed volunteers.

Supported by: Allied Irish Bank (GB)

the children's charity

NCH
www.nch.org.uk
Tel: 020 7704 7000
Registered Charity No: 4764232

NCH is the leading UK provider of family and community centres; children's services in rural areas; services for disabled children and their families; and services for young people leaving care.

NCH runs more than 500 projects, supporting over 178,000 of the UK's most vulnerable and excluded children, young people and families, many of whom face difficulties such as poverty, disability and abuse.

We believe that all children and young people have unique potential and that they should have the support and opportunities they need to reach it. We have been working to make this vision a reality for over 135 years.

Supported by: Allied Irish Bank (GB) and Travis Perkins

Cruelty to children must stop. FULL STOP.

NSPCC
www.nspcc.org.uk
www.childline.org.uk
Child Protection Helpline: 0808 800 5000
ChildLine Helpline: 0800 1111
Registered Charity No: 216401 and SC037717

The National Society for the Prevention of Cruelty to Children (NSPCC) is the UK's leading charity specialising in child protection and the prevention of cruelty to children.

The NSPCC's purpose is to see a society where all children are loved, valued and able to fulfil their potential. The society has 180 community-based projects and runs the Child Protection Helpline

and ChildLine in the UK and the Channel Islands. Most of the NSPCC's direct work is with children, young people and their families, but they also work to achieve cultural, social and political change – influencing legislation, policy, practice, public attitudes and behaviours and delivering services for the benefit of young people.

Supported by: JCB

RICHARD
HOUSE
Children's
Hospice

Richard House Children's Hospice
www.richardhouse.org.uk
Tel: 020 7511 0222
Registered Charity No: 1059029

Richard House Children's Hospice in east London, supports children and young people aged 0-19 with life-limiting and life-threatening conditions. Our highly trained care team help the children and their families with the medical and emotional challenges that these conditions bring.

The core purpose of Richard House's work is to make the children's experiences as positive, comfortable and fulfilling as possible during the progression of illnesses, during death and for the lives of those who are left behind. We aim to foster many positive memories along the way, in seeking to give these families the most precious gift of all: a little time together. All services including respite and residential care are provided completely free of charge to families and with limited Government funding – we are very much reliant on voluntary income to continue providing this vital care.

Supported by: Hiscox

SAMARITANS

Samaritans
www.samaritans.org
Helpline (UK): 08457 90 90 90
Helpline (Republic of Ireland): 1850 60 90 90
Registered Charity No: 219432

With over 13 million working days lost to stress, depression and anxiety each year and one in five children affected by psychological problems, Samaritans is more relevant than ever. As the UK's 24/7 emotional support service, Samaritans relies on 17,000 volunteers who respond to someone in distress every six seconds.

Samaritans remains as innovative as when it took its first call in 1953, pioneering an email service and SMS text messaging service, to stay relevant to the communication needs of young people – especially young men who are particularly vulnerable.

Samaritans aim is to promote better emotional health in the community. Samaritans DEAL and Skills for Life programme equips young people in schools to develop positive coping skills to deal with difficult life situations, whilst the Worklife programme and Samaritans annual Stress Down Day on the 1st February supports employers to address the serious issues of stress in the workplace.

Supported by: Lloyd's

Save the Children
www.savethechildren.org.uk
Tel: 020 7012 6400
Registered Charity No: 213890

We are the world's independent children's charity. We are outraged that millions of children are still denied proper healthcare, food, education and protection. We are working flat out to get every child their rights and we are determined to make further, faster changes. How many? How fast? It's up to you.

Supported by: BSI and First

SPARKS
www.sparks.org.uk
Tel: 020 7799 2111
Registered Charity No: 1003825

SPARKS funds pioneering medical research that has a practical, positive impact on the lives of babies and children.

Since 1991, SPARKS has funded more than 180 cutting-edge medical projects in the UK, committing over £15 million to tackle conditions as diverse as cerebral palsy, meningitis, the dangers of premature birth, spina bifida, cystic fibrosis, club foot, childhood arthritis and cancers.

In the UK, many important areas of paediatric research depend heavily on funding from charities like SPARKS rather than the public purse. It's this knowledge that motivates the dedicated SPARKS team.

Supported by: Deutsche Bank

The Place2Be
www.theplace2be.org.uk
Tel: 020 7923 5500
Registered Charity No: 1040756

The Place2Be is uniquely placed inside primary schools to support and nurture troubled children, helping them to move past their problems, and build the foundations for a successful life.

Today's school children face all kinds of challenges that threaten to derail them, from gang culture on our streets to abuse at home. Unless they are given the means to cope, their feelings of sadness, fear and anger can easily spill over in the classroom – and into society. Whilst some children may become disruptive, others will withdraw completely, shutting everyone out.

The Place2Be provides one-to-one and group counselling sessions, plus a lunchtime drop-in service inside schools. We also support parents, carers and school staff members with dedicated counselling and training.

The Place2Be is currently supporting 40,000 children in 120 UK primary schools. We are poised to expand into six new parts of the country with plans to support 80,000 children by 2010.

Supported by: Deutsche Bank

The Prostate Cancer Charity
www.prostate-cancer.org.uk
Helpline: 0800 074 8383
Registered Charity No: 1005541

Prostate cancer is the most common cancer in men, with 35,000 men diagnosed every year. Ten thousand men die from prostate cancer each year, which equates to one every hour.

The Prostate Cancer Charity is the UK's leading charity in the field of prostate cancer. We fund research into the causes of, treatments for, and impact of living with prostate cancer. Over recent years we have invested over £6 million in vital medical research.

We work to raise awareness of prostate cancer within both the general public and the media. Through our campaigning we are a leading force in lobbying Government for improved NHS services. The Charity also runs the UK's only dedicated prostate cancer phone line, which is staffed by specialist nurses. This provides support and information to men and their families living with prostate cancer in communities across the UK.

The Prostate Cancer Charity has a vision of a world where lives are no longer limited by prostate cancer.

Supported by: Snap-on

War Child
www.warchild.org.uk
Tel: 020 7916 9276
Registered Charity No: 1071659

War Child is the only international child protection agency to operate in south Iraq where we help children go to school, to separate children from adults in prison in Afghanistan, and to help ex-child soldiers establish income-generating projects in northern Democratic Republic of Congo.

We assume resilience among these children. On this basis we invest in their capacity to protect themselves, while working with their communities and local organisations to develop a protective environment for them.

Sixty-six per cent of all fatalities during war are children. This enrages us. And we know it enrages many young people in the UK, who we enroll through music events, CDs and innovative use of online technologies. We use this support to leverage the attention of the press as well as politicians. In this way we are able to influence policy and so benefit many more children than we could possibly help directly.

Supported by: Weber Shandwick

affected by cancer. In addition to funding the Cancer Care Centre at York Hospital, we have funded important research with The University of York and education projects involving the local community.

Recently, we raised money for a mini bus to transport patients from York Hospital to Cookridge Hospital, Leeds, for radiotherapy and chemotherapy treatments.

We have done all this with incredible support from local people – including local businesses. In the coming months we plan to focus our fundraising efforts on Give as You Earn schemes and other forms of corporate giving.

The phrase we use to sum up what we do is: local people raising money to help local people affected by cancer.

Supported by: Portakabin (Shepherd Group)

York City Knights Foundation
www.yorkcityknights.co.uk
Tel: 01904 758234
Registered Charity No: 1112571

The main objective of York City Knights Foundation is the promotion of community participation in healthy recreational activities for the benefit of the inhabitants of York, North Yorkshire and their surrounding areas.

This is achieved by providing facilities for playing rugby league as well as other sports, recreational and leisure pursuits. These facilities have benefited many in the community who need extra care such as the young, infirm or disabled as well as those living in poverty or with difficult social and economic circumstances.

The Foundation is currently working with approximately 110 schools spread across York, Easingwold, Tadcaster and Selby and in 2007 engaged with more than 25,000 children in the form of rugby league coaching sessions, festivals, inclusion assemblies and health assemblies. This included working with children with disabilities as part of the ever-growing tag-ability programme.

Supported by: Portakabin (Shepherd Group)

York Minster Fund

York Minster Fund
www.yorkminster.org
Tel: 01904 557245
Registered Charity No: 252157

As with all ancient buildings, York Minster is in a state of constant restoration and conservation. The present project concerns the East Front. Decay caused by pollution and weather has meant that some 2,500 stones have to be replaced. This in turn has meant that the whole of the Great East Window, installed in 1408, and about the size of a tennis court, has to be removed. The cost of the project is around £23 million. Support has come from many sources including the Shepherd Group and the Heritage Lottery Fund, but there is a never-ending need for money, and the Minster receives no direct help from either central Government or the Church of England.

Supported by: Portakabin (Shepherd Group)

THE UNIVERSITY of York

Community and Volunteering Unit
Careers Service, The University of York
www.york.ac.uk/careers/volunteering.cfm
Tel: 01904 432685

The Community and Volunteering Unit (CAVU) seeks to encourage greater University involvement in the city of York, primarily through volunteering.

It provides an environment for students and staff to realise their ambitions with regards to community engagement, harnessing their enthusiasm, creative energies and distinct skill set and channelling these to provide an important resource for the community.

For example, university volunteers have set up music workshops for local schools, a community sports coaching programme, an oral history project with the National Railway Museum, York Carnival, exhibitions with galleries and museums, a youth conference, social research projects and more.

CAVU helps students and staff bring their ideas for new community projects to life by providing pump-prime funding and brokering introductions to over 200 local community and voluntary organisations.

Since 2002, the Unit has supported over 40 enterprising community projects, led by students or staff, and created more than 500 opportunities to volunteer.

Supported by: Portakabin (Shepherd Group)

Woodland Trust
www.woodland-trust.org.uk
Tel: 01476 581111
Registered Charity No: 294344

The Woodland Trust is the UK's leading woodland conservation charity, owning more than 1,200 woods which are open free of charge for the public to enjoy. Our vision is to protect what we have, restore what has been spoilt and create new woods for the future, to make our countryside friendlier for people and wildlife.

The UK has only 12 per cent woodland cover compared to a European average of 46 per cent. To tackle this, the charity works with communities to plant millions of trees throughout the UK. It also campaigns for better protection of ancient woodland which is the UK's most precious wildlife habitat and home to threatened species such as the dormouse and red squirrel. Trees and forests also stabilise the soil, generate oxygen, store carbon, transform landscapes and provide one of the richest habitats for flora and fauna.

Supported by: Yellow Pages

York Against Cancer
www.yorkagainstcancer.org.uk
Tel: 01904 764466
Registered Charity No: 518478

Since 1987 York Against Cancer has made a significant difference to the lives of people

Business Superbrands Council 2008

Jonathan Allan
Managing Director
OMD UK

Jonathan graduated from Newcastle University in Economics and immediately joined a full service agency, Cravens Advertising, in the City. After a year planning and buying across all media for Northern Rock, Allders and the Halifax, he joined OMD as a trainee TV buyer in 1995.

After a number of years working on clients such as Barclaycard, Boots, American Airlines and AXA, Jonathan was appointed to the board in January 2000.

In 2002 he broadened his role into that of business director, responsible for running a number of accounts including PepsiCo, easyJet and Barclaycard.

In February 2005 Jonathan was appointed deputy managing director and in January 2007 he became managing director.

Anthony Carlisle
Executive Director
Citigate Dewe
Rogerson

In his current role, Anthony acts for companies such as T-Mobile, Yell, Legal & General, Carphone Warehouse, National Grid and Iberdrola. He is also a non-executive director of CSR, the global leaders in Bluetooth wireless.

Anthony began his career at Lintas Advertising, working on FMCG accounts. He helped found Dewe Rogerson, later becoming chief executive and then chairman, building it into a leading international marketing and communications group, before creating Citigate Dewe Rogerson, now part of Huntsworth Group. He led around 90 per cent by value of UK privatisation marketing and communications, pioneering wide share ownership.

Anthony has advised numerous companies in the UK and abroad on their marketing, branding and communications strategies; their positioning with corporate and investor audiences; and on capital raising and bid defence as well as acquisitions. He was also in the core adviser group in creating Orange.

Steve Cooke
Marketing Director
BMRB

For the past 10 years Steve's responsibilities have been in corporate and service marketing. In his current role he is responsible for developing the communications strategy for BMRB and the KMR Group. Steve manages all central aspects of brand development which includes advertising, PR, corporate events, conferences, website, internal comms and marketing collateral. He recently headed up a rebranding programme, resulting in the launch of a new identity for BMRB.

Steve has a wealth of experience in business to business marketing and market research, gained from his current role and previous positions at television sales house TSMS and media independent BBJ. He holds a postgraduate diploma in marketing.

Nadia Cristina
Partner
Practice Management
International LLP

Nadia is a partner in Practice Management International LLP, an organisation which encourages professionalism in marketing and management in professional service firms worldwide through founding and organising influential trade associations. To this end they run the Managing Partners' Forum (MPF) and the Professional Marketing Forum (PM Forum). She joined the organisation 14 years ago and has been instrumental in its growth and direction.

Nadia's main focus is Professional Marketing, the worldwide magazine for marketing professional services from the PM Forum. She is the managing editor, responsible for commissioning, editing and design, a role which she continues to enjoy immensely.

Jonathan Cummings
Director
Start Creative

Jonathan joined Start Creative in early 2007 after four years as marketing director of the Institute of Directors (IoD). A top-10 independent UK brand and digital design agency, Start's clients include Virgin, adidas, BBC, Royal Mail, Bentley, Hertz and Hilton amongst others. Jonathan is responsible for marketing and business development strategy and delivery across the agency's portfolio of services. Start recently created the identity for the 2007/08 CoolBrands programme.

At the IoD Jonathan was responsible for the marketing of its diverse range of activities; from top-end hospitality to publishing and from business information and advice to director-level training. Jonathan sits on various advisory boards and collaborative bodies and presents regularly on e-business and marketing issues. A key theme for Jonathan is to communicate the benefits of a holistic brand engagement strategy, and the importance of ensuring that every stakeholder in an organisation truly understands the brand and their influence on it.

BJ Cunningham
Director
Georgina Goodman

Whilst still a teenager BJ started his first enterprise, importing classic cars and Harley Davidsons from LA to London. This stopped abruptly when the market collapsed!

Taking his considerable debt with him, BJ decided to launch DEATH™ Cigarettes. His Enlightened Tobacco Company gained such a foothold that it found itself taking on the combined might of the industry. Then, with a growing reputation for challenging norms, BJ set up a brand marketing agency with clients including Volkswagen, B&O and Fairline Boats. Having sold the agency, he is currently developing the luxury shoe designer Georgina Goodman.

BJ is also an established speaker.

Michelle Dewberry
Founder
Michelle Dewberry Ltd

Michelle is an inspirational business woman who shot to national fame in 2006 after competing against 15,000 people to win The Apprentice, becoming Sir Alan Sugar's right hand lady.

Following a year of intense learning from Sir Alan, Michelle branched out and established her own consultancy; Michelle Dewberry Ltd (MDL). MDL offers outsourcing, project delivery and consultancy services.

Prior to The Apprentice, Michelle had progressed up the ranks of some of the biggest telecoms and ISP providers in Europe. At the age of 24, she became a self employed consultant delivering multi-million pound offshoring and outsourcing programmes across the globe.

In 2007, Michelle wrote her first book, Anything is Possible, and ran her first London Marathon, raising vital funds for the NSPCC. She has a number of business projects in the pipeline and currently writes for both Glamour magazine and Daltons Business Magazine.

Paul Edwards
Chairman
Research
International UK

Paul worked at Bartle Bogle Hegarty on a range of FMCG and retail accounts, before a spell as head of planning at Young & Rubicam and Still Price Lintas. He then became chairman and chief executive of The Henley Centre, working on future strategic direction for a wide range of blue chip clients and developing new working techniques for management groups. Whilst at Henley, Paul was a frequent commentator on TV and radio on branding, consumer and new media matters. More recently he was the group chief executive for Lowe & Partners and the chairman of the London agency, taking particular responsibility for serving clients' integrated marketing needs.

After a year avoiding corporate life where he consulted for a bewildering range of clients (from Sugar magazine to Challenger tanks) he joined Publicis in October 2004 as chief strategy officer. In August 2007, Paul joined Research International UK as chairman.

Simon Gruselle
Corporate
Marketing Director
Datamonitor

Simon was appointed Datamonitor's corporate marketing director in 2002 with responsibility for the company's brand development. He has since overseen a number of rebranding projects for companies newly acquired by Datamonitor. He has also played a key role in the development of Datamonitor's latest brand values, in conjunction with the launch of the Knowledge Centers.

Prior to this appointment, Simon ran a number of the business units within Datamonitor. Simon was one of the first people to join Datamonitor shortly after it was founded in 1989, starting his career in the information industry as an analyst.

Joel Harrison
Editor
B2B Marketing

Joel is founding editor and co-owner of B2B Marketing, and director of its publishing company Silver Bullet Publishing. Launched in June 2004, the B2B Marketing brand has since been expanded to encompass a range of associated products, including the B2B Marketing Awards.

Joel began his career in professional publishing at Incisive Research, now part of publishing giant Incisive Media, managing its portfolio of newsletter titles targeting the financial services sector – including Financial IT and Financial Marketing. He moved to Trades Exhibitions in 1999 to edit Incentive Today, and during his four year tenure focused it towards the emerging field of motivation, launching The Motivation Awards in 2002.

Joel is a high profile commentator on all matters relating to business marketing, and an enthusiastic champion of its cause. He is a regular speaker at industry events, and chairs B2B Marketing's quarterly Great Debate series.

Joanna Higgins
Group Editor
Director Publications

Joanna is group editor of Director Publications and oversees the day-to-day output of the Institute of Directors' (IoD) small publishing arm. She is also full-time editor of Director magazine, the IoD's monthly flagship for business leaders, a role she has held since 2000. Under her editorship, she has led a highly praised and radical redesign, launched the website, overseen the development of new editorial products, and in 2004 spun out leisure and lifestyle publication After Hours, now a successful quarterly title.

Joanna has sat on the judging panel for a number of prestigious business awards for organisations including Business in the Community, Working Families, the Scottish Institute for Enterprise, Shell and Sage. She is frequently asked to comment on issues relating to the small and medium-sized enterprise sector, business leadership, and enterprise in Britain.

Darrell Kofkin
Chief Executive
Global Marketing
Network

Darrell began his career in marketing management with London Underground and InterCity before entering a career in professional education and development. In 2002 he combined his passion for marketing and teaching and founded London School of Marketing. Between 2002 and 2005 he led this to become one of the leading providers of professional marketing education programmes in both the UK and Russia. He subsequently sold his stake in the company in 2005. In 2007 he launched Global Marketing Network, a new global professional development and membership organisation for the marketing profession.

Passionate about getting more people engaged in the marketing profession and putting marketing at the heart of the boardroom agenda, he speaks regularly at conferences and business schools and was a senior judge of the 2007 Marketing Week Effectiveness Awards, presenting the Chief Executive Award for Marketing.

Kate Manasian
Managing Director
Saffron Consultants

Kate is a director and owner of Saffron, a brand consultancy formed in 2001 by Wally Olins. Before joining Saffron, she worked at Wolff Olins for 12 years where she was a partner and owner.

Starting out in branding over 20 years ago at a small design firm in Chiswick, Kate's early career also encompassed freelance speechwriting and work for various design journals such as Design Magazine and Interior Design.

Her experience is wide and varied – retail design, packaging and corporate design for industries including automotive, oil, food retailing and telecoms as well as NGOs and professional service organisations. Clients have included Unicef, Cadillac, Tesco, PricewaterhouseCoopers, Cooperative Retail Services, House of Fraser, AOL, BP, Shell, BT, Weil Gotshal, Smith & Nephew, Thames Water, Mitsubishi and Nissan.

Kate launched Wolff Olins' American business in 1998 and is now leading Saffron's US business.

John Mathers
Ex-CEO, UK
The Brand Union

John was CEO of The Brand Union in the UK until January 2008. Part of WPP, The Brand Union is one of the world's leading brand and design specialists. John has a broad mix of experience, on both the client and agency sides. On the client side, this ranges from relaunching Lyons Ground Coffee to a comprehensive rebranding of Safeway in the mid 1990s, which encompassed everything from the identity through to complete new store design as well as an internal brand engagement exercise with all 56,000 employees.

On the agency front, John spearheaded the complete branding of the Sheffield Supertram system; helped to reposition BP as an energy organisation; and revamped the Belgian Post Office network.

John is also a director of the Design Business Association, having been its President for the last three years. He is also active on a number of Design Council committees.

Ruth Mortimer
Editor
Brand Strategy

Ruth is editor of Brand Strategy magazine, the leading global business magazine for senior marketing executives. She is also a regular columnist for Marketing Week magazine. She often appears on the BBC or Sky News to report on branding issues.

Ruth was previously freelance, writing about business issues for a large number of magazines and newspapers in the UK and Australia. She still contributes to Channel 4 on issues concerning music, film, TV and design.

Prior to this, Ruth had a former existence as an archaeologist, based in south east Turkey, specialising in the Middle East.

Lee Murgatroyd
Director
Cohn & Wolfe

Lee is a board director at one of the UK's leading PR consultancies, Cohn & Wolfe.

He leads a team of 20 people in the Corporate Affairs division, providing communications services to clients such as Diageo plc, Barclays Wealth Management, Picture Financial, the Learning and Skills Council (LSC) and London Underground.

In a 12-year career, Lee has worked as a journalist, in the press office of a regional development agency and for a number of PR consultancies in London. He has advised some of the world's biggest brands including Microsoft®, Starbucks, Mitsubishi, British Gas, Sky, Royal Mail and Coca-Cola.

Lee's work has won and been nominated for a series of industry awards from PR Week, the Public Relations Consultants Association (PRCA) and the Chartered Institute of Public Relations (CIPR). He is also an occasional contributor to a number of communications titles including The Marketer and The Public Affairs Newsletter.

Marc Nohr
Managing Partner
Kitcatt Nohr
Alexander Shaw

Marc is managing partner at DM Agency of the Year, Kitcatt Nohr whose clients include Waitrose, Virgin, Citroën and Friends Reunited. Marc is an honorary fellow of the Institute of Direct Marketing (IDM), and one of the Institute's most popular speakers. He has spoken at marketing conferences around the world. Marc also regularly contributes to debates on marketing in the media, and was one of the founding columnists in Financial Times Creative Business. He now has a column in the leading DM monthly title Marketing Direct and is Number One in their DM Power 100.

Phil Nunn
Partner
Trinity

Phil launched the media company, Trinity, in September 2007 with two partners Simon Timlett and Amy Lennox. Trinity already has six clients including Sling Media, Charles Trywhitt and New Look. The business focuses on unifying communication solutions across digital, brand and direct channels.

Phil has spent a total of 18 years in media starting at BBC Worldwide and then at Publicis's Optimedia. Here he launched Interactive@Optimedia in 1998, running accounts including Hewlett-Packard as global Agency of Record for Online, Allied Domecq across Europe, COI online buying in the UK, BA Holidays and MBNA.

He joined Manning Gottlieb OMD in 2003 as director of direct, digital and data.

Most recently he was managing partner of Manning Gottlieb OMD, responsible for and actively involved in John Lewis, Virgin Media's launch, Virgin Mobile, and also charged with all new business delivery over the past 18 months.

David Parsley
Editor
City A.M.

David has been the editor of the free London business daily City A.M. since its launch on 5th September 2005. In just 18 months City A.M. has become the widest read newspaper in the City of London and Canary Wharf, London's primary business districts.

Before joining the City A.M. launch team in July 2005, David worked on a number of newspapers. In November 2001 he became Fleet Street's youngest business editor when he joined the Sunday Express at the age of 29. Before that, he worked on the business desk at The Sunday Times for almost five years.

During his career David has broken some of the biggest business stories in recent memory, including the Government induced collapse of Railtrack in October 2001 and the US$100 billion merger of Texaco and Chevron in 2000. He was also Fleet Street's leading journalist on the drama at MG Rover.

He is currently working on a book about the collapse of the last British-owned mass car manufacturer.

Andrew Pinkess
Strategy Director
Rufus Leonard

Andrew has 20 years' experience in brand and marketing consultancy. His specialisms include: brand strategy and development; digital strategy; integrated communications; and internal communications as a catalyst for organisational change. His client experience spans business to business, business to consumer and the public sector.

He joined brand and digital media consultancy Rufus Leonard in 1998, and key clients include: BBC, BT, COI, Foreign & Commonwealth Office, Identity & Passport Service, Lloyds TSB, Morgan Stanley, Royal Mail, Royal Bank of Scotland, Shell, UK Trade & Investment, and the Wellcome Trust. Before joining Rufus Leonard, he was planning director at financial services advertising agency CCHM, and also managing consultant at P. Four Consultancy.

His early career was spent in international marketing and the travel industry. Andrew is an Oxford graduate with an MBA from Warwick University.

Shane Redding
Managing Director
Think Direct

Shane is an independent consultant with over 20 years' international business to business and consumer direct marketing experience. She provides strategic direct marketing advice and practical training to both end-users and DM suppliers; clients include The Financial Times, HBOS, the IoD and Royal Mail. Specialising in data, databases and analysis, Shane enjoys helping large and small businesses use direct marketing to significantly improve the bottom line.

In addition to her consultancy business, Shane also holds a number of non-executive directorships and board advisory roles including Livingston Guarantee, Cyance and Total Hotspots.

Shane was recently awarded an honorary fellowship of the Institute of Direct Marketing (IDM). Futhermore, she is the current chair of the IDM's B2B Council. She also lectures on topics including CRM, lead generation, and B2B analysis; as well as speaking around the world on international direct marketing.

Tom Stevenson
Journalist
The Daily Telegraph

Currently a columnist at The Daily Telegraph, Tom has been a financial journalist for nearly 20 years and has a particular interest in investment strategy and economics.

He began his career at Investors Chronicle – where he was companies editor – and has worked at Hemscott and The Independent, where he was both city editor and financial editor.

Tom is also the author of How to Become a Millionaire (Texere, 1999).

Matthew Stibbe
Writer-in-Chief
Articulate Marketing

Matthew is writer-in-chief at Articulate Marketing. His clients include HP, Microsoft®, eBay and HM Government. He helps them talk to non-techies about technology and also writes the popular blog, BadLanguage.net.

Before starting the agency in 2005, he worked as a freelance business and technology writer and was a regular contributor to Wired, Popular Science and Director. He also reviewed business jets for The Robb Report and still flies for fun; but in much smaller and cheaper planes.

In 1992 Matthew started a computer games company which has developed over 20 games for publishers such as EA, Sony and LEGO®. He ran the business until 2000 when he sold it to his management team. Prior to this, he read Modern History at Pembroke College Oxford.

Morvah Stubbings
Managing Director
BPRI

Morvah began her career at Frank Small and Associates in Melbourne, Australia's largest locally owned Market Research Company at the time. Here she specialised in service industry research for blue chip clients in the airline, banking and telecommunications industries. Joining Nett Effect – the division set up to focus on customer service and satisfaction offers – at its inception, she helped develop and package proprietary methodologies for use within the wider group.

Later she joined TNS in Sydney, ultimately running the Business Services division. Leaving to set up the Asia Pacific office of BPRI, Morvah travelled extensively helping international clients understand and respond to regional challenges. Moving back to the UK in 2003 with BPRI she is now a managing director. BPRI is the specialist B2B brand within Kantar – WPP's research, insight and consultancy arm.

Jack Wallington
Programmes Manager
Internet Advertising
Bureau

In 1999 Jack began working in online advertising when he established his own web production business and consultancy in the entertainment industry. He managed music and television campaigns before moving into communications for the charity sector.

In his current role, Jack manages the Internet Advertising Bureau's (IAB) Working Groups to address key industry issues and initiatives. This is achieved by liaising directly with the companies that form the IAB's membership.

Daily contact with advertisers, media owners and agencies on Working Group projects has offered him a unique overview of the internet advertising industry and the brands within it.

The primary aim of the projects that Jack works on is to drive growth of the internet advertising market, which has now reached £2 billion, overtaking radio.

Tim Weber
Business Editor
BBC News Interactive

Tim is the business editor of BBC News Interactive, responsible for the BBC's business news on the internet, teletext, digital text and mobile platforms. The BBC News website has a monthly reach of about 36 million readers, while the business pages have more than 9.8 million readers a month (summer 2007) and continue to show strong growth.

Before joining the team that launched the BBC News website, Tim worked as a producer and editor at BBC World Service. He is a graduate of the German School of Journalism, Munich, and holds a PhD from Free University Berlin.

Simon Wylie
Founding Partner &
Managing Director
Xtreme Information

Simon is a founding partner of Xtreme Information. Launched in 1983 as the TV Register, Xtreme Information is the leading media intelligence source of global TV, press, radio, cinema, outdoor and internet advertising. After graduating with a degree in History & French from Goldsmiths, Simon joined the TV Register in 1985. In 1989 he founded the company's first international office in Italy, returning to the UK in 1995. He became sales and marketing director in 1996 and then took on the same role in the newly formed Xtreme Information in 1997. He is currently managing director of the Advertising Division London HQ.

Stephen Cheliotis
Chairman
Superbrands
Councils UK

Stephen began his career at global brand valuation and strategy consultancy, Brand Finance, where he advised companies on maximising shareholder value through effective brand management. In addition he produced significant studies, including comprehensive reports on global intangible assets. His annual study of City Analysts was vital in understanding the importance of marketing metrics in forecasting companies' performance.

In 2001 Stephen joined Superbrands UK, becoming UK managing director in 2003 and overseeing two years of significant growth. Given a European role in 2005, his expertise was used across 20 countries.

He has been a freelance consultant since 2006 and in 2008 set up The Centre for Brand Analysis, which is dedicated to understanding the performance of brands and is contracted to run the Superbrands selection process. Stephen chairs the three independent UK Superbrands Councils.

He speaks regularly at conferences and also comments for international media on branding and marketing, with frequent appearances on CNN, the BBC and Sky.

Business Superbrands YouGov Election

By Panos Manolopoulos
Managing Director
YouGov

About YouGov

YouGov is a full service online market research agency pioneering the use of the internet and information technology to collect higher quality in-depth data for market research and public consultation. YouGov operates a diverse panel of more than 230,000 UK residents, with similar operations in the US and the Middle East.

Based on its past record, YouGov is the UK's most accurate political opinion pollster and dominates Britain's media polling. YouGov is one of the most quoted agencies in Britain and has a well-documented and published track record illustrating the success of its survey methods and quality of its client service work. Based on its work

in the consumer research and opinion polling sector, the agency has one of the fastest growth rates in the industry.

YouGov is a pioneer of online research and e-consultation, using its strong market research skill set and industry expertise to support its clients. The agency's full service work extends across industry sectors including consumer, financial, healthcare, media, new media and technology. A range of research types and data collection methods are used in survey designs tailored to individual client requirements. YouGov offers innovative and tailored market research solutions, quality of service and insight that allow its clients to make effective decisions about their business.

YouGov and Business Superbrands

YouGov has worked with the Superbrands organisation over the past few years in providing comprehensive data which reflects the opinions of consumers and, in the case of Business Superbrands, business professionals. The aim of the Business Superbrands YouGov Election was to establish which business to business brands respondents rated most highly. The survey results are reflective of industry in Great Britain and play a key role in the Business Superbrands selection process, which establishes the 500 strongest business brands in Britain. These brands are awarded Business Superbrand status. YouGov also conducts online elections for the organisation's other UK programmes – Superbrands and CoolBrands.

At the beginning of this publication you will find a step by step explanation of the Business Superbrands selection process, however you will find to follow details of the methodology used by YouGov for the completion of the Business Superbrands YouGov Election.

The survey, which took place for Business Superbrands 2008, was conducted using an online interview system. This was administered to members of the YouGov GB panel of individuals who have previously agreed to take part in surveys for the company.

Online research has proved to be the best medium for quantifying the perception of Business Superbrands amongst business professionals. Its inherent qualities mean that extremely useful data can be delivered. This type of research has been found to be engaging and the questionnaire process stimulating. The process is intuitive, so it can be quick and enjoyable for participants. In addition, online research is non-intrusive as the questionnaires are completed by invitation. It is representative as there are sufficient numbers of individuals online to compensate for the biases in the online community when sampling. Furthermore, it is faster and elicits a considered response to the questions from participants, thus generating good quality data. Finally, online research is more cost effective than conventional approaches.

The sample of respondents was drawn from senior business professionals – defined as those individuals who are decision makers or have company purchasing responsibility – across a wide range of industry sectors and employee bands. The final responding sample was approximately 1,500 individuals.

As business professionals have begun to take a more active interest in the brands they consume in recent years, they are inherently qualified to aid in the judging process. This allows brand owners a direct insight into consumer perspectives about their brands. Some further analysis of the data can also help brand owners to better understand some of the key demographics that play a role in driving perceptions of their brands as well as the market in which they operate, and how these perceptions compare with other brands in their competitive landscape.

An email was sent to the sample inviting them to take part in the survey and providing a link to the survey. YouGov normally achieves a survey response rate of between 35 per cent and 50 per cent, however this varies depending upon the subject matter, complexity and length of the questionnaire.

Within a typical Business Superbrands election, business professionals are asked to choose the brands that they view as Business Superbrands. The definition of a Business Superbrand that the respondents consider when scoring is 'a brand that represents quality products and services, is considered reliable, i.e. it delivers consistently against its promises, and is distinctive, i.e. well known in its sector, suitably differentiated from its competitors and has a personality and values that makes it unique within the market place in which it operates'. Sectors that are considered for Business Superbrands are wide ranging and include utilities, general financial, healthcare equipment, insurance, media, automobiles, pharmaceuticals, support services, travel and leisure, mining and computer software.

When the online election has been completed the final scores are sent to Superbrands, to be incorporated with the scores given to the brands by the Business Superbrands Council (see selection process details at the beginning of this publication).

YouGov executives are members of the Market Research Society and ESOMAR. YouGov is a member of the British Polling Council. YouGov is also registered with the Information Commissioner.

www.yougov.com

The Business Superbrands Results, 2008

By Stephen Cheliotis
Chairman, Superbrands Councils UK
& Chief Executive, The Centre for
Brand Analysis

THE CENTRE FOR
BRAND
ANALYSIS

The Centre for Brand Analysis is an organisation dedicated to understanding the performance of brands. It provides market intelligence on brands and insight into what is new and what is working in brand marketing.

From mid 2008, The Centre for Brand Analysis will manage the research process for all Superbrands programmes in the UK. They will appoint the expert councils, co-ordinate the independent researchers, and manage the partnership with YouGov who will continue to canvass consumer opinion.

www.tcba.co.uk

Last year the methodology for selecting the Business Superbrands was modified and enhanced to incorporate the views of more than 1,500 business professionals, as well as the independent and voluntary council of media, marketing and business experts (see selection process on page nine).

As a result of this change the selection process has become more robust and independent, increasing the transparency and credibility overall. A key element of these changes is the publication of the top 500 'league table' (available at www.superbrands.uk.com).

Top Performers
The results last year clearly showed a significant halo effect enjoyed by those brands operating in both business to business (B2B) and consumer (B2C) markets, meaning brands such as Vodafone and Apple performed extremely strongly; in these cases entering the overall top 10.

Indeed the number one business brand was deemed to be BBC Worldwide, the commercial arm of the BBC. There is no doubt that universal awareness of the BBC brand in the UK and the high affection in which it is held by consumers, recent controversies aside, meant that while many of the business council and business professionals may have had no direct experience of BBC Worldwide, they still rated it highly in a B2B context – a reflection

Business Superbrands Top 10

2007	2008
BBC Worldwide	**Google**
Microsoft®	**Microsoft**®
British Airways	**BP**
BT	**BBC Worldwide**
Google	**GlaxoSmithKline**
BP	**Rolls-Royce Group**
Vodafone	**FT**
Apple	**British Airways**
Rolls-Royce Group	**FedEx Express**
Hertz	**Hertz**

of the BBC's overall brand power. This year BBC Worldwide continued to perform strongly, falling only slightly to fourth place.

Microsoft® retained second place in the rankings; again this could be due, in part, to the ubiquitous awareness it enjoys, but also the result of continued innovations such as Windows Vista.

In third place last year, British Airways fell slightly to number eight – a commendable performance considering the difficulties and bad publicity it has experienced in recent times; from its fine for colluding in price fixing to topping the lost luggage worst performers list published by the Association of European Airlines in November 2007.

Brands with a significant heritage, such as British Airways, seem to benefit from greater forgiveness from consumers as a result of the trust they have built up over the years. Of course, if the brand fails to learn any lessons or continues to make mistakes then that forgiveness will not last; in the short term though, these brands are often given the benefit of the doubt.

Falling out of last year's top 10 are BT, Vodafone and Apple, replaced this year by GlaxoSmithKline, the FT and FedEx Express; seven of the top 10 brands remained the same, reflecting their continued strength.

Four of this year's top 10 brands are FTSE100 companies, while BBC Worldwide is a subsidiary of another British goliath, the publicly owned BBC, and FT is part of FTSE 100 constituent, Pearson. Although a significant percentage of the top 500 brands are not owned by British organisations, business professionals in the UK did largely rate locally owned companies in their top 10. While the UK is perceived to be less sensitive to issues of nationality, for example having a more open market approach and not defending local champions from foreign takeover, affection for national hero brands is perhaps not so dissimilar here in the UK than on the continent. Fifty-four per cent of the top 50 brands are owned by non-UK based enterprises but this drops to just 40 per cent in the top 10.

Heritage is a factor that assists the performance of brands in this ranking with all those in the top 50, bar three, founded before 1990. The majority are considerably older with 15 founded before the 20th century. One of the three new brands, GlaxoSmithKline, is new merely as a result of a merger; the separate brands have significantly older origins. The other two youngsters, Google and eBay, are internet based brands.

An interesting revelation is that all bar one of the top 10 are corporate brands, i.e. their products or services share the corporate name. Only the FT, owned by Pearson, is a stand-alone product name.

Indeed few product brands make the top 50, most notably the FT in seventh place, Teflon in 29th place, Dulux in 41st place and LYCRA® in 49th place. Of those four, three outperform their parent company brand. Teflon owner, and former LYCRA® owner, DuPont is down in 60th place. LYCRA®'s new owner Invista fails to make the top 500. Conversely Dulux owner ICI, in 24th

place, outperforms its product brand; perhaps due to the high levels of exposure it received as a blue chip British company.

Size is clearly another influence on Business Superbrand status. The top 10 have huge market capitalisations, with the exception of BBC Worldwide, which is publicly owned. The smallest market capitalisation amongst the top 10 is British Airways, which at the time of writing was still capitalised at close to £4 billion. Three at the time of writing had market caps above the £100 billion mark and another three were worth more than £10 billion.

Expert Council vs Business Professionals

Last year only three brands featured in both the council top 10 and that of the business professionals – BBC Worldwide, Microsoft® and British Airways. Perhaps surprisingly the council seemed more influenced by the previously mentioned 'consumer halo effect' scoring brands such as Sony, Nokia, Apple, The Economist and Virgin Atlantic into their top 10 – none of which made the business professionals' top 10. Conversely, the professionals added brands solely operating in B2B markets such as Boeing and PricewaterhouseCoopers into their top 10. Two competitors swapping places in the council and professionals tables last year were the two major UK airlines, with Virgin Atlantic making the council's top 10 ahead of British Airways but British Airways alone making the professionals' list.

The council scored Google in first place last year and kept the brand in pole position this year. Meanwhile, the business professionals added it into their top 10 for the first time, in sixth place, giving it overall first place in the combined score this year.

The difference of opinion this year between the council and the professionals has continued; only two brands feature in both top 10s – Microsoft® and Google. Brands operating across both B2B and direct B2C markets perform strongly again with the council voting no pure B2B brands in its top 10, while the professionals ranked only two – PricewaterhouseCoopers and the Rolls-Royce Group. This count is correct if you assume that the GlaxoSmithKline branding on its direct consumer products is noteworthy to purchasers and that Goldman Sachs private banking unit is a B2C operation.

There are some that suggest that our process should only monitor pure B2B players, but I do not believe you can omit brands simply because they have been successful in both a B2C and B2B channel. Inevitably brands that have a direct consumer interface may rise to the top but they have done so through their own hard work and deserve to be recognised in both channels if they have built sufficient equity. Equally those pure B2B players performing well in the table enjoy their success all the more for being acknowledged alongside brands like Microsoft® and BP, rather than just niche B2B players.

Overall Movers and Shakers

Out of last year's bottom 50, 30 failed to re-qualify in this year's top 500 – including four advertising agencies, two media companies, a PR agency, two media planning agencies and a design agency. This continues the relatively poor showing of marketing based companies, proving that it is not always easy to practise what you preach. Utilities Southern Water and Severn Trent also fell from the top 500 while

Comparative Top 10s

	2007 Results			2008 Results	
Rank	Business Professionals	Business Superbrands Council		Business Professionals	Business Superbrands Council
1	BT	Google		BP	Google
2	Microsoft®	BBC Worldwide		GlaxoSmithKline	BlackBerry
3	BP	The Economist		Shell	Apple
4	British Airways	Apple		Microsoft®	BBC Worldwide
5	BBC Worldwide	Nokia		Hertz	The Economist
6	Hertz	FT		Google	Nokia
7	Vodafone	Virgin Atlantic		PricewaterhouseCoopers	FT
8	Shell	Sony		Visa	Virgin Atlantic
9	PricewaterhouseCoopers	British Airways		Rolls-Royce Group	Microsoft®
10	Boeing	Microsoft®		British Airways	Goldman Sachs

defence companies Thales and Quinetiq dropped out of the rankings – the latter maybe suffering from negative publicity surrounding its controversial privatisation.

Those having considerably more success from last year's bottom 50 include Pitman Training, which rose 102 places to 370, Regus Group which rose 101 places and Moody's which rose 91 places. Conversely, falling further were Invensys – dropping 33 places from 467 to last place (500) – and Lex, which fell three places from 478 to 481.

Of this year's bottom 50, 20 are new entrants, seven have risen up the rankings and 23 are fallers. The biggest faller in the bottom 50 is credit card company MBNA, which dropped a staggering 256 places. It was followed by branding consultancy Wolff Olins, which fell 198 places, no doubt harmed by the negative criticism surrounding its London 2012 Olympic logo.

Nevertheless, it remains one of only two brand consultancies in the top 500, the other being Interbrand.

Of the new entrants in the bottom 50 the highest placed was media owner CBS, which came in at 451. The rebranding of Viacom Outdoor to CBS Outdoor and the resulting high coverage of the brand name in its media space may explain its strong entrance. Banham Alarms at 452 and couriers City Link at 453 followed closely.

Overall in the top 500 there are 206 fallers, seven that remain in the same position, 143 risers and 144 new entries. The biggest faller is the previously discussed MBNA. The largest riser is Stanley, which moved up 307 places, although this was partly as a consequence of being re-categorised. The highest genuine riser, ignoring changes in categories, was stationery brand Viking, which rose 178 places.

Brands that remained in exactly the same position from last year are car rental firms Avis (31) and Hertz (10), banking giant HSBC (39), software giant Microsoft® (2), researchers Mintel (207), energy company Shell (17) and technology firm Hewlett-Packard (32). Two hundred and nine of the 352 brands featuring in the list in both years did not move more than 50 places.

Sector Performance
There are brands from 58 different sectors in this year's top 500. Categories with the most entrants are 'technology – hardware & equipment' (31 brands), 'financial – bank' (22 brands), followed closely by 'retailers – office equipment & supplies'. Other sectors performing strongly are 'travel & leisure – business hotels'; 'construction & materials – tools & equipment'; 'construction & materials'; and 'travel & leisure – airlines'.

Following last year's results and market feedback some categories were amended this year. As a result of sub-dividing and merging certain sectors it is hard to compare sector success without going into detail, which would not be appropriate for this summary. It should be noted however that a few brands' positions may have been affected due to these amendments. We do not expect this to reoccur as categories will now remain consistent year-on-year.

Select Category Winners and Interesting Battles

The top performer in the aerospace & defence category is the Rolls-Royce Group, with fellow British defence giant BAE Systems over 90 places below it, perhaps reeling somewhat from the allegations of bribery in relation to its business in Saudi Arabia, notably the Al Yamamah deals. Sandwiching it are the two giants in aircraft making, Boeing and Airbus – the former beating its European rival by more than 60 places.

While the commercial success of both Boeing and Airbus are closely matched, in brand value terms Boeing is still the clear winner. One could speculate that negative coverage of ongoing boardroom battles in relation to the future of Airbus, particularly in respect of its corporate structure and potential job losses, outweighed any positive coverage of Airbus' commercial and technical successes. At a more basic level the Boeing brand is more established thus heritage is possibly playing a key role – Airbus was founded in 1970, Boeing in 1916. The rest of the sector's qualifiers are UK subsidiaries of American defence giants such as General Dynamics UK and Lockheed Martin. Compared with last year,

five fewer companies from this sector made the overall top 500. Nine aerospace and defence companies featured in total.

In automobile & parts the top performers are the big tyre makers, exactly as they were in the 2007 results. Toping the 2008 sector ranking is Michelin, followed closely by Pirelli and Goodyear. Bridgestone, the official tyres of Formula One from 2008–2010, trails its big rivals for now. As the popularity of Formula One in the UK gains momentum and as Bridgestone's exclusive contract begins, we can examine whether this affects its rating. Of course, in the 2007 Formula One season Bridgestone was in effect the sole tyre supplier as a result of Michelin concluding its involvement. An extra eight brands from this sector made the top 500, improving the sector's performance overall.

The chemical sector has exactly the same number of entrants this year as last. Yet again it is topped by ICI with strong performances also from DuPont, BASF and BOC, all of whom finished in the top 200. BASF jumped above BOC and one ponders whether the latter losing its status as a British blue chip, having been taken over in

September 2006 by German group Linde, had any effect on its ranking. That is not to say that foreign ownership is a bad thing – BASF, which took BOC's place, is a German company itself – merely that in 2006 BOC enjoyed considerable exposure in the UK financial press from a markets perspective and now has a lower profile as part of a multinational of a different name.

There was a large increase in the number of construction companies making the top 500, with seven additional entrants from last year taking the total to 17. Perhaps the slow realisation that branding does matter even in traditionally non-branded fields has started to pay dividends for categories like construction. The field is currently led by Pilkington, Blue Circle and Tarmac – two of these iconic British brands have recently been acquired by Lafarge and NSG respectively, while Tarmac is currently for sale by its Parent Anglo American (at the time of writing). Lafarge itself is in 443rd place, compared to Blue Circle at 150 – the group is currently, sensibly, maintaining the Blue Circle name in the UK market.

Other sectors with notable changes in the number of constituents in the top 500

Top Performing Categories 2008

Category	Brand Total
Technology – hardware & equipment	31
Financial – bank	22
Retailers – office equipment & supplies	21
Travel & leisure – business hotels	17
Construction & materials – tools & equipment	17

include advertising services, which shed 11 members from the top 500. Only seven advertising agencies made the top 500 compared to 18 last year! Is this a reflection of the dwindling influence of the large advertising groups or a one-off? It will be interesting to see how the sector performs next year.

Software & computer services lost 12 members, with 13 brands making the top 500 compared to 25 last year. Microsoft® tops the list followed by Cisco Systems and Adobe, with Sun Microsystem and Sage taking the final places in the top five for the category.

The clash of the oil giants shows that BP outperforms Shell in the sector rankings, although both considerably outperform third placed brand EXXON MOBIL. The top two again possibly benefit from higher exposure due to their UK stock market status but also their more favourably perceived environmental credentials.

Nokia and Sony clearly lead the way in the electronic & electrical equipment category; the rest of the players in the sector are some way further down the list.

Visa outperforms Mastercard but only by seven places with American Express a further three places down. In the battle of the retail banks, 10 in total make the top 500, with HSBC nudging Barclays out.

In the B2B delivery sector FedEx Express scores most highly, entering the top 10 in ninth place. Incredibly, in the top 500 two of its biggest rivals, UPS and DHL, sit next to each other in 21st and 22nd place respectively. In the delivery of bulk goods Eddie Stobart tops the logistics, distribution & freight services category.

Reflecting their relatively low profile, only three mining companies make the top 500

with Rio Tinto ahead of Anglo American and Rio Tinto's proposed merger partner BHP Billiton.

Vodafone dominates the battle of the mobile operators ahead of Orange, which sits in second place in its category.

Surprisingly, the law firms perform badly on the whole. Only eight made the top 500 with Linklaters highest at 259th. Clifford Chance also made the top 300 with the other six firms finishing between 300-500.

What Makes a Business Superbrand

Brands are rated on the three factors:
▓ Quality – does the brand represent quality products and services?
▓ Reliability – can you trust the brand to deliver consistently against its promises and maintain product and service standards across all customer touch points?
▓ Distinction – is the brand well known in its sector? Is it suitably differentiated from its competitors, with a personality and values that make it unique within its marketplace?

All three factors are considered essential ingredients in a Business Superbrand. In addition all highly rated brands must stand up against the following definition:
'A Business Superbrand has established the finest reputation in its field. It offers customers significant emotional and or tangible advantages over its competitors, which (consciously or sub-consciously) customers want, recognise, and are confident about investing in. Business Superbrands are targeted at organisations (although not necessarily exclusively so).'

Of course in reality this is a subjective process and therefore ultimately a whole myriad of influences are affecting people's perceptions of each brand, from their

personal experience of the brand to the companies' environmental and corporate responsibility and from the personality exuded by a brand's sales force to the creativity of their marketing campaigns.

Business Superbrands does not go into detail on specific sectors, rating a wide range of brands across diverse sectors by taking a snapshot of opinion both from experts, in the form of the council, and from business professionals. While the professionals surveyed have purchasing responsibility for their companies they may not have experience of many of the brands featured in the list. Invariably, these factors mean that the Business Superbrands process favours higher profile sectors and those brands bridging both B2B and B2C markets. Business Superbrands aims to celebrate overall branding successes and while there are no doubt stories of smaller brands in niche markets building exceptional reputations, they are not deemed to be Business Superbrands.

Conclusions

All the brands featuring in the top 500 have performed incredibly well, considering the thousands of brands initially considered across so many sectors. All deserve Business Superbrands status. For many brands in the top 500 it is their very presence in this elite group, rather than their specific placing within it, which is their greatest achievement, particularly when you consider the brands that failed to make the grade, from catering giant Sodexho to telecommunications and satellite operator Inmarsat. The challenge in 2009 for this year's top 500 will be to maintain or improve their position in the official Business Superbrands survey.

Qualifying Business Superbrands 2008

3
118 118
3COM
3i
3M
AA
Abbey
Abbott Mead Vickers BBDO
ABN AMRO
ABTA
ACAS
ACCA
Accenture
Accountancy Age
Acer
ACNielsen
Adecco
Adobe
ADT
AIG
AIM
Air France
Airbus
Akzo Nobel
Alamo
Alfred McAlpine
Allen & Overy
Alliance Boots
Allianz
Allied Irish Bank (GB)
Alstom
AMD
AMEC
American Airlines
American Express
Amtrak
Anglo American
Apax Partners
Apple
Arriva
Arup
Ashridge Business School
Ask.com
Associated British Ports
AstraZeneca
Atkins
Avery
Avis
AXA
AXA PPP Healthcare
B&Q
BAA
BACS
BAE Systems
Bain & Company
Balfour Beatty
Banco Santander
Banham Alarms
Bank of America
Bank of Scotland
Barclaycard
Barclays
BASF

Basildon Bond
Bayer
BBC Worldwide
BBH
BDO Stoy Hayward
Belkin
BG Group
BHP Billiton
BIC
Biffa
Big Yellow Self Storage
Black & Decker
BlackBerry
Blackstone
Bloomberg
Blu Tack
Blue Circle
Bluetooth
BMI
BMRB
BNP Paribas
BOC
Boeing
Bosch
Bostik
Boston Consulting Group
BP
Bridgestone
Bristol-Myers Squibb
British Airways
British Gas Businesss
British Gypsum
British Land
Brook Street
Brother
Brunswick
BSI
BT
Budget
BUPA
Business Week
Calor
Campaign
Canon
Capgemini
Capita
Carbon Trust
Carlton Screen Advertising
Carphone Warehouse
Casio
Caterpillar
Cathay Pacific
Cazenove
CBI
CBS Outdoor
Charterhouse
Chubb
CIMA
Cisco Systems
Citigroup
City Link
Clifford Chance
CNBC

CNN
Compass Group
Conqueror
Continental
Continental Airlines
Co-Operative Bank
Corus
Costain
Coutts
Cranford School of Management
Credit Suisse
Crown
Crowne Plaza
CVC
D&B
Datamonitor
De La Rue
Dell
Deloitte
Dennis
Deutsche Bank
Deutsche Post
DeWalt
DHL
Dolby
Dow Chemicals
Draper
Drapers
Dresdner Kleinwort
DTZ
Dulux
Dunlop
DuPont
E.ON
Easyjet
Ebay
EC&O Venues
Eddie Stobart
EDF Energy
Emirates
Enterprise Rent-A-Car
Epson
Ericsson
Ernst & Young
Estates Gazette
Europcar
Eurostar
Eurotunnel
Eversheds
Excel London
Expedia
Experian
Exxon Mobil
Fairtrade
Fedex Express
First
Flybe
Ford (Transit Vans)
Four Seasons Hotels
Freshfields Bruckhaus Deringer
FT
FTSE Market Information Service
Fujitsu

Fujitsu Siemens
Fyffes
G4S
Gallup
Gatwick Express
GE
General Dynamics UK
Getty Images
GFK NOP
GKN
GlaxoSmithKline
Goldman Sachs
Goodyear
Google
Grant Thornton
Great Portland Estates
Gulf Air
Gulfstream
H.R. Owen
Hanson
Harris
Hays
Heathrow Express
Henley Management College
Herbert Smith
Hertz
Hewlett-Packard
Hill & Knowlton
Hilton
Hiscox
Hitachi
Hogg Robinson Group
Holiday Inn
Honeywell
Hoovers
HSBC
HSS Hire
IATA
IBM
IBM Business Consulting Service
ICC Birmingham
ICI
Inchcape
ING
Intel
Interbrand
InterContinental Hotels & Resorts
Interlink Express
Invensys
Investec
Investors in People
IoD
Ipsos MORI
Iveco
Jarvis
Jarvis Hotels
JC Decaux
JCB
Jewson
Jiffy
John Laing
Johnson & Johnson
Johnson Matthey

Jones Lang LaSalle
JP Morgan
JVC
JWT
Kall Kwik
Kelly Services
Kier Group
Kimberly-Clark Professional*
Kitemark
KKR
KLM
Knight Frank
Korn/Ferry International
KPMG
Lafarge
Land Securities
Lazard
Le Meridien Hotel & Resorts
Legal & General
Lehman Brothers
Letts
LEX
Lexmark
Leyland
LG
Lilly
Linklaters
Lloyd's
Lloyds TSB
Lockheed Martin
Loctite
Logica CMG
Logitech
London Business School
London City Airport
London School of Economics and Political Science
London Stock Exchange
Lovells
Lufthansa
LYCRA
Lynx Express
M&C Saatchi
Maersk
Makita
MAN
Management Today
Manchester Business School
Mandarin Oriental
Manpower
Marketing
Marketing Week
Marriott
Massey Ferguson
Mastercard
MBNA
McAfee
McCann Erickson
McKinsey & Company
Mercedes (Trucks)
Merck
Merrill Lynch
Michael Page International

Michelin
Microsoft
Millennium & Copthorne
Mintel
Monster.com
Moody's
Morgan Stanley
Motorola
MSN
Multimap
National Express
National Grid
Nationwide
Natwest
NEC
NEC Birmingham
Nectar
Netgear
Nissan (Commercial Vehicles)
NM Rothschild
Nokia
Nomura
Nortel
Norwich Union
Novartis
Novell
Npower
O2
Office Angels
Ogilvy & Mather
Olympus
Oracle
Orange
Oxford Black n' Red
P&O
PA Consulting
Palm
Panasonic
Papermate
Parcelforce Worldwide
Parceline
Paypal
PC World
Peal & Dean
Pearson Longman
Pendragon
Permira
Pfizer
Philips Medical Systems
Pickfords
Pilkington
Pirelli
Pitman Training
Pitney Bowes
Polycell
Portakabin
Pratt & Whitney
Press Association
PricewaterhouseCoopers
Pritt
Prontaprint
Property Week
Prudential

Qantas
Quark
RAC
Radisson Edwardian Hotels
Ramada Jarvis
Reed
Reed Elsevier
Regus
Rentokil
Retail Week
Reuters
Rexel
RIBA
Ricoh
Rio Tinto
Roche
Rolls-Royce Group
Ronseal
Rotring Pens
Royal & Sun Alliance
Royal Bank of Scotland
Royal Mail
Ryman
Saatchi & Saatchi
Sage
Saint Gobain
Salvesen
Samsung
SAP
Savills
Scania
Schering-Plough
Schroders
Scotch
Scottish Power
Securitas
Sellotape
Shangri-La Hotels & Resorts
Sharp
Shell
Sheraton
Siemens
Singapore Airlines
Sir Robert McAlpine
Skanska
Skype
Slaughter & May
Smith & Nephew
Snap-on
Sony
Sony Ericsson
Staedtler
Stagecoach
Standard & Poor's
Standard Life
Stanley
Staples
Streetmap
Sun Microsystems
Swiss Re
Symantec
Tarmac
TDK

Teflon
Terra Firma Capital Partners
Tetra Pak
Texas Instruments
Thames Water
The Banker
The Carlye Group
The Daily Telegraph
The Economist
The Grocer
The Guardian
The Law Society
The Observer
The Open University
The Queen Elizabeth II Conference Centre
The Ritz Carlton
The Sunday Times
The Times
Thistle Hotels
Thomson Directories
Thomson Financial
Thyssen Krupp
Ticketmaster
Tipp-Ex
T-Mobile
TNT
Toshiba
Total
TPG
Travelocity Business
Travelodge
Travis Perkins
UBS
Unibond
Unisys
United Airlines
Unix
UPS
VAIO
Velcro
Velux
Vent-Axia
Verisign
Viking
Virgin Atlantic
Virgin Trains
Visa
Vodafone
Volvo (Trucks & Buses)
Warburg Pincus
Warwick Business School
Weber Shandwick
Wickes
Wincanton
Wolff Olins
Xerox
Yahoo!
Yellow Pages
YKK
Zurich

The 'And' in Brand

By Anthony Carlisle
Executive Director
Citigate Dewe Rogerson

We're certainly not short of definitions of brand.

Agencies of all disciplines extol 'its' values with fervour.

Consultants symbolise 'it' with precise circles and pyramids.

Accountants value 'it'.

Even some lisping thwee-year-olds are aware of 'it'.

Which is all well and good as far as it goes. But it's all too often missing the one person who can actually – and should, actually – control 'it'.

Brand is a reflection of personality. It's a reflection of what a business, a product, an organisation aims to be. Fundamentally, and above all, it's a direct reflection of corporate strategy.

Which is a somewhat serious point.

And… a genuine CEO responsibility.

Which makes it mildly surprising that so many companies let it be played with – often by those who show little corporate understanding.

There's a whole list of excuses. The CEO is too busy. He or she doesn't understand. His or her skill set is elsewhere. It's a big area…

Yet the evidence is that when the CEO does enter the brand world – usually in response to a specific corporate need

– there can start to be a charmed and magic circle.

The brand is more focused. It knows what it has to achieve – quite often in a limited timescale.

That means the messages are clear – dictated by corporate purpose and strategy.

As a result, the creative execution is often distinctive and confident. Because

the brand has something to say – it departs from the empty 'comfort factor' measures of others in its sector.

And with one clear internal line of communication, the consistency is often less diluted.

So message, language (tone of voice), as well as look, flow clearly across all communications – including the bits that CEOs know are important but which often get just lip service from traditional marketeers.

Timing – and top-down handling – eliminates the salami slicing death by a thousand cuts by well meaning, but ultimately destructive, layers of 'decision makers'.

All of which means that – assuming a fair wind and a team with talent – the brand stands a good chance of getting its messages over. It stands out – because it stands for something.

It becomes a conviction brand – firm and consistent in its positioning and in its handling of, and reaction to, events. Not a confection brand – endlessly trying to re-shape itself to the next fickle fashion or nod of focus group approval, ending up standing for little or nothing.

OK for the theory. The practice is more pertinent.

Once long ago…

There was a bank that, despite being a substantial player in its market, was, courtesy of its history, seen as a low level lender of last resort. Far from being thought of as up there with the big four, it would have been lucky to have been seen in the small 27. That's the kind of thing that focuses the mind of a CEO of a newly floated company.

So he withdrew all product advertising – focused on creating the brand he wanted, telling people the hard facts. Fast.

The resulting campaign constantly topped the awareness polls, produced the 'most-liked' TV ad in its sector – and, indeed, saw sales of products across the offering soar – as well as expanding the sector phrasing to 'the big five'.

(Sadly, not all the bank's decisions were as successful; but on brand, they played a blinder.)

In years of British Gas advertising, when did it arguably receive its most high level focus?

When it was privatised and needed to sell billions of pounds of shares to millions of individuals. Enter Sid, who performed his task with immense popularity, efficacy and a single mindedness second only to She who was – almost always – obeyed.

The Scottish Widow was born when a chief exec (and a determined marketing manager) challenged the wisdom of

changing the name to SW to 'modernise and differentiate' the brand – and enabled the creation of one of the best known visual mnemonics in its sector – one that has endured for over 20 years. (Though noticeably at her strongest before new acquirers allowed slightly careless treatment of her.)

Orange entered its market with a CEO who passionately believed in a future (beyond phones) that was wire-free, a dictate that small things (like customers!) mattered – and a certainty that you simply didn't get to win in a market dominated by established players by being the same. His last act – floating the company for France Telecom – saw Orange rise to be number one by customer base, in a campaign (without product advertising) to promote the 'Orangeprint for the future'.

And, of course, many of our more meaningful brands today are still shaped – and crafted – by those who created the company. Ever felt that the spirit of the Pret A Manger brand lives best in the small details…. The back of its vans distributing its food to the homeless… the message on the bags … the info on the sarnie. Even after McDonald's became a major strategic investor, it's still the founding CEO who firmly influences his brand – including writing many of its materials.

And some, when faced with crisis, do successfully re-invent – re-discover the fundamentals that re-ignite customer enthusiasm and loyalty – 'Your M&S'…

So why is it that when companies aren't forced to react to a crisis, or when they become a big player in their market, so many CEOs seem to abandon their brands to expensive arms-length mediocrity?

Some who successfully build the brand argue that they simply have to 'let go' as a company grows. But it's often at that point that they see the initial investment – and brand authority – dissipate. Brands are fragile – far easier to dent than to build. The DNA easily mutates.

Others suggest CEOs don't have a creative bone in their body. But, in truth, brand empathy is often found as strongly in the boardroom as in the marketing department. No-one is suggesting giving up the day job – but intelligent insight to guide accurate communication of key messages doesn't require becoming a severe threat to Leonardo da Vinci.

Perhaps it's in the naming? Many call it Marketing and Advertising.

If we just said M and A, would CEOs pay more attention?

Creativity in B2B

By Kate Manasian
Managing Director
Saffron

When asked to write about 'creativity in B2B', I thought – I'm either the best person to do this or the worst person. That's because I don't like the concept of 'B2B' and I'd like it if people stopped using the term. More importantly, I'd like it if people stopped thinking in those terms. I don't mean the practice of B2B, but the B2B mindset – the assumption that B2B demands a different approach. Because it doesn't.

Creativity in B2B isn't a different kind of creativity – it's just creativity.

I've never really understood why people find the distinction between B2B and B2C important. I've never found it helpful. There is an underlying assumption that people are different when wearing their business hats. And they're not.

I don't think it's about B2B or B2C. I think it's about B2P – the 'P' being people.

I'm most likely to hear the 'B' phrase when a client says to me, "yes, but this is B2B". Then I think "oh no" – because that's

code for... "make sure it's benefit-specific, fact-based, value-driven, stakeholder-targeted and grounded in evidence".

I understand that some businesses sell to consumers, while others sell to other businesses, but I don't accept that this means they should change the way they tell their story. Whether people are deciding what car to buy or what auditor to appoint, they take in information and make decisions in the same way – rationally and emotionally – and the two can't be separated.

I find it puzzling when clients are reluctant to apply their own experiences to the way they talk to customers. No-one likes being bored – so why do people approve boring copy?

No-one likes being confused – so why do we swamp people with information that is important to us, but not to them? Sometimes I look at the PowerPoint presentations my clients have written and wonder – "would you like to sit through

this?" I don't know how people survive it – and I wonder what they learn from it.

A few years ago one of my clients was a New York law firm.

I was interviewing one of the senior partners and he was explaining the difference between real advice and what passes for advice. He said that when he was starting out as a lawyer, a young entrepreneur consulted him – he was launching a business and wanted to know if he should form a corporation.

This lawyer – my client – said he went through the options, the pros and cons of each, the legal and tax implications, the advantages and disadvantages of starting a business in one form and changing it to another later on – and so on. He outlined the options in meticulous detail – but he didn't tell his client which was best for him.

He said he thinks the young man left his office so confused that he never started a company. To quote him – "the answer to his question – 'should I form a corporation?' –

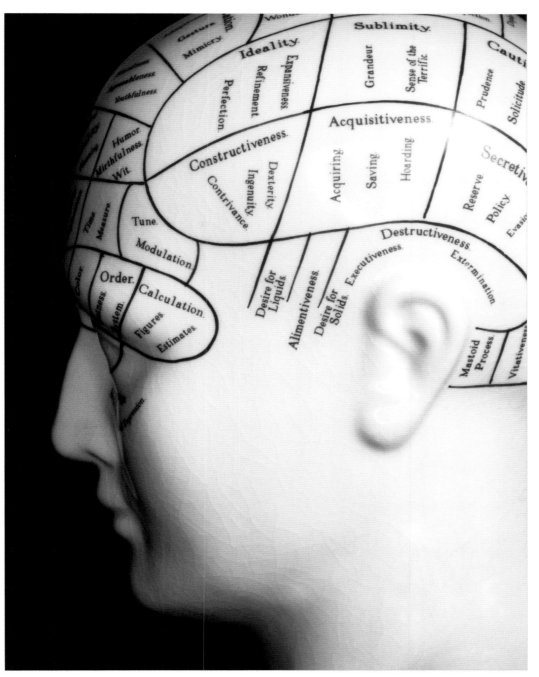

was 'yes' – but I got so lost in the minutiae that I forgot what he'd come to me for – a simple answer to a simple question."

When we're trying to talk to our customers, we can make the same mistake. And when we think 'B2B' we're more apt to make that mistake – because it leads us down the wrong path.

Everyone in business should read the The Economist Style Guide.

B2B material would improve overnight if they did – as would business meetings and all PowerPoint presentations.

The guide reminds us to say 'guess' rather than 'guesstimate'.

And that critique is a noun, not a verb – if you want a verb, say 'criticise'. It says, 'readers are primarily interested in what you have to say. By the way in which you say it, you may encourage them either to read on or to give up. If you want them to read on, do your best to be lucid'.

One of my colleagues is a stringer for the Wall Street Journal – he wrote a piece on nation branding that attracted the attention of a strategy consultancy. They wanted him to ghost an article on nation branding for an audience of insurance brokers. He wrote a stimulating piece – full of anecdotes and quotations that made the points in a readable and colourful way.

His draft article came back with every anecdote and quotation stripped out. The covering email said, 'our audience is the strategy wing of a major global insurance company and as a result they expect a certain dry style'.

So – is it true that we take information more seriously when it bores us?

You may have heard of Peggy Noonan, a well-known American journalist and speechwriter. She is known for her simple, elegant prose. She wrote the moving speech given by Ronald Reagan 20 years ago when Challenger exploded after take-off. It replaced Reagan's State of the Union address – this is the last paragraph…

'The crew of the space shuttle Challenger honoured us by the manner in which they lived their lives. We will never forget them, nor the last time we saw them, this morning, as they prepared for their journey and waved good-bye and slipped the surly bonds of earth to touch the face of God.'

In her autobiography, Noonan tells stories of the wrangles she had with White House and State Department lawyers when they were editing her speeches. They were always telling her "you can't say that" or "that's not strictly the case" or "this could get us in trouble".

The vetting process was about scores of staffers adding and deleting things until the speeches became soggy and the messages obscure. While she favoured plain speaking, the lawyers and bureaucrats were more comfortable with qualification and ambiguity. Anything interesting or opinionated was cut out.

You may be surprised to know that Peggy Noonan is an admirer of George Bush's style of delivery. She likes what she calls his "thudding bluntness" when speaking impromptu. She approves of him when he says that he wants Osama Bin Laden "dead or alive" or that congress will raise taxes "over my dead body".

She thinks this tendency might stem from a boyhood in Texas, where a valid murder defence still on the books has been boiled down to 'he needed killin''.

Illustrations © John Woodcock

Why does she approve of Bush's vivid use of language? For the same reason she admires John F Kennedy for saying "Ich bin ein Berliner" instead of "I support Berlin" (according to her, that's what the State Department lawyers would have had him say).

She believes these two presidents have something in common – when they said what they said, they wanted people to understand what they meant and that they meant it. And in her view, if you want people to know what you mean, "use words that pierce, not words that cloud".

Saying things simply and well is good practice whatever you are saying and whoever you are saying it to. Adjusting the way you talk because you are talking to a business audience is bad practice.

In 'Blink', Malcolm Gladwell tells the story of Gary Klein, an American consultant who wrote a book called 'Sources of Power' – a classic work on decision-making. Klein did a study that involved nurses, intensive care units, firefighters – people who make decisions under pressure. One of his conclusions was that when experts make decisions they don't logically and systematically compare all available options.

That's how they're taught to make decisions, but in real life it's too slow. The nurses and firefighters in his study all sized up situations immediately and acted – drawing on experience and intuition. That's what decision-making in business is like – it's complex, it isn't all rational and it's done at speed and under pressure.

Detail is important, but judgments are usually made against a bigger backdrop. And that backdrop is made up of the things you already know and what you think about those things.

Maybe that's my problem with the concept of B2B. It encourages people to separate detail from the bigger picture. And that's what takes the heart out of things.

I spend a lot of time in airports. In particular, I spend a lot of time in passport queues looking at B2B ads – good ones and bad ones.

I like SAP's ads – the ones that show black and white images of SAP customers going about their daily work – selling toys, or cutting hair or delivering parcels. The ads say – 'The Body Shop runs SAP' or 'UPS runs SAP'. And they add a strapline – 'the best run businesses run SAP'. That's all they say.

SAP is a B2B brand – why does it choose to run simple, human ads that don't even mention that they're in software? Because the ads form one of those backdrops that lives in purchasers' minds.

What is SAP communicating in its ads? Reassurance. They're saying, "it's OK – it's SAP". "It may be more expensive – but it's SAP". They want customers to think – "these other people look OK, but I'd feel better going with SAP".

At one time Intel was considered a B2B brand. It has what – maybe 500 customers? Before the 1990s it was a second-tier electronics player lagging well behind Texas Instruments in microprocessor sales. It certainly was an undistinguished brand. Few purchasers – B or C – knew or cared about their specialised components.

Then in 1991, whoever was given the task of marketing their microchip, figured out that the best way to do it was to create some grassroots pressure for this wonderful piece of technology. They launched a US$100 million co-operative campaign with PC makers – Intel Inside – that ran round their primary customers straight to the end users.

Well, they shot past Texas Instruments after that. Intel Inside is their backdrop. However much detail they provide on their various products – and I'm sure they provide a lot – it's all seen against this backdrop.

That's why Pirelli ran those calendars for years. Ninety nine per cent of tyre sales are direct to manufacturers. Did young men look at those calendars and then go out and buy four tyres? Probably not.

The calendars raised Pirelli's profile – they associated it with something slightly risqué. Like Intel, they created upward pressure on manufacturers. Car makers would say, "this is a fast, sexy car – we want to sell it to young men – let's supply Pirellis as standard".

I know it's easy to cite famous, successful examples and I'm aware that I've glided over a few practicalities – like the fact that not all businesses have budgets for airport campaigns. I've used these stories to make a few simple points…

There is good B2B work out there – but it's just good work – not good B2B work.

There's creative B2B work out there – but it's just good creative work.

The distinction between B and C isn't the important thing. Creativity is the important thing. Forget about the distinction and you'll find that the creativity comes easier.

Saffron

Saffron was formed in 2001 by Jacob Benbunan and Wally Olins. It was founded on a simple premise: to build a brand consultancy where strategy and creativity are equal and excellent. Saffron people value thought and relationships over process. The business is independent, so it sets its own agenda. It only takes on work it believes in, so its involvement with and commitment to clients is total.

It has offices in three locations – London, Madrid and New York – across which it operates as one company. Saffron is young and fast growing. All of its people are accomplished brand professionals, and its principals – Jacob Benbunan, Wally Olins, Kate Manasian, Ian Stephens and Eric Scott – are experienced players in the world of branding having worked over their careers with Volkswagen, Tata, Fedex, PricewaterhouseCoopers, Linklaters, Unilever, Lloyd's of London, Tesco, HP and BT.

Saffron's chairman, Wally Olins, is recognised as one of the world's foremost brand practitioners. His recent book, 'Wally Olins On Brand', has been published in more than 15 countries.

www.saffron-consultants.com

How B2B Brands can use Digital Channels to Build Brand Value

The role of digital in the B2B marketing mix

By Andrew Pinkess
Strategy Director
Rufus Leonard

Digital has had a chequered history in B2B marketing over the last few years, with some marketers embracing it enthusiastically as a god-send, helping to improve awareness, cut costs and reach more customers, whereas others remain resolutely sceptical – preferring to rely on tried and trusted ways of doing business. For example, a senior partner in a professional services firm, during a recent round of stakeholder interviews for the redesign of the company's website, came up with the jaw-dropping comment: "I think the web has had its day!"

Thankfully this sort of attitude is very much the exception these days. Most B2B companies have got the basics of online brand communications pretty well sorted. They have gone through the stages of using the web as a directory, and have now put most of their brochures and product/service data online as well. They have even got to grips with the importance of search engine marketing and in some cases have begun to experiment with digital advertising, focusing on online marketplaces which are specific to their sector. So where do they go next?

In our view there is still plenty of opportunity for B2B marketers to build their brands online, and we see them moving forward on four different fronts:

■ Managing and protecting brand reputation
■ Creating compelling online brand experiences
■ Using the web to make money and save money
■ Building long term relationships with key clients and accounts

All of these can build real brand value for B2B organisations who master them over the next few years.

Managing and protecting brand reputation

For B2B marketers brand value is intrinsically linked with brand reputation. As many B2B sectors are relatively opaque, it can take a long time to build a strong reputation and a long time to lose it. Poor service experiences could in the past be contained and kept out of the public gaze. But not any more.

If product quality or service delivery does not match expectations then blogs and discussion forums can spread the word in a matter of hours. Although blogs may only be read by the minority, they remain a great source of leads for trade journalists, who can then amplify messages and create embarrassing headlines.

Larger B2B organisations are already tuned in to this, and are tracking comments in the blogosphere. United Airlines has been forced to respond to a branded blog called 'Untied' which became a magnet for disaffected business travellers, fed up with consistently poor service.

Companies such as General Motors and Boeing have sought to forestall this kind of criticism by monitoring discussion forums and creating their own blogs. The latter are used to engage with priority audiences in a more informal way – adopting a personal tone, but amplifying it quickly across the marketplace.

The web is also a great vehicle for telling the company story on corporate and social responsibility (CSR) in a compelling way. In the past CSR was seen as a niche activity, but B2B companies are rapidly moving away from printed annual reports, towards more frequent online reporting. For instance we have worked with both O2 and BT on the creation of award-winning corporate responsibility sites as part of a wider corporate communications programme.

A further very impressive example is General Electric's (GE) Ecomagination microsite, which is accessible from the main GE website, and tells the story of the company's efforts to use the threat of global warming as a trigger for profitable new product development activity.

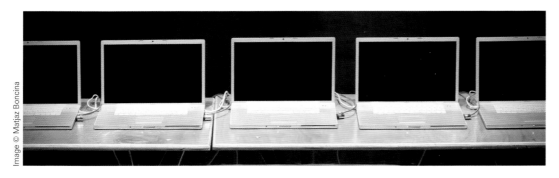

Image © Matjaz Boncina

Creating compelling online brand experiences

The rapid growth of broadband access to both business and consumer audiences has opened up an opportunity to create really compelling, near broadcast quality video and rich media experiences. B2C companies have been quick to spot the promotional potential for this, but B2B is only now beginning to catch on.

And yet, this facility is particularly appropriate to B2B marketers, many of whom struggle with explaining complex propositions to hard to reach audiences. A recent example features the online 'technology showcase' created by science research consultancy QinetiQ, which specialises in security and defence. This puts in an online shop window, sexy new products such as the security body scanner now being introduced at airports to combat terrorism, and robots able to defuse bombs.

On a more accessible level, payments and fuel card services specialist Retail Decisions has used Google Maps to create a site selector for its fleet manager customers, showing them exactly where across Europe their cards will be accepted. Not only does this provide a valuable

service, it also acts as a value-added differentiator and retention tool in a competitive and promiscuous market.

Another example of creating online brand experiences comes in the presentation of case studies, and the telling of stories about company successes and culture.

IBM is a leader in this space with its Executive Interaction Channel. It uses flash animation on its website to introduce themes and topics, allowing the user to select a relevant case study. The story of the project is then told using audio and video, including client commentary and endorsements. Clearly, as a technology oriented business with deep pockets, they are well-placed to exploit this opportunity, but it also gives them stand out against other competitors such as Accenture, who still favour text-based examples.

As TV and internet start to converge in the mind of the consumer, the rich media style of presentation is likely to become the norm in B2B. Yet few B2B organisations are currently prepared for or resourced to take advantage of what the web has to offer in this area.

The current Wild West frontier for online brand experiences is virtual worlds, such as World of Warcraft and Second Life. At

the moment these are more the preserve of image conscious teenage and twenty-something consumers. But B2B marketers are beginning to experiment – often to generate PR or to entice future recruits. They certainly have the potential to play a role in product demonstration, partnership building and collaborative working, but for the moment at least, they need more business traffic to justify much B2B time or investment.

Using the web to make money and save money

Many areas of B2B still offer bespoke solutions or services which are hard to deliver online. But plenty more lend themselves well to rapid sourcing of specific products, which in the past could only be found through brokers or intermediaries.

The latter segment has taken a real battering as B2B ecommerce has grown rapidly, effectively by-passing them and their offer.

But this in turn has led to the creation of new 'eBay' style business models for low cost and low overhead operations which piggy-back off other sectors in a parasitic way. Many of these are unbranded but use their knowledge of search engine algorithms to outsmart the search engines and position their offer at the top of the list when particular keywords are requested.

This might suggest that the power of brands in an online world is in decline. Certainly online has had a major impact on the way brands are perceived and consumed. And yet brands remain as powerful as ever on the web, particularly where money is changing hands. Payment organisations such as PayPal and Visa have moved in to provide reassurance to purchasers, but both B2B and B2C online customers remain wary of buying from those they do not know.

Setting aside direct B2B ecommerce services, there is still much that the web has to offer B2B marketers who remain reliant on personal selling. Much good work is being done in the creation of saleforce extranets (e.g. O2 and BT), which take the administrative hassle out of B2B selling. These tools provide quick and easy access to a wide range of information including:

- Best practice sales presentations
- Product/service reference material
- Datasheets
- Real-time order status

Websites are also getting better at actually closing the sale, or at the very least making the purchasing process less painful. Office supplies, equipment hire, and computer equipment are now mainly ordered online, but purchasing forms are still painful to complete with many frustrated users simply abandoning the process and picking up the phone – or worse still, buying elsewhere.

Again there are interesting developments here with the introduction of presentation-layer technologies (e.g. AJAX), which allow brand-owners to create new condensed concertina-style forms. Information is updated in real-time within the browser, rather than the customer having to step through multiple screens to reach the end of the process. Direct Line has recently launched its Direct Line for Business service using AJAX, and market reaction seems to be very positive. Interesting to note that they trialed the new service with B2B customers, before even considering rolling it out to a B2C audience.

Other areas of opportunity for helping to close the sale include: branded widgets, which can be launched onto the desktops of registered site users, and provide a vehicle to push offers and reminders to prospects without them having to return to the website; email reminders can perform a similar function, ensuring that the target is fully aware of your best deal at the point when they are ready to purchase; and finally, secure payment facilities provide additional reassurance once they have made the decision to buy.

Building long term relationships with key clients and accounts

Finally the Holy Grail for B2B web marketers is full-blown e-CRM, with the web acting as a backbone for long term multi-channel relationships. These tend to rely on integration with some form of customer database, which may be accessed through a web interface. Provided that sales and customer service staff can be motivated to share valuable customer information, these tools provide the potential to offer more joined up team-based customer service and improved client retention.

Other useful online relationship building tools include:

- Cross-selling and up-selling
- Customer newsletters
- Webinars
- Reducing customer service costs
- Customer wizards
- FAQs
- Online chat

Conclusion

Digital is an integral part of the B2B marketing mix and is here to stay. But does it build brand value, rather than just reflecting what is happening offline? Only if you use your imagination to identify ways of doing things faster, cheaper or better...

The beauty of digital marketing is that it is measurable, and that should be the ultimate means of judging how much value it can add to your brand. Personal relationships will invariably remain a key part of the B2B marketing mix, but there is still plenty of upside potential for digital channels to do more for your business.

Writing as Branding

By Matthew Stibbe
Writer-in-Chief
Articulate Marketing

Companies lavish great sums on ads, branding and websites. But they give less thought to the everyday writing they create. I'm not talking about copywriting in adverts. That's poetry. I'm talking about prose. The humdrum stuff of daily business life: press releases, contracts, marketing collateral, website content and the rest.

I believe that writing is a fundamental part of a brand. Finding a corporate voice and using it consistently adds weight and distinctiveness to a brand. Companies that neglect their writing risk short-changing their brand.

Google is a role model. It is no coincidence that it has a very consistent style and that its writing echoes the brand. Google's home page is nothing but words, after all. Most people concentrate on the button 'Google Search.' Those two words define what Google does but the other button, 'I'm Feeling Lucky', is more subtle. It reassures me that I'll find what I'm looking for. It tells me 'I' am in charge. It

radiates optimism. These few words tell me a lot about the Google brand.

Google's word-branding goes deeper than its home page – it permeates everything they do. Its terms and conditions also talk straight to the reader ("Thank you for trying out Google Desktop! Google Desktop is made available to you by Google Inc...."). It tells you what's important (when you enable advanced features it says 'Please read this carefully, it's not the usual yada yada').

Reinforcing the brand
Good writing, like Google's, enhances a brand in different ways. It can reinforce the reader's idea of what the brand stands for. For example, Virgin Atlantic shares the Virgin brand's cheeky irreverence. Tired by a long flight? "Pretend you're already there," says Virgin Atlantic. Bored by safety announcements? Watch a cartoon instead.

On a more practical level, good writing can increase sales. Amazon's login screen has a big friendly button which says

'Sign in using our secure server'. This reassures me that Amazon will keep my details safe. Similarly, on the penultimate page of the checkout process it says 'you can review this order before it's final' right under the 'Continue' button. Amazon has analysed where and why people stop buying and they've added these cues to get more people through the process.

Breaking faith
In contrast to Amazon, Virgin and Google's success, most corporate-speak is bland, undifferentiated and hard to read. Meaning is obscured by jargon, waffle, hype, verbiage, legalese and conventionality.

The cost of bad writing far outweighs the value created by good writing. A typical example is the heavily-promoted 'free' online trial that opens with a daunting click-through contract. Another common problem is website copy that just doesn't answer your questions. Yet another is the pious press release that takes 200 words to clear its throat and get started. My pet peeve is application forms that might as well be written in Medieval Latin. In fact, once you start looking for bad business writing, it's easy to spot.

It is possible to track the impact of clear product descriptions on sales, well-written manuals on support calls and snappy website copy on traffic. On the other hand, it is very difficult to add up the costs that come from obscure press releases, poor marketing collateral, or badly-worded letters.

The cost of bad writing is two-fold. First, you lose the money you spent delivering the words to the reader. Expensive website? Waste of money. 50,000 brochures? Recycling fodder. Second, you lose the hoped-for result. Have you ever read a brochure that bored or confused you? Did you buy the product afterwards?

Once you get past the glossy ads and shiny exterior, most companies sound like a headmaster, bank manager or lawyer. Is this how you want your company to sound to its customers and employees? In a wider sense, a company breaks faith with a reader any time a company's words don't match its brand. It's like a witness squirming under cross-examination. The truth will out.

What is good writing?

Good grammar, punctuation and spelling are necessary but not sufficient. Business writing is about hooking and persuading the reader. The best way to engage a reader is to use stories because human beings are wired for them. We look for believable details, natural speech and a flow from beginning to end. Journalism has evolved ways of creating credible, persuasive and readable stories and books like Donald Murray's Writing to Deadline have a lot to teach the business world. But journalism stops short of persuasion and that is the objective of a business writer. The 'call to action' often

I've just made a few last minute changes to the brief... so... everything you've done so far is... err... wrong.

Illustration © Thom Vincent

comes at the end of a piece but good business copy has a logical thread running through it that persuades the reader as it goes.

Writing for the web

We're all internet entrepreneurs now. The internet has done what technology always does. It has gone from being gee-whizz to ho-hum, from avant-garde to comme il faut. Business writing – so important in this new medium – has not caught up with the change. The BBC has got it right, though. They know that people don't read web pages the same way they look at newspapers or books and they write accordingly. Their website uses short paragraphs, short sentences, scannable text (clearly labeled links and headlines), hype-free language (in the journalistic tradition) and crisp micro-content ('Falklands return. How going back 25 years later helps heal veterans' scars').

One of the problems with less switched-on websites is the low priority given to web copy during development. A 2006 survey of digital agencies found that over half of them blamed delays on content problems but only 10 per cent said that content was a priority. They thought that design, development and search engine optimization were much, much more important. To me, this is like building a missile but forgetting the payload. The gap is filled by 'lorem ipsum' placeholder copy. If you see this on a development website, consider it a warning sign.

We're all writers now

Thanks to email, blogs and social networks like Facebook, we're all business writers now. Microsoft® positively encourages its employees to blog. Its thousands of employee-bloggers put a human face on their business. But most companies prefer to muzzle employees rather than develop their writing skills and embed a corporate tone of voice across the business. As these new media burst into life, we have a chance to embrace every written word as a tool that can make a brand strong, fresh and different. Otherwise it's just the usual yada yada.

Image © Eugene Kuklev

ARTICULATE

Articulate Marketing helps companies to talk about technology in good, everyday English. The agency's clients include Hewlett-Packard, Microsoft®, eBay and HM Government. It creates original content for websites, blogs, marketing and in-house magazines. It also gives advice on strategy, tone of voice and style guides.

Matthew Stibbe is owner and writer-in-chief at Articulate Marketing, as well as the author of the BadLanguage.net blog.

www.articulatemarketing.com

Seven types of bad writing

Everyone can write. But not everyone can write well. The result? Bad writing that...

1

Thinks too much of itself.
Private Eye's regular column on 'solutions' has it spot on. Prefer 'bandages' to 'innovative solutions for wound management'. Word inflation devalues meaning and arouses the scepticism of readers.

2

Is too clever by half.
Nervous writers want to sound big, grown-up and clever. So they use big words and long sentences. Ironically, scientists have proved that grandiloquence and circumlocution make you sound dumb.

3

Gets hyped up.
Press releases often include frankenquotes. These are made-up quotations that bear no resemblance to normal speech. Write how you talk. It sounds more natural.

4

Tells lies.
In the UK, journalists score low in public trust – somewhere near politicians and estate agents. However, good journalists are obsessive about research, accuracy, good reporting, details and, yes, truth. Do thou likewise.

5

Ignores the reader.
As a writer, the greatest skill is to think about what the reader needs to hear, not what you need to say. It takes an imaginative leap.

6

Needs to go on a diet.
Most writing can be improved by liposuction. Antoine de Saint-Exupery said it best: "A designer knows he has achieved perfection not when there is nothing left to add, but when there is nothing left to take away."

7

Has no direction.
My favourite tutor at Oxford told me that I had to take my essays and drive them like Ayrton Senna. Good writing has direction and pace.

Working Towards a CarbonNeutral® Future

By Ben Hudson
Chief Executive
Superbrands (UK) Ltd

As illustrated by the case studies in this, our sixth annual volume of Business Superbrands, the sheer spectrum of business to business (B2B) brands qualifying for inclusion is remarkable. Members include international conglomerates and niche B2B operators, sectors range from engineering to business education to trade associations (and everything in between), and ownership varies from public sector to FTSE 100 to private equity.

This diversity is all the more remarkable for the fact that members are united by more than just branding expertise; a further common denominator is a shared belief in the importance of sustainability, environmental awareness, and social responsibility. Ten years ago it might have been possible to pay lip service to these areas without undertaking a significant shift in business practice. In 2008 it is beholden on these B2B leaders to put corporate social responsibility (CSR) at the heart of their decision-making – and it is fascinating to observe how our members are approaching this challenging area.

It is immediately evident that members are eager to share knowledge and collaborate with other leading brands. To this end we have been working closely with Conqueror and their 'Blank Sheet Project' which aims to inspire businesses to think about the steps they can take to reduce carbon emissions. As part of the campaign, a blank sheet of Conqueror paper has been sent to over 40,000 SMEs, FTSE 100 CEOs and CSR directors, asking them to write down their thoughts on how to deal with the threat of climate change. The aim is to engage debate; the most inspiring results will be published on an online forum and sent to Government for consideration later this year.

David Cook, UK and Ireland sales and marketing director at Arjowiggins, owner and manufactuer of Conqueror, comments, "We launched the Blank Sheet Project because we really wanted to engage businesses in a high-profile environmental debate. The campaign coincided with the

Conqueror range becoming CarbonNeutral® in the UK and following a reduction of our carbon emissions by five per cent during the last two years. As a business, we constantly work to identify further energy saving opportunities.

"For many brands, using environmentally-sound products is now integral to their company culture or larger corporate social responsibilities. Whilst it is the responsibility of us all to reduce paper wastage, taking a small step such as using carbon neutral paper can make a big impact. For example we calculated that if all companies switched to using CarbonNeutral® paper, UK businesses alone could save over 23,000 tonnes of CO_2 each year, which is equivalent to the annual emissions of almost 4,200 households."

What is clear from the Blank Sheet Project and other initiatives like it is that the 2008 Business Superbrands – by definition, amongst the leaders in their respective fields – see the need to invest, innovate, and inspire. Examples abound (and much can be learned from the aforementioned case studies), but dialogue with members has allowed me to cherry-pick a few interesting examples for the purpose of this article:

Invest On the back of years of sustained investment, Corus has become one of the UK's largest recyclers, every year turning some 4.3MT of steel scrap into new steel

products, saving 6.5 million tonnes of CO_2 emissions.

Innovate FirstGroup – which carries more than 2.5 billion passengers on their buses and trains each year – aims to reduce carbon dioxide emissions by between 20 and 25 per cent by 2020. These tough objectives will require a wide series of innovative initiatives from investing in new technology to developing and trialling alternative fuels and changing the way it operates.

Inspire The Royal Institute of British Architects (RIBA) uses its considerable sphere of influence to encourage and assist architects, their clients and other professions, to understand the role that buildings play in climate change, and to provide a guide to the principles, tools and techniques to build low carbon buildings.

A practical issue for many businesses is that of measurement – both in terms of assessing current greenhouse gas

emissions and also in establishing future targets and measures of success. Two of our members, BSI and the Carbon Trust, are currently leading the development of a standard for a method for measuring the embodied greenhouse gas emissions from products and services across their lifecycle. The single standard, due to be published in June 2008, will help companies understand the impact that climate change has on their products' lifecycles and highlight opportunities to cut carbon emissions.

As you will see in the following pages, we have also been working closely with Business in the Community (BITC) to incorporate a dedicated CSR section into the Business Superbrands book for the first time. There is no doubt that this section of the book can be expected to grow in 2009 and beyond. As Brendon May, managing director of Planet 2050, Weber Shandwick's corporate responsibility and sustainability practice, succinctly concludes: "No organisation, Superbrand or not, can afford to ignore the challenges of sustainability. For in those challenges lie vast, often untapped, opportunities. The Superbrand is surely the company that attracts and retains the best people, shifts agendas, applies new thinking to old problems, and manages its business, day in, day out, with due care for the natural environment and the resources it brings us all."

QUALITY RELIABILITY DISTINCTION

Superbrands/BITC Corporate Social Responsibility (CSR) Project

When we launched Business Superbrands in 2000 it would have been a challenge for many UK organisations to articulate their approach to Corporate Social Responsibility across two pages of our book. How many businesses (or brands) could comment authoritatively on their carbon footprint, supply-chain management, and local community engagement? Eight years later, CSR sits firmly on the corporate agenda of large and small businesses across the land – and every business has a story to tell.

Hence, this dedicated section of Business Superbrands 2008 – itself the result of a new project that we have undertaken in conjunction with Business in the Community (BITC). The objective was quite simple: to showcase a number of positive and inspiring CSR stories from some of the UK's most respected organisations. Mallen Baker, development director of BITC kindly chaired the CSR Advisory Panel and explains the process in the following pages.

For our part, we must endeavour to practice what we preach. Superbrands (UK) Ltd publishes about 100,000 books each year and from January 2008 has been printing all of them in the UK using a one site operation. We have contracted with new printers who use ISO 14001 environmental management systems and vegetable based inks. Moreover, all our books (including the one you are holding) are printed on FSC-approved papers comprising (six per cent) de-inked post-consumer waste and (94 per cent) virgin fibre.

I hope you find this section of the book interesting, informative, and inspiring. As always, I welcome your comments and feedback.

Ben Hudson
Chief Executive, Superbrands (UK) Ltd
ben.hudson@superbrands.uk.com

The Rise of Corporate Social Responsibility

By Mallen Baker
Chairman
Superbrands/BITC CSR Advisory Panel

Expectations on businesses are still changing. Amidst a constant drip-feed of bad news, people find it harder to trust corporations or their products. Without the trust of its customers, no company can flourish.

And there are new problems to overcome. The growing awareness of climate change has been the biggest feature on the landscape during the last year. It has challenged companies to innovate in order to change the impact of their products on society. It has demanded of them that they be leaner and fitter to an extent previously unimaginable. It is not going to go away any time soon. So rather than representing the latest fashion or fad, it is beginning to redefine what it means to be a successful business in the modern age.

And as if that wasn't enough, issues around child labour, working conditions, bribery and corruption across the world have been a big part of life for a number of companies. Dealing with such issues has made for an essential 'hygiene factor' for a number of at-risk brands. The internet age has left nowhere to hide on such matters, even when they are buried deep within the supply chain. And at the other end, the relationship with customers is under strain. For instance, the trick of advertising to children used to be to do so with the trust and permission of parents. But will we soon see a time when no company can advertise to children at all?

On the positive side, business is seen as a key partner in addressing poverty. If society is to achieve the UN Millennium Development Goals, it will require business to do what it

does best – create enterprising solutions to problems and find ways to use these solutions to create wealth.

Successful businesses have always been those that adapted most quickly to change in the external environment. So we have seen a wave of companies moving towards a new way of understanding their business, engaging different stakeholders of the business and adopting mission or values statements that acknowledge that their positive impact on society is part of their reason for being. The best of them already have positive stories they can tell about what they have actually done as a result.

Corporate social responsibility (CSR) has become the most used term for this movement of change within business. It is about how companies organise their activities

The UN Millennium Development Goals

Eradicate Extreme Poverty and Hunger

Achieve Universal Primary Education

Promote Gender Equality and Empower Women

Reduce Child Mortality

Improve Maternal Health

Combat HIV/AIDS, Malaria and other Diseases

Ensure Environmental Sustainability

Develop a Global Partnership for Development

Business in the Community

Business in the Community (BITC), founded in 1982, is an independent business led charity. Its objective is to create a public benefit by inspiring companies to improve the positive impact of business in society and to be a platform for dialogue, collaboration and for sharing best practice concepts.

Its president is HRH The Prince of Wales and it has a current membership of more than 750 companies. This includes 71 of the FTSE 100 and 82 per cent of the FTSE's UK leading companies in their sector. Together BITC members employ 12.4 million people in over 200 countries worldwide, including one in five of the UK private sector workforce.

BITC is the largest national network of its kind, with over 100 partnerships across the UK and more than 60 international partner organisations sharing their experiences from around the world with the aim of translating policy into practice. Its strategy is driven by over 200 business leaders from companies at the forefront of social and environmental responsible business practice.

Mallen Baker is BITC's development director.

www.bitc.org.uk

---

to seek to have a positive impact on society. It is something that supports a healthy business in how it makes money, it is not a cost imposed from the outside (although that can often be the consequence of failure).

So a number of businesses have embraced CSR. Some merely pay lip-service to the concept. "What is the least amount of this stuff I have to do?" is a question heard from one CEO in the last two years.

But others have found serious ways to build it into their business model. They have involved employees in how they manage their environmental impact, or the way in which they decide to invest in the local community. They have reviewed their products to see what needs to be done to protect the interests of potentially vulnerable customers. They have started to produce CSR reports, identifying targets for performance in those areas that are easiest to measure (such as carbon emissions) and providing some sort of story-telling narrative in those areas that are impossible to measure, but remain important to success.

Superbrands/BITC CSR Project
It has been a pleasure, therefore, to see that one of the premier platforms for recognising the achievement of effective B2B brands – Business Superbrands – has chosen to introduce a CSR section into its book. This move gives appropriate recognition to the growing importance of this area to the future success of brands, whether they be business to business brands, or business to consumer.

I was delighted to be invited to chair the CSR Advisory Panel for this project, and to convene a panel of knowledgeable experts and business practitioners to help guide the selection of the pool of companies from which the initial example case studies would be drawn. We were lucky enough to have a strong panel, who gave a robust commentary on how to define the criteria for who would make it onto the list of companies with an interesting story to tell.

The Advisory Panel was asked to identify organisations that have made CSR a key focal point of how they go about their business, particularly in terms of how they build the value of their brand. The aim was to use the Business Superbrands book to tell a number of positive and inspirational stories that show what businesses are now doing in a way that might serve to inform and inspire others.

Once CSR became defined around core business issues – how you make your money – it inevitably led into difficult grey areas, and controversial ones. What constitutes best practice is always under review, and there are plenty of groups, some with an anti-corporate agenda, others simply fuelled by healthy scepticism, who are ready to question the sincerity or value of every initiative. So the Panel was not asked in the short time available to tread into overly murky waters!

The Superbrands/BITC CSR project is not a 'best of the best' league table. It pulls out a number of leading organisations that have relevant and motivational stories to tell. All the companies concerned have received other recognition for their work. Nevertheless, in some cases organisations may have been qualified for inclusion by majority vote, and hence not all panellists approved the inclusion of all the organisations featured herein.

Selection Process
A list of potential organisations was constructed based upon the constituent members of respected CSR indices. The indices used were:

- AccountAbility Rating
- Business in the Community CR Index
- Carbon Disclosure Project Members
- Covalence Ethical Quotation
- Dow Jones Sustainability Index
- Ethibel Sustainability Index
- FTSE4Good Index

The resulting 'long list' was circulated to all panellists for their review.

At a subsequent Panel meeting, the members reviewed and shortened the list with a view to increasing the probability of finding inspiring examples of CSR activity. The panel also agreed the addition of some smaller organisations, public institutions and NGOs.

Superbrands then approached organisations on the resulting list in a 'top down' fashion – i.e. those that appeared on the greatest number of CSR indices and/or those that had been specifically commended by the Panel were contacted first.

The organisations that subsequently chose to accept the invitation to tell their CSR story were subject to an editorial process designed to ensure that the totality of the organisation's CSR activities are reflected; an independent freelance writer was commissioned to write the case studies.

Seeking Inspiration

Having dealt with many companies over the years that are committed in some way to CSR, one frequent feature I have found is the difficulty companies find in telling their own story. Very often, they know they are doing good things, but these things are poorly communicated – often to the extent that the company's own staff remain unaware of great strides that have been made.

Partially, this is because companies are very sensitive to the charge that 'they are only in it for the PR'. But they also know that journalists and the sceptical campaign groups are unlikely to give credence to the good news stories, convinced as they are that these constitute merely a smokescreen designed to mask the bad. The number of credible channels that are open for the conveyance of good news are still relatively few and far between.

I hope that the stories told in these pages will help as just one extra way to spread the word of what successful companies can achieve in this space. It is only a start – an illustration of what is to come. We hope to see larger numbers of such stories in subsequent editions.

In the mean time, all that remains for me is to thank all the members of the CSR Advisory Panel for their input and for their support for the project, and also to give my special thanks to John Luff for his involvement and support which was particularly helpful to me on a number of occasions.

I hope you find the results of their labours make for an interesting and inspiring read.

Mallen Baker
Development Director
Business in the
Community
Chairman
Superbrands/BITC CSR
Advisory Panel

Mallen is the development director for Business in the Community (BITC), and a frequent writer, speaker and strategic advisor on corporate social responsibility. He is the editor of the email CSR newsletter Business Respect, a member of the CSR Europe board, a member of the expert advisory group on CSR reporting for the United Nations Conference on Trade and Development and was a representative on the UK Government's Sustainable Procurement Task Force. He is a member of the Ethical Corporation advisory board, as well as being a regular columnist for the magazine.

Mallen's work at BITC focuses particularly on marketplace issues. He was the principal author of the Marketplace Responsibility Principles, and is leading the workstreams on responsible marketing and supply chain strategies.

Superbrands/BITC CSR Advisory Panel

David Bent
Principal Sustainability
Advisor, Business
Programme
Forum for the Future

David leads Forum's work on business strategies and models for a sustainable future. He works with businesses on how they can profit from the up-coming operating context – having dynamic economies that enable nine billion people to choose how they live, within environmental limits. In addition, he uses inquiry and learning methods to create change in organisations.

David is a chartered accountant and is vice-chair of the Corporate Responsibility Committee for Europe's largest accounting institute, the Institute of Chartered Accountants of England and Wales (ICAEW). He was invited to contribute in the latest revision of the Global Reporting Initiative (GRI), first on the economics working group and also on the committee co-ordinating development of all the indicators. David has published on corporate strategy for sustainability and measuring the business case. He has spoken at academic and practitioner conferences, including at EU Presidency events.

Lauren Branston
Director, Corporate
Identity, Public Affairs &
Communications
Coca-Cola Great Britain

Lauren is currently director of corporate identity, public affairs and communications at Coca-Cola Great Britain.

Prior to working for Coca-Cola, Lauren worked at the environmental management consultancy Dames & Moore (now URS) in their reputation risk management group, and at the PR agency Ketchum (part of Omnicom).

She has worked with clients from a wide range of sectors, on corporate reputation and social responsibility.

Lauren has a degree in Ecology from University College London.

Barnaby Briggs
Head of Social
Performance
Management
Shell

Barnaby joined Shell as a corporate planner, moving later into the Public Affairs section of the company. He left Shell to join the Royal Society for the Protection of Birds (RSPB) as energy and transport policy officer, where he worked for six years on climate change, and other policy issues, including setting up global ecological networks on climate change and biodiversity. He then joined Environmental Resources Management (ERM) as a consultant working on environmental and social issues. He rejoined Shell as its chemicals issues manager five years ago, and now runs the Social Performance Management Unit in the Corporate Affairs team. The Unit provides policy, best practice and guidance on managing social performance across Shell as well as hands on support for individual projects and assets.

Prof David Grayson CBE
Founding Director
Doughty Centre for
Corporate Responsibility,
Cranfield School of
Management

David is a former managing director of Business in the Community (BITC) and remains a part time director where he particularly focuses on sustainability and small businesses. He chairs the UK's Small Business Consortium and speaks, writes and advises on business, society, and entrepreneurialism, around the world.

Amongst his books are 'Corporate Social Opportunity – Seven Steps to make Corporate Social Responsibility work for your business' and 'Everybody's Business' – both with Adrian Hodges.

David is also chairman of Housing 21 – one of the leading providers of sheltered housing and home care for older people in the UK. He is a patron of the disability charity Scope as well as a trustee/ambassador for several other national charities.

David was educated at Cambridge and Brussels universities and has held visiting fellowships from a number of Business Schools. He is currently a visiting senior fellow at Harvard's Kennedy School of Government in the US.

Louella Eastman
Group Corporate Social
Responsibility Director
Aviva plc

In her current role, Louella is accountable for implementation of vision and strategy for Aviva's CSR programme. She has been responsible for leading initiatives to carbon neutralise the company's operations globally and developed and implemented the Think Again diversity campaign, which won Opportunity Now's City Award, as well as the Respect Diversity Toolkit, which won a Global Diversity and Innovation Award at the United Nations in New York.

Prior to this, Louella was executive vice president of human resources and communications for Aviva Canada. In this role she was responsible for championing the rebrand to Aviva and the internal embedding of its four corporate values.

Louella has extensive experience in all areas of human resources; her earlier career encompassed several years in senior HR roles at Northern Telecom and Connaught Laboratories, and eight years as vice president of human resources at Johnson & Johnson.

Richard Ellis
Group Head of Corporate
Social Responsibility
Alliance Boots plc

Richard has spent the past 25 years working for a range of companies on all aspects of the CSR agenda.

The early part of his career was spent in Banking before he became involved in CSR after the inner city riots of the early 1980s. Following this he held CSR related positions at HSBC, TSB and British Aerospace and ran his own CSR consultancy for five years.

In 2003 he joined Boots and became responsible for all of the Company's CSR activities. Following the merger between Boots Group and Alliance UniChem in 2006 he was appointed into his current role.

Sarah Howe
Senior VP of Consulting
Text 100

Sarah has worked with the Text 100's parent company, NextFifteen Communications Group, in various senior management roles since 1994. Prior to joining NextFifteen, she worked with IBM and two other leading London PR consultancies. Overall, she has over 15 years of high level consultancy experience across a broad range of industry sectors and has been based in North America and Australia, as well as the UK.

Sarah has consulted major corporations such as IBM, Canon, Sony, Dell, Microsoft® and Xerox at local and international levels. Most recently, Sarah has developed much broader corporate and consumer advisory skills and has worked with clients including: The Department for Education and Skills (DfES), The Central Office of Information (COI), TOTAL, More Th>n Business, The Commonwealth Bank, Orange, Whirlpool and One Water.

Sarah has developed specific expertise in advising public sector clients and also developing CSR and ethical campaigns. She works closely with executive client teams and counsels them on broad PR requirements such as brand and crisis communications, corporate communications planning, stakeholder campaigns and, of course, CSR.

Geoff Lane
Partner
PricewaterhouseCoopers
LLP

Geoff is responsible for Sustainability issues and leads a multidisciplinary team of 40 people working full time on a range of Sustainable Development and Corporate Responsibility related projects.

He joined PricewaterhouseCoopers LLP in 1991 and has worked on a wide range of policy, management and risk appraisal projects for private and public sector clients and international institutions, both in the UK and internationally.

Geoff has worked extensively throughout Western and Eastern Europe, Central Asia, North America and Africa during his time with the firm, which has taken him to over 35 different countries.

In addition to his client facing work he is involved in the development of emerging standards and guidelines relating to corporate responsibility, representing the firm for example on the World Business Council for Sustainable Development, the Council of the Institute of Social and Ethical Accountability, and on the relevant committees of the UK and European Accountancy associations. He also contributes regularly to the media and speaks at conferences in the UK and internationally.

Simon Lidington
Chief Exchanger
The Insight Exchange

Simon's early career was in research before setting up his own agency at the age of 31. Four years later he was a co-buyer of Quadrangle, and then became one of the first Insight management consultancies in the 1990s.

In 2004 he was appointed CEO of Research International UK. During his tenure he initiated fundamental change in the business, reorganising it from a traditional sector-based to a client-centric organisation.

In early 2006 he set up The Insight Exchange to help clients put customers at the heart of their businesses. The consultancy works with clients such as American Express, Audi UK, FT Business, BMJ Publishing Group, and Volkswagen Group Services to innovate and improve brand and customer experience.

He is currently chairman of the UK Market Research Society, a fellow of the RSA, and sits on the Advisory Council for the Economic & Social Research Council's 'Cultures of Consumption' Programme.

John Luff
Founder
Sustainable Marketing

John specialises in helping organisations identify and promote their brand and CSR credentials and is a frequent speaker worldwide on the topics of brand, CSR and communications. Recent/current clients include major financial institutions, major construction companies, mobile telecoms and TV brands, cities, Government and UN departments.

Previously John was head of global CSR and head of global brand at BT. In these roles he helped BT achieve its third top rating on the Dow Jones Sustainability Index – the first time BT had achieved this on a global basis.

He developed the brand positioning for BT and its joint ventures worldwide. He is proud to have lead BT sponsorship of the Global Challenge – 'The World's Toughest Yacht Race'.

John's other senior roles have been in the fields of occupational psychology and organisational development. He is an alumnus of the prestigious Prince of Wales Business and the Environment programme.

Neil Makin
External Affairs Director
Cadbury Schweppes plc

Neil has been with Cadbury for 20 years, taking on his Group-wide current role in 1997. As such, he manages the Group's governmental affairs programme in Brussels, Westminster and Washington, and co-ordinates relationships with trade associations and a number of other industry-wide bodies.

Corporate social responsibility occupies a key position in his role, supporting the Main Board CSR Committee, and he chairs the Group's Human Rights and Ethical Trading Group. Neil is also a board member of the International Cocoa Initiative, the new multi-agency foundation established by the global confectionery industry, the ILO and a number of NGOs. Neil directs the affairs of the Cadbury Schweppes Foundation and its charitable giving programme with a particular focus on education and enterprise activities in schools.

He is also a director of Birmingham and Solihull Connexions Partnership, a member of BITC's National Education Leadership Team and a fellow of both the Institute of Personnel and Development and the Royal Society of Arts.

Glenn Manoff
Communications Director
O2

Glenn has been communications director at O2 since 2003. As coach for a 40 strong team of comms professionals responsible for corporate responsibility, public relations, internal communications, public affairs, charity partnerships, community relations and sponsorship exploitation, his role is to put an integrated approach to reputation and brand management values at the heart of O2's strategy.

O2 has consistently been recognised as an innovator in this field and has received various awards for the effectiveness of its communications brand and corporate responsibility campaigns. Glenn remains motivated by a desire to help O2 become one of the very best loved brands, very best places to work and very best corporate citizens in the UK.

Prior to O2, Glenn was responsible for Corporate Communications and Marketing Communications internationally for Ebone, Global TeleSystems and Esprit Telecom. Previously, he worked as a journalist, teacher, aid worker and basketball coach.

Mike Peirce
Deputy Director &
Head of Development
CPI

Mike is deputy director and head of development at CPI. He has a background in strategic consultancy and commercial due diligence. He also spent five years with the NGO, AccountAbility, at first managing the development of its corporate accountability framework, AA1000, and later as chief operating officer.

Mike has a degree from Oxford University and a postgraduate diploma in international relations from Johns Hopkins University.

Hilary Parsons
Global Public Affairs Manager
Nestlé

Hilary was head of corporate affairs for Nestlé UK at the time of joining the Advisory Panel. She has since moved to Nestlé headquarters, based in Switzerland, taking on the role of global public affairs manager.

Solitaire Townsend
Co-Founder &
Managing Director
Futerra Sustainability
Communications

Solitaire co-founded Futerra in 2001 and now oversees worldwide consultancy work with business and Government, including internal communications, media management and communications strategy for climate change and corporate responsibility.

Passionate about making sustainable lifestyles more desirable, she led Futerra's work on the Climate Change Communications Strategy for the UK Government. She is an expert advisor to companies such as BT and Microsoft®, and also works closely with the United Nations (UN) and numerous professional bodies. Solitaire is a member of the UN's Sustainable Lifestyles Task Force, a Board member of Tomorrow's Company and sits on the Chartered Institute of Marketing (CIM) Steering Group on CSR.

Andrew Vickerman
Global Head of
Communications &
External Relations
Rio Tinto, London

Andrew has overall responsibility for media, corporate communications, public affairs, corporate social responsibility and community relations at Rio Tinto, London.

Andrew has a BA, MA and PhD from Cambridge University. Prior to joining Rio Tinto in London in 1991 he worked as a development economist and as a consultant for international organisations, including the World Bank. Andrew travelled extensively for Rio Tinto on commercial negotiations in the early 1990s.

From 1994 to 1998, Andrew was responsible for finance, supply, personnel, community affairs, and investor & public relations aspects for the Lihir gold project in Papua New Guinea. He was a leading participant in the successful raising of US$750 million in debt and equity for Lihir in 1995.

In his current role Andrew played a leading role in the Global Mining Initiative, a mining industry exercise focused on addressing the contribution of the industry to the transition to sustainable development.

About
The Writer

The Superbrands CSR
Project was written with
the help of the corporate
responsibility team at
The Writer

Are you making the most of your CSR story?

The Superbrands/BITC CSR Project was written with the help of the corporate responsibility team at The Writer.

The Writer is a language consultancy. Set up in 2000, it exists to change organisations by changing their approach to writing.

Over the last seven years, The Writer has built up a client list that ranges from small and mid-sized corporates, to high street names and multi-nationals. The team deals with a huge range of language issues: from naming for BT, M&S and US-based Air Products, right through to writing corporate responsibility, marketing and graduate recruitment material for the likes of RBS, Sky and Molton Brown.

The team has built a particular expertise in the development of tone of voice for brands like O2, Standard Life, Toshiba and Radox. So far The Writer has trained more than a thousand people to write more creatively at work – in offices from Croydon to Canada.

"We started The Writer to change organisations through the words they use," says The Writer's managing director Martin Hennessey. "Companies are under mounting pressure to increase the amount and depth of their corporate reporting. This is particularly true when it comes to proving their credentials as a genuinely responsible business."

The Writer argues that this is where the importance of writing and tone of voice is absolutely critical. "Reporting on your sustainability as a business isn't just about reeling off facts," says Hennessey. "It is about understanding how to shape and to tell an engaging story – that doesn't make any over claims.

"Too much corporate responsibility writing is dull," says Hennessey. "At its worst it's confusing. When it's not confusing, it comes across as distant or formulaic. Nobody really enjoys writing it, so nobody will enjoy reading it – whether that's staff, shareholders, customers, the media, or the world at large.

"And we think every boring piece of writing is a missed opportunity to make the most of a company's real commitment to being a more active corporate citizen."

The Writer does three things:

■ **Writing** They write almost anything in CR, find specialist writers, and manage writing projects.
■ **Brand language** They help define brands, develop tone of voice for projects, and come up with names.
■ **Training** They train people to become more effective and creative writers at work.

www.thewriter.co.uk

TheWriter™

Martin Hennessey

Martin co-runs the CR team. He is The Writer's founder and managing director. A former print and broadcast journalist, he advises national and multi-national corporations on their brand communication strategy. He is co-author of the Investor Relations Handbook published by LexisNexis, a founder member of business writers' group 26, and a former judge of the Writing for Design category at the D&AD Awards.

Ed Sowerby

Ed is an award-winning writer and corporate responsibility specialist. He writes for BT, Sky, RBS, Ernst & Young and Clifford Chance – among many others.

Introduction and Background

In July 2006, healthcare giants Alliance UniChem and Boots merged to form Alliance Boots – Europe's largest pharmacy-led health and beauty group. The group is split into two divisions: a wholesale division (based on what used to be Alliance Healthcare), which serves over 120,000 pharmacies, dispensaries, hospitals and health centres across 14 countries, and a retail division made up of 2,500 outlets in the UK, and around 500 more spread across the world from Norway to Thailand.

Alliance Boots is now no longer a publicly quoted company, following the completion in June 2007 of the private equity acquisition led by KKR and Stefano Pessina.

Alliance Boots believes that a responsible business is a healthy business. As a result, CSR is an important factor in the group's long term business planning. That said, its focus on CSR in the short term since 2006 is equally impressive. The period after a merger is always challenging. Yet at the same time as integrating two companies, Alliance Boots managed to agree an aligned CSR strategy. Not only is it relevant to the two different parts of its business, it also contains four clear priority areas: carbon management; community healthcare; stewardship and integrity; and employee well-being. These have helped to give the group's CSR activity a clear and meaningful direction.

Environmental Issues

As a product developer, manufacturer, retailer and wholesaler, Alliance Boots has the potential to reduce the carbon footprint of every stage of a product's journey right through the supply chain. It is something that will help the group reach its ambitious target of reducing its carbon emissions by 30 per cent by 2020.

However, reaching this target isn't something Alliance Boots is leaving for tomorrow. The group has already made some important steps forward by:

Getting employees on board Creating awareness among employees can be just as effective a way of reducing carbon emissions as large, sweeping initiatives. At Alliance Boots this has meant that decisions at every level of the business are now made with their environmental implications in mind. Much of this is about providing employees with digestible and relevant information, and that's what Alliance Boots has done. For example, in 2007 the group sent out energy saving packs to every member of staff in its Health and Beauty stores, offering tips on how to reduce energy use at work and at home, and explaining why it is a good idea to do so.

Developing low-carbon products Alliance Boots has just completed a pilot project to analyse the emissions given off in the manufacturing and distribution of two shampoos in its Botanics range. The result was a 20-25 per cent reduction in both products' carbon footprints and, more importantly, a valuable understanding of how to make similar savings across many other products in the Boots range.

Streamlining the supply chain In 2007, Alliance Boots expanded its double-deck trailer fleet from 16 to 41 vehicles, helping to save around 3,100 tonnes of CO_2 and 5.25 million product kilometres per year (the equivalent of 130 trips around the world). Furthermore, it also started collecting goods from suppliers rather than the other way around – a move that helped save in the region of 1,700 tonnes of CO_2 and 2.2 million product kilometres.

Saving energy Alliance Boots has been working with the Carbon Trust since 2002 to improve the energy efficiency of its stores, and with great success: in 2006/07 alone it managed to reduce energy use by 6-7 per cent (adding up to a £1.5 million saving on its energy bill). New 'edge-of-town' stores are also 10-15 per cent more energy efficient than before 2002, and the group is now working with the Carbon Trust to achieve similar results in its community pharmacies.

Reducing waste Alliance Boots has made a big effort to reduce the waste it produces. For example, through recycling redundant shop fittings and making sure all shrink-wrap and cardboard is recycled, the group's Health and Beauty business has reduced its reliance on landfill by 14 per cent since 2002/03.

Suppliers, Procurement and Commercial Partners

Within the highly competitive health and beauty market, few brands are as widely trusted as Boots. To maintain this trust, and to make sure all its suppliers live up to its own high standards, the group completed a major assessment of 650 of its Boots brand product suppliers in April 2006.

Alliance Boots also aims to go one step further: since 2006, the group has been working with the Ethical Trading Initiative to look at how it can make positive changes to its supply chain. It is a project that has taken its procurement experts as far away as northern India to talk to the homeworkers who make necklaces for the Boots accessories range.

Community Engagement

Community involvement is part and parcel of what Alliance Boots does every day, and nowhere is this more apparent than in its community pharmacies. Often located near local surgeries, these pharmacies supply communities with all the medicines and health-related services they need. Recently, the group has also introduced 677 private consultation rooms into these community pharmacies, and opened 50 midnight pharmacies.

The Boots partnership with Breast Cancer Care is now in its 12th year and still going strong. £500,000 was raised last year alone, and the awareness raised by the Boots support has helped contribute to improving survival rates beyond five years. Research shows there has been a 20 per cent fall in breast cancer mortality in the last 10 years (1993-2002) which can be attributed to breast awareness, early detection and improved treatment.

In 2007 Boots strengthened its support for women's cancer with a new partnership with the Eve Appeal, focused on ovarian cancer.

On a corporate level, Alliance Boots supports a wide range of public health campaigns including the stop-smoking charity QUIT and Macmillan Cancer Support. It also raised more than £1 million for BBC

Children in Need in 2007, donated around £200,000 to local community-based charities in Nottinghamshire through the Boots Charitable Trust, and formed a partnership with Médecins du Monde to help displaced people get access to healthcare in Tower Hamlets. All in all, it raised £1.7 million for charity in 2007.

Boots aims to encourage all its employees to share their expertise to help people lead healthier lifestyles, and to build happier, more cohesive communities. To that end, in 2007 the group set up a new volunteering programme with Home-Start, the UK's leading family support organisation, to encourage Alliance Boots employees to spend time helping their local communities. It has been a great success with six per cent of employees getting involved in voluntary work over the last year. It is in these individual actions that one can find some of the most striking examples of what community support really means. Take, for example, the free beauty makeover workshops the Boots No7 consultants are involved within hospitals. Called 'Look Good... Feel Better', these workshops gave a morale boost to over 5,000 women undergoing treatment for cancer.

Internal Practices

Employee well-being is one the four key CSR priorities for Alliance Boots. In the last two years many small steps forward have been taken on a local level that, combined, make a big difference to the group overall. For example:

Health and fitness Alliance Boots has extended the Boots 'Change One Thing' campaign – a campaign encouraging its customers to improve their health by doing one thing differently – to promote well-being for employees.

Support Alliance Boots community pharmacies recently formed a partnership with the Retail Trust, a charity providing help and support to people working in the retail industry and their families.

Training Every year around 15,000 people start working in Boots stores alone, and they all now receive a one-day, off-the-job induction called a Red Carpet Day.

Flexible working A job-share register has recently been reintroduced to help provide more flexible work patterns for workers and managers in central teams.

Accolades and Achievements

In 2007, the Boots life-cycle approach, called the Product Journey, received a Major Commendation at the 2007 Business Commitment to the Environment Awards. This concept takes a holistic approach to product sustainability, embracing the whole product lifecycle, from concept and design, through to customer use and final disposal of packaging and waste product. At every stage, measures to improve the environmental and social performance of the products are considered.

www.allianceboots.co.uk

Alliance Boots CSR Quick Facts

At the Be Gorgeous Ball in June 2007, Boots employees and suppliers raised £200,000 for Breast Cancer Care and The Eve Appeal.

In 1911, Boots became one of the first companies to employ welfare workers. More recently Alliance Boots has been among the pioneers of flexible working practices such as job sharing, career breaks and term time working.

For more than 50 years Boots has been running staff consultative bodies – its latest is called the Forum, with meetings held four times a year. Before the meeting Forum reps talk to the people in their area and bring together their feedback.

Introduction and Background

BP is one of the world's largest energy companies and provides fuel, energy and petrochemical products in over 100 countries.

BP has been very aware of the climate change issue over recent years and has since tried to incorporate this agenda into its business operations by producing more fossil fuels more efficiently today, making better use of them and beginning the transition to a low carbon future. In 1997, BP Group chief executive, Lord Browne, became the first CEO of an oil company to publicly acknowledge the link between human action and climate change.

Historically, BP was active in corporate responsibility long before the phrase was coined. As far back as 1909, BP staff set up a medical clinic to treat the local community at its Persian refinery. In the 1920s, 1930s and 1950s, BP was creating new homes, recreational centres and schools, both at home and abroad. Building a better society,

especially through education, has always been part of the BP story.

Environmental Issues

In the 21st century, BP has sought to explore business focused on finding alternative sources of energy that are cleaner, lower-carbon and sustainable (wind, solar and biofuels), while raising public awareness of this important issue at the same time. It is also working to reduce its own greenhouse gas emissions, setting aside US$350 million over five years to help reduce CO_2 emissions by up to a million tonnes each year.

BP advocates a multi-pronged approach to tackle environmental challenges, through public policy, research/innovation and education. In terms of public policy, the Group has been supportive of mandatory emissions caps, and a global carbon market for trading emissions.

In research/innovation, in 2006 BP announced an investment of US$500 million,

over 10 years, to set up the BP Energy and Biosciences Institute for bioscience research, based in Berkeley, California. BP is also funding major research projects and university programmes around cleaner energy in India, China, the UK, US and Algeria. It is also working with DuPont to develop advanced biofuels.

BP has also used its advertising to raise public awareness on environmental issues. As well as making a public commitment to reducing its own carbon footprint, BP has been working to encourage the public at large to rethink their own use of energy, day-to-day. On BP's website, for example, is a simple carbon footprint calculator that anyone can use to work out their own emissions. On a larger scale, BP was part of the Clean Cities campaign in Europe.

Suppliers, Procurement and Commercial Partners

Many of BP's operations are in emerging economies. At the same time, the Group's global supply chain is estimated to be worth US$40 billion a year. For local communities, this combination represents a tremendous opportunity for economic development, but one that has to be managed carefully to make sure this development is sustainable and ethical.

Mutual Advantage, one of BP's key values, is a concept which recognises that working with local suppliers, and investing in their ongoing training and development, benefits both BP and the local community. On a purely commercial level, having a strong pool of local talent is also more cost-effective, reliable and simple to manage. Earning the trust and respect of local communities is also essential to the Group's longevity.

Recently, for example, BP has worked with the Angolan and Azerbaijani governments to strengthen ties with local businesses. In Angola, BP's investment has already

translated into 15 locally-awarded energy contracts. In Azerbaijan, BP has doubled its local spending, to US$500 million a year.

Community Engagement

BP believes in making sustainable investments in the communities in which it operates and seeks to provide solutions to communities which are aligned to the company's needs. Its support ranges from primary schools and higher education programmes, as well as community healthcare programmes – from training local villagers in health care in Indonesia, to sponsoring primary, secondary and higher education programmes in over 30 countries in the last year.

In 2007, the Group also drew up a set of 'social requirements' that are used to guide the assessment of the social impact of new projects. These are designed to safeguard aspects of human rights of the people and communities where BP operates, including

due care, concern and protection for their culture and resources.

BP also contributes to charitable causes. For example, in the wake of disasters like Hurricane Katrina in the US, and the devastating earthquake in Indonesia, the Group gave more than US$3.1 million in aid. The group also matches time or money donated by its own staff, adding up to another US$11 million in 2007.

Internal Practices

For a company under such constant public scrutiny, fair dealing and total transparency are absolutely critical to BP. Its Code of Conduct reinforces these values, by spelling out for all employees and suppliers what constitutes fair play. The Code was launched two years ago. As well as industry-leading safety standards, the code also covers ethical issues, like race and gender, and even anti-trust issues.

Crucially, the Code of Conduct protects not just the company, but its suppliers as well. If a supplier or contractor believes BP is operating unfairly or against industry standards or local laws, they can phone a confidential and independently-run helpline, called OpenTalk.

Accolades and Achievements

Diversity is one of BP's major strengths and it was awarded a Catalyst Award for Diversity and Inclusion in 2007 as well as a Corporate Equality Award from the Human Rights Campaign.

BP also picked up several other prestigious awards last year, including 10 IR Magazine Awards (including the Grand Prix), a Gold Quill Excellence Award and an Excellence in Communication Leadership (EXCEL) Award from the International Association of Business Communicators, as well as an R Gene Richter Award for Leadership and Innovation in Supply Management.

BP's CSR work in Vietnam was also recognised with an award for its contribution

to the community. The Group's internship and work experience schemes won both a UK Target and a National Council for Work Experience award.

On top of these, and many other awards given to BP every year, the Group also hands out awards to its own people. The BP Helios Awards not only honour teams within the company, but also contractors and suppliers, who embody the BP brand which is defined as 'performance-driven, innovative, progressive and green'.

Frequently held up as a particularly good example of how to engage employees in CSR activity, the awards are another way BP manages to spread and reinforce its brand values throughout the organisation, on a global scale.

www.bp.com

BP
CSR Quick Facts

In 1998, BP set targets to reduce GHG emissions from its operations to 10 per cent below 1990 levels by 2010. It achieved the target by 2001.

In 2005 BP launched Alternative Energy and committed US$8 billion investment by 2015.

In 2006 BP's contributions to communities in need around the world totalled US$106.7 million, compared to US$95.5 million in 2005.

In 2007 construction began on five wind power generation projects in the US, which are expected to deliver a combined generation capacity of some 550MW.

let's make a
better
world

Introduction and Background

From its roots as a traditional telco, BT has turned into one of the world's leading providers of telecommunications, broadband, internet services and IT solutions.

Despite being in one of the most complicated markets in the world – worth trillions of pounds each year – BT's philosophy is simple: people and businesses everywhere need to connect with each other. So the company's aim is to help everyone benefit from improved communications. Doing this in a responsible way is what BT's CSR commitment is all about.

It's a commitment that goes right back to the 1930s, when BT first produced telephones for hearing-impaired customers. While the technology used might have changed, BT's involvement in CSR activities has remained constant since then.

Environmental Issues

BT is one of the UK's largest users of electricity, but it has managed to lower its overall CO_2 emissions by 60 per cent since 1996. It is also now one of the world's largest purchasers of green energy – meaning it can meet almost all of its UK energy needs from environmentally friendly sources like hydro and wind power as well as combined heat and power plants.

The company has also launched initiatives to get its customers to cut waste. For example, it's now possible to choose online billing and directory services instead of getting a printed bill sent through the post. Furthermore, in association with the Woodland Trust, BT has planted thousands of saplings across the UK – one for every customer who signs up for paper-free billing.

Video conferencing and broadband technology allow people to reduce the amount they travel, so BT is able to help improve its business customers' carbon footprints. They also practice what they preach: currently over 12,000 BT employees work at home some or all of the time; and audio or video conferencing is used as much as possible. All these initiatives are profitable as well as eco-friendly, and BT's total environmental cost saving for the 2006/07 financial year was £229 million.

Suppliers, Procurement and Commercial Partners

Ethical sourcing, fair trade, working conditions in the developing world – they're big issues for any global company, and justifiably so. BT runs a 'Sourcing with Human Dignity' programme that investigates overseas suppliers to make sure their employees are treated well. The company was also an original signatory to the UN Global Compact, and makes sure that all its policies and procedures go well beyond the requirements set out in the United Nations Universal Declaration of Human Rights.

Community Engagement

BT is committed to maximising its positive impact on society and time and again, BT has shown that this commitment is more than a set of promises. It gives a minimum of 0.5 per cent of its UK pre-tax profits to direct activities in support of society and more than a further 0.5 per cent via in-kind activities. In the 2006/07 financial year, that equated to £21.8 million given to community projects.

BT's support for charities focuses on causes that have the most to gain from its communications expertise. These include ChildLine, which BT has supported since it was founded, and UNICEF, with whom BT has just launched a £1.5 million global charity partnership to invest in education and community programmes in South Africa, Brazil and China. BT's technology is also put to regular use during telethons such as Comic Relief and Children in Need, helping to raise millions of pounds every year.

One problem with the rapid advance of communication technology is the 'digital divide' it creates between those who have access to it and those who don't. BT plays an important role in narrowing this gap, by actively working in UK communities where internet take-up is low, to introduce people to the benefits of online communication. On an international level, BT also sponsors ICT education in a deprived area of Delhi, where over 10,000 children so far have been trained in key communication skills.

The BT Education Programme – one of the UK's most significant corporate investments in education – also provides free online and classroom learning resources to help teach thousands of children the importance of good, clear communication. BT also sponsors

Tate Online – the UK's most visited arts website with over 650,000 visitors every month – and works with the National Theatre, the British Film Institute and the Philharmonic Orchestra to make theatre, film and music easily available, particularly to school children. At the same time, BT is a board member of the Internet Content Rating Association (ICRA), and has developed BT Safe Surf – a programme which provides information for parents on protecting their children when online, and user-friendly training for the children themselves.

BT also has an Age and Disability Action Unit that helps the elderly and disabled use modern communication technology. The unit developed Text Direct, a national telephone service run by the Royal National Institute for Deaf People to help deaf, hard-of-hearing and blind people make and receive phone calls. By working with the Royal National Institute of Blind People, BT has also created new products for those who had previously been excluded from the world of texting – products such as BT's text-to-speech system and Personal Digital Assistant that reads text messages aloud when they are received.

Internal Practices

BT values the importance of getting the basics right internally, and making sure employees maintain the right work/life balance. For BT, this means using its own technology to make home working possible, and providing the tools to enable even more people to work from wherever suits them best – 64,000 at the last count. It has also introduced mental health programmes that have successfully reduced stress by 30 per cent.

BT people are heavily involved with the company's CSR activities, whether that be through manning the phones for Comic Relief or joining the BT Volunteers programme and teaching communications skills in schools. The company also rewards employees that are active in their local communities through its 'Community Champions' and 'Chairman's Awards' schemes.

Accolades and Achievements

In recognition of all the work it has done over the years, BT has been named the number one telecommunications company in the Dow Jones World Sustainability Index for seven years running, and is the holder of the Queen's Award for Enterprise for Sustainable Development.

In 2007, Business in the Community named BT its Company of the Year for its positive impact on society. BT has also been named one of the Global 100's Most Sustainable Corporations in the World and, in Spain, was ranked in the top 30 best companies to work for by the weekly business magazine Actualidad Economica.

Importantly too, in a 2007 survey 62 per cent of BT employees said that BT's CSR programme made them feel proud to work for the company, and 22 per cent of new graduates said that BT's reputation for CSR had influenced their decision to apply for a role with the company.

www.bt.com/betterworld

BT CSR Quick Facts

BT and its employees have raised over £6.1 million for ChildLine since 2002, enabling 700 more children to get through every day.

Through BT's Lifelines project, farmers in 591 remote villages in India can get information on agriculture, animal husbandry and agribusiness. They call Lifelines and record a question on an automated system and expert answers are then left as a recording for the farmer to pick up.

Ninety nine per cent of women who take maternity leave return to BT, compared to the national average of 40 per cent.

BT published its first Environment Report in 1992.

By the end of 2016, BT aims to have reduced its carbon dioxide emissions (measured in tonnes CO_2 equivalent) to 80 per cent below 1996 levels.

Approximately three million school children benefit from BT's free communications skills resources each year.

First
transforming travel

Introduction and Background

As a provider of public transport, there is a measure of social responsibility in everything that FirstGroup does. That is why the company goal – to provide safe, innovative, reliable and sustainable transport – is also the foundation of its CSR programme.

Transporting over 2.5 billion passengers a year, with 135,000 employees and annual revenues of more than £5 billion, the company is the world's leading transport operator.

As such, First is in a prime position to support the move towards more sustainable travel and encourage changes in public attitudes to public transport.

Environmental Issues

As a company FirstGroup offers significant opportunities to reduce emissions by attracting more people to use public transport. This objective is central to its vision to 'Transform Travel'. However, the company also recognises that it is a significant contributor to atmospheric emissions, including carbon dioxide (CO_2), and is committed to reducing these.

In May 2007, First unveiled a new Climate Change Strategy – the first of its kind in the sector – setting both short and long term carbon emission reduction targets.

Reduce emissions More than 95 per cent of First's CO_2 emissions in the UK come from its vehicles. Reducing carbon dioxide emissions from the vehicle fleet is therefore a central part of the Climate Change Strategy. Over the past 12 months FirstGroup has reduced the total carbon dioxide emissions from its UK bus fleet by three per cent which equates to 26,756 tonnes of carbon dioxide.

Through its Climate Change Strategy, First is also working to improve the fuel efficiency of its existing fleet, exploring alternative fuels and investing in more efficient vehicles. First already uses sulphur-free diesel and five per cent biodiesel in its UK bus fleet. New buses now have EURO IV engines that are 10-15 per cent more fuel-efficient than their predecessors. In 2008, the company will also be trialling new hybrid buses in London.

Through these combined measures FirstGroup is seeking to achieve long term reductions in carbon emissions from the train fleet of 20 per cent and from the UK bus fleet of 25 per cent by 2020. This will reduce its CO_2 emissions by 250,000 tonnes each year.

Using less energy FirstGroup is also committed to reducing its energy consumption year-on-year. Indeed, during 2006/07 energy consumption was reduced by 18 per cent in its bus depots.

Energy reduction is also an important consideration in new building design. First's new global HQ in Aberdeen includes plans for ground-source heat pumps and movement-responsive lighting.

First is currently working towards accreditation under the Carbon Trust's Energy Efficiency Accreditation Scheme (EEAS).

Get more people using public transport Encouraging greater use of public transport is a key element of the Climate Change Strategy. First's initial step has been to practice what it preaches. Each one of its 38,000 UK employees has received either a free First bus or rail pass.

Following the opening of the new global headquarters each member of headquarters staff will receive a 'green travel plan' which will encompass individually tailored options of how employees can get to and from work – this will include bus and train routes and times, cycle paths and estimated walking times. Moreover, First is committed to continue to provide ever more safe, innovative, reliable and sustainable transport services. By continuing to improve its services, the greater the number of people that will be persuaded to opt for public transport.

Suppliers, Procurement and Commercial Partners

FirstGroup also seeks to apply its CSR principles and commitments through the procurement process. First's approach to procurement is a collaborative one, and the basis of its Supplier Relationship Programme. As part of this programme, First has introduced a range of recent improvements in partnership with suppliers, including a local sourcing policy and increased use of biodiesel, Fairtrade products, energy-saving equipment and 100 per cent recycled paper.

The company has recently completed ethical and environmental risk assessments on its key

products. It has also introduced new software that makes it easier to evaluate suppliers' ethical and environmental credentials.

Community Engagement

As the UK's largest provider of public transport, First's operations touch all members of the community including customers, neighbours, employees, businesses and residents. After all, First is responsible for making sure millions of people get to work every day and keeping people safe when they travel. Safety is First's number one priority. The motto for its Injury Prevention Programme is 'If you cannot do it safely – don't do it'. It's a simple rule which has been proven to work: over the past year the programme has reduced the number of employee injuries by 22 per cent, and the number of passenger injuries by 16 per cent.

First engages with the community through its 'First into Management' scheme. This is an NVQ2 programme, run in association with Business in the Community (BITC), that has doubled the number of voluntary hours given by First employees over the last year, and helped many good causes.

First is also involved with national charity initiatives, for example its corporate partnership with Save the Children will see the charity benefit by around £1 million.

This is supported by local level initiatives such as free ticket schemes for disadvantaged families. The company's community work also involves support to a number of wide ranging community projects on a local level. These range from First Great Western's work experience programme for students with disabilities, to First's sponsorship of the Short Film Festival in Hull and its 'adopt a station' scheme which runs throughout the country.

In the US, First Transit worked closely with the Baltimore Washington Thurgood Marshall International (BWI) airport in Maryland to help repatriate US citizens uprooted from Lebanon after fighting broke out in 2006. Furthermore, when Wal-Mart donated leftover holiday stock to local charities across the US, First student volunteer drivers delivered them.

Internal Practices

FirstGroup sees its employees as its most important asset as they are key to the operation of safe, reliable, customer-focused services. The company is therefore committed to investing in its employees to ensure it recruits, develops and retains the best people in the industry.

Learning and development opportunities

First UK Bus' Learning and Development programme is one of the most sophisticated in Britain's bus industry. Every First UK Bus employee has a continuous improvement programme called a 'learning and development ladder'. The learning programme, which is open to all employees, leads to recognised qualifications – drivers are encouraged to work towards S/NVQ qualifications and the company's leadership development programme, launched in March 2006, leads to a Diploma in Company Direction.

In 2007, First was among eleven major employers invited by the Department for Education and Skills to sign the 'Skills Pledge' – a Government-led initiative to improve adult learning. But First's focus on employee training goes back much further. The company pioneered the idea of lifelong learning centres with the Transport and General Workers' Union to help staff learn new skills. Located in depots or mobile units, and used by more than 55,000 people, there's now a network of 40 learning centres in First's bus division alone.

First has also been responsible for other groundbreaking new schemes, such as First ScotRail's award-winning 'earn as you learn' programme that gives employees an extra hour's pay for every hour they spend on a course.

Representation and company involvement

Thanks to popular share-ownership schemes, First employees and ex-employees make up 57 per cent of First shareholders. There is also an employee director on First's plc board, and on the board of 70 per cent of all

its UK operating companies (it is aiming to increase this to 100 per cent). In total, 90 per cent of its workforce in the UK and 40 per cent in the US are unionised. First's strong relationships with these unions have resulted in joint initiatives, such as their award-winning 'lifelong learning centres'.

Accolades and Achievements

First has won a raft of industry awards over the years. Since 2006, these have included the Continuing Environmental Excellence award at the Network Rail Environmental Awards, and the National Green Apple award for environmental best practice in the Transport and Freight Industry Awards. Among many local awards, First's bus division won the UK Bus Award for Successful Partnership for its work with Glasgow City Council. First TransPennine Express received the North West National Training Award and the Group as a whole was awarded 91.1 per cent in the BITC Environmental Index in 2007 – a score that puts it in the gold performance band.

www.firstgroup.com

FirstGroup CSR Quick Facts

In 2006/07 First reduced its carbon dioxide emissions by 22,000 tonnes.

In 2006/07 First's Injury Prevention Programme saw a 22 per cent reduction in all injuries.

First plants 1,500 new trees every year as part of its commitment to support biodiversity.

In 2007 FirstGroup nominated Save the Children as its Charity of Choice – a partnership that is worth more than £1 million to Save the Children.

Kimberly-Clark

Introduction and Background

Kimberly-Clark was founded in Neenah, Wisconsin in 1872. Its founders based their new company on the three principles of quality, service and fair dealing. These principles still guide the way Kimberly-Clark operates. They are principles that have helped it become one of the largest health and hygiene companies in the world, with a turnover of US$16.7 billion and over 55,000 employees.

Kimberly-Clark's products are divided into three main categories – consumer brands, health care and professional products. Consumer brands include household names such as KLEENEX®, ANDREX®, HUGGIES®, KOTEX®, DEPEND® and FIESTA®. Kimberly-Clark's Health Care products are used in pain management, digestive health, surgery as well as for healthcare associated infections. Meanwhile, the KIMBERLY-CLARK PROFESSIONAL* product range encompasses washroom products and protective clothing. In addition, its DIY business includes products such as shop towels, protective gloves and overalls.

Sustainability is a company-wide priority for Kimberly-Clark, with the presidents of all its global businesses sitting on its Corporate Sustainability Steering Committee. In addition, the company consults an external Sustainability Advisory Board.

In 2006 it set up a dedicated corporate sustainability team, to co-ordinate the many initiatives that Kimberly-Clark is involved with around the world, including charity partnerships and joint projects with global retailers such as Wal-Mart.

Environmental Issues

Kimberly-Clark launched its Vision programme in 1995, which set five-year targets to reduce the impact of its products and processes on the environment. In 2006, this programme moved into its third five-year phase, Vision 2010, which is based on the environmental concerns identified by the UN Environmental Programme and the World Business Council for Sustainable Development (namely energy-related emissions, climate change, the availability of clean water, and land use and degradation). Vision 2010 has tangible and challenging targets which set out to:

■ Reduce energy use – by setting targets to improve the efficiency of Kimberly-Clark's production process. Since 2000 its energy efficiency has improved by more than 19 per cent.
■ Reduce carbon emissions – by developing cleaner methods of both production and distribution. Already, between 2005 and 2006, Kimberly-Clark's overall CO_2 emissions per tonne of production fell by two per cent.

■ Minimise manufacturing waste – by reducing waste per unit of output by 10 per cent, and making sure none of it ends up in landfill (currently 17 per cent of waste goes to landfill).
■ Reduce freshwater use – by looking at water efficiency on a site-by-site basis. In this area, 50 per cent of Kimberly-Clark's sites have already met their Vision 2010 targets.
■ Improve wastewater quality – all of Kimberly-Clark's sites are regulated closely and often. In 2006, 83 per cent of them hit their 2010 Vision wastewater quality targets.
■ Roll out the combined management system – recently introduced, this system integrates environmental and safety management, helping each site see how they're doing against their targets, and how sustainability and site safety fit together.
■ Introduce country-specific programmes – particularly to help maintain the fragile eco-systems in developing countries like Brazil, India, China and Indonesia.

At the same time, Kimberly-Clark is also designing more sustainable products using less packaging and more recycled material. Since 2000, it has reduced its levels of packaging by 10 per cent, and further progress in this area has the potential to make a massive difference. To put this potential into context, compressing the package size of its Pull-Ups® training pants saved 160 tonnes of poly packaging, 590 tonnes of corrugate packaging, 290,000 gallons of fuel, and greenhouse gas emissions equivalent to taking nearly 1,000 cars off the road.

Suppliers, Procurement and Commercial Partners

Kimberly-Clark aims to ensure that its suppliers meet its own high standards. In 2007, the company also published a set of supplier guidelines to encourage each of its suppliers to sign up to its sustainability agenda.

Wherever possible, Kimberly-Clark also sources materials locally – particularly in developing countries. The exception is its sourcing of natural fibres, which are used in many of its products. These come from hard and soft wood, and because of the sensitivity around sources of timber, Kimberly-Clark has a very strict fibre-procurement policy. Its aim is for 100 per cent of the virgin fibre

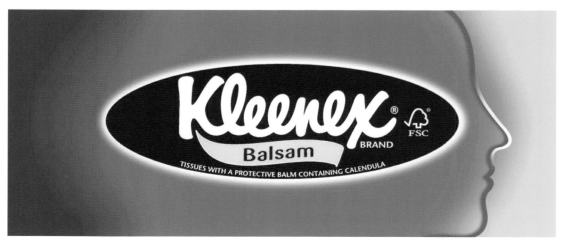

it uses to be certified by an internationally acknowledged forest certification system.

Community Engagement

With nearly a quarter of the world's population using Kimberly-Clark products, it's almost impossible to overstate the company's responsibility towards community health.

It is a responsibility that the company takes extremely seriously, regularly using its expertise to help tackle health issues around the world. For example, it recently formed a partnership with the Surgical Care Improvement Programme to research new product innovations that could help reduce the spread of infections.

The company's charity record is also impressive. Since it was established in 1952, the Kimberly-Clark Foundation has formed a series of hugely successful charity partnerships. Currently these include a partnership with UNICEF, to whom it has given US$6 million since 2001, and Medshare International, who were supplied with US$2 million of products in 2006 to help them in Latin America. In total in 2006, the foundation donated US$24.3 million of cash and products. This included US$1.3 million to match donations made by employees, and US$1.1 million to match time volunteered by employees – both as part of its Matching Gifts Programme.

The company also supports a wide variety of local community projects, often in conjunction with small groups of its employees. These range from Teenage Cancer Trust in the UK to Comic Relief, to In Kind Direct which re-distributes new goods donated by some of Britain's best-known manufacturers and retailers to hundreds of voluntary organisations. Kimberly-Clark was presented with the charity's Founders Award by its Patron Prince Charles in 2007.

Internal Practices

Kimberly-Clark is a big employer in both developing and developed countries. But when it comes to corporate governance and employee welfare, the same standards apply across the board. These include providing a wide range of employee benefits from flexible working options to social networks. In 2008, it also scored 85 per cent in the Human Rights Campaign Foundation's Corporate Equality Index, putting it firmly in the top half of the retail- and consumer-products companies involved. Furthermore, in a global survey looking at what percentage of staff felt engaged in the workplace, Kimberly-Clark scored 56 per cent against an average of 52 per cent.

Accolades and Achievements

Kimberly-Clark has recently been named as sustainability leader in the personal products sector of the 2007 Dow Jones Sustainability World Index for the third year running. Other examples in 2007 include:
- Being named industry leader in GMI's (GovernanceMetric International) global accountability ratings, which measure corporate governance and accountability.
- Being awarded the EPA's (Environmental Protection Agency) SmartWay Transport Partnership Award for its work reducing fuel use and emssions in its distribution network.
- Being named as one of the paper industry's 10 Best Corporate Citizens by CRO (Corporate Responsibility Officer) magazine.
- Kimberly-Clark China being named as 2007's Most Admired Corporate Citizen by the China Social Worker's Association.
- Kimberly-Clark Australia achieving first place in the personal care and cosmetics packaging category and 'best in show' at the Packaging Evolution Awards for its work improving the environmental impact of its packaging.
- Kimberly-Clark Russia being named as one of Russia's top 10 employers, coming ninth among 64 international and national companies in a study by the human resources consultancy, Hewitt Associates.
- Yuhan-Kimberly being named Korea's most admired company by the Korea Management Association, the most

sustainable company by the Korean Government and the best company for CSR by the East Asian Institute.
- Being included in the London Stock Exchange's FTSE4Good index for corporate responsibility.
- Ranking 14th out of 152 brands in the GolinHarris Corporate Citizenship Index (CCI).

What is equally impressive is how well Kimberly-Clark's founding principles of quality, service and fair dealing have been translated into a meaningful sustainability vision for a company of such size – one that should help it reach its 2010 sustainability targets and beyond.

www.kimberly-clark.com

Kimberly-Clark CSR Quick Facts

Since 2001 Kimberly-Clark has committed more than US$6 million to UNICEF's programmes, providing life-saving supplies and healthcare, education and skills training to more than 350,000 children in 24 countries.

The KLEENEX® brand in the UK is now FSC certified and began to label on-pack, across most of its range, from January 2008. The ANDREX® brand in the UK will be in a position to label its mainline range as FSC certified later in 2008.

Kimberly-Clark is taking part in the Carbon Trust's pilot to test a draft methodology for establishing the Carbon Footprint of products in the UK and potentially for the industry to move towards carbon labelling. Kimberly-Clark has committed to work with its ANDREX® and HUGGIES® brands on this project.

Clydesdale Bank   Yorkshire Bank

Members of the **National Australia Bank** Group

Introduction and Background

If the National Australia Group isn't a household name here in the UK, its two main UK retail brands – Yorkshire Bank (www.ybonline.co.uk) and Clydesdale Bank (www.cbonline.co.uk) – certainly are. That's not to say National Australia Group itself isn't well-known; starting life as the National Bank of Australasia back in 1858, it's now a financial services organisation of international repute with over AUS$564 billion in assets, more than 10 million customers, and nearly 40,000 employees across Australia, New Zealand and the UK.

National's CSR approach is centred around the impact which it has on people. The aim is to make a positive contribution to society by operating in a responsible way, encouraging communities to protect their local environments and by helping the communities in which their employees are involved.

Environmental Issues

National Australia Group has committed to meeting the enormous challenge of becoming carbon neutral by September 2010.

Significant steps have already been made in several important areas, nowhere more so than in the UK:

Energy consumption In April 2006, Yorkshire Bank and Clydesdale Bank started buying 'green' electricity from renewable sources such as wind farms, and from sources exempt from the Climate Change Levy, such as hydro-electric power stations. By the following May, 100 per cent of their electricity was coming from renewable sources.

Energy and water efficiency Yorkshire Bank and Clydesdale Bank have also managed to reduce their total energy consumption by about 10 per cent, and their water consumption by seven per cent over the last 12 months. This is thanks to: upgrading the technology used in heating, ventilation and cooling systems; replacing old boilers with high-efficiency gas alternatives; installing energy-efficient lighting; switching to instantaneous water heaters instead of storage heaters; buying energy-efficient office equipment; and making sure all new and

refurbished properties include energy-saving measures, such as intelligent lighting systems, sensor-controlled taps and water meters.

Recycling As part of the Toptree scheme, Yorkshire Bank and Clydesdale Bank paid for more than 4,800 trees to be planted in 2007 to help offset the paper used for its customers' bank statements.

Sponsorship In September 2007, Yorkshire Bank announced that it was sponsoring The National Trust, Europe's leading conservation charity, to help raise awareness of important environmental issues.

Suppliers, Procurement and Commercial Partners

In 2007, National Australia Group's global supply chain involved over 56,000 suppliers, spread from New Zealand to the UK. Many goods are sourced on a global scale. However, National has a good track record of using local suppliers whenever possible, particularly in the UK. Even when goods are sourced from different parts of the world, its CSR Procurement Policy and support for global human rights means that it only selects suppliers who have sound social and environmental practices and procedures in place.

Community Engagement

When a community involvement programme really works, it's often because it focuses on a cause close to the company's area of expertise. National Australia Group's community programme in the UK is a good example of this, with much of the money it invests in the community spent on improving people's numeracy skills and financial literacy. This involvement takes the form of community partnerships, charity partnerships, corporate donations and direct staff involvement.

The community partnerships include two programmes:

The first is the award-winning Count Me In initiative. Now in its third year, it promotes

children's numeracy skills in 18 local authorities across England and Scotland. The nuts and bolts of the scheme involve a collection of over 3,500 bags filled with numeracy tools and games that nursery groups, child minders and parents can borrow from their local library. It's been a great success and has prompted the launch of a pilot scheme (in partnership with Hull City Council) called the Count Me In VIP programme, for visually impaired children.

The second is the Count and Grow project, featuring 'Superspud' the potato superhero. His mission? To help bring maths to life among six- to eight-year-olds in 320 schools across Scotland. During the 10-week project, children are encouraged to grow and monitor their own potato crop. They also get the chance to visit local farmers to get a better understanding of where their food comes from.

The biggest of the charity partnerships is the support of the British Heart Foundation, which started in 2005. Money is raised mainly through direct employee fundraising, but for every pound raised by an employee, the company donates another pound. In the last three years, more than £500,000 has been raised.

The Banks' Employee Volunteer Grants Programme is just one example of the support National gives to employees' direct action and community work. It does this by giving grants (of up to £500) to charitable organisations that its employees are involved with.

Internal Practices

Like any successful service-led organisation, National Australia Group knows that its own employees need to be happy and engaged if they are going to deliver excellent customer service. To ensure this is the case, it recently put together an employee welfare plan with three aims: firstly, to give its people the opportunity to play an active role in their communities; for example, in April 2007 National's board unveiled the employee volunteering programme. This programme offers each employee the chance to undertake two days of voluntary work each year, with full pay.

Secondly, to create a working environment where people can develop their skills, and be more innovative and effective at work. The company encourages flexible working and provides flexible working toolkits. It also puts on training modules and master classes on topics such as leadership style. Furthermore, its 'Two Tick' employer status shows the level of its support for employees with disabilities.

Finally, it aims to build a culture of co-operation and strong leadership. It's often the small things that can make a difference here. For example, Yorkshire Bank and Clydesdale Bank recently worked closely with Unite, their union, to introduce childcare vouchers for employees returning to work. Over the last 18 months, these vouchers have helped the two banks see a 17 per cent increase in the number of new mothers returning after maternity leave.

Accolades and Achievements

National Australia Group UK received a bronze ranking in the 2006 Business in the Community Corporate Reporting Index Survey and was listed in the Top 100

Companies that Count, while its community activity received a silver ranking. The company was also ranked in the Top 50 Places Where Women Want to Work by The Times in October 2007.

Over the past year, National in the UK has also won awards including the World Call Centre of the Year award in October 2006 and the Best CSR Programme of the Year award at the Credit Card Awards in November 2006. It also won Credit Today's Responsible Lender of the Year award in April 2007, and an ASA HR Excellence award (large category) in 2007.

The company has also won awards for its activity on a local level – awards such as the UK Arts & Business Brand Identity Award for its sponsorship of Leeds Grand Theatre and Opera North, and the Community Award from Scottish Arts & Business for the Count Me In 123 scheme with Dundee City Council in October 2006. These awards reflect the depth of the National Australia Group's community commitment in the UK, and are a true measure of its success.

National Australia Group CSR Quick Facts

In the last 12 months, the company has decreased its total energy consumption by approximately 10 per cent and has reduced water usage by seven per cent. Furthermore, in the next 12 months all properties will be metered so that water consumption can be measured more accurately and additional water saving measures implemented.

Since 2005, Yorkshire Bank and Clydesdale Bank have raised more than £500,000 for the British Heart Foundation.

In October 2006, National won the World Call Centre of the Year award.

RWE npower **RWE**

Introduction and Background

RWE npower is the UK energy business of the RWE Group, one of Europe's leading electricity and gas companies. With more than 6.8 million domestic and business customers, npower is the UK's largest electricity supplier.

As such, it knows it has an enormous responsibility to address major social and environmental challenges. Therefore, moving to a low carbon economy and providing a sustainable, secure and affordable energy supply for the future is top of its corporate responsibility agenda.

Environmental Issues

RWE npower is in a unique position when it comes to environmental issues: developing more efficient energy production will make a huge difference to its own carbon emissions. But through educating and helping its customers, the company can also assist them in lowering their own carbon footprints. With this in mind, it has developed a two-pronged approach.

The first is about generation and includes significant investment in:

Power stations In 2007 RWE npower announced plans to cut its CO_2 emissions by one third from 2000 levels. Investments totalling £1.7 billion form part of this commitment.

Renewable energy RWE npower leads the UK wind energy market, operating 18 onshore wind farms and the UK's first major offshore wind farm, North Hoyle, off the North Wales coast.

The second approach involves helping customers become more energy efficient. This encompasses:

Sustainable energy npower works with business customers – including BT, Marks & Spencer, Sainsbury's and Wembley Stadium – to reduce their carbon dioxide emissions and use energy more efficiently. In addition, in August 2007 npower business launched the 'Big Switch Off', which aimed to encourage companies to save thousands of pounds by switching off lights and equipment left on overnight to reduce their energy consumption.

Juice RWE npower has developed a 'green' electricity product for its domestic customers which supplies non-premium priced environmentally friendly energy, Juice. For every customer who stays with Juice for the year, the company donates £10 to a fund for long term research into other forms of renewable energy. Currently, this fund is supporting the development of wave and tidal technologies.

Suppliers, Procurement and Commercial Partners

Despite the scale and complexity of its varied operations, RWE npower has worked hard to reduce the environmental and social impact of its procurement activities.

It is keen to improve awareness of its sustainable procurement policy, and has developed a series of supplier surveys to gain feedback on its effectiveness and visibility. It is also mapping supply chains to work out the best ways to make them more sustainable.

In addition, RWE npower has developed a risk assessment tool to identify products and services where there might be cause for concern, and has agreed action plans with suppliers to mitigate the risks.

Community Engagement

The development of more sustainable energy is a major part of RWE npower's corporate responsibility plan. But it is definitely not the only part. Its community work is award winning and involves a number of different aspects:

Voluntary work The number of npower employees working in their local communities has grown every year since 2001, and now over 10 per cent of the workforce are actively involved in community volunteering projects. All together they contribute more than three working years in voluntary hours. E-mentoring also formed part of npower's volunteering programme in 2007. The scheme provides extra support for children and allows all employees the opportunity to volunteer without leaving their desks. It works by linking local pupils at Key Stage 2 level with individual mentors from npower, who then help them improve their literacy and ICT skills through programmes sent via email.

Tackling fuel poverty RWE npower's Health Through Warmth (HTW) scheme – in partnership with the National Health Service (NHS) and National Energy Action (NEA) aims to assist vulnerable people whose health is adversely affected by cold, damp living conditions. The scheme trains community workers who can then identify people of all ages in need and refer them to the scheme. HTW supports the installation of insulation and heating measures and seeks funding

through grants and charities as well as using the unique npower HTW crisis fund. HTW has received over 36,000 referrals and for many people it is the first time that they have managed to heat their home properly – making a positive impact on their health, comfort and quality of life.

Sponsorship Over the last few years, npower has become synonymous with English cricket, and its sponsorship of the game runs right through to a grassroots level with the 'npower Urban Cricket' project. In 2006, this project announced plans to build five big indoor arenas, and turn five playgrounds into 'Urban Cricket zones', to give local kids the chance to develop their cricketing skills.

Education RWE npower has launched the Greener Schools programme, which is a five-year initiative aimed at making at least 2,500 UK schools more sustainable. It provides 'green makeovers' for the schools themselves, including free energy audits and advice on how to reduce their carbon footprints. It also teaches children simple ways to save energy in an interesting way through its 'Climate Cop Academies' (www.climatecops.com).

The 'npower enthuse' programme helps students learn about engineering and addresses the challenges that the industry faces in inspiring young people to enter a science, technology or engineering related career. This interactive education programme is targeted towards 13-14 year-olds and is delivered through workshops which also offer opportunities for employees to volunteer and share their interest in engineering. In addition, employees are actively engaged in the SETNET Science and Engineering Ambassadors Programme.

Internal Practices

RWE npower places great importance on the well-being of its employees and believes that a healthy and diverse workplace is an important part of job satisfaction. RWE npower has therefore put in place a programme aimed at:

Supporting a diverse and inclusive workplace RWE npower's diversity and inclusion programme supports the recruitment and retention of talented people in the energy industry. During the last two years npower raised awareness of diversity through a series of workshops attended by over 2,000 senior managers, line managers and team leaders. This was supported by an online e-learning training tool and diversity video available to all employees. Positive effects have been seen – for example, women now make up over 40 per cent of RWE npower's workforce, with more than 900 in management or team-leader roles. This is rare for a company of its size and kind, and has resulted in RWE npower being ranked in The Times Top 50 Places Where Women Want To Work.

Creating a healthy working environment RWE npower actively promotes flexible working and runs 'well-being programmes' that advise employees on how to be healthy at work. It also encourages them to think about everything from the hours they work to their diet and daily exercise. More than 1,000 managers have attended stress workshops to learn how to identify and support colleagues in their teams who may be at risk.

Providing top-class training RWE npower provides educational and recreational courses for contact-centre staff and has opened resource centres at customer services locations. Hundreds of members of staff have now benefited from open-learning courses.

Accolades and Achievements

RWE npower's corporate responsibility work has not gone unnoticed. Over the last year, its recognition includes:

■ The Charities Aid Foundation's award in recognition of its community investment.
■ Achieving platinum status in Business in the Community's (BITC) Corporate Responsibility Index.

■ Receiving a BITC 'Big Tick' standard of excellence in the Impact on Society Award for Large Companies.
■ Being awarded a 'Silver Big Tick' by BITC for its npower Active programme, which is run in partnership with the English Federation of Disability Sport to promote sport for all abilities.
■ The HTW scheme topping the 'Investing in Social Change' category at the Directory of Social Change Awards as a result of a public vote.

www.rwenpower.com

RWE npower CSR Quick Facts

RWE npower has made low carbon investment commitments of £1.7 billion, which will collectively reduce its carbon intensity by one third from 2000 levels.

The HTW scheme helps vulnerable people in the community who are living in cold, damp homes. Since HTW began in 2000, £2.9 million has been spent from the npower HTW crisis fund which is specifically for vulnerable people who are ineligible for other grants and funds. In addition, HTW has levered funds of £29.5 million from a range of sources including charities.

RWE npower is the largest wind farm operator with 18 onshore, as well as the UK's first major offshore wind farm and a total generating capacity of more than 400MW – equivalent to approximately 20 per cent of the UK installed wind capacity.

In 2006, employees volunteered a total of 9,775 hours of their time to help with community projects – the equivalent of more than three working years.

Introduction and Background

Yell is a leading international directories business operating in the classified advertising market. Since the launch of the Yellow Pages directory in 1966, its aim has been to put buyers in touch with sellers by anticipating, understanding and meeting their changing needs.

In the UK, Yell provides a range of simple to use information services: Yellow Pages, its printed directory; Yell.com, its online directory service; and 118 24 7, its telephone information service.

Acting responsibly as a business is one of Yell's core values and it believes that this also helps to manage the expectations of its advertisers and consumers. Its dedicated team of 4,000 people in the UK ensures that it continues to make an increasing contribution to the environment and communities in which the company operates.

Environmental Issues

Yell has been registered to the environmental standard ISO 14001 since 1998 and its environmental policy commits it to reducing, reusing and recycling resources throughout its operations.

With more than 28 million Yellow Pages directories delivered last year to households and businesses across the UK, its biggest environmental commitment is to manage the impact of its printed directory.

Yell works closely with its supply chain in the production of its directories, aiming to strike a balance between its environmental impact and ensuring the directories remain fit for purpose. To reduce the amount of paper used, Yellow Pages directories are made from a low weight paper (34gsm) and annual production includes 25,000 tonnes (51 per cent) recycled fibre content. The remaining 49 per cent is virgin fibre – sawmill dust and off cuts – from sustainably managed forests in Finland.

Since 1993 Yell has worked with all UK local authorities to assist them – financially and in-kind – in increasing the number of old directories that are recycled. Currently, 99 per cent of councils in the UK provide recycling facilities for old directories and Yell continues to look for solutions with the remaining one per cent. Old directories are recycled into new products including animal bedding, cardboard, insulation materials and newsprint. Research conducted in 2007 showed that 66 per cent of UK households recycled their old directory, the highest level to date.

In more than 100 council areas in the UK, Yell enhances residents' recycling facilities with its environmental campaign for schools – the Yellow Woods Challenge – which is run in partnership with the Woodland Trust and local authorities. Since its launch in 2002, more than two million children have been involved in the campaign.

School children recycle old Yellow Pages directories and compete with other schools to win cash prizes for recycling the most directories per pupil. For every pound Yell awards to schools, it gives a matching pound to the Woodland Trust. Since 2004, these funds have supported the Trust's 'Tree For All' campaign – the most ambitious children's tree-planting project ever launched in the UK. The funding from the Yellow Woods Challenge to date has enabled the Trust to plant the equivalent of 19 hectares (48 football pitches) of native woodland.

Free curriculum-linked resources, created especially for the Challenge, are given to every participating school. Kirk, the campaign mascot, visits schools and features in all educational activities. He aims to make lessons about recycling, woodland conservation and caring for the environment fun for children.

Since 1998, the environmental impact of Yell's everyday office work has been driven by targets and measures as part of its annual environmental scorecard. The 'Think Again' programme is run by environmental representatives who champion the reduction, re-use and recycling of all office consumables. Yell also donates all its old laptops to local schools and nurseries.

In 2006, Yell introduced 'Liftshare' to all its employees in the UK – a car-sharing scheme designed to reduce its employees' CO_2 emissions and cut congestion whilst reducing their travel costs.

Suppliers, Procurement and Commercial Partners

Yell aims for high ethical and environmental standards, both within the business and throughout its supply chain. All suppliers are required to commit to Ethical Guidelines for Suppliers and to promote the same high standards in their own supply chains.

Yell focuses on building long term, mutually beneficial, sustainable relationships with its suppliers and partners not only to improve

the way it works but also to add value to its business. This can be best demonstrated through its 25-year relationships with its paper supplier, UPM-Kymmene; its pre-press partner, Pindar Set; and its printer, RR Donnelley.

Community Engagement

In 2007, Yell Group contributed £1.13 million to the community through donations and in-kind support.

Since 1999, Yellow Pages has sponsored Marie Curie Cancer Care's annual fundraising campaign, the Great Daffodil appeal. In addition to helping the charity to increase the appeal's profile, it also covers the promotional costs of the campaign, which means that all money raised goes directly to the work of the Marie Curie Nurses. Yell has helped to raise more than £20 million for the charity, which equates to one million high-quality nursing hours provided free of charge to terminally ill people in their own homes.

Since 2006, Yell has encouraged 446,000 school children to fundraise for the charity by taking part in 'Mini Pots of Care' – an activity that has helped raise £740,000. School children plant a daffodil bulb in their own 'mini pot' in autumn and when the flowers bloom in spring, pupils decorate their pots and take them home to someone they care about in exchange for a donation to the charity.

Since 2004, Yell has also donated £60,000 to Marie Curie Cancer Care through offering Yellow Pages advertisers the option to donate £50 to the charity in exchange for their participation in market research, rather than receive the equivalent in shopping vouchers.

In 2006, Yell became a patron of the Prince's Trust – a charity that supports 40,000 disadvantaged young people every year who lack the self-belief and practical skills to get into the world of work.

Yell has held more than 10 workshops for Prince's Trust businesses covering finance, marketing, design, selling and planning.

The 'Yell Raisers' – a 13-strong team of Yell volunteers – raised £67,000 for the Prince's Trust in 2007 and, in recognition of their contribution, four members of the team were nominated for the Prince's Trust Employee Development Awards.

Yell has since strengthened its support for businesses mentored by charities and organisations like the Prince's Trust by launching 'Yell for Enterprise' – a web-based programme to provide free business information. To date, 150 new businesses have joined and a group of Yell volunteers have been trained as mentors.

Yell also works with local Education Business Partnerships to mentor pupils from local schools, share skills and discuss any issues or concerns they have about further education or being in the workplace.

Yell's group of 'Community Champions' are volunteers based at offices across the UK who champion and support local charities of their choice through fundraising activities and in-kind support. By adopting this approach as a company, Yell is able to support local organisations as well as its national charity partners.

Internal Practices

Yell is one of only 36 organisations with Investors in People 'Champion' status, recognising its award-winning approach to people management and development.

The company gives its employees the flexibility to manage their commitments through different working options. Currently, one in five Yell employees are participating in this scheme which includes carers leave, special leave for community work, home-based and term time working, job sharing, part-time working and career breaks.

Yell has recently signed up to the Healthy Workplace Challenge for 2008 – a programme running in the South East which aims to increase morale, improve productivity and reduce absenteeism in employees.

Yell's employees are encouraged to get involved with the company's CSR activities in a number of different ways. This can range from leading assemblies in schools to manning the phones for Comic Relief, helping to paint a local community centre or organising a beach clean.

Accolades and Achievements

In recognition of Yell's commitment to CSR, it has been included in the Dow Jones Sustainability Index for the fourth year running and is also a member of the FTSE4Good Index.

In 2002 and 2007 Yell was awarded the Queen's Award for Enterprise for Sustainable Development by demonstrating an approach to business that fosters strong economic growth whilst benefiting society, encouraging protection of the environment and efficient use of resources.

In 2007, Yell was acknowledged as one of the world's most sustainable businesses for a second time through inclusion in the Global 100 and in 2006 it received a Green Apple Award for its environmental management.

www.yellgroup.com

Yell CSR Quick Facts

More than 50 per cent of the paper used to make Yellow Pages directories is made from recycled fibres. The remainder is sourced from sawmill dust and off cuts from sustainably managed forests.

Yell's support for Marie Curie has helped them raise more than £20 million, equating to one million nursing hours.

Yell has given more than £300,000 to UK schools and donated the same amount to the Woodland Trust through their recycling competition for schools – the Yellow Woods Challenge.

In 2007, Yell employees donated more than £75,000 to charities of their choice through the 'Give as You Earn' scheme.

Brands, CSR and Sustainability

By David Bent
Forum for the Future

The last two years have seen a number of issues break into the mainstream, and people have begun to change what they buy and why. Campaigns such as 'Make Poverty History' and 'Stop Climate Chaos' have been matched with the rise of Fairtrade coffee, organic food and green energy. In 2005, people in the UK spent some £29.3 billion on 'ethical' products and services – that's more than on beer and cigarettes.

The issues may be familiar to business people as CSR or 'Corporate Social Responsibility', though many experts place CSR within the wider agenda of sustainable development. Whatever the jargon, it is clear that people are making higher demands of brands, or they stop trusting them. And, there are businesses using their brands to grab the opportunity of sustainability.

What is this 'CSR'?

"Whether it is the world's rapidly growing population or the worsening problem of global warming, we see the need for sustainable business practices as increasingly urgent. And perhaps more than anything else, we see sustainability as mainstream."
Lee Scott, Chief Executive, Wal-Mart, 2007

Finding an agreed meaning to CSR is a rich terrain for hair-splitting. It's possible to spend many fruitless hours comparing and contrasting Corporate Citizenship, Corporate Social Responsibility and Corporate Responsibility. But at its heart is the question: what is the role of business in society today?

We know that expectations of business have been increasing over the last decade. Consumers demand better products at lower prices – creating the competitive pressures in the market place. People as citizens support campaigns that demand higher social and environmental standards. Brands such as Nike and Gap have been subjected to campaigns on supply chain labour standards. People as voters pressure governments to demand that business addresses social issues. The EU REACH and End-of-Vehicle Life directives are but two examples.

"Many CEOs recognise the underlying tension between business models wedded to increasing patterns of consumption and the reality of limited natural resources."
McKinsey & Co, Shaping the New Rules of Competition, 2007

At the same time, there is growing scientific evidence that many of the things we do in our daily lives put our ability to continue into the near and far future at risk. The products and services we buy contribute to environmental problems like climate change, and to social inequalities across the globe.

The largest challenge for society today is to meet the needs of the present generation without compromising the ability of future generations to meet their own needs. The challenge of sustainability is setting the

forum for
the **future**
action for a sustainable world

Forum for the Future is the sustainable development charity which works in partnership with leading organisations in business and the public sector. The charity's vision is of business and communities thriving in a future that is environmentally sustainable and socially just. It believes that a sustainable future can be achieved, that it is the only way business and communities will prosper, but that we need bold action now to make it happen.

Forum for the Future plays its part by inspiring and challenging organisations with positive visions of a sustainable future; finding innovative, practical ways to help realise those visions; training leaders to bring about change; and sharing success through its communications.

David Bent leads Forum for the Future's work on business strategy.

www.forumforthefuture.org.uk

context for business. Basic services and resources that the natural world now provides cheaply will become more and more expensive. Rising expectations of business' role will translate into new regulation, changed consumer behaviour, new norms in the supply chain and investor pressure.

So, to answer the question at the heart of CSR, the role of business today is to find profitable ways of creating a sustainable future. What that means for particular businesses is no longer the domain of the CSR department (or equivalent) but part of the core of the business, from product and service innovation through to branding and marketing.

Risking the trust in brands

A brand symbolically encapsulates all the information associated with a product. The brand serves to create associations and expectations around it. In a market where many consumers have an astonishing range of choice, brands are fundamental to business success. The experience of what the product actually delivers – whether it meets the expectations around it – can make or break the brand, and so the business.

As we have seen, people's expectations of business are increasing. As long as businesses and brands meet those expectations then they remain trusted. When brands mess up then the effects can be severe.

The most dramatic recent example is Northern Rock, where, ironically, it was the announcement that savers could trust that their money was safe that highlighted that their savings had been at risk. They queued around the block to get their money out.

Nike, the sports equipment brand, suffered a fall in sales and share price over allegations of the use of child labour in developing world factories working as third-party suppliers in the manufacture of its sportswear. Its response was a 'product stewardship' strategy that improved working conditions and reported transparently on its actions. The threat to the brand has declined.

Image: npower

In 2005 Jamie Oliver's TV show attacked junk food in school dinners. The catering company at the centre of the row, Compass, reported an eight per cent fall in half-year profits and its shares fell six per cent.

Grabbing the opportunity

"Having studied consumer behaviour all my working life, I believe that we are standing on the threshold of something very exciting and positive – nothing less than a revolution in green consumption."
Sir Terry Leahy, Chief Executive, Tesco, March 2007

For a long time CSR has been about risk management, reporting and stakeholder engagement. Now it is about opportunity. The gap between what people say they will buy and what they actually buy is closing – just ask Tesco who have seen

sales of organic food go up a phenomenal 39 per cent year-on-year.

Guardian News and Media, publishers of The Guardian and The Observer, worked with the Henley Centre Headlight Vision on project 'Green Light', to segment the UK population along ethical parameters. The research included examining consumer motivations and examples of 'green' advertising, in addition to input from GNM's own Total Audience study, fused with TGI and TGI Net. Not surprisingly, the smallest groups are the Principled Pioneers and Vocal Activists, both four per cent, who are proactive in taking a stand in their consumption. More surprisingly the next smallest group is Onlookers at 26 per cent, who believe the issues are exaggerated and action is not their responsibility.

The remaining two groups are of similar sizes. The Conveniently Conscious, (35 per cent) are concerned and, while they won't make any sacrifices, they will make small changes. A full 31 per cent of consumers are Positive Choosers, who believe there are serious issues where they can make a difference and use their money proactively.

That means almost 40 per cent of the UK population is proactive on ethical consumption, and a further 35 per cent will act if it is easy. Not surprisingly, companies are using their brands to grab the opportunity. We can see companies growing the size and sophistication of demand in mature markets.

Companies are increasing the sophistication of consumer demand to shift customers from saying they'd like to buy ethically to actually doing so. Companies that proactively shape demand can respond to changing purchasing habits faster than their competitors.

In 2005 Marks & Spencer launched a ground-breaking marketing campaign called 'Look behind the label' which informed customers of M&S's long commitment on social and environmental issues such as fish sourcing, animal welfare, Fairtrade

and reducing salt and fat levels in food. A Citigroup report in the middle of 2006 said that the campaign contributed to the ongoing sales recovery and would underpin M&S brand performance going forward.

In 2007 Marks & Spencer has pushed on with 'Plan A', the five-year, 100-point plan to tackle 'some of the biggest challenges facing our business and our world'. Plan A is extensively promoted in store, in PR campaigns and in adverts. M&S is building on its brand strengths of trust and making it easy for the consumer. Plan A effectively says "come inside our store, we'll take care of all the difficult decisions".

Cafédirect is another example of the whole company brand approach. It has achieved double-digit growth by putting quality and fair treatment of producers (accredited by the FAIRTRADE Mark) at the heart of its hot beverage offering.

innocent drinks won the 2006 Brand Campaign of the Year at the Business XL Awards. As one journalist put it: "It's no great surprise that innocent has become one of the

Image: innocent

biggest zeitgeist brands of the noughties. Pick any right-on issue – food miles, kids' health, ethical trading, environmental awareness, and the smoothie-maker were championing it long before it became a bandwagon."

Other companies have gone down a route of creating 'hero' products. The Toyota Prius has been an astonishing success: Car of the Year in North America (2004) and Europe (2005), and selling 750,000 by June 2007. The Prius has defined a category and opened up a new market, defying all expectation. Customers were initially attracted by the fuel-efficiency in a time of high petrol prices, but it has now become a fashionable item to own.

The Toyota brand is benefiting from the halo effect of the Prius, according to the president of Toyota Motor North America. Certainly other car-makers are jealous of how the Prius helps Toyota avoid criticism for its other vehicles.

GE's Ecomagination is an example of creating an umbrella brand for a range of hero products. GE describes Ecomagination

as 'a business strategy to help meet customers' demand for more energy-efficient, less emissive products and to drive growth for GE – growth that will greatly reward investors'. In 2006 GE had launched some 45 products with a revenue of US$12 billion.

At the same time companies have been linking their products and services to growing public concerns. Virgin Trains promotes itself with the slogan 'Go Greener. Go Cheaper'. A number of brands are collaborating on an initiative, 'We're in this together'; B&Q, Barclaycard and others offer easy ways to combat climate change – from insulation with B&Q to low rates on green purchases with Barclaycard Breath.

There are also growing brands that allow business to tell consumers they can trust their products or service. These product labels tend to cover specific issues – the Carbon Trust Carbon Reduction label, the Soil Association's organic stamp or the FAIRTRADE badge.

In the future...

Sir Terry Leahy is right: we are standing on the threshold of something very exciting and positive. The challenge of sustainability will initiate a wave of creative opportunity for

marketing and branding new products. Incumbents will fail, and be replaced by new entrants who have some aspect of sustainability in their business model and in their brand. The 'currently niche' will be the successes of the future.

Profound questions remain. How will we meet the needs of a growing population within environmental limits? Can brands be part of giving people experiences that satisfy their needs and wants, without consuming precious planetary resources? We would say yes, and the examples above are the first in that direction.

How will brands jump ever-higher hurdles in order to be trusted? Nike's product stewardship and transparency offer one possible answer.

In the future I would expect sustainability issues to play in integral role in the context of every company's brand – so much so that activities will be covered in the main Superbrands entry, and a separate 'CSR' section will not be needed. Either companies will ignore the issues, and risk their brand, or they will ensure that their brands grab the opportunity of sustainability – and take a leading societal role.

Image: Carbon Trust / Walkers